Dōwa Policy and Japanese Politics

This book locates the development of Dōwa policy projects within their historical and political context, offering examples of human rights protection in a non-Western society.

Charting Dōwa policy from its origins in the pre-war period to its revival after 1945 up to the turn of the 21st century, chapters in this study provide a social and historical review supplemented by detailed analyses of policy process and implementation at both national and local levels. No previous publication on the 'Buraku Problem' has focused on the direct impact of Dōwa policy in overcoming prejudice and economic inequalities. Topics covered range from left-wing Buraku Liberation League demands in the late 1950s, the Special Measures Law for Dōwa Policy Projects (SML) in the 1960s, and the evolution of a human rights based Dōwa policy into the 1970s, 1980s, and 1990s. Through its evaluation of the relative successes and failures to improve local infrastructure and opportunities for marginal communities, this book invites comparative analysis with policies in other Asian and Western polities which seek to mitigate descent-based and racial discrimination.

Dōwa Policy and Japanese Politics will prove a valuable resource for students and scholars of international relations, human rights, politics, and Japanese studies.

Ian Neary is an emeritus fellow of the Nissan Institute and St Antony's College, Oxford University. He has previously published *Human Rights in Japan, South Korea and Taiwan*, 2002 and *The Buraku Issue in Modern Japan: The Career of Matsumoto Jiichiro*, 2010. The second edition of his textbook, *The State and Politics in Japan*, was published in 2019.

Nissan Institute/Routledge Japanese Studies

Series Editors:
Roger Goodman, Nissan Professor of Modern Japanese Studies, University of Oxford, Fellow, St Antony's College
J.A.A. Stockwin, formerly Nissan Professor of Modern Japanese Studies and former Director of the Nissan Institute of Japanese Studies, University of Oxford, Emeritus Fellow, St Antony's College

The Liberal Democratic Party of Japan
The Realities of 'Power'
Nakakita Kōji

Japan's New Ruralities
Coping with Decline in the Periphery
Edited by Wolfram Manzenreiter, Ralph Lützeler and Sebastian Polak-Rottmann

New Directions in Japan's Security
Non-U.S. Centric Evolution
Edited by Paul Midford and Wilhelm Vosse

Child Guidance Centres in Japan
Alternative Care and the Family
Michael Rivera King

Gradual Institutional Change in Japan
Kantei Leadership under the Abe Administration
Karol Zakowski

Tenkō
Cultures of Political Conversion in Transwar Japan
Irena Hayter, George T. Sipos, Mark Williams

Rethinking Locality in Japan
Edited by Sonja Ganseforth and Hanno Jentzsch

Dōwa Policy and Japanese Politics
Ian Neary

For more information about this series, please visit: www.routledge.com/Nissan-Institute-Routledge-Japanese-Studies/book-series/SE0022

Dōwa Policy and Japanese Politics

Ian Neary

Routledge
Taylor & Francis Group
LONDON AND NEW YORK

First published 2022
by Routledge
2 Park Square, Milton Park, Abingdon, Oxon OX14 4RN

and by Routledge
605 Third Avenue, New York, NY 10158

Routledge is an imprint of the Taylor & Francis Group, an informa business

British Library Cataloguing-in-Publication Data
A catalogue record for this book is available from the British Library

Library of Congress Cataloging-in-Publication Data
Names: Neary, Ian, author.
Title: Dōwa policy and Japanese politics / Ian Neary.
Description: Milton Park, Abingdon, Oxon ; New York, NY : Routledge, an imprint of the Taylor & Francis Group, an Informa Business, 2021. |
Series: Nissan Institute/Routledge Japanese studies series | Includes bibliographical references and index. |
Subjects: LCSH: Civil rights—Japan. | Human rights—Political aspects—Japan. | Minorities—Legal status, laws, etc.—Japan. | Discrimination—Law and legislation—Japan. | Buraku people—Civil rights. | Buraku people—Japan—History.
Classification: LCC KNX2460 .N43 2021 | DDC 323.0952—dc23
LC record available at https://lccn.loc.gov/2021009862

ISBN: 978-0-367-65134-3 (hbk)
ISBN: 978-0-367-65136-7 (pbk)
ISBN: 978-1-003-12799-4 (ebk)

DOI: 10.4324/9781003127994

Typeset in Times New Roman
by codeMantra

For Joseph and Abigail: always in my thoughts

Contents

Illustrations

Figures

Tables

Foreword

Having spent most of my academic career teaching and writing about post-war Japanese politics and doing research about Buraku issues, there is in retrospect a certain inevitability in my turning to focus on the formation of Dōwa policy as the place where post-war Japanese politicians embraced the Buraku problem. The idea for the project only crystallised in a conversation with Tim Amos at a Japanese studies conference held in Sydney in 2009 when we remarked about how little had been written either in Japanese or in English on the Dōwa policy – its formation, implementation, and impact. From that point, the question was less whether I should take on this project than how I could avoid it.

However, I still had my biography of Matsumoto Jiichirō to complete and, that done, found myself with an administrative load that made sustained research difficult. However once freed from that burden, I was granted a year of sabbatical leave in 2015 which I spent in Japan first based at Kyushu University and then at Keio University. That gave me the time to focus on collecting and reading the basic documents that had been produced by the government on Dōwa policy administration.

It soon became clear that the national narratives of Dōwa project policy were only part of the story and that how those policies were implemented at the local level was an essential part of the picture. There has been some work published on Dōwa policy in Osaka, Kyoto, and Nara. I was introduced to colleagues in Osaka and Nara who were generous with their sources and time providing me with material that makes up the first two parts of Chapter 8 in what follows. However, I felt that I should also try to capture the story of how Dōwa policy was implemented outside the Kansai region and, being based in Kyushu and also a long-time member of the Fukuoka Jinken Kenkyūkai, it seemed obvious that I should try to find a local case study. Following some tentative enquiries, I was introduced to material on Dōwa policy in a small city in the Chikuhō region that for the purposes of this book we will refer to as Q city.

During the five years that I have been actively involved in this research, I have incurred a number of academic debts that I would like to acknowledge. First, to the Japan Foundation who funded me for nine months in 2015 and Professor Hachiya Machiko who was my host in the Faculty of Law, Kyushu University during that time. Second, to Professors Tamai Kiyoshi and Oishi Yutaka who invited me to spend the final three months of that year at Keio University as a visiting professor. Many people in Osaka, Nara, and Fukuoka prefectures have spent time with me talking about Dōwa policy but in particular I would like to thank Oga Masayuki and Kanai Kōji in Osaka and Ioka Yasutoki in Nara for providing me with material and answering my questions. Kawamoto Kazuhiro of the Buraku Liberation and Human Rights Research Institute helped with several aspects of this project. I am particularly grateful to Tomonaga Kenzō who at short notice took the 'After' photographs that appear in Chapter 1. Many members of the Fukuoka Jinken Kenkyūkai have supported my research over the last 40 plus years but Moriyama Senichi and Horiuchi Tadashi have been particularly generous with their time in helping to understand how Dōwa policy was administered in the Chikuhō region.

Indirect but no less important academic support for this project came from Oxford colleagues in the Nissan Institute and St Antony's college with whom I discussed many of the ideas that appear in the following pages. Colleagues at Kyushu University, in particular Ed Vickers, Ted Boyle, and Mark Fenwick, organised seminars at which I tried out some of my first thoughts before a Japanese audience and lent a sympathetic ear to my frustrations. Tim Amos of the National University of Singapore was responsible for first sparking the notion of writing a book on Dōwa policy and has read most of the final manuscript making comments and asking questions which have made me rethink some sections. Christopher Bondy at the International Christian University in Tokyo has also provided helpful comments. Closer to publication, Robert Jones, a friend for more than 50 years, read through the manuscript and not only made some helpful observations but also introduced me to Elizabeth Gaskell's work on the Cagots of western France which suggests some intriguing parallels with Burakumin (Gaskell, 2005).

Family support has been important across the years of this project as ever. Andy and Masashi, Rose and Tomas, Joseph and Abigail, and of course Suzuko, have accompanied me and distracted my thoughts in productive ways. I fear that my thanks to them all, but especially to Suzuko, have too often gone without saying.

Despite all this assistance, on completing the final draft I became increasingly aware that it leaves many questions both unanswered and unasked about Dōwa policy and indeed the broader 'Buraku Question'. I hope that as readers spot these lacunae, at least some of them will be moved to fill the gaps. To quote from Elizabeth Gaskell:

> What faults you saw in me,
> Pray strive to shun;
> And look at home; there's
> Something to be done.
>
> (Gaskell, 2005, 39)

Ian Neary
New Yatt
January 2021

Bibliography

Gaskell E. C., (2005) *An Accursed Race*, The Project Gutenberg eBook. (Originally published in *Household Words*, 1855).

General Editors' preface to Ian Neary, *Dōwa Policy and Japanese Politics*

Few topics are as sensitive in the study of Japan as that of the *hisabetsu burakumin* (literally, 'the discriminated people of the hamlets'). Sometimes referred to as Japan's 'invisible race', the fact that communities of the *hisabetsu burakumin* are generally found in western Japan, particularly around the Kansai, Chugoku, Shikoku, and Kyushu areas, means that it is still possible for Japanese growing up in Eastern Japan, Tokyo, and further north, to not even know about their existence until they reach adulthood. The Japanese State's refusal to acknowledge their minority status plus the desire for many members of the *hisabetsu burakumin* communities to 'pass' undetected in society has rendered discussion of their history and status highly complicated and, in certain contexts, almost taboo. Despite this, it would not be correct to assume that the Japanese State did nothing in the post-war period to alleviate many of the economic and social problems which faced the *hisabetsu burakumin* communities. Unlike the civil rights-based policies which were being developed at that time in many Western countries, however, the Japanese government in the 1960s implemented a policy to improve the lot of these communities through the provision of funding that would improve housing and infrastructure designed to 'level up' living conditions and life chances of their residents.

Indeed, under the guise of support under the banner of '*dōwa*' (literally 'equalisation' or 'levelling up'), the Japanese State invested huge amounts of money to raise the living standards of *hisabetsu burakumin* communities; the Special Measures Law for Dōwa Policy Projects (SML) which was passed in 1969 provided ¥14 trillion (approx. $140 billion) of funding over the next 33 years. By the end of the 1990s, even the programme's sternest critics conceded that, while discrimination itself had not been expunged, the living environment of most of these communities had been transformed.

The author of this volume, Ian Neary, is the leading scholar in the field of 'Burakumin studies' and he has dealt with the sensitivities around writing about these communities for over 40 years. His work has encouraged others to follow in his footsteps and there is now a much stronger literature on the topic than there was even a decade ago. It is this background that allows Ian Neary to provide the first full account of exactly what the Japanese State did do in the post-war period in relation to what is widely called the '*buraku mondai*' (problem of the hamlets). In *Dōwa Policy and Japanese Politics*, Neary brings together, for the first time, a complete history and overview of the *dōwa* policy process and implementation at both national and local levels, in an account which is sure to serve as the key text on this topic for many years to come not just in English but also in the Japanese edition which is sure to follow. In many ways, this book ties together the work on Burakumin studies that has been produced over the past decade by placing the mobilisation of people, civil society, and government policies in a much broader framework and across the whole history of modern Japan since the Meiji Restoration of 1868.

Neary's account is much more, though, than just a historical record of *dōwa* policy. It provides important insights into the Japanese policy making system more generally in the post-war period and the State's ability to incorporate – critics might say 'co-opt' – the interests of marginalised groups without officially according them minority status. It also provides an important example of human rights protection and promotion and affirmative action in a non-Western society. The number of such accounts, we suspect, is vanishingly small, not necessarily because there are no similar cases elsewhere but because there is little academic interest in examples of where the State has delivered for its marginalised communities to such an extent. This, in turn, invites comparison with policies devised to mitigate discrimination elsewhere and forces us to question some of our own assumptions about whether the way such issues are tackled in our own societies in the end has the greatest impact for those communities for whom those policies have been designed.

The above reasons explain why, as the joint editors of Nissan Institute/Routledge Japanese Studies series – which has published well over a hundred volumes since its inception in 1986 – we are proud to include *Dōwa Policy and Japanese Politics*.

Roger Goodman
Arthur Stockwin
Oxford February 2021

1 Dōwa policy projects and the problems for which they were a solution

> Owing to discrimination which was formed based on social status in the course of the historical development of Japanese society, some Japanese people have been forced to endure a lower status economically, socially and culturally, and they are still subject to various kinds of discrimination in their daily lives even today. This is the Dōwa issue, which is a unique Japanese human rights problem.
>
> ...the State, together with local public entities, has been working since 1969 on measures for regional improvements ...in order to improve the impoverished environment of the Dōwa districts ... and the regional disparity has become considerably smaller.
>
> However, discrimination in marriage and employment has not ended....
>
> Ministry of Justice website 2015 (since deleted)

After being mostly overlooked by overseas scholarship, more has been written recently in English about the 'Buraku Problem'. Since 2000, some 15 academic monographs focusing exclusively or partially on Buraku issues have been published in the USA or the UK. However, most of them deal with historical topics; only three consider Buraku issues in the context of postwar Japan. A search of publications in academic journals reveals a slightly wider variety of articles that seek to explain the persistence of the Buraku issue in the context of contemporary Japan but none explore the origins or impact of the Dōwa policy that the state launched in 1969 to address, even solve, the 'Buraku Problem'.

There are of course many policy areas that have for whatever reason received scant attention in the English language literature. Japan is a large and complex political economy and the number of non-Japanese scholars working on it is relatively small and usually focused on topics relevant to their polities. Even in such circumstances one might expect to find more research published in Japanese about the Dōwa policy which had not, yet, been examined by overseas researchers. Now there was a time when this was true. As I will discuss in a little more detail later in this chapter, during the 1980s, there was a wave of interest in Dōwa

DOI: 10.4324/9781003127994-1

policy that led to a series of publications about what had been done, what remained to be done, and how effective it had been. Entering the 1990s, however, as the implementation of Dōwa policy drew to a close, that interest quickly evaporated. Most of what has been published on the topic since then has taken the form of compilations of government documents reproducing the legislation, regulations, and budgets of the Dōwa Projects Policy. But this did not stimulate researchers either in Japan or outside it to enquire what had been done or to assess what had been achieved. Exactly why this is at a time when there has been an increase in academic research about Japan is an interesting topic but not one that will be addressed here.

This book is a first step towards such an analysis. The historical focus for this study is the period between publication of the report of the Dōwa Taisaku Shingikai (Dōwa Policy Commission of Enquiry) in 1965 which set the parameters within which Dōwa policy was developed, and 2002 when it was brought to a close. Through these policies, the Japanese state aimed to improve the living environment and life chances of the residents of Dōwa districts and by the early twenty-first century most people, even Burakumin activists, would have agreed with the MoJ 2015 statement quoted above that 'the impoverished environment of the Dōwa districts' had been improved even though 'discrimination in marriage and employment has not ended…'.

The body of this volume will consider the background to Dōwa policy, how it was implemented over the course of 33 years, and what has replaced it. I will provide a summary of its contents shortly but first let me try to convey in a few paragraphs something of the nature of the discrimination being encountered by residents of Buraku communities/Dōwa districts at the time the Dōwa policies were being implemented.

Discrimination against Burakumin in the late twentieth and early twenty-first century – some selected examples

The Ministry of Justice website quoted above talks about the continuation of discrimination in marriage and employment, so we will focus on examples on those topics beginning with a vignette which introduces both issues[1]:

> Y M, was born in 1980, from Daiki town, Watarai-gun, Mie Prefecture. When she was in her second year of junior high school, the Civics teacher came to her house because her class were learning about the buraku issue. After the visit, she learned from her parents for the first time that they live in a discriminated buraku area. After graduation, the high school introduced her to a company hoping she could get work, but they did not hire her because she was from a Dōwa district. After she finished school, she started dating, but when they talked

> about marriage two years later, her boyfriend's mother was against it. M thought: 'We'd better break up then. But next time I go out with somebody, it will probably happen again. What's the point of my life?' and she mindlessly cut her wrists. Fortunately, her family was nearby and prevented a tragedy.
>
> (Šturdík, (Kurokawa) 2017, 709)

A slightly more detailed account illustrates some of the psychological and social complexity of discrimination when such a marriage takes place:

> Hiroko and Kenichi, married each other in 1984 when they were both 22. They started seeing each other in middle school and continued to see each other in high school. Hiroko called Kenichi's house frequently and even met his parents several times. Hiroko figures that Kenichi's parents found out that she was a Burakumin because her father is a well-known Buraku liberation movement leader in the area. From the time they started dating, Hiroko had doubts about the relationship: 'I kept thinking that if I can't explain [the essence of what it means to be Burakumin] to my boyfriend and make him understand, then who can I explain it to? So, it was more than just the fact that I liked him, but my own pride and stubbornness kept me from giving up.' After graduation, they saw little of each other except on weekends. Hiroko was content to continue dating Kenichi and to go out with her friends, but when her mother decided it was time for her to get married, she went along with it. This is when Hiroko and Kenichi found out that Kenichi's parents were against the marriage. They said, 'We have a lot of relatives, and we are not going to be able to see them [if Kenichi marries a Burakumin].' In addition, Kenichi's parents believed that Kenichi and Hiroko's marriage would adversely affect Kenichi's younger sister's chance of marrying. Kenichi's sister told her parents that she thought this was absurd. She also went to the same middle and high schools as Hiroko and Kenichi and had many Burakumin friends. She had no prejudiced attitudes and stood up for Hiroko and Kenichi. During this time, Hiroko had difficulty dealing with the discrimination: 'I felt like it would all be OK if I just gave up. I knew that discrimination was bad, yet somewhere in the back of my mind, I had this feeling that I was somehow to blame because I am a Burakumin.' Meanwhile, Kenichi and his parents fought almost every night about the upcoming wedding. Kenichi told Hiroko that he would marry her even if he defied his parent's wishes or they disowned him. Kenichi's parents eventually gave in, mostly because they realized they could do nothing to stop the marriage. Even so, only Kenichi's mother and sister came to Kenichi and Hiroko's wedding. After their marriage, they rented a house in the Buraku area against the wishes of Kenichi's parents, who objected because Kenichi and their children would be perceived as Burakumin.

> Only Kenichi's mother ever visited them in the Buraku area, and this was ... only after her grandchildren were born. Kenichi's father died without ever visiting his son's house.
>
> (Morgan, 2007, 32–3)

Both of these scenarios played out during the last decades of the twentieth century while Dōwa policy was being implemented by central and local governments. But there is evidence that similar discrimination continues and does not only involve young adults:

> In 2015, a divorced middle-aged man was considering proposing to a co-worker. He first revealed his Buraku background to her, as he had experienced marriage discrimination before. The woman was not, herself, deterred from accepting the man. She decided to mention him, little by little, to her mother—omitting his intentions, and of course his Buraku origin. The mother ... immediately took the man's name to a detective agency. The budding romance was nipped in the bud.
>
> (Kobayakawa, 2020, 13)

Few companies would admit to practising employment discrimination and examples are hard to find but Kobayakawa cites the case of a manager who was quite explicit:

> One branch manager of a company with its headquarters in Tokyo said to a career counselor that 'it is better to tell you now rather than later and get into trouble. My company absolutely does not hire Koreans or Burakumin.' The publication of another company taught branch managers that Burakumin were the class of employee most to be avoided... *shafū* is the usual reason for rejecting applicants. *Shafū* means a company's atmosphere, a corporate culture, a company style, and [the company] rejects applicants from minorities such as Burakumin and Koreans, former convicts, the disabled, and so on. On top of the shame of associating with Burakumin, there is the 'common knowledge' that Burakumin are less productive than non-Burakumin.
>
> (Kobayakawa, 2020, 14)

When marriages have taken place, the non-Buraku partner may often find themselves subject to 'micro-aggressive' discrimination if they choose to live in the Buraku community:

> The first time I felt like I was discriminated against was a small thing, but happened when my first child was entering elementary school and I wanted to get dressed up for the ceremony... I put on my Kimono (formal dress) and went to a hair salon located just outside the Buraku area.

> Other elementary schools around the area were also having ceremonies, so while the beautician was cutting my hair, she was asking me if my child went to one of the schools outside of the Buraku area and was naming the various schools. I said no and as soon as I told her the name of the school [this school is located in the Buraku area and most people know it is a Buraku school] her face changed: she shut up and gave me a cold look. After I went home, I thought that the beautician probably didn't think a Buraku woman would go to her shop to get her hair done for a school ceremony...That's when I really felt that people look down on the Buraku school, as well as the school children's parents.
>
> (Morgan, 2007, 47)

Moreover, discrimination can follow a person throughout their careers. The following instance relates to an event that took place between 2001 and 2003, just as the Dōwa programmes were coming to an end, and involved a leading politician:

> Nonaka Hiromu, born 1925 in a Buraku in Kyoto prefecture, became one of the most prominent members of Liberal Democrat Party in the 1990s rising to the post of secretary-general by 2001 at which point he was a possible contender to become party leader and thus PM. Asō Tarō, another contender for the leadership, strongly opposed Nonaka's ambitions at a meeting in 2001 and then again at the executive council of the Liberal Democratic Party in 2003. In 2001 he is reported to have said: 'Nonaka, A and B are all Buraku people. So what's going to happen if people like that become Prime Minister of Japan. (Laughs).' Asō denied the reports at the time but Nonaka has since repeated the allegations.
>
> (Šturdík, 2017, 704–5 quoting Kurokawa; Nonaka and Shin 2009, 164)

Each of these vignettes deserves greater exposition that there is no space to provide here. If the reader is interested to learn more, they should refer to the original sources. However, I think that they serve to demonstrate first how prejudices and discrimination persistently constrained the daily lives of those born into Buraku communities and those who associate with them in the late twentieth century, the era of the Dōwa policy projects. And, second, that they affect the lives of a broad swathe of Japanese people, from a non-Buraku heritage mother at the hairdressers to a potential leader of the ruling party. As we will see, the origins of these prejudices can be traced back into Japanese history but they are not a problem of the past alone and have been recreated within Japanese society such that they continue to influence how mainstream Japanese regard Burakumin and how they see themselves.

A note on definition and size of population

Burakumin cannot be distinguished from mainstream Japanese people ethnically, religiously, or linguistically. Some Western analysts refer to them as descendants of outcastes of the early modern, Edo period in order to indicate their location both geographically and normatively outside 'normal' society and to suggest the possibility of comparison with the plight of outcaste communities in South, Southeast Asia, and even Africa. Others suggest that it is more productive to think of them 'as if' they were a 'racial' group (Brown 2013; Kurokawa 2016). There are a number of difficulties that arise from the problem of definition which will be explored in the following text but for the moment I want to focus on the more basic question of how many of them there are? Across the twentieth century, successive government surveys indicated that around 1% of the Japanese population reside in Buraku communities and are descendants of outcastes of the pre-modern period, suggesting a population of around one million. However, those who have campaigned on their behalf frame their constituency as all those who, if their background were known, would be vulnerable to discrimination, such as in marriage or employment, whether or not they reside in Buraku communities bringing the likely figure to over three million although this figure is widely disputed. Moreover, as we will see later, they are not distributed uniformly across the islands of Japan meaning that while there are no Buraku communities in some regions, in some towns and cities, for example, in northern Kyushu, they comprise up to 20% of the population. We will return to the problem of definition and identity across the body of this text and in the conclusion.

Dōwa policy – a summary

Dōwa policy had antecedents in the Yūwa policies devised mainly from the late 1920s which themselves can be traced back to the 'social policy' of the final years of the Meiji era that were essentially the state's response to a perceived imminent threat from the emergence of a small number of social movement organisations, some of which were linked to the even smaller number of socialist groups. Yūwa policy in the 1920s continued to be characterised by its attempts to deter Buraku communities from supporting 'socialism' but it also contained some measures that improved their living conditions. National coordination of these programmes was reinforced in 1935 with the launch of a Ten-Year Yūwa Plan which, while embracing some efforts to improve education in schools and reduce unemployment, increasingly did so in coordination with the mobilisation of the whole population in support of war. National coordination of Yūwa policy, by now called Dōwa policy, ceased in 1945.

Some local governments revived Dōwa projects as early as 1946 and 1947 in the face of the indifference of both central government and the

US Occupation. More and more local governments adopted similar, albeit small-scale, programmes until by the early 1950s every prefecture with a significant Burakumin population had a Dōwa policy of some kind. Moreover, they began to convene regular conferences which among other things would request central government to provide coordination and funding. Parallel to this, the Burakumin social movement evolved to create the Buraku Liberation League in 1955 which also demanded that the state should take some responsibility for resolving their problems.

These demands were transmitted through the democratic process and during the 1950s Diet members, at first from the JSP but later in the decade also from the LDP, started to petition the government to formulate a clear Dōwa strategy. In fact, one ministry, the Ministry of Health and Welfare which pre-war had been the lead ministry for Yūwa policy, made its first budget allocation for Dōwa projects as early as FY1953 and a few more followed later in the decade but there was little coordination. The major breakthrough occurred in 1959–60 when government conceded to a Diet request to establish a committee of enquiry (*shingikai*) into the problem known as the Dōwa Taisaku Shingikai. After almost four years of deliberation it produced its report, the Dōtaishin, that recognised that there was discrimination against Burakumin and that it amounted to 'an infringement of their civil rights and freedoms' which it was the duty of the state to eliminate.

This was followed by another four years of debate within the Diet and in society more generally about what kind of policy package might best deal with this. Finally, in the summer of 1969 a Special Measures Law (SML), initially set to last for ten years, was adopted that provided an outline legal framework for the creation of the Dōwa Policy Programme (*Dōwa Taisaku Jigyō*). The law emphasised that this policy was to be implemented through the cooperation of central and local governments which in effect meant that the initiative had to come 'bottom up'. No central government agency was formed and indeed the amount of central government coordination was minimal. Over the course of the 1970s, more than one thousand local government units, both prefectures and municipalities, devised Dōwa programmes for their communities funded by central and local taxation and loans. The initial SML was extended for three years. Then, after further debate, in 1982, it was renamed the Chiiki Kaizen Taisaku (Regional Improvement Policy) but continued essentially unchanged for another five years with slightly different terms of reference. In 1986 although some conservatives wanted the Dōwa programme to be discontinued, it was argued that there were still some projects that were incomplete and even some Buraku communities which had not benefited from any Dōwa improvements. Therefore, following some minor changes to its title, the policy was further extended for five, then another five years until in 1996 it was decided that the remaining capital projects should be completed and that responsibility for the welfare aspects of Dōwa policy should be transferred to the 'general' social welfare budgets. Dōwa policy then would cease at the end of FY2001–2. However, the document produced in 1996 that approved the process by which the Dōwa programmes would be wound down explicitly noted that just because state funding was ending did not mean that that the problem was solved. Moreover, as long as discrimination against Burakumin continued to exist so would the duty of the state to take action to eliminate it.

Dōwa policy – its cost

It is difficult to provide an accurate figure of how much was spent on Dōwa projects despite the existence of some very detailed budget tables provided in government documents. Over the 33 years of the SML, FY1969–2001, the total burden born by the national government was just over ¥4 trillion (to be precise ¥4,291,031 million). For comparison, before that, between FY1953–68 the total Dōwa spend had been ¥17,803 million. However, despite the stipulation in the SML of 1969 that the state would provide up to two-thirds of funding for many of the projects, it was a constant complaint that the implementation of Dōwa policy was a serious drain on local government finance that was not being properly supported by the central government. We will comment further and in some detail about this in Chapter 8 but overall estimates suggest that total spending by prefectures and municipalities on Dōwa policies was more than twice that of the central state. This would make total Dōwa spending by all levels of government in the range of ¥14–5 trillion.

Dōwa policy – its geographical scope

There never were any Buraku communities in either Hokkaidō or Okinawa but the 1935 census, which is widely regarded as having been the most comprehensive, found Buraku communities in 41 of the remaining 45 prefectures. Mizuuchi and Jeon, two urban sociologists, have provided the best summary of the impact of Dōwa policy and translated data from surveys of Dōwa project expenditure and Buraku population in 1974 and 1975, respectively, on to a map which is reproduced below (Mizuuchi and Jeon, 2010) (Figure 1.1).

Although total Dōwa spending increased rapidly after the 1970s, the pattern of spending remained more or less constant across the country. As is clear from the map, the six prefectures that make up Tōhoku, Yamanashi, Toyama, and Ishikawa reported that they had no Buraku communities and therefore received no Dōwa funding. Overall, the amount of money distributed to fund Dōwa projects, predictably perhaps, was concentrated in those prefectures where their population was the densest. However, funding was not allocated simply on the basis of the presence of Buraku communities. Local governments had, in collaboration with their Buraku communities, to formulate a plan for Dōwa projects. This required those communities to communally 'come out' as a Buraku community which some, especially smaller communities, refused to do. We will return to this.

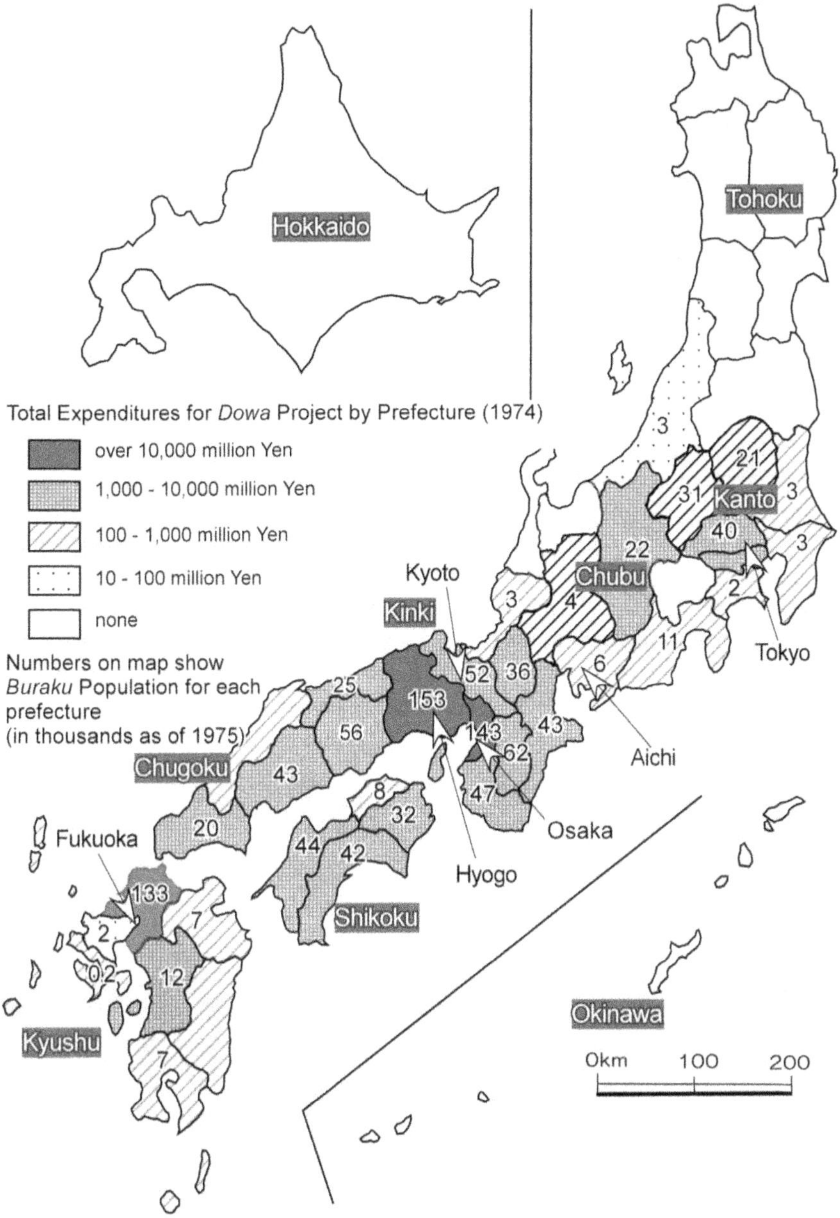

Figure 1.1 Total expenditure on Dōwa policy in 1974 and estimates of Buraku population by prefecture.

Dōwa policy – its impact on urban areas

In many urban areas, the impact of Dōwa policy was to transform the appearance of the built environment of Buraku districts. In some parts of Fukuoka, for example, as the city was modernising in the 1960s and 1970s, the Buraku communities were much slower to change meaning that even an uninformed outsider could roughly tell where they began and ended by the fact that their buildings were low level, usually not more than a single storey, shabby and unimproved with only narrow lanes providing access. It was one aim of the Dōwa programmes to change this. The following short series of 'Before' and 'After' photographs gives an impression of what living conditions looked like in the later 1950s and early 1960s and how they had changed by the twenty-first century. They were taken in a Buraku community in Osaka city before the Dōwa programmes began and in 2020 (Figures 1.2–1.7).

With more than one thousand local authorities engaged in the implementation of Dowa programmes across central and western Japan, there was considerable variation in how Dōwa policy was interpreted and implemented. However, at least in urban areas, the transformation that is suggested by this series of photographs was replicated in many areas of Japan. The improvements have been a physical manifestation of the intention to eliminate the vicious circle that was reproducing discrimination based on the perception that living conditions in Buraku communities were not only poor but in some way being left behind. While there may remain issues that affect the residents of these areas and the location of the Buraku

Figure 1.2 Before 1: Street level view of the Sumiyoshi area, Osaka, 1959.

Figure 1.3 After 1: Photograph of the same area of Sumiyoshi, Osaka, 2020.

Figure 1.4 Before 2: View over the rooftops of buildings in Sumiyoshi area, Osaka, 1962.

Figure 1.5 After 2: Photograph of the same area in Sumiyoshi, Osaka, 2020.

Figure 1.6 Before 3: Sumiyoshi, to the south of apartment building 11, Osaka, 1962.

Figure 1.7 After 3: Sumiyoshi, to the south of apartment building 11, Osaka, 2020.

communities will still be known by long-term residents, the Dōwa policy rehousing programmes have done a great deal to ensure that Buraku communities blend into urban landscapes.

Dōwa policy – the existing literature

So, what have the main sources of information had to say about the development of Dōwa policy? Among the early coverage of the Buraku issue in English, one book edited by George DeVos and Hiroshi Wagatsuma, *Japan's Invisible Race*, stands out as, in Hankin's words, 'iconic' mainly by virtue of being an attempt to provide a multi-disciplinary overview of the issue combining perspectives from history, anthropology and psychology with cross-cultural approaches to 'caste'. Although published in 1966 (with a revised edition in 1972), the historical narrative only runs up to 1961. Brief mention is made of the creation of the *shingikai* but the author (Wagatsuma) expresses doubts, '…whether the government's conciliatory attitude towards outcaste minority demands will result in large-scale ameliorative measures' (DeVos and Wagatsuma, 1972, 84–5). In 1977, Yoshino and Murakoshi produced a relatively short volume which attempts to update DeVos and Wagatsuma and suggested that Burakumin are not quite so invisible, as hinted at in their enigmatic title, '*The Invisible Visible Minority – Japan's Burakumin*'.

Although it provides a brief summary of the 1965 Dōtaishin and the passage of the SML in 1969 is mentioned in one paragraph, it has nothing to say about the content of Dōwa policy (Yoshino and Murakoshi, 1977, 83–7, 89).

During the 1970s, the Buraku liberation movement became divided between a mainstream group within the BLL and a group that was critical of the BLL leadership. The latter worked at first (from 1970) to try to reform the movement from within before splitting off to create an independent organisation in 1976, called the Zenkoku Buraku Kaihō Undō Rengōkai (Zenkairen). Suginohara Juichi worked within this latter tradition and in 1982 published *The Status Discrimination in Japan* as a response to Yoshino and Murakoshi who were associated with the BLL. Suginohara has more to say about the Dōwa administration in particular about improvements made to housing and the living environment, 'remedying the scars of discrimination' as he puts it. But he is strongly critical of the way the state has evaded responsibility and pushed onto local governments the duty to execute Dōwa policies. Moreover, he warns that it is necessary to 'thoroughly destroy their reactionary influence and to strengthen struggle for conquering the negative side of the *shingikai* report and the SML and making the most of their positive side' (Suginohara, 1982, 75).

At this point, we encounter the pioneering work of Frank Upham, a legal scholar now teaching in NYU whose analysis of Dōwa policy set a high standard. He begins his review of the first ten years of the Dōwa policy with the comment that 'there is very little written in English about recent government efforts to eliminate discrimination…' (Upham, 1980, 39). Focusing mainly on legal issues, he summarises the main elements of the Dōwa projects as they were implemented in Osaka city and prefecture improving the physical living environment, promoting welfare and employment opportunities, encouraging educational achievement, and enhancing human rights protection. But, despite the SML mandating central government support for these projects up to two-thirds of their cost, he noted that between 1969 and 1975 the state only re-imbursed 12.12% of Osaka prefecture's Dōwa expenditure (Upham, 1980, 50). He is the first to comment on the central role played within the implementation process by the Dōwa Jigyō Sokushin Kyōgikai (Dōsokkyō) which, while having no formal legal status, acted as an intermediary between the local administration and Burakumin, not only making demands and drafting plans on behalf of the Buraku communities but also screening their applications for the various benefits provided through the projects, particularly the provision of goods or services to individuals or households. As he remarks, this worked well until the movement split. He takes a particular interest in the case brought by the JCP supported Zenkairen in which in 1972 an Osaka woman filed for Dōwa benefits *without* Dōsokkyō endorsement. The court judgement provided elements which enabled both sides to claim vindication. While the court praised the Dōsokkyō role as adding to administrative efficiency and ensuring the provision of Dōwa benefits were not seen as simple charity, it also argued that Osaka city should provide an alternative route for applicants who were refused Dōsokkyō endorsement for some reason (Upham, 1980, 58). We will discuss this judgement and the problem of *Madoguchi Ippon* (Single Window) in more detail in Chapter 8.

Of more interest at the moment is Upham's provisional assessment of the programmes after the first ten years. He concludes that while they do appear to be improving the lot of Burakumin as a group in a narrow sense, they do little to facilitate their entry into modern life. At worst, they work against residential integration by concentrating Burakumin into high rise apartments leaving non-Buraku families behind in sub-standard housing or totally displacing them. He suggests that affirmative action in the employment market or statutes that made discrimination illegal were unlikely as the government would be reluctant to enforce it. At best, then, the urban renewal programmes amounted to visible signs of an LDP commitment to social justice but they left basic problems untouched. Dōwa policy, he concludes, has little more than symbolic importance (Upham, 1980, 73).

The chapter that Upham published in 1987 focused much less on Dōwa policy than on the 'denunciation strategy' (*kyūdan*) that Burakumin activists used to persuade discriminators to apologise and to illustrate the existence of embedded prejudice. However, he does refer to Dōwa policy commenting that the SML 'gave broad authority for government action while mandating virtually nothing' (Upham, 1987, 86). As a result, the scope of the improvement projects, the level of welfare payments, and the way they are distributed – means tested or not, requiring BLL endorsement or not – depended greatly on the power and activism of the local BLL chapter. From the evidence he gathered in Osaka from the 1970s, he concluded that, on the one hand, the BLL chose not to pursue the protection of equal opportunity but rather the improvement of material conditions which suited the government; on the other hand, it created a system that mandated 'no legal duties on the part of government agencies and legal rights for individuals…' (Upham, 1987, 86). And that was pretty much the final word about Dōwa policy written by English-speaking academics in the twentieth century.

There was, of course, discussion of the implementation of Dōwa policy in Japan, although by no means as much as one might have expected. The peak for such publications was the 1980s, not coincidentally the peak of spending on Dōwa projects. This was, first, because alongside provision for improvement projects of various kinds, it was possible to persuade local government to channel Dōwa funding in support of the activities of groups of local activists and academics interested in Buraku history. For example, the Fukuoka Burakushi Kenkyūkai (Fukuoka Buraku History Research Association) was set up in 1974 supported by Fukuoka city and prefecture and it began to publish a journal a year later. Over the next decade, similar groups were established in many areas. Second, there were social scientists who became involved in Dōwa policy implementation and built on their experiences to analyse the scope and effectiveness of these projects. We will briefly discuss

Isomura Eichi below but the Osaka-based urban sociologist Yamamoto Noboru also served on the Dōwa Taisaku Kyōgikai between 1966 and 1992 and published articles and books about the policy. There were numerous other social scientists and historians who published about Buraku issues during the 1980s some of whom commented on Dōwa policy. However, with one or two exceptions this interest waned during the 1990s almost in parallel with the winding down of the Dōwa projects.

In the rest of this chapter, we will consider in a little more detail the work of three Japanese authors whose writing on Dōwa policy and projects has been fundamental to understanding of the policy: Isomura Eichi, Kanai Kōji, and Suginohara Juichi, the latter two of whom maintained their interest in Dōwa policy and have published it about into the twenty-first century. Their writing reflects the three strands of writing and thinking about Dōwa policy.

As we will see, Isomura Eichi was a key figure in the development of Dōwa policy. Born in Tokyo in 1903, he reports first having encountered the Buraku issue as a child when he became aware of a Buraku community close to where he lived. After graduation from Tokyo University, he embarked on career as an employee of the Tokyo municipality in 1928 where he worked throughout the war but was forced to resign his post by the occupation purge. He began teaching at Tokyo Metropolitan University (TMU) in 1949, becoming full-time there in 1953 specialising in urban sociology and working on urban slums both in Japan and elsewhere. He retired from TMU in 1966 but took up a similar post in Tōyō University later serving as its president between 1969 and 1982, taking on the latter post at the height of student radicalism. He became a member of the Dōwa policy *shingikai* that was formed in 1961 and was re-appointed in 1966 to the Dōtaikyō which was charged first with overseeing the development of government policy in response to the report and then with the implementation of the SML after it was passed in 1969. In 1972 he was appointed its chair, a position he retained for 20 years until 1992 by which time he was almost 90 years old. In the course of his academic career, he published prolifically including several volumes on Dōwa policy issues and was the editor of a series of five volumes entitled *Dōwa Gyōseiron* (Research on Dōwa Administration) published between 1983 and 1986 which brought together articles on the impact of Dōwa policy on particular Buraku communities alongside overviews of Dōwa policy administration often written by Isomura himself. He set out his approach to the issue clearly in a book published in 1982 in which he argued that the 'Dōwa problem' should be regarded as a 'human rights problem' and suggested that the three sections into which the Buraku movement had divided should come together on that basis (Isomura, 1982, 151). In 1986, writing on the prospects for an extension to the SML, he noted that although Dōwa policy had incorporated some human rights ideas that set it apart from the general social welfare policies, it needed to develop 'horizontal solidarity' to create communities that crossed Buraku boundaries. While he conceded that this was difficult in Japan given its 'vertical society', he suggested that a way forward might be to include respect for human rights into the plans for '*machizukuri*' (neighbourhood planning/urban renewal) that many municipalities were devising (Isomura, 1986, 7, 26). He argued that it is appropriate to consider the Buraku problem as a 'transient' issue that can be resolved before the end of the twentieth century by completing the remaining Dōwa project improvements at the same time as passing a law to penalise discrimination that would move the focus away from communities and to the individual. Such an approach would be consistent with the increased influence of international human rights standards on Japanese practice as seen following ratification of CEDAW in 1985 (Isomura, 1986, 24). These are the views of a liberal scholar-administrator trying to ensure progress amid a reluctance to commit to further policies within the government and fierce antipathy between the rival wings of the liberation movement.

Kanai Kōji published the first, and so far, only single volume account of Dōwa policy in 1991. It traces the policy from its origins in the occupation period up to the early 1990s providing the most comprehensive account of the policy process. He has since supplemented it with two recent additions which focus in more detail on the policy process from the publication of the Dōtaishin to the passage of the SML (December 2018) and the development of Buraku policy under the occupation (December 2019). Although published by the Kaihō Shuppansha he does not (at least in my reading) take a line close to that of the BLL but rather seeks to stick to a simple view that by learning from history we can learn about the future (Kanai, 1991, 2). In his conclusion, he suggests that although there is more that Dōwa administration could have done, the Buraku problem will never be resolved without changes of attitudes among the Japanese people at large, for example, in companies, in schools, and in religious organisations. He suggests that this will require a re-examination of Japan's social structure and the creation of new social values based on respect for human rights and the implementation of freedom and equality to guide society as a whole, including those involved in Dōwa administration (Kanai, 1991, 302–3).

Finally, the only other attempt to provide a complete overview of the development of Dōwa policy was published by Suginohara Juichi in 20 parts in the journal *Jinken to Buraku Mondai* between April 2006 and November 2007. Like Kanai, he begins with the occupation period but, having the advantage of being published 15 years later and 5 years after the expiration of the SML, he is able to provide a more complete picture of the policies' final years and their immediate aftermath. He sets out his position clearly in his first sentence, 'The Buraku Problem which is based on the residue of feudal status discrimination is approaching the final stage of its solution…' (Suginohara 744, 2006, 74) In his earlier work, he had stressed the way in which 'reactionary power' used the Dōwa administration to divide the Buraku liberation movement and that 'struggle to dissolve discrimination against Burakumin' needed to be part of the 'struggle for checking and destroying the despotic rule of monopolistic capitalism' (Suginohara, 1982, 128–9). While he seems to have modified his political perspective, his underlying argument clings to the Marxist framework and remains that Buraku discrimination is a feudal remnant which can be and is being resolved within the framework of capitalist society. In the absence of any material or ideological basis for discrimination the Buraku problem is rapidly disappearing and as such any further 'special' measures will only serve to perpetuate awareness of the issue (Amos, 2020). However, although he misses no opportunity criticise the actions and theory of the 'Asada group' within the BLL during the 1970s and the alleged excesses of BLL demands, Suginohara provides a balanced and well thought-through account of the development of Dōwa policy and the years that immediately followed the expiration of the SML.

Between 2010 and 2011, a five-volume series with the title *Buraku Mondai Kaiketsu Katei no Kenkyū* (Studies on the Process of the Resolution of the Buraku Problem) was published by the Buraku Mondai Kenkyūsho which sounded as though it might be about the Dōwa policies. However, while it included some essays that were relevant to the context within which Dōwa policy was devised and implemented, disappointingly few of them provide details or analysis of those policies or programmes.

To summarise: there has been no significant attempt to analyse the background or content of the Dōwa policy projects written in English since Upham's publications in the 1980s. In Japanese, Isomura provided accounts of the evolution of Dōwa policy from his position as a liberal academic inside the policy making process, Kanai made a major contribution to the literature when he published in 1991 his critical account that emphasised the deep-rooted nature of prejudice, while Suginohara's rather less easily accessible journal articles provided an account that emphasised that the problem if not yet solved was close to resolution. There is however no more recent academic analysis of Dōwa policy in Japanese.

Dōwa policy – this book

Building on the work done by Isomura, Kanai, and Suginohara and using the data and documents that have been published in works such as *Dōwa Gyōseishi* (A History of Dōwa Administration, 2002), this book amounts to a first attempt to fill that gap.

The next chapter will suggest the themes that will guide the analysis over the course of the volume as a whole. I propose five approaches to the problem each of which will contribute in different ways to our understanding of the form and content of Dōwa policy. First, I argue that at the most abstract level, our account of the evolution of Dōwa policy illustrates the evolving narratives about the implications of the constitutional and international commitments to human rights standards for the domestic policies of states, which enables us to ask questions about how seriously Japan has taken those commitments. Second, and relatedly, I want to enquire about the international context to the formulation of Dōwa policy and how the international dimension has informed domestic decision making. Most accounts focus on the national debates but, as we have seen, Isomura who was at the core of the Dōwa policy process emphasised the importance of the UN human rights regime from at least the early 1980s. Thirdly, the domestic context was also important, in particular the parallel processes in which broader strategies of Japanese welfare policy were being discussed and defined at the same time that Dōwa policy was being considered and formulated. Fourthly, as mentioned in the summary above, the response to the report of the mid-1960s was not to create a new agency of central government to administer the programme but rather to insist that the initiative be taken by local government which raises questions about the size of the Japanese state and its relations with local government. Finally, noting that the ultimate test of Buraku identity is that of 'common knowledge', there being no ethnic, religious, or racial markers that distinguish them from other Japanese, it is particularly appropriate to ask how far the 'Dōwa problem' and solutions to it have been socially constituted and how that process of social construction has influenced policy.

Having set out those themes, Chapter 3 locates the post-war development of Dōwa policy within its historical context. The militarist wartime regime, often referred to as 'fascist' by post-war critics, cast a deep shadow across post-war society. Many feared that the Cold War-inspired policies of conservative governments in the 1950s were rolling back the liberal reforms of the Occupation era, thus recreating the basis for a revival of an authoritarian nation state. Yūwa policy had been devised primarily as a means to deter activity independent of the state even if during the 1930s it also provided some funding for livelihood improvements. It was not surprising then that Burakumin activists examined proposals for a national Dōwa policy for evidence that they too were more about control than genuine concern about their living conditions. Moreover, both at the national level and within local government, many of those who had been involved in the administration of pre-war Yūwa projects took up similar duties within post-war Dōwa programmes. Chapter 3 summarises the development of Yūwa administration in order to better understand the origins of the Dōwa policy.

To the extent that Dōwa policy has received any analytic attention, it has largely been regarded in Galapagos-like isolation of the rest of the policy process. However, the process through which policy proposals passed was not dissimilar to many other policies of the same period. Chapter 4 looks at the initial stages of that process from the first, mainly local government-based, policies adopted in response to concerns about Buraku living conditions to the attempts made by Diet members to urge government to formulate a national response to the demands being expressed by their constituents, local governments and the Buraku Liberation League. However, by 1960 all this had produced was a poorly planned and inadequately funded Ten-Year Plan that reminded many of the similarly named programme launched in

1935, and a law that authorised the creation of a *shingikai*. At that point, many would have agreed with Wagatsuma who doubted that its conclusions would result in any large-scale ameliorative measures. However, contrary to the expectations of many, the *shingikai* report of 1965 came very close to the demands being made by the Buraku activists even if the law finally passed in 1969 fell short of their hopes. Chapter 5 pays close attention to tracing this policy process.

Chapter 6 describes the three phases of the implementation of Dōwa policy:

Phase I, between 1969 and 1982 the Dōwa Taisaku Jigyō was characterised by a rapid increase in the amount of funding provided in response to programmes of Dōwa projects that were devised in and by Buraku communities across the country. When it became clear that the policy aims could not be completed within the initial ten-year time frame, it was relatively easy to persuade government to allow an extension, but only for three years. In terms of administrative control, what began under the supervision of the MHW was transferred to the Sōmuchō in 1984. Meanwhile, the advisory body formed in 1966, the Dōwa Taisaku Kyōgikai (Dōtaikyō), was reformed in 1982 to exclude all representatives of the Buraku liberation movement.

Phase II, 1982–7, began with a change in the name of the programme to Chiiki Kaizen Jigyō Taisaku (Regional Improvement Project Policy) but the nature of the projects supported remained the same. In fact, this five-year period was the peak in terms of number of projects funded and their cost. Within the LDP there was some resistance to any further extension of Dōwa policy but in the end it was renewed with more or less the same levels of funding but a commitment to reduce the number and scope of the projects.

Phase III, 1988–2002, the programme's name was formally changed once more to Chiiki Kaizen Taisaku Tokutei Jigyō (Regional Improvement Policy Designated Projects) by legislation that emphasised the special financial provision being made to support the programmes. This time the discussion of extension assumed that all outstanding projects would be completed in the near future but that there might be a small number of new projects started in those Buraku communities which had benefited little or not at all thus far. In the end, the Dōwa programmes were extended twice more in a process that looked increasingly routinised. The final document of the advisory committee published in May 1996 discussed the termination of the programme but firmly endorsed the view that it would continue to be the duty of the state to take action to eliminate discrimination for as long as it continued, and looked forward to the development of policies that would extend human rights protection within Japan such that it would protect the interests of a wide range of vulnerable communities, including Burakumin.

Up to that point, the narrative follows the leads provided by Kanai and Suginohara explaining the evolution of policy at the national level. However, Dōwa policy was only ever loosely coordinated at the level of the national government. Chapters 7 and 8 provide more detailed accounts of how policy was carried out by the main ministries and at the local level. Very detailed descriptions exist of the budgets and programmes of each of the ministries. Chapter 7 summarises the projects that each ministry implemented.

Given that there were over one thousand local authorities that were involved in devising and then implementing Dōwa Project Programmes, it is impossible to give a full picture of how policy worked out on the ground. And yet since Dōwa projects were primarily local responses to specific conditions it seemed important to give some kind of description of Dōwa policy at the rice-roots level. Fortunately, there is a single volume narrative account of Dōwa policy in Nara prefecture and sufficient material about Dōwa policy in Osaka prefecture and city for it to be possible to provide an overview of how Dōwa policy worked there. In addition, I was allowed access to records of Dōwa policy administration in a city in Fukuoka prefecture which I will refer to as Q city in order to provide some anonymity. This allows us to see the evolution of Dōwa policy in very different circumstances to those in the Kansai region.

There have been repeated accusations across the years that significant amounts of Dōwa funding were wasted on unnecessary projects or been channelled into the hands of Buraku bosses with links to organised crime (*yakuza*). It is difficult to ascertain the extent of this but in a brief penultimate chapter, I review some of the discussion that lies in the public domain before concluding that, at least in part, it is just one aspect of the broader systemic corruption endemic within the Japanese construction industry.

Finally, I return to the themes outlined in Chapter 2 and argue that using these complementary perspectives as frames of reference enables us to extract Dōwa policy from its domestic Japanese context and draw lessons about not only the policy making and human rights in Japan but also about the influence of the international contexts.

*****

Section 1 of the Dōtaishin, the definitive report on the issue published in 1965 is entitled the 'Basic Nature of the Dōwa Problem' and contains the following passage in the section on 'discrimination in modern Japan':

> Buraku discrimination in modern Japan in brief is nothing other than the infringement of civil rights and freedoms. Civil rights and freedoms include the freedom to select occupation, the right to be assured equality of opportunity in education, freedom of residence and mobility, and freedom in marriage. That these rights and freedoms are not completely protected in the case of residents of Dōwa districts amounts

> to discrimination...Accordingly, the central topics for Dōwa problem policy are to ensure complete protection of equality of opportunity in employment and education for residents of Dōwa districts and planning to increase the stability of their lives and the level of their social status by having the accumulating surplus population that exists in the Dōwa districts enter the production process of major modern industries.
>
> (Dōwa Gyōseishi Henshū Iinkai, 2002, 233)[2]

The core task of this book is to explore why and how the Japanese government responded to this report and assess its consequences for the Buraku communities.

Notes

1 Each of these vignettes has been edited for length.
2 Unless otherwise indicated, all the translations from Japanese are by the author.

Bibliography

Amos T., (2020) 'Contested Liberation: The Japanese Communist Party, Human Rights Groups, and the New Anti-Discrimination Law', *Japan Forum*, vol. 32, no. 2: 220–43.

Brown E. S., (2013) 'Racialization in a 'Homogenous' Society? The Case of Buraku People in Japan', *Asian Ethnicity*, vol. 14, no. 1, 1–28.

Buraku Mondai Kenkyūsho, (2010–1) *Buraku Mondai Kaiketsu Katei no Kenkyū* (Studies on the Process of the Resolution of the Buraku Problem), Vol. 1–5, Kyoto: Buraku Mondai Kenkyūsho Shuppanbu.

De Vos G. and Wagatsuma H. (eds), (1972) *Japan's Invisible Race, (Revised edition)* Berkeley: University of California Press.

Dōwa Gyōseishi Henshū Iinkai (Dōwa Administration History Editorial Committee), (2002) *Dōwa Gyōseishi* (A History of Dōwa Administration), Tokyo: Sōmuchō Daijin Kanbō Chiiki Kaizen Taisakuhitsu.

Hankins, J. D., (2014) *Working Skin, Making Leather, Making a Multicultural Japan*, Berkeley: University of California Press.

Isomura E., (1982) *Dōwa Mondai to Dōwa Taisaku* (Dōwa Problem and Dōwa Policy), Osaka: Kaihō Shuppansha.

Isomura E., (1983–6) *Dōwa Gyōseiron* (Research on Dōwa Administration), Vol. 1–5, Tokyo: Akashi Shoten.

Isomura E., (1986) 'Dōwa Gyōsei no Gendai to Tenbō', in E. Isomura (ed) *Dōwa Gyōseiron V: Tokusohō jūhachinen no sōkatsu to tenbō*, Tokyo: Akashi Shoten, pp. 3–35.

Kanai K., (1991) *Dōwa Gyōsei: Sengo no Kiseki* (Dōwa Administration: The Postwar Path), Osaka: Buraku Kaihō Shuppansha.

Kanai K., (2018) *Tokusōhō Jidai no Makuhirake* (The Opening of the SML Era), n.p.

Kanai K., (2019) *Senryōki to Buraku Mondai* (The Buraku Problem in the Occupation Period), n.p.

Kobayakawa A., (2020) 'Japan's Modernization and Discrimination: What Are Buraku and Burakumin?' *Critical Sociology*, Vol 47:1, 2021, 111–132.

Kurokawa M., (2016) *Tsukurareta 'Jinshu': Buraku Sabetsu to Reishizumu* (A Fabricated 'Race': Buraku Discrimination and Racism] Tōkyō: Yūshisha.

Mizuuchi T. and Jeon H. G., (2010) 'The New Mode of Urban Renewal for the Former Outcaste Minority People and Areas in Japan', *Cities*, vol. 27, Supplement 1, June, 525–34.

Morgan C. V., (2007) 'A Case Study of Buraku and Non-Buraku Couples in Japan', *Journal of Comparative Family Studies*, vol. 38, no. 1, 31–54.

Nonaka H. and Shin S., (2009) *Sabetsu to Nihonjin* (Discrimination and the Japanese), Tōkyō: Kadokawa Shoten.

Šturdík M., (2017) 'Gradual Disappearance of the Hisabetsu Buraku Story', *ASIA*, vol. 71, no. 2, 697–711, [A translation of part of Kurokawa M., (2016) *Tsukurareta 'Jinshu': Buraku Sabetsu to Reishizumu* (A Fabricated 'Race': Buraku Discrimination and Racism)...... Tōkyō: Yūshisha].

Suginohara J., (1982) *The Status Discrimination in Japan*, Kobe City: Hyogo Institute of Buraku Problem.

Suginohara J., (from April 2006 to November 2007) 'Sengo Dōwa Gyōsei no Tenkai to Shihai Seisaku' (The Evolution of Postwar Dōwa Administration and Ruling Policies), *Jinken to Buraku Mondai*, Kyoto: Buraku Mondai Kenkyūjo, in twenty parts, No. 744–66.

No. 744, April 2006, pp. 74–9.

Upham F., (1980) 'Ten Years of Affirmative Action for Japanese Burakumin: A Preliminary Report on the Law on Special Measures for Dōwa Projects', *Law in Japan*, vol. 13, 39–73.

Upham F., (1987) *Law and Social Change in postwar Japan*, Cambridge, MA: Harvard University Press.

Yoshino R. and Murakoshi S., (1977) *The Invisible Visible Minority – Japan's Burakumin*, Osaka: Buraku Liberation Institute.

2 Approaches to the problem

The opening chapter provided a summary of the main contours of the evolution of the Dōwa issue through a review of some of the existing literature on the topic. The main body of this work will focus on the process of the formulation of policy to address this problem and how that policy was implemented up to its formal end in 2002. There is no single, parsimonious theory that explains the various twists and turns in the narrative I will present and instead I propose five approaches to the problem each of which will contribute in different ways to our understanding of the form and content of Dōwa policy:

- The evolving narratives about the implications of the constitutional and international commitments to human rights standards for states and how seriously Japan has taken those commitments.
- The international context to the formulation of Dōwa policy and how the international informed domestic decision making.
- The domestic context of the Dōwa policy process, in particular the parallel process in which broader strategies of Japanese welfare policy were being discussed and defined at the same time that Dōwa policy was being considered and formulated.
- The size of the Japanese state and its relations with local government.
- Finally, noting that the ultimate test of Buraku identity is that of 'common knowledge' there being no ethnic, religious, or racial markers that distinguish them from other Japanese, it is particularly appropriate to ask how far the 'Dōwa problem' and solutions to it have been socially constituted and how that process of social construction has influenced policy.

I will discuss each of these, in turn, in a little more detail.

Taking rights seriously – the 'positive duties' of a state

The authors of the post-war Japanese constitution were insistent that it should contain unqualified commitments to human rights. However, the idea that citizens had rights was not completely new. The Meiji constitution of 1889 had contained a chapter on the Rights and Duties of the Subjects

DOI: 10.4324/9781003127994-2

(articles 18–32) but most of the rights listed there were qualified in some way such as 'within the limits of law' or 'within limits not prejudicial to peace and order'. In the new constitution, articles 10–39 protect what was probably the most extensive range of rights promised by any constitution anywhere at that time. It is well-known that Beate Sirota, a member of the drafting team, insisted on the explicit inclusion of women's rights (Takemae, 2002, 277–8). Less well-known is that there was frequent interaction between this American group and Japanese scholars and politicians which resulted, for example, in the adoption of a JSP suggestion to include a commitment to welfare rights as expressed in article 25 (Takemae 2002, 288–9).[1] It is further claimed that the 'only' in article 24 which begins, 'Marriage shall be based *only* on the mutual consent of both sexes…', was included at the insistence of Matsumoto Jiichirō, at the time a member of the JSP and leader of the National Buraku Liberation Committee although Sirota herself always disputed this.

Many left-of-centre politicians active in the late 1940s and 1950s were optimistic about the prospects for a better life in Japan because of the commitments of the new constitution. Matsumoto himself would always carry a copy of it with him. But it was not clear how these abstract commitments could make a difference to everyday life. For this reason, Matsumoto encouraged the formation of the Japan Civil Liberties Union in the hope that it would play this role. However, it struggled to have an impact.

The re-organised court system did prove capable of protecting equality as a civil/political right in the sense of restraining the state 'from treating similarly situated individuals differently' (Fredman, 2008, 176). However, if we focus more on the social dimension of rights such as in employment or marriage where 'equality consists in the equal ability to participate in social life' the state was much less effective. Where inequality defined in this way continues, it often arises from cultural value patterns which constitute some people as subordinate, excluded, or invisible. Where these patterns result in, or justify the continued existence of unequal distribution of wealth in a society, status hierarchies will map on to or be supported by economic hierarchies. In such circumstances, a state that takes rights seriously would find itself committed to not just the protection of equality by restraint but to take *positive measures* to protect and promote equality. And, as Amartya Sen has pointed out, 'Equal consideration for all may demand very unequal treatment in favour of the disadvantaged' (quoted by Fredman, 2008, 178). In such circumstances, the elimination of social disadvantage goes beyond the elimination of individual acts of prejudice. It further entails:

- Breaking the cycle of disadvantage associated with out-groups
- Facilitating full social participation
- Accommodating/positively affirming/celebrating their identity with the community
- Promoting respect for the equal dignity and worth of all.

(Fredman, 2008, 179)

With this in mind, we want to enquire whether such a rights-based framework that includes both the civil/political and the social was being consciously adopted as a guide for decisions made in Japan in the later twentieth century as policymakers discussed, decided on, and then reviewed Dōwa policy. Can we see in the demands being made on the state and the positive measures that it devised a working out of what a constitutional commitment to equality might mean in a Japanese context? This might also suggest a possible checklist that we could use to assess the continuing need for a Dōwa policy in the twenty-first century.

International human rights commitments

It is of course no coincidence that the rights-replete Japanese constitution was adopted in November 1946 only two years before the UNGA adopted the Universal Declaration of Human Rights (UDHR). All around the world, the reaction to the defeat of fascism was to commit to the principles of human rights. F D Roosevelt's notion of 'four freedoms'[2] finds echoes in the preamble to the Japanese constitution, 'the right to live in peace, free from fear and want'. And Eleanor Roosevelt as the chair of the UN committee on Human Rights was instrumental in ensuring that these ideas were elaborated into the UDHR. But this was simply a declaration, not an international treaty with authority to oblige members of the UN to incorporate its standards into their domestic legal practice, even though a few Scandinavian countries did so as early as the 1950s. In Europe, and a little later the Americas, a framework was created that could provide transnational oversight of human rights protection and promotion. However, this did not develop anything like teeth until the 1970s and after. Indeed, even then outside Scandinavia very few countries seemed minded to take human rights seriously.

Change within the UN began in the 1960s. Until then, progress in developing the human rights agenda had been blocked by the Cold War stalemate in which neither the USA nor the Soviet Union nor their allies encouraged discussion on how to implement these ideas. To the limited extent that they did, one side, the USA, criticised the other for their lack of respect for civil and political rights, while the Soviet Union responded by attacking the American record on economic and social rights. Following the process of de-colonisation in the 1950s and early 1960s, the number of 'third world' states which had no strong ties to either Cold War hegemon increased. Moreover, their leaders in the campaigns against colonialism had often legitimated their struggle through reference to human rights, particularly anti-racism. Once they became full members of the UN, they became critical of South Africa which was adopting a series of racist, apartheid policies. UNGA resolutions condemning apartheid and racism provided the context for debates on the two basic covenants on human rights, one on civil and political rights and one on economic, social, and cultural rights which had been prepared in the mid-1950s. They were finally approved in 1966 to become effective when ratified by 35 states, something that did not occur for another ten years.

Meanwhile, at the level of individual states, it is possible to trace a parallel process in which states were forced to take rights seriously in a variety of contexts. In the USA in 1954, the Supreme Court decision on *Brown v the Board of Education, Topeka* ruled racially separate educational provision to be unconstitutional giving encouragement to the civil rights movement. Their demands resulted in the Civil Rights Acts of 1964 and 1968 and the Equal Employment Opportunity Commission of 1972. In the UK, the state's response to the rise of discrimination against immigrants from the Commonwealth, mainly from the Indian sub-continent and the Caribbean, was to pass the Race Relations Acts of 1965, 1968, and 1976. Across the channel, the French state sought to re-enforce constitutional commitments to citizens' rights in the law of 1972 which prohibited discrimination based on race or nationality and incitement to racial hatred.

The policy process to be explicated in subsequent chapters will enable us to locate Japan within this international context. It is surely no coincidence that Dōwa policy was being devised at the same time that both the UN and states to which Japan looked to for inspiration were ratifying the various international covenants and creating positive measures to protect and promote racial equality. Most of the existing narratives about Dōwa policy focus on the domestic train of events that lead from the BLL demands of the mid-1950s through the Dōwa Policy Council report of 1965 and legislation of 1969 which provided the legal foundation for 33 years of Dōwa programmes. It is only in the Iken Gushin of 1996 that there is any explicit reference to the international human rights regime. Nevertheless, we want to enquire whether the development of Dōwa policies should be regarded as part of a transnational process even if for most of the period of its implementation it was not recognised as such within Japan.

Dōwa policy as welfare policy

If existing narratives of Dōwa policy – those few that exist – tell their story with almost no reference to the international context, it is perhaps more surprising that they also pay little attention to the domestic context. This was not always so. Several writers, both at the time and subsequently, commented on the way that the Yūwa Ten-Year Plan launched in 1935 was, by 1937, serving the interests of the now dominant military. In that year, the army had made its support for Konoe's cabinet conditional on a commitment to launch the Ministry of Health and Welfare in the context of its concern about the poor health of many conscripts, especially those from rural regions. As mobilisation of the population behind the war effort became the core element in government policy, the state adopted the slogan of 'all people are soldiers' which had, of course, an egalitarian element that was central to Yūwa policy.

However, few people have sought to demonstrate the connection between the development of Dōwa policy and other policies post-war, not even social welfare policy. So, was it simply coincidence that Japan constructed a system of universal health care coverage by the early 1960s (only the fourth country in the world to do so) at the same time that the Dōwa Policy Council was turning its attention to how the state should act? Commentaries on the evolution of social policy in the 1960s note that the rapid economic growth after 1955 was the necessary pre-condition for expansion of more generous health care provision. The decade of the 1960s saw the LDP caught in an apparently inexorable decline in its electoral support that it sought to address by expanding welfare provision. Moreover, the egalitarian ethos fostered during wartime, now shorn of its military connotations, continued to be present in the attitudes of many state officials and politicians from the centre right as well as the leftist parties (Kasza, 2011).

In a broad sense, both Dōwa policy and welfare policy were made possible by a similar set of background factors. In 1962, the Advisory Council of Social Security published a report proposing to divide Japan into three categories according to income group: middle income, lower income (just above the poverty line), and poor income (below the poverty line). Social welfare work should, it concluded, prioritise the problems of the latter (Tamai in Izuhara, 20, 2003). This turn towards addressing those who had not so far benefited from the rapid economic growth set the context for the discussions that would shortly commence within the Dōwa Policy Council.

Meanwhile, costly public programmes were being devised to support employment and income levels in several of the less efficient economic sectors. The most obvious and costly of these was the rice price support policy which sought to minimise the difference between the average incomes of the rural farming households and those of urban residents engaged in manufacturing industry. The Large-Scale Retail Store Law restricted the development of large supermarkets, thus protecting small- and medium-sized retailers, particularly 'corner shops'. The construction industry that had traditionally been an LDP supporter was another employer of large numbers of workers 5.27mn in 1984, 9% of the total employed workforce[3] (Levy, 1990, 220–1). Probably as a means of ensuring their continued support, regulations were passed in 1966 that required central and local governments to award public works contracts to local SMEs. In fact, many local governments excluded non-local firms from even bidding for these contracts. As a result, there were by 2001 over 586,000 construction firms with an average of 12 employees each (Kingston, 2004, 124–5). These cannot be considered social welfare policies by any strict definition but might be considered to be 'functionally equivalent' to them in the sense that their main impact was on those in the 'poor-income' category as defined in the 1962 report.

A third theme in what follows will be to investigate whether and to what extent Dōwa policy, or better, the various strands of Dōwa policy can be regarded as functionally equivalent to a form of time-limited social welfare policy. If so, the questions are first why were the general social welfare strategies (and their functional equivalents) thought to be insufficient to deal with the issues faced by Buraku communities and how effective they have been in dealing with poverty in Buraku areas since 2002.

The Japanese state – big, small, or what?

It has been a common complaint of Japanese politicians over the last 40 years that the Japanese state is large, too large. This was a core theme within PM Nakasone's policy agenda which in part may be explained by his desire to identify with his US and UK equivalents, Ronald Reagan and Margaret Thatcher, both of whom talked of the importance of reducing the size of the state. Nakasone used this rhetoric when engaged in reducing the generosity of the social welfare budget which was said to be promoting welfare dependency and the rapidly increasing budget deficit. Then in the late 1990s, the Administrative Reform Council established by PM Hashimoto Ryūtarō produced a set of recommendations for reform of the structure of central government which was based on the premise that government in Japan had grown 'extremely large and rigid' making it essential to streamline the Japanese government structure. However, it is not difficult to demonstrate that by international comparison the Japanese state is small whether measured by the number of personnel employed by the state or the proportion of GDP that it consumes. For example, employment in the public sector as a percentage of total employment in 2009 in Japan was 7.9% compared to 15.4% in Germany, 24.7% in the UK, and 20.1% in France (OECD, 2015). So how is it possible for it to be so pervasive?

There are several ways to approach this apparent paradox but I want to suggest that one way in which the Japanese state is able to project its authority so widely despite its small size is by creating or adapting non-state structures to implement and supervise policies decided at the ministerial level. There are a number of examples of this across government. Here, I will just outline a few examples.

Agriculture policy is decided by MAFF within what anyway is the largest ministry judged by number of direct employees. Implementation of policy however is largely done at the local level through the Nōkyō farming cooperatives which in the late twentieth century employed another 300,000 staff (George-Mulgan, 2000, 289). As George-Mulgan has voluminously documented, the various structures which became Nōkyō in the late 1940s and 1950s were built on foundations established in the pre-war period and extended MAFF control of policy deep down into rural communities. It is only recently that Abe Shinzō was able to weaken the power of the MAFF-Nōkyō alliance which had been able to frustrate attempts to reform agriculture policy but even now, and certainly for all of the post-war period, the agriculture policy structure can only be explained by describing the combination of state and non-state structures.

We can see something similar in the implementation of social welfare policy. Garon and Goodman – historian and social anthropologist, respectively – have described how the *minsei iin* system was re-created in the late 1940s on the basis of a model that originated in the 1920s (Garon 1998; Goodman, Kwon and White, 1998). This developed into an extensive, intrusive, and very cheap system of social welfare provision based on 'volunteer' social workers numbering 238,349 as of March 2017. They are attached to local government offices but are under the ultimate control of the MLHW. As analysts routinely suggest, they function not so much to enable potential claimants to obtain what state aid is available but rather, fearing encouragement of welfare dependence, they act as gatekeepers so as to limit access to benefits. Soeda estimated that in 1990 less than 25% of low-income families took up their entitlement to welfare benefits and take up rates for some specific benefits were much lower than this (quoted in Goodman, Kwon, and White, 1998, 148).

However, *minsei iin* form just one of a number of semi-voluntary organisations that have been created on the boundaries of the state and civil society. For example, there are 13,000 Civil Liberties Commissioners (*Jinken Yōgo Iin*) who are charged with the promotion and protection of human rights. They are organised within prefectural and municipal local government structures but ultimately work under the Ministry of Justice through its local branches and are quite strictly controlled by them (Neary, 1997). Similarly, the probation service, crime prevention groups and traffic safely organisations act as extensions of the police influence within society. Indeed, there may be as many as 30 different organisations of 'volunteers' who take an interest in such topics as well as consumer affairs or environmental issues. Their total membership probably extends to several hundred thousand citizens although some people will serve in more than one role. Taken together, they amount to a substantial section of mainly middle-class people and organisations which, particularly before 1998 and the changing of restrictions on NGO activity, controlled the social space usually inhabited elsewhere by social movement organisations.

There are several other examples that one could cite but the point is that assessing the authority of the Japanese state is not a matter of just looking at its size, whether measured either in terms of manpower or spending but rather requires focusing on its pervasiveness. This is best explained, I am arguing, by the way it creates or co-opts structures apparently outside its formal structure which can influence, maybe even control how policy is made and then implemented.

A second way in which the state can project its authority is through local government. The overall size of local government in Japan in terms of people employed was virtually untouched by the reforms that took place in central government at least until the Great Heisei consolidation of 1999–2006. Moreover, as the welfare system was developed post-war, it did so on the basis of the structures established in the late 1930s mentioned above which placed responsibility for its administration at the level of local government, mainly the municipalities. In this way, Japan was able to develop a functioning 'welfare state' of sorts without expanding the central administration by pushing responsibility for welfare down to local government and even there the tasks were shared between professionals and those from the voluntary sector such as the aforementioned *minsei iin*.

What I am suggesting here is that when it came to decisions about how Dōwa policy was to be implemented there was an 'obvious' existing pattern of policy management at the local level that could be used. Most policy initiation seems to have come from local government, either the prefecture or municipality, and it was at that level that coordination did, or did not take place. This was welcomed by local politicians and administrators as it increased the amount of resources available to them and also by the local Buraku communities as it enabled them to play a part in making decisions about how those resources were used. However, one might suggest that some of the wasteful excesses amounting at times to corrupt practice derive from, or at least became possible because of, the high degree of decentralisation of the Dowa policy implementation process.

The Buraku issue as a socially constructed problem

Fifth, and finally, to focus on an approach to the problem from the perspective of the social construction of the Buraku problem to which Dōwa policy was a solution. This approach argues that social problems are not so much objective, identifiable societal conditions but rather emerge through a process of definition embedded within prevailing political language and cultural symbols. Political language shapes the understandings of what officials, activists, and the general public perceive to be legitimate, while cultural symbols are the concepts, images, objects, and actions that both represent and serve as vehicles for communicating shared values, norms, and beliefs. Between them, they provide the central organising ideas that provide the frame within which the 'problem' is interpreted and 'solution' proposed. Different actors will compete to influence the process of problem recognition often in the context of national development strategies. One key aspect of this is the way the essence of the problem is equated to the characteristics of the social group. Policy will aim to provide ideological measures and material incentives to persuade them to undertake behavioural change imposing sanctions where incentives are ineffective. To quote Murphy,

> ...social problems are commonly defined in terms of the deficiencies of the policy beneficiaries. This is so that solutions entail the provision of help to ameliorate these deficiencies rather than enact changes to the wider institutional order. At the same time, the use of help or care to address the social problem mitigates the need for the use of coercion

> in the exercise of social control because expressions of affection for the policy beneficiaries encourage them to buy into the élite's definition of the nature of the problem and the solution.
>
> (Murphy, 2014, 782)

In liberal democracies, civil society actors may resist the process of problem definition by the élite, refuse to undertake the required behavioural changes, and insist on the necessity of wider institutional change to embrace their vision of themselves and their 'problem'.

This approach is particularly attractive for thinking about the Buraku issue as one could argue that the core nature of the Buraku problem is its 'social constructed-ness'. That is to say that a major difference between the position of Burakumin in Japan and minority groups in other societies, African-Americans in the USA or immigrant communities in the UK or France, is that there is no visible marker that distinguishes them from the mainstream community whether language, religion, or ethnicity. The only thing that is said to set them apart from the majority community are their 'deficiencies' – lack of hygiene, lack of education, lack of self-discipline, lack of employment – which, once resolved, will eliminate the problem.

Nevertheless, there are some analysts who have suggested that Buraku discrimination shares many features with racism. Kurokawa Midori, a Japanese sociologist who works on Buraku history has suggested that Buraku identity resembles in many ways the racial identities of groups in other advanced industrial societies while acknowledging that 'race is a social construction' and that 'race in a biological sense does not exist' (Kurokawa, 2016). Meanwhile, E S Brown, an American sociologist, has independently argued that the development of Buraku outcaste status can be usefully analysed through a 'racialisation approach' showing that 'racialisation of group inequalities ... often occurs in situations where the groups are not "phenotypically" different' (Brown, 2013, 21). The main focus of this book will be on the process which led to the formation and impact of Dowa policy but in the twenty-first century, after the formal Dowa programmes have come to a close, considerations of what a Buraku identity might consist of have become more important. We will return to consider identity issues in the closing chapter.

The constructivist literature is also helpful in its labelling of different parts of the policy process. For example, it neatly distinguishes between the interrelated levels of state intervention once it has acknowledged a problem's existence: political, administrative, and operative. The first is directed at the passage of a law and creation of a new organisation or the restructuring of an existing one, a process that will be accompanied by much media attention. Next is the administrative phase when the policies and laws are converted into administrative rules that determine the technical task of applying the resources. Third, there is the operative stage when those rules and directives are applied to situations (Jamrozik and Nocella, 1998, 49). However, this three-stage process will often be preceded by the conduct of research by the state in which it will control the research agenda, appoint politically reliable people to the advisory committees, and prescribe the methods of enquiry. Jamrozik and Nocella comment that, 'commissioned research into social problems serves to validate political and administrative measures and can produce trivial results usually presented in an impressive array of statistics' (Jamrozik and Nocella, 1998, 106). They suggest that following the first phase of administrative action there will be a strong tendency to convert what was placed on the agenda by political activity into a technical administrative problem or even a private problem to be resolved by individuals.

Thus, the social constructivist literature suggests a research agenda which can identify stages in the process of policy formation and implementation, identifies different types of actors who become involved in that process and suggest a way to think about the evolution of that process that might be particularly helpful in analysing the Dōwa policy process that has a clear start, middle and end. But it also regards it as axiomatic that the state is not a neutral actor in this process and that we need to be alert to how the state's priorities are expressed both in what policy says and how policy is implemented. How successful and by what means were the groups representing Burakumin able to influence or resist it?

Concluding remarks

There is only a short distance between an eclectic approach to issues and being indecisive or unfocused. And yet while shining a light from one angle can result in revealing patterns which might otherwise be hidden, the same process can also hide important features in shadow. By approaching the Dōwa policies as attempts to resolve the Buraku problem from a fixed number of perspectives, I am indicating features of both their domestic and international dimensions in a way that makes it possible to compare them with other, similar solutions to social problems elsewhere. This is not primarily conceived of as a comparative exercise, and indeed the narrative will dive deep into some of the detail of the policy process at state and local government levels. However, in addition to shining a light into an areas of Japan's policy process that will inform those who already know something about Japan, I hope to enable non-specialist readers to 'make sense of' Dōwa policy in a way that enables them to compare its implementation to affirmative action policies in states they are more familiar with.

Notes

1 'All people shall have the right to maintain the minimum standards of wholesome and cultured living...

(2) In all spheres of life, the State shall use its endeavors for the promotion and extension of social welfare and security, and of public health'.

2 Freedom of speech, freedom of religion, freedom from want, freedom from fear.
3 This compares to 6.6% and 6.4% in the USA and the UK, respectively, in the same year.

Bibliography

Brown E. S., (2013) 'Racialization in a 'Homogenous' Society? The Case of Buraku People in Japan', *Asian Ethnicity*, vol. 14, no. 1, 1–28.

Fredman S., (2008) *Human Rights Transformed: Positive Rights and Positive Duties*, Oxford: Oxford Scholarship Online.

Garon S., (1998) *Molding Japanese Minds: The State in Everyday Life*, Princeton, NJ: Princeton University Press.

George-Mulgan A., (2000) *The Politics of Agriculture in Japan*, London: Routledge.

Goodman R., Kwon H. J., and White G., (1998) *The East Asian Welfare Model*, London: Routledge.

Jamrozik A. and Nocella L., (1998) *The Sociology of Social Problems: Theoretical Perspectives and Methods of Intervention*, Cambridge: Cambridge University Press.

Kasza G. J., (2011) 'The Rise(and Fall?) of Social Equality: The Evolution of Japan's Welfare State', in A Gaunder (ed) *Routledge Handbook of Japanese Politics*, London: Routledge, pp. 189–211.

Kingston J., (2004) *Japan's Quiet Transformation: Social Change and Civil Society in the Twenty-first Century*, London: RoutledgeCurzon.

Kurokawa M., (2016) *Tsukurareta 'Jinshu': Buraku Sabetsu to Reishizumu* (A Fabricated 'Race': Buraku Discrimination and Racism), Tōkyō: Yūshisha.

Levy S. M., (1990) *Japanese Construction: An American Perspective*, Heidelberg: Springer.

Murphy R., (2014) 'Sex Ratio Imbalances and China's Care for Girls Programme: A Case Study of a Social Problem', *China Quarterly*, vol. 219, Sep, 781–807.

Neary I., (1997) 'The Civil Liberties Commissioners System and the Protection of Human Rights in Japan', *Japan Forum*, vol. 9, no. 2, 217–232.

OECD, (2015) *Government at a Glance 2015*, Paris: OECD Publishing.

Takemae E., (2002) *Inside GHQ: The Allied Occupation of Japan and Its Legacy*, New York, London: Continuum International.

Tamai K., (2003) 'Development of Social Policy in Japan', in M Izuhara (ed) *Comparing Social Policies: Exploring New Perspectives in Britain and Japan*, Bristol: The Policy Press, pp. 35–48.

3 A brief review of modern Buraku history and the formation of Yūwa policy

In the eighth month of 1871, the *Senmin Haishirei* (Declaration to Eliminate Senmin Status) was promulgated.[1] It decreed that:

> The titles *eta* and *hinin* and others of the kind shall be abolished. Henceforth the people belonging to these classes shall be treated with the same manner both in occupation and social standing as commoners.
>
> (Ninomiya, 1933, 109)

If the state had an obligation to address the special circumstances of those affected by adverse social and economic circumstances in the 1960s, as would be argued in the Dōtaishin, then the same obligation should have applied to the government at the start of the Meiji era when it briefly turned its attention to the plight of those who had been marginalised in the course of the preceding period of Tokugawa government. In fact, one of those who had been peripherally involved in the process of formulating the *Senmin Haishirei*, Oe Taku, did advocate the provision of some kind of compensation for those '*senmin*' who as a result of the abolition of their status would lose the benefits of such craft monopolies as leather making.

However, Kurokawa argues that we should think of the *Senmin Haishirei* of 1871 as the formal abolition of a 'status line' within Japanese society and that to have created some kind of compensation scheme immediately afterwards would have been to recreate that 'line' albeit in a different form. It was therefore as well, she suggests, that no special, even positive, attention was given to these groups. Whatever we may conclude about this, it points towards a core dilemma that lay within the process of making and implementing an affirmative policy intended to favour communities who cannot be distinguished from the majority by any kind of objective characteristic: there is always the possibility that the rules operating such a policy make more visible those differences that it is the aim of the policy to reduce. This was not a major concern of policymakers in the early part of the twentieth century when the scale of the projects was quite small but it becomes increasingly important after 1965 as the government began to formulate Dōwa policy. It is a dilemma to which we will return.

DOI: 10.4324/9781003127994-3

Our main aim in what follows is to account for the evolution of the Dōwa policy in the second half of the twentieth century using the perspectives outlined in the previous chapter but we need to be aware that it was not constructed from new. On the contrary, local governments had been puzzling about whether and how to address the problems being encountered by Buraku communities within their boundaries since at least the start of the twentieth century and central government set its first, tiny budget for Yūwa policy in 1920. Yūwa policy was closely controlled by the Home Ministry (Naimushō) and evolved rapidly over the next decade both in terms of the amount of funding being provided and the ambition of its aims. It was developed still further in the 1930s such that in 1935 the central Yūwa organisation launched a 'Ten Year Programme for the Completion of the Yūwa Projects' (Yūwa Jigyō Kansei no Jūkanen Keikaku) which set out plans for the distribution of funds that aimed to improve living conditions in the Buraku communities. Without going into any great detail, this chapter will review the Meiji background to developments within Buraku communities before providing a critical introduction to this precursor to the post-war Dōwa policy.

Burakumin in Meiji Japan

Despite their formal 'liberation' from feudal restrictions, there was ample evidence of lingering resentment towards former outcastes. During the 1870s, there were many popular disturbances protesting about the government's modernising policies such as the land tax, the compulsory school system, conscription, and the new currency which would often also include criticism of the *Senmin Haishirei* for assigning commoners the same status as *eta/hinin*. This resentment sometimes led to murderous attacks. To mention just two examples: the Mimasaka Blood Tax rebellion of 1873 destroyed several outcaste communities and resulted in the deaths of 18 individuals (Bayliss, 2013, 35; Howell, 2005, 89–109). In the same year, the *Takeyari Ikki* in Fukuoka prefecture involved more than 100,000 people who attacked over 4,500 houses of which more than 90% are thought to have been in former outcaste communities (Neary, 2010, 12).

The Family Registration Law passed in the fourth month of 1871 slightly preceded the status abolition law and had envisaged the creation of a separate register (*koseki*) for the various marginal groups. These plans for a separate register were abandoned but when the following year local officials began to devise replacements for the temple registers of the Tokugawa period, they foresaw that doing so would hinder identifying '*eta*, *hinin* and others' in the future. Some of them therefore adopted measures to make them identifiable: inserting 'new' (*shin* 新) by their names indicating that they were 'new' commoners, or adding a red mark, or insisting that all residents of these communities adopt the same surname (Chapman and Krogness, 2014, 93–110; Krogness, 2008, 218–9). An unintended consequence of this was to concretise the formal discrimination against non-outcaste commoners who from earlier in the nineteenth century had moved into or resided close to established *eta* or *hinin* communities either forced to eke an existence from begging or having taken up one of the outcaste occupations. Whatever their regional or caste origins may have been prior to this migration, from 1872 they were indelibly identified with the pariah community in which they now resided.

Enlightenment scholars, such as Nishimura Kanefumi and Yokokawa Shoto in 1873, criticised the view, not uncommon in the Edo period, that *eta* were 'another species', arguing that they were 'without doubt human' and that to treat them differently from other human beings would be contrary to the laws of nature. In the following decade, the Freedom and Popular Rights Movement (Jiyū Minken Undō) propagated similar liberal ideas. Perhaps the best known of its activists was Nakae Chōmin. He was expelled from Tokyo in 1887 and moved to Osaka where he lived in Watanabe-mura, a large former outcaste community. The following year, he became the editor of the Shinonome Shimbun in which he exposed the hypocrisy of the rights activists who criticised aristocratic élitism while themselves discriminating against former outcastes. He was probably the first person to express the idea that, 'the time has come when one can be proud to be *eta*'.

Others sought to investigate the origins of these marginal communities. Prominent among them were members of the Anthropological Society formed in 1883 (known from 1886 as the Tokyo Anthropological Society). As well as being interested in the Ainu and Okinawan communities, these anthropologists soon turned their attention to outcaste groups, publishing articles such as Fujii Kansuke's 'The *eta* must be foreigners' in December 1886. They were interested to find differences between *eta* and 'normal' Japanese whether by reference to myths or texts from the pre-modern period or more 'scientific' methods based on measurement of physiological features. Torii Ryuzō, for example, carried out surveys in the mid-1890s in Buraku communities in Tokushima and Hyōgo prefectures. He concluded that their residents' bone structure, beard patterns, and eye shapes resembled those of Malayo-Polynesians rather than the Mongolian race. At that time, much scholarship on the origins of the Japanese people subscribed to the view that they were a composite of many races, so Torii may not have been claiming that Burakumin had a uniquely different racial origin still less justifying discrimination. However, when the Hinode Shimbun reported on these surveys, it commented on the similarity of these groups to 'aboriginal people of the islands of Malaya and Polynesia' in ways that stressed that they were not 'normal Japanese' (Teraki and Kurokawa, 2019, 135).

The economic depression which began in 1881 increased poverty across the country, especially in rural areas. This affected former outcaste communities with particular severity but even mainstream tenant farmers and urban dwellers found themselves thrust into poverty and many were forced to take refuge in slums located in or near these settlements. They may have begun by emphasising their differences from the long-term residents of these communities but they soon found themselves identified as belonging to them. Thus, the number of people vulnerable to discrimination increased. Newspapers reported on their 'coarse customs' and 'hereditary peculiarities'. Intellectuals, such as Takahashi Yoshio, a student of Fukuzawa Yukichi, argued that although former *eta* and *hinin* were now to be regarded as commoners, it might still be wise to avoid marrying into their bloodline. For example, it was feared that among these people '...families in which leprosy runs are not rare... Experts on such matters tell us that leprosy cannot be eradicated from a family line even with the passage of five generations' (Kurokawa, 1999, 44). When, later in the decade, there was a series of cholera outbreaks, nationally circulating newspapers such as the Choya Shimbun falsely hinted that they originated in former *eta* communities. Such ideas clearly encouraged the continued dissemination of ideas of defilement and pollution that lingered on from the pre-Meiji period (Bayliss, 2013, 53–6).

And formal procedural discrimination continued in other ways. In 1887–8 when new regulations restructured local government, one important principle was to fix the size of the new towns and villages at no smaller than 300 households. However, one exception to this rule permitted the formation of smaller administrative units 'where it was not possible to peacefully merge a former *eta* village with another town or village' (Kurokawa, 1999, 58). In this way, Buraku communities were excluded from newly created local government units and often, at the same time, from school zones. Not only did this mean their children attended separate schools but as the poorest communities in any area, they had difficulty adequately supporting them. This separate and unequal educational provision was not eliminated until the 1920s.

Prejudice and discrimination were not only perpetuated in the administrative infrastructure of late Meiji, they were also recognised by the courts. In 1902, a Hiroshima woman petitioned her local court for the annulment of her marriage on the grounds that her husband had lied about his family background. He had claimed that he was from an upright and wealthy family which prior to the restoration had been permitted to use a surname and carry a sword, when in fact he was from an outcaste community. The court accepted the woman's petition arguing that 'Former *eta* were a low-class race from olden times' and 'even in the present day an aversion to engage in marriage with a 'former *eta*' is a normal state of affairs' (Teraki and Kurokawa, 2019, 139).

Such views remained in circulation in the early twentieth century as shown in Shimozaki Tōson's novel, *Hakai*, published in 1906. The protagonist, Ushimatsu Segawa, hides his status background to gain entry to a teacher training college and then finds a post in a primary school. However, he is not able to sustain his subterfuge and finally confesses his background in front of his class before fleeing to Tokyo, perhaps planning to migrate to Texas. The novel reports various commonly held ideas such as, 'Their skin is darker than ours...', 'being shut off from society has made them terribly warped inside...', and '...*eta* have a special smell...' (Shimazaki, 1974, 194). So, although the legal framework that supported discrimination had been abolished in 1871, deeply held customary prejudices recreated new forms of discrimination in the latter part of the nineteenth century and early twentieth century.

The Emergence of Yūwa Policy – 1905–20

Pre-modern prejudices evolved into modernised versions which described Burakumin as having 'strange customs', suffering a lack of hygiene, and plagued by criminality. Overall, the former outcaste communities encountered increased impoverishment in the final decades of the nineteenth century but there were some pockets of wealth where sections of the better-off Buraku élites had invested in traditional industries post-Meiji restoration and were able to take advantage of the cheap and captive labour supply. This Buraku bourgeoisie began to recognise that the discrimination and prejudices that they encountered locally were part of a pattern that was replicated across the country. While starting to make demands of wider society emphasising their similarity to other Japanese, they began to buy into the idea that the continued existence of discrimination was at least in part the result of the lack of hygiene, laziness, and poverty that characterised the majority within their own communities. Therefore, they launched improvement campaigns that aimed to change habits and clean up their communities. However, these attempts at self-improvement (*kaizen*) were often frustrated by newly created institutional barriers such as the lack of equal access to schools.

Attempts to encourage 'self-improvement' in the 1880s and 1890s combined with an embryonic patriotism and spirit of public service led a group of younger Buraku businessmen and community leaders to meet in Osaka in the summer of 1903 to create the Dainippon Dōhō Yūwakai, as a nationally coordinated 'self-improvement' movement which sought to teach Burakumin to behave more like proper Japanese citizens so they could be accepted by majority society. However, the restrictions on political activity made it difficult to sustain the organisation particularly after the outbreak of the Russo-Japanese war in February 1904 and it did not survive.

Official policy towards the Buraku issue was referred to as Yūwa – assimilation/reconciliation – policy, which, in general, was framed as improving Burakumin customs and behaviour and providing some economic support. It was launched in Mie prefecture in 1905 when the governor launched a Yūwa programme that became a model for other local governments. Funding was provided to create groups that were set up in Buraku communities, sometimes organised from the local police station, which encouraged improvements in customs and living standards. There was a strong element of control but very few resources provided to address the underlying poverty. When, perhaps predictably, these policy initiatives failed to improve living conditions or reduce prejudice, blame was ascribed not to the policy or lack of resources but rather to the irremediable inferiority of the residents in these communities.

The broader context of Yūwa policy was the creation of a 'social policy' at the national government level that aimed at limiting the impact of an emergent but small civil society sector and an even smaller socialist movement through considerable repression and a small measure of benevolence. The repressive aspect of this policy culminated in the High Treason Incident of 1910 in which 24 socialists and anarchists were sentenced to death, having been found guilty of plotting to assassinate the emperor. Most of them were innocent of any wrong doing but 12 were executed, the rest sentenced to imprisonment for life. At the same time, it was announced that the Meiji emperor, in an act of benevolence, would endow a foundation to support hospitals to provide health care for the poor.

Of those arrested, one was a doctor, Ōishi Seinosuke, who operated a free clinic in the Buraku community of Shingū-machi Wakayama prefecture and another, Takagi Kenmei, was a Buddhist priest at the Jōdo Shinshu temple serving the same community. Although neither of them were from that, or indeed any, Buraku community contemporary reports suggested that they were 'descendants of the tormented *eta*' (Fujino, 1984, 82). This created the suspicion within government that there was a link between the Buraku communities and the socialist movement, a fear that spurred the state to develop a national Yūwa policy. In November 1912, a conference on the 'Improvement of the Buraku of Poor People (*saimin*)' (Saimin Buraku Kaizen Kyōgikai) was held in Tokyo bringing together many of those involved in the administration of Yūwa and representatives of the Buraku élite who had been advocates of self-improvement policies (Teraki and Kurokawa, 2019, 152). Discussion at the conference was dominated by the government officials who were less interested in promoting measures that might reduce discrimination or improve the living conditions of the mass of the Buraku community and rather sought ways to make Burakumin more useful to the state. One particular set of policy proposals, which would be repeatedly suggested over the next 25 years, suggested that Burakumin should migrate, in this case to Hokkaido. This would disperse the Buraku communities, send their residents to a place where there was no embedded prejudice, and enable them to serve the nation and their emperor by increasing the population of the underdeveloped island and farming the land there (Fujino, 1984, 89).

Meanwhile in August 1912, an organisation called the Yamato Dōshikai was formed in Nara city with the support of the mayor and prefectural governor. Matsui Shōgoro (1869–1931), who had taken part in the ill-fated conference of the Dainihon Dōhō Yūwakai ten years earlier, provided not only leadership but also much of the funding for this group. His wealthy family had supported him at Tokyo Imperial University where he had studied agriculture. On his return in 1902, he took over the family meat business and participated in local improvement groups. The Yamato Dōshikai produced a journal, *Light of Meiji (Meiji no Hikari)*, that circulated among the Buraku élite mainly, although not exclusively, in Nara prefecture. While critical of continued discrimination in education, for example, it was by no means a radical group. As the title of its journal hints, the group urged Burakumin to express their gratitude to the Meiji emperor who had liberated them from status restrictions (Bayliss, 2013, 91–9).

This link between the imperial institution and Yūwa policy became even more explicit in the agenda of another group, the Imperial Way Society (Teikoku Kōdōkai) formed in 1914, which listed Itagaki Taisuke and Shibusawa Eichi among its titular leaders and Oe Taku in its leadership team.[2] Their approach to the Buraku problem was to regard it as similar to that of transforming Taiwanese and Koreans into imperial subjects. The Kōdōkai sought to work with the Yamato Dōshikai and similar groups in order to serve the interests of the Japanese empire. For example, the Kōdōkai established programmes to encourage Burakumin to migrate either to Hokkaido or to one of the 'new lands' of the empire where they would not only escape from prejudice but also, by settling there, serve the emperor.

However, other events continued to raise concerns that, unless the government provided more relief, Burakumin anger would disrupt political and social life. The Rice Riots of 1918 shocked the governing classes in a number of ways, including their perceptions of Burakumin participation. Burakumin made up 10% of those arrested in the disturbances although they formed less than 2% of the overall population. Government officials thought Burakumin were unusually militant – taking advantage of the situation to take their revenge for years of discriminatory treatment – but Burakumin themselves argued they were treated as scapegoats. At the same time, there was some evidence that Buraku communities where a Yūwa group existed were less likely to take part in the rioting. The Russian revolutions of 1917/18 suggested that urban and rural workers' discontent could contribute to the overthrow of an imperial regime. Moreover, many, including Oe Taku, believed that the violent peasant protests that had precipitated the revolution in Russia had been manipulated by Russian Jews (Fujino, 1984, 137). These Rice Riots suggested the possibility of similar levels of discontent in Japan among marginal groups like Burakumin who were susceptible to manipulation by political forces. Home Minister Mizuno Rentarō requested the Teikoku Kōdōkai to redouble its efforts to exert social control.

Meanwhile in Paris in 1919, Japanese government officials argued for the inclusion of a racial equality clause in the text of the Versailles Treaty. They framed their case as a moral battle against white racism. Articles in *Meiji no Hikari* criticised this as hypocritical and a group in Nagano, for example, noted the inconsistency in demanding the abolition of racial discrimination in Versailles while doing nothing about discrimination against Burakumin in their own country.

Thus, both domestic and international circumstances suggested a renewed interest in Yūwa policy. A Teikoku Kōdōkai conference in February 1919 brought together politicians, scholars, religious leaders, bureaucrats, and Buraku leaders and concluded that '...to create a situation where there is no discrimination it will be necessary to improve the people in the Buraku communities...' This movement remained completely external to the Buraku communities at best sympathetic to their plight and benevolently suggesting ways in which they might improve. The following year, the Hara Kei cabinet allocated ¥50,000 for Yūwa policy of which ¥43,000 was set aside for improvement projects in the 17 prefectures with the largest Buraku populations. This was to be managed through the newly created Social Affairs Bureau of the Home Ministry and was the first provision of central government funds that aimed to improve the living conditions in Buraku communities (Bayliss, 2013, 139).

The first two decades of the twentieth century witnessed on the one hand the self-mobilisation of the Buraku wealthier classes to improve their situation, while on the other the state devised Yūwa policies to control their activities. In their different ways, both of these trends served to generate a sense of identity that was shared between these marginal groups in different parts of the country who prior to the start of the Meiji period had had very little contact with each other. They began to realise that they were encountering similar kinds of discrimination as they attempted to make their way in modernising Japan. In those years, the Buraku-based groups tended to share with government leaders the assumption that the main problem was located in the Buraku, not mainstream society, although they were becoming increasingly critical of and frustrated by government policy, a trend that would intensify over the next decade.

The Yūwa movement and Suiheisha activism: 1920–45

The amount of money budgeted for Buraku improvements increased a little over subsequent years but until the 1930s it was far less than what government spent on the Yūwa movement's administration. Yūwa policy mainly aimed to exert control over Buraku communities rather than to improve the living conditions or life chances of those resident in them. However, in a pattern that would be repeated many times across the twentieth century, the decision to launch a new Buraku policy in 1920 was followed by surveys to assess the size and circumstances of the Buraku population. This was the first time such a national survey had been attempted and apart from estimating the total population at 872,720, most of whom still resided in the 4,890 Buraku communities, the researchers found, for example, that only 84% of their children were attending primary school regularly, sometimes in separate schools or in different buildings from other pupils. Only 3% of marriages crossed the 'status line' (427 of 11,912 marriages) (Noguchi and Ishimoto, 2014, 90–2). Getting a job and buying or renting property depended on personal references and copies of one's family register which often clearly showed an individual's status origins (Bayliss, 2013, 114–6). Large firms avoided employing them. About half were engaged in some form of agriculture (48.5%), followed by manual labour (15%), miscellaneous occupations (13.3%), commercial activity (12.2%), or were industrial workers (8.3%). More detailed studies showed that most of the first group were landless farm labourers. Many of them earned additional income through the production or repair of traditional forms of footwear. Even where Burakumin worked in modern industries, such as the coal mines of the Chikuhō district of Fukuoka prefecture, they encountered segregation and discrimination. So, despite Yūwa administrators arguing that they should be treated just like other citizens, there was ample evidence that employers and other workers were treating them differently.

The tsunami of interest in left-wing ideas that swept over Japanese society in the 1920s also affected Buraku communities. The Japan Communist Party (JCP) was formed in July 1922 and that same year several labour and tenants' movements began organising. In parallel, Burakumin began to form new groups inspired by the same concepts of freedom, equality, and self-liberation. In Nara prefecture in 1919, a group of young men formed the Swallow Association (Tsubamekai) that initially planned to escape discrimination by 'flying away' to the Celebes islands (Sulawesi, Indonesia) where they believed swallows spent their winters. Later, influenced by radical ideas such as those expressed by Sano Manabu, a founder member of the JCP, they began to see a solution to their problems through the creation of a socialist society and, inspired by anti-colonial movements in India, Ireland, and Africa, they resolved to create a national movement for and of Burakumin that they decided to call the Suiheisha, the Leveller's Society.

It was launched at a conference held in Kyoto on 23 March 1922 and adopted as its key notion, 'liberation by our own efforts'. The Suihei Declaration (*Suihei Sengen*), which was probably the first statement of human rights within Asia, rejected the reformism and the patronising support of the Yūwa activists, on the grounds that 'The movements acting on our behalf … have yielded no appreciable results'. They also rejected the way earlier Buraku groups had assumed that there was something basically wrong with them. They asserted instead, 'The time has come when we can be proud of being *eta*', echoing Nakae Chōmin. Therefore, they proposed to launch 'a new collective movement to emancipate ourselves by promoting respect for human dignity'.[3]

Over the next few years, Suiheisha groups established themselves across the country and waged hundreds of campaigns against discrimination. Many young Burakumin trapped in poverty responded enthusiastically to the call for 'liberation by our own efforts' and to the encouragement to protest against discrimination through direct confrontation. Unfortunately, these protests often ended in violence, provoking a disproportionate response from the police and typically resulting in more severe punishment of

Suiheisha activists than the discriminators. Such events reinforced negative images of Burakumin in newspaper reports of the incidents, so from the mid-1920s the movement became more strategic in the way it selected which incidents to campaign about and tried to ensure that the campaigns were less about criticising an individual and more about encouraging changes in local practices to eliminate discrimination and prejudice.

It is possible to identify three strands of thinking within the Suiheisha movement. The first conference selected as its chair Minami Umekichi, at the time in his mid-40s and a former member of the Yamato Dōshikai. Minami was among the group of liberals who were prepared to work with those involved in Yūwa groups such as Arima Yoriyasu and his Dōaikai (Mutual Love Society) which had been formed in 1921. Arima was the son of the former daimyo of Kurume and a follower of Tolstoyan Christianity. He feared that Buraku discontent, as had been evident in the Rice Riots, might lead to Bolshevik-style revolution. The Dōaikai hoped to avert this by reforming government policy, arguing that ending discrimination required improving Buraku economic circumstances. In 1925, the Dōaikai went as far as to propose legislation to make discrimination illegal (Bayliss, 2013, 156).

A second group was mostly composed of younger activists who were attracted by the idea of a socialist revolution that would radically restructure society and thereby eliminate status discrimination. This group was particularly influential in the Kansai area. They developed a class analysis that emphasised the identity of interest of Buraku activists with fellow proletarians, both workers and peasants, and criticised Yūwa policy for aiming at undermining this solidarity. They argued that campaigns against discrimination should be directed not at individuals but rather at the ways that government and social institutions reproduced prejudices. A third group was equally critical of the Yūwa programme and as keen to promote class consciousness but feared that the Suiheisha under Marxist leadership would become subordinate to the JCP. This so-called 'anarchist faction' faded away during the 1930s but in emphasising 'taking pride in being *eta*' they seem to have prioritised a form of 'identity politics'.

In different circumstances, the interplay of these three perspectives might have led to a productive discussion about the nature of discrimination within Japanese society and creative strategies to oppose it. However, mass arrests of radical activists, especially those associated with the JCP, in March 1928 and April 1929 resulted in the imprisonment of the Suiheisha's most energetic young leaders. Matsumoto Jiichirō, who had succeeded Minami as the leader of the movement in 1926, had already been arrested and imprisoned by then on what were almost certainly trumped-up charges. After the mass arrests, all discussion and social activism took place within state-controlled parameters that gradually tightened.

Funding for Yūwa/Regional Improvement projects increased rapidly after the first provision of ¥50,000 in 1920 – to over ¥100,000 in 1921 and then to ¥490,745 by 1923, the year after the formation of the Suiheisha (Fujino,

1984, 127). However, as Bayliss points out, this was still only a small fraction of the imperial household budget and some in the Teikoku Kōdōkai suggested that as much as ten million yen per year would be needed to address the problem properly (Bayliss, 2013, 139).

Meanwhile, the Yūwa movement was brought under direct state control. In February 1925, Arima invited the various regional Yūwa groups to merge into a coordinated national movement called the National Yūwa League (Zenkoku Yūwa Renmei) which was initially willing to work with the Suiheisha and called on the government to do more to improve Buraku living conditions and eliminate discrimination. In September that same year, the Home Ministry's Social Affairs Bureau launched the Central Yūwa Project Association (Chūō Yūwa Jigyō Kyōkai) which in July 1927 took control over the League and its member organisations such as the Dōaikai, the remnants of the Teikoku Kōdōkai, and the local groups. Arima became its deputy chair but the leading post was held by Hiranuma Kiichirō, prosecutor at the High Treason Trial, a former Minister of Justice and founder of an ultranationalist organisation, the Kokuhonsha. Hiranuma, who Arima criticised as having 'no experience of the Buraku problem and knowing nothing' about it (Bayliss, 2013, 157), initially insisted that discrimination was just a moral issue; no additional funds were needed to improve the material circumstances within Buraku communities.

However, Arima and the liberal views that had been expressed by his supporters in the Dōaikai such as Yamamoto Masao continued to exert some influence on the formation of Yūwa policy. In December 1928, a committee of 13 composed of members of both houses of the Diet, senior military officials, bureaucrats from the Home and Education ministries and three representatives of the Yūwa association including Arima, launched a new set of Yūwa policies that aimed to unify the Yūwa movement and provide more funding for Yūwa projects. The accompanying documents talked about the need to ensure equality of opportunity in employment across both public and private sectors and in education. They discussed the need to remove obstacles to equality in marriage, at funerals and in general social intercourse, and in the provision of such services as the renting of land, housing and financial institutions (Fujino, 1984, 190).

By the end of the 1920s, Japan's domestic economic crisis precipitated by the global Great Depression was so dire that not even Hiranuma could sustain the view that there was nothing the government should do to support Buraku communities economically. Already in November 1929, a survey carried out by the Central Yūwa Project Association had shown that at a time when the average household in a farming village paid ¥20 a year in taxes, the average Buraku household paid only between ¥3 and ¥8, indicating a big gap in incomes (Kurokawa, 1999, 212). For the next few years, living conditions in Buraku communities only got worse. In 1930, the Yūwa association launched the Buraku Economic Regeneration Movement (Buraku Keizai Kōsei Undō) with fresh funding to focus on economic improvement.

Through the combined strategy of the promotion of self-esteem and provision of financial assistance, the Yūwa association hoped to replace the Suiheisha that was by then at a low ebb following the mass arrests of 1928 and 1929.

Entering the 1930s, a new emphasis was placed on the encouraging *naibu jikaku* or *jiriki kōsei* – 'enlightened self-esteem' and 'starting anew through one's own efforts'. These ideas were very reminiscent of the notion of 'liberation by our own efforts' that had proved so popular in encouraging the emergence of the Suiheisha some ten years earlier, as some Yūwa activists acknowledged (Bayliss, 2013, 243). The Central Yūwa Project Association (Chūō Yūwa Jigyō Kyōkai) also started to call for the creation of cooperatives within Buraku communities 'guided' by local Yūwa leaders but run by Burakumin.

Meanwhile, those socialist Suiheisha activists who remained at liberty were suggesting a new strategy. Pursuing their class analysis, in late 1931 they proposed taking solidarity with the other proletarian movements to its logical conclusion by dismantling the Suiheisha. Burakumin activists, they argued, should henceforth work alongside their comrades within the labour or tenants' unions (Bayliss, 2013, 210–1). Two things happened that prevented the 'dissolution' strategy being adopted. First, Matsumoto Jiichirō was released from prison in December 1931 shortly after a Suiheisha conference approved the proposal to merge into other working-class movements. His first priority was to oppose the move and he was eventually able to get the proposal dropped. Then in 1933, protest began about a court case in Takamatsu city where two Burakumin had been found guilty of the 'abduction' of a local woman. The core accusation was that one of them had proposed marriage to the woman without revealing his status background. The court ruled that in this the men had committed criminal deceit. The Suiheisha feared that this ruling would place a legal obligation on Burakumin to disclose their status background. Although the Ministry of Justice refused to respond formally to the Suiheisha's protests, the judge and public prosecutor were transferred to another region and the two Burakumin were released before the end of their prison terms. But more significantly, the court's decision reminded Burakumin that their struggles differed from those of other Japanese. As many as two-thirds of Buraku communities took part in this campaign which revived the Suiheisha movement. It continued to be active into the late 1930s although admittedly under increasingly strict constraints. Under Matsumoto's guidance, the movement adopted a more pragmatic strategy, the Buraku Iinkai Katsudō, which urged local Suiheisha groups to, for example, create consumer cooperatives and to ensure that the government-funded Yūwa projects genuinely improved their material circumstances (Bayliss, 2013, 267). One Buraku in Hiroshima reported that only 30% of its allocated Yūwa funding was spent to improve general conditions with the rest being used to build a house for the leader of the Yūwa group. In Mie prefecture, there was opposition in 1934 to a plan which would reclaim a plot of waste land as this would only benefit the landlord.

Instead, they wanted the money spent on improvements to the community's drainage system which would be of general benefit (Neary, 1989, 178–9).

Meanwhile that same year, the government restructured its Yūwa policy by transforming the Emergency Economic Regeneration strategy into a 'Ten Year Plan for the Completion of the Yūwa Projects'. It defined the basic spirit of these Yūwa Projects saying 'Even though the name used is reconciliation (Yūwa) the aim in fact is assimilation or rather that Buraku will no longer exist'. And,

> The process of enhancing the economic and cultural standards in the Buraku will be a process in which discriminatory concepts disappear. In the same way we can regard the process of reconciliation as being one which leads in the direction of the natural resolution of the problem.
>
> (Quoted in Kurokawa, 1999, 242)

Plans for the projects were to be based on data acquired in a new national survey of Buraku communities, population, households, and occupations carried out in 1935. A detailed budget for the decade was set out at a total cost of ¥49,797,870 – approximately five million yen each year. However even in the first year, FY1936, only ¥1,234,484 was spent on the projects, about the same amount as spent on Regional Improvements the previous year. Matsumoto Jiichirō, by now an MP, in one of his first Diet speeches argued that at least ten million yen per year would be needed to make a difference (Fujino, 1984, 252). In the end in no year was more than ¥2 million spent on Ten-Year Plan projects and indeed the amount spent on Buraku improvement projects increased hardly at all following the launch of the plan.

The impact of the Yūwa Ten-Year Plan has not been studied in detail but it seems to have consisted of the upgrading of roads or sanitation facilities, projects to increase rural productivity through the improvement of irrigation systems and in urban areas to promote 'economic revitalisation'. Overall aims were set at a national level but local groups were encouraged to take a lead in creating specific improvement agendas for their own communities. This fitted in well with the encouragement being given by the Suiheisha leadership. However, there continued to be allegations of Yūwa money ending up in the hands of the Buraku élite.

Yūwa movement policy on education emerged from around 1932 and the following year, the first Yūwa educators meeting was held in Tokyo. It set out in 1934 to cultivate 'the spirit of unity among the people of the nation' (Bayliss, 2013, 246). In particular, it sought to undermine the widespread view that Burakumin were racially different to the Japanese mainstream and to propagate the idea among the population that loyalty to the emperor required all Japanese to set aside their prejudices against Burakumin. A Yūwa Reader (*Yūwa no Dokuhon*) was adopted in Nara in 1938 and in 1939 a *Wa no Dokuhon* began to be used in a 'designated Yūwa education research school' in Mie prefecture (Bayliss, 2013, 246; Kurokawa, 1999, 253).

By 1940, there were 18 such nationally designated schools and others set up by prefectures making as many as 200 in all. Nevertheless, it is unclear how many schools outside this number used the texts or what impact this research had. In August 1942, the Ministry of Education produced a new text for use in school *Kokumin Dōwa e no Michi* (The Path to Assimilation of the People) which, reflecting the propaganda of the time, explained the diverse racial origins of the Japanese people and described discrimination against Burakumin as a 'mistaken contradiction' that would gradually be overcome and eliminated with the creation of the 'New Order in East Asia' (Kurokawa, 1999, 267). However, once again we do not know how widely this text was used.

During the 1930s, the margin for permitted political activity narrowed still further. The 'liberal' grouping within the Yūwa movement came under criticism from the nationalist mainstream represented by Hiranuma Kiichirō. Yamamoto Masao who had supported the approach of encouraging 'enlightened self-esteem' (*naibu jikaku*) and contributed to the formulation of the Ten-Year Plan resigned from his position in 1937 as did several other 'liberals'. Approaches to the Buraku problem based on ideas of rights, in any case always a minority position within the Yūwa organisations, were replaced entirely by 'national ethics' (Kurokawa, 1999, 243). In other words, Buraku discrimination was unacceptable because it impeded the larger national agenda. Universal principles such as love for humanity or liberalism were rejected as 'foreign' (Kurokawa, 1999, 235).

Something similar was happening within the Suiheisha. It dropped its Marxist rhetoric and told its members to demand that the state accept responsibility for the discrimination they were facing and do something about it by funding projects within Buraku communities. In 1935, the annual Suiheisha conference adopted a motion calling for 'national reconciliation and the protection of the livelihoods of the oppressed Buraku masses'. The movement was still divided but now the division was marked by one side, mainly Matsumoto and his supporters, who continued to stress the importance of Buraku identity compared to a group around Asada Zennosuke who bought into the national identity arguments and the prospects for an elimination of the problem within the New Order. The fact that the Suiheisha's leader was an elected politician enabled the movement to survive at a time when most other social movements had been closed down but even so most grass-roots activity ground to a halt. The Suiheisha ceased activity in January 1942. Matsumoto continued to serve in the Imperial Diet throughout the war and most of the other core leaders of the Suiheisha lent their support to the war effort (see Bayliss 2013; Neary 2010).

Then, in June 1941, the Yūwa movement was restructured to create the Dōwa Hōkōkai as 'a powerful reconciliation movement of state officials and people', in which discrimination was defined as 'unpatriotic activity'. This was the first official use of the term Dōwa to replace Yūwa. Why the name was changed at this time is not clear although Bayliss suggests it was to divert attention away from the fact that it dealt with a 'minority problem'. Dōwa (harmonisation) had been used hitherto in association with enterprises and organisations unconnected with Yūwa policy but in this context it is said to have been derived from the text of the rescript issued on 28 December 1926 on the occasion of the accession of the new emperor. 'Dōwa' had even been one of the candidates for the era name that in the end became 'Shōwa'. Emphasising this connection with the Emperor certainly fits in with broader changes taking place in Yūwa policy in which discrimination was being regarded as 'un-Japanese'. It is somewhat less than totally persuasive however in that there was news sheet published in the early 1920s featuring articles on Buraku and minority problems which was called the *Dōwa Tsūshin* (Harmonisation News) suggesting that the word was already linked to Buraku issues several years before the death of the Taishō emperor (Bayliss, 2013, 261–2). Whatever the case, the change of name marks the point when previous leaders of the Yūwa movement with the exception of Hiranuma were moved aside and control passed into the hands of senior civil servants. By the end of the year, the movement had been completely absorbed into the IRAA.

From 1938, the Yūwa programmes had become closely integrated into the overall plans for war mobilisation. Government estimated that around 35% of the residents of Buraku were either completely or partially unemployed. Their situation deteriorated further when the import of hides became more difficult, causing problems for leather production. Yūwa groups created cooperatives of leather producers, suggested new sources of raw materials such as dog hides, or recruited Burakumin into the munitions industry. At the same time, policies were revived that encouraged Burakumin to migrate to Manchuria, and later Mongolia, a policy that Matsumoto in summer 1939 criticised as 'clearly a policy to exile Burakumin overseas' (quoted in Bayliss, 2013, 218).[4] Meanwhile, discrimination was still in evidence at the official ceremonies held to send off new recruits into military service or receive the remains of the war dead (Teraki and Kurokawa, 2019, 219).

Funding for Yūwa/Dōwa policy had in theory been designated for the decade starting FY1935/6 but how much was spent on Dōwa projects during the Pacific War is difficult to assess. One might have expected the programme to have been dropped entirely given the other, more urgent priorities. And yet precisely because there was evidence of continuing discrimination despite the 'national emergency' and because there were some doubts about the patriotism of Buraku residents it is possible that Yūwa/Dōwa policies were maintained to demonstrate the commitment of the state to overcoming discrimination and also as a way of ensuring Burakumin employment.

Conclusion

We can see how the definition of the 'problem' changed across the first half of the twentieth century. During the period 1900–20 the discourse was dominated by administrators who regarded the problem(s) as existing within the Buraku communities. Their residents were dirty, backward, unruly, and drank too much. Policy was designed to control their unruliness and they were exhorted to address their own faults in order to make themselves acceptable to the majority community. The blame for discrimination, then, lay with them not the prejudices of the majority. Some of the Buraku élite had agreed with this diagnosis of the problem as early as the 1880s and joined with the initial Yūwa policy administrators in urging their fellow Burakumin to sort themselves out. Allied to this were sets of ideas about their origins. These varied from racial theories – that they were the descendants of a racially distinct group (or perhaps even groups) which had arrived in Japan at some time in the past – to ideas that explained that they were shunned as a result of Tokugawa status policies reinforced by their associations direct and indirect with occupations that were regarded as in some way polluted by the Buddhist and Shinto religious traditions.

Some of the attitudes of the Yūwa administrators suggested that they subscribed to some sort of racial origin theory. And although racial origin theories were definitively rejected during the 1910s by historical research, they continued to circulate as plausible explanations of 'difference', even in some cases within Buraku communities. The dominant definition of the 'Buraku problem' was that their patterns of poverty reproduced prejudice and discrimination but still the responsibility for resolving the problem was placed squarely on the communities' residents. This was challenged by members of the Suiheisha who argued that they were 'proud to be *eta*' and equal to any other Japanese. They regarded their problems as being caused by the prejudices held by the majority community that constrained their social interaction and economic activity. The more radical among them thought that only fundamental social change – socialist revolution – could root out these prejudices but there was a range of opinion from democratic socialists who, without necessarily disagreeing about the need for revolution, felt that it was the responsibility of the contemporary state to undertake measures that might mitigate the consequences of policies pursued by their Tokugawa predecessors, to various kinds of liberals who were committed to ideas of equality whether this was a notion of equality before God (the Christians), a vaguer notion of the equality of all humanity, or a more specific notion of the equality of all 'children of the emperor' (*heika no sekishi*).

All historical enquiry about the origins of the Japanese race in general or any part of it became difficult during the 1920s, so it is no surprise that theories about the origin(s) of the Buraku community (or communities) were not explored.[5] The theory which informed Yūwa policy as it became more sophisticated towards the end of the 1920s largely slipped back to that of the pre-Suiheisha period and once more located the essence of the problem within the Buraku communities. By now though the underlying problem was regarded as largely socio-economic, the legacy of poverty was deemed to have been a product of a 'Buraku lifestyle'. So, as we move into the 1930s and more cash was provided for improvements to the Buraku living environment, the belief of those like Hiranuma, Arima, and even Yamamoto was that Buraku poverty could be overcome with a little outside help and 'rejuvenation by one's own efforts' (*jiriki kōsei*). This made it possible, indeed necessary, that the Yūwa projects should not be administered 'top down' but that the local communities should be able to influence to some degree what the Yūwa funding was spent on – Buraku communities were granted some degree of agency in how projects were implemented at the local level.

Activists such as Matsumoto, Asada, and others within the Suiheisha insisted on the need for positive engagement by the state to mitigate the dire poverty and seemed to get a positive response with the launch of the Ten-Year Plan in FY1935/6. However, because the national agenda was soon overtaken by the need to focus all resources on waging war, only a small proportion of the amounts promised for these programmes was ever delivered. At the same time, all traces of the liberal policy agenda were left behind as Buraku discrimination was defined at first as an obstacle to uniting the nation behind the war effort, then as something to be resolved in the course of mobilising human resources to serve the war effort and finally something that would disappear in the course of the creation of the New Order, whatever that might be. By the early 1940s, even Matsumoto and Asada seemed to be persuaded by the notion that Burakumin would be absorbed into the harmoniously unified Japanese nation and accepted as full equals.

Although ultimately impotent in the face of the power of the authoritarian Japanese state as it emerged in the 1930s, one clear achievement of the Suiheisha and its associated activists was to forge a sense of identity among residents of the Buraku communities across the whole of Japan. This had been almost entirely absent at the time of the Meiji restoration. It was starting to develop at the beginning of the twentieth century but by the mid- to late 1920s thanks to the efforts of the Suiheisha and the administrators of the Yūwa groups and programmes, the existence of a 'Buraku problem' was undeniable. In this sense, while the Yūwa administrators had tried to create a definition of the 'Buraku Problem' which in an almost racial way emphasised their deficiencies, Burakumin within the various groups that preceded the formation of the Suiheisha and then in the course of its debates about appropriate tactics and strategy constructed a rival narrative that suggested that their predicament was the result of policies and prejudices that derived from mainstream society. It was that, they argued, that had to change. Curiously, the state narrative began to bend in this direction when it argued that the creation of the East Asian Co-prosperity Sphere would change the nature of Japanese society.

There is a major debate in the political history of Japan as to the importance of 1945 as a turning point. While some, particularly an earlier generation of American scholars, regarded defeat in war and the subsequent reforms of the occupation as amounting to a democratic revolution, others point out that many of the structural features that characterise the post-war Japanese state and made rapid post-war economic growth possible derive from reforms introduced in the period 1935–42. They point to not only the restructuring of the banking system, including the Bank of Japan Law of 1942, but also the creation of a national health insurance system controlled by the MHW set up in 1938 and the rice price support system created to ensure a steady flow of food during wartime (see Francks 2003; Garon 1994; Noguchi 1998). In this context, it is tempting to wonder whether or how far post-war Dōwa policy derives from or was conditioned by the pre-war Yūwa experience.

Notes

1 This is sometimes also referred to as the 'Liberation Declaration' or *Kaihōrei.*

2 Oe Taku (1847–1921) was born in Tosa han with a lower samurai background and unsuccessfully petitioned the early Meiji government to provide economic aid to the newly 'liberated' *senmin.* He then had a career that included involvement in the *Maria Luz* incident in Kanagawa in 1872, imprisonment for involvement in the Satsuma rebellion of 1877, election to the Diet 1890–2, and participation in various business enterprises in Korea and China. In the final decade of his life, he once more took up an interest in Buraku issues but is well-known to have always taken with him a set of eating equipment – chopsticks, rice bowls, etc. – when visiting Buraku communities so he would not have to share with them (Fujino, 1984, 100).

3 For a full English version, see Hankins, 2014, 80–1; Appendix 1.

4 It is not clear how many actually emigrated but the figures supplied by Fujino (1984) for 1939, e.g. 434 to Manchuria, suggest that it was likely to have been hundreds rather than thousands.

5 The one sustained attempt to explore this theme was a book written by Takahashi Sadaki, *Tokushu Buraku Issennenshi* (A Thousand Year History of the Special Buraku) originally published in 1924 and banned almost immediately on publication. It was republished in the 1990s as *Hisabetsu Buraku Issennenshi.*

Bibliography

Bayliss J. P., (2013) *On the Margins of Empire: Buraku and Korean Identity in Prewar and Wartime Japan*, Cambridge, MA: Harvard University Asia Center.

Chapman D. and Krogness K. J. (eds), (2014), *Japan's Household Registration System and Citizenship: Koseki, Identification and Documentation*, London: Routledge.

Francks P., (2003) 'Rice for the Masses: Food Policy and the Adoption of Imperial Self-Sufficiency in Early Twentieth-Century Japan', *Japan Forum*, vol. 15, no. 1, 125–46.

Fujino Y., (1984) *Dōwa Seisaku no Rekishi* [A History of Dōwa Policy], Osaka: Kaihō Shuppansha.

Garon S., (1994) 'Rethinking Modernization and Modernity in Japanese History: A Focus on State-Society Relations', *The Journal of Asian Studies*, vol. 53, no. 2, 346–66.

Hankins J. D., (2014) *Working Skin, Making Leather, Making a Multicultural Japan*, Berkeley: University of California Press.

Howell D. L., (2005) *Geographies of Identity in Nineteenth-Century Japan*, Berkeley: University of California Press.

Krogness K. J., (2008) *The Koseki System and 'Koseki Consciousness': An Exploration of the Development and Functions of the Modern Japanese Household Registration System and how it Influences Social Life*, PhD Dissertation, University of Copenhagen, Institute of Cross-Cultural and Regional Studies, Japanese Section.

Kurokawa M., (1999) *Ika to dōka no aidan* (In between Alienation and Assimilation), Tokyo: Akashi Shoten.

Neary I., (1989) *Political Protest and Social Control in Pre-war Japan: The Origins of Buraku Liberation*, Manchester: Manchester University Press.

Neary I., (2010) *The Buraku Issue in Modern Japan: The Career of Matsumoto Jiichiro*, Abingdon: Routledge.

Ninomiya S., (1933) 'An Enquiry Concerning the Origin Development and Present Situation of the Eta in Relation to the History of Social Classes in Japan', *Asiatic Society of Japan*, vol. 10, 47–154.

Noguchi M. and Ishimoto K., (2014) *Buraku Jittai Chōsa no Shoshiteki Kenkyū* [A Bibliographical Study of Surveys in Buraku Conditions], Kyoto: Sekai Jinken Mondai Kenkyū Sentaa.

Noguchi Y., (1998) 'The 1940 System: Japan Under the Wartime Economy', *The American Economic Review*, vol. 898, no. 2, 404–7.

Takahashi S., (1992) *Hisabetsu Buraku Issennenshi* [A Thousand Year History of Discriminated Buraku], Tokyo: Iwanami Bunko.

Teraki N. and Kurokawa M., (2019) *A History of Discriminated Buraku Communities in Japan*, trans. Ian Neary) Folkeston: Renaissance Books.

Tōson Shimazaki, (1974) *The Broken Commandment* (Hakai), trans. Kenneth Strong, Tokyo: University of Tokyo Press.

4 From the Occupation to the new Ten-Year Plan

Dōwa policy and the reconstruction of Japanese politics, 1945–60

The USA had decided well before the Occupation began that its preference was to rule the country indirectly through the existing machinery of government, all of which remained intact, unlike in Germany. At the same time, it was committed to the notion that Japan should be prevented from posing a threat to international peace in general and the US interests in particular and that this could be achieved through a process of democratic reforms. Exactly how fundamental those reforms proved to be is, as mentioned at the end of the previous chapter, a topic of extensive and intensive academic debate. There can be no doubt that the new constitution went much further, especially in its protection of rights, than most Japanese conservatives would have liked, while land reform and reforms of the structure and content of education had long-term consequences. However, the reforms hardly touched the core role played by the bureaucracy in the policymaking process as has been demonstrated by studies of the evolution of industrial policy, welfare policy, and agricultural policy from the late 1940s into the 1960s. At their broadest level, the histories of these policy processes are about the reconstruction of the political system to serve a different Japan. It is in that context that this chapter will address the question of how Yūwa/Dōwa policy was reconstructed within these new political structures in order to show how that framework set the scene for the policy created at the end of the 1960s.

Dōwa policy under the Occupation

Immediately after Japan's surrender was announced, Matsumoto Jiichirō headed back to Tokyo to attend meetings of the Imperial Diet. Over the coming months, he would make speeches there in which he urged the government to pay attention to the plight of the homeless and starving who were eking out a living in the bombed-out cities across the country. In November, he took part in the founding meeting of the Japan Socialist Party (JSP) acting as its first treasurer and, it is said, providing much of the party's initial funding. The following month, as the Americans turned their attention to the constitution, he spoke in Diet debates in support of the

DOI: 10.4324/9781003127994-4

promotion of democratic practice and human rights and the abolition of old structures such as the Privy Council and peerage which institutionalised status privilege.

Meanwhile, other former members of the Suiheisha were meeting to discuss how to revive their movement. Their plans came to fruition in February 1946 with a founding conference held in Kyoto to launch the Zenkoku Buraku Kaihō Iinkai (National Buraku Liberation Committee – NBLC). This was attended by 240 people from 23 prefectures, mostly former Suiheisha activists but also including former members of the Yūwa administration such as Yamamoto Masao. It elected Matsumoto as the new chair of its central committee composed of ten men, four of whom were members of the JCP which had been re-formed the previous December. The following day, the Buraku Kaihō Jinmin Daikai (Buraku Liberation People's Conference) was held in support of the new movement and attended by a broad range of politicians and activists, liberals such as Miki Kiyoshi, later a member of the LDP and prime minister during 1974–6, as well as Nosaka Sanzō, a leading member of the JCP just back from exile in China. There was an optimistic view that a broad, non-partisan movement might be created that would work for 'the complete liberation of the Buraku masses' but even at this early stage there were clear divisions between those who took a radical view that the elimination of status discrimination should entail the abolition of the emperor system and those who supported its retention (see Neary, 2010, 141–3; also Amos, 2017). The NBLC struggled to recreate a viable movement during the Occupation period as, quite apart from these internal ideological tensions, the inhabitants of the Buraku communities were facing dire poverty and unable to spare much time to engage with a political movement. Meanwhile, ideas that they had some kind of 'foreign' origin became widespread once more and the use of such discriminatory language as 'Tokushu Buraku' in magazines and newspapers became as bad if not worse than before the formation of the Suiheisha (Kurokawa, 1999, 288–9).

The Yūwa policy Ten-Year Plan launched in 1935 had, in theory, continued even after the outbreak of the Pacific War but by January 1945 all Dōwa policy activity had ceased and on 20 March 1946, the MHW issued a memo to all local governments formally noting its termination (Kanai, 2019, 17; Suginohara 744, 2006, 76). The US Occupation had no clearly stated policy to address the Buraku issue. It used to be argued that the American occupiers of Japan knew little if anything about the Buraku issue and were positively opposed to any continuation of the Dōwa policy at the national level.[1] Kanai has considered this in some detail and argues that there is no documentary evidence to support that view. There was, for example, no memo originating from SCAP banning Dōwa policy and plenty of evidence of knowledge about the Buraku issue, for example, among such *occupationnaires* as Herbert Passin, Beate Sirota, Charles Kades, and Frank Rizzo. They will have known about the efforts by local governments to revive Dōwa projects from 1946 onwards which they did nothing to prevent. It is true that there was no formal recognition of the problem as one which required specific policy attention. GHQ seems to have taken the view that as the constitutionally guaranteed rights, particularly the notion of equality before the law, became embedded in social practice Buraku discrimination would disappear. Any social welfare policy was to be implemented on the 'principle of non-discriminatory equality' such that any remaining issues of poverty and unemployment would be dealt with through the general programmes. In sum, the view of the Occupation seems to have been that the Buraku problem would fade away as the state and society implemented democratic reform. This may simply reflect the Tokyo-centric focus of the US command that was unaware of the extent of discrimination in Osaka and areas to the west of Japan but we should also remember that the notion that 'affirmative action' might be required to deal with embedded discrimination was even in the USA a product of the civil rights movement in the 1960s.[2]

However, some of the fundamental structural reforms which were carried out as part of US efforts to democratise Japan were having a differential impact across Japanese society. For example, land reform: in order to qualify for any land that was being re-distributed from landowners to tenant farmers, they had to already cultivate a minimum of three *tan* (just over 0.7 acre) but there were many in rural Buraku communities who worked less than this minimum amount and therefore did not qualify to receive any re-distributed land. In some areas, Burakumin organised to negotiate with the land commissions to get themselves entitled to land re-distribution despite only having two *tan* (DeVos and Wagatsuma, 1972, 74). Nevertheless, Yamamoto Masao estimated that overall only 10% of Burakumin tenants benefited from this land reform.

In the first election held under the new constitution in April 1947, Matsumoto Jiichirō and two other Burakumin were elected to the upper house and another six to the lower house. Alfred R Hussey, head of the SCAP political division, proposed to Matsumoto that both houses of the Diet should create a standing committee on civil liberties. Petitions were sent to the Diet and presented to the speakers of both houses but to no avail (Kanai, 2019, 12; Morooka I, 1980, 73). Another 27 Burakumin had been elected to prefectural assemblies and there was a suggestion that they might constitute a special committee on 'status liberation issues' composed of all democratically elected Buraku-origin politicians (Kanai, 1991, 26–7). It is not clear why these proposals failed. Imoto Rinshi, then secretary to the NBLC who led the initiative, said that the authorities opposed the moves since to have accepted them would have implied the existence of a problem that they were reluctant to recognise (Kanai, 1991, quoting an interview with Imoto Rinshi in 1983, 27–8). Tanaka Shōgetsu, a Diet member at this time, later suggested that if such a committee had been convened, Burakumin would not have had to wait until the 1960s for the issue to be properly addressed. During the debate on the constitution in the Diet in summer 1946, he specifically questioned the minister of state Kanamori Tokujirō on Buraku matters and seemed to elicit an answer that promised an active policy but in the end nothing happened[3] (Kanai, 1991, 18; 2019, 46–8).

Despite the apparent lack of interest at the national level, local governments soon revived the policy. A Dōwa Jigyō Kondankai (Dōwa Project Discussion Group) was convened in Kyoto in October 1946 by representatives of the seven prefectures of the Kinki region (Nara-ken, 2003, 63–4). Only Nara and Kyoto set a Dōwa budget for FY1946 but Osaka set a budget the following year and by 1950 nearly all prefectures where there were a significant number of Buraku communities had initiated Dōwa projects (Table 4.1).

In June 1947, the Kinki Dōwa Jigyō Kyōkai requested through the Diet that MHW conduct a national survey on living conditions in Buraku communities and asked for support for community-based improvement projects such as trachoma clinics (Kanai, 1991, 60; Nara-ken, 2003, 64). On 20 October 1949, the group met in Okayama now with eight more prefectures represented and changed its name to the Nishi Nihon Dōwa Jigyō Kyōkai. Once more it asked for central government support for the projects that its members had started at the local level. In November 1951, it changed its name to become the Zen Nihon Dōwa Taisaku Kyōgikai (Zendōtai). Thereafter, it would meet most years to discuss policies, share ideas, and demand the state provide more money, conduct surveys, and establish an advisory council to propose a comprehensive policy (Nara-ken, 2003, 74).

In its final years, the Occupation's main priority changed from enthusiastic support of democratising reforms to strengthening the economy and making the Japan a reliable ally in the Cold War world. Many of the Occupation's liberal 'new dealers' who knew about and were sympathetic to the problems faced by Burakumin such as Passin or Kades had returned

Table 4.1 Dōwa Budget Appropriations 1946–50 – by Prefecture

Prefecture	*1946*	*1947*	*1948*	*1949*	*1950*
Mie			1,129,500	539,000	
Shiga	5,000		94,300	800,000	
Kyoto	148,793	490,710	17,1760	5,707,700	9,694,461
Osaka		1,740,000	2,300,000	1,200,000	2,130,000
Hyogo		360,000	2,200,000	1,750,000	5,000,000
Nara	100,000	290,000	629,128	300,000	
Wakayama			1,290,650	2,500,000	5,150,000
Tottori					400,000
Shimane	338		14,000	15,200	304,500
Okayama		741,875	1,100,000		1,200,000
Tokushima			162,000	4,087,500	20,000,000
Kagawa				3,235,000	
Kochi			780,000	300,000	1,900,000
Fukuoka					10,000,000
Nagasaki	3,360		1,104		

Source: Shiryō: Senryōki no Buraku Mondai (1991, 446–7).

to the USA leaving the US administration dominated by career soldiers. Matsumoto, having been elected deputy speaker of the Upper House, was pre-occupied with Diet politics and rivalries within the JSP leaving little time to focus on Buraku issues. It remained his deeply held view that discrimination against those at the lowest level of the status system was linked to the excessive reverence paid to those at the top. He consistently argued for the abolition of the emperor system from the end of 1945 and on the occasion of the opening of the Diet in January 1948, he refused to walk 'crab-wise' before the emperor (Neary, 2010, 149–52). This upset many on the conservative right, including Yoshida Shigeru. Yoshida became PM in October 1948 and by the end of the year had persuaded General Whitney to extend the purge to disbar Matsumoto from all political activity (see letter from Yoshida to Whitney dated 1 January 1949, Senryōki no Buraku Mondai, 1991, 32). The purge order was issued on 24 January 1949, the day after the second lower house election held under the new constitution. It covered Matsumoto and nine others, including the recently re-elected Tanaka Shōgetsu (Neary, 2010, 153).

Matsumoto's purge can be seen in retrospect as the first stage in a systematic effort to reduce the influence of the left-wing in Japanese politics which later would be referred to the 'Red Purge'. This was formalised on 3 May 1950 when MacArthur announced that he would step up the drive to root out 'destructive communist elements'. By the end of the year, about 22,000 public and private employees had lost their jobs. At the same time, and not coincidentally, the US authorities endorsed the 'Dodge Line' which aimed to reduce the cost of the Occupation and revive the economy. It amounted to a policy of austerity in order to achieve a balanced budget. The short-term impact was to put more than a million people out of work and impose wage cuts on between 15% and 20% of the working population. About 250,000 civil servants and 410,000 municipal employees lost their jobs (Takemae, 2002, 468–70). These were not circumstances in which central government was able to respond positively to requests from local government to fund poverty alleviation programmes among marginalised communities.

As the Occupation came to a close, one might not have expected the government to pay much attention to the problems of minority groups either but in September 1951 a *Report on the Prevention of Discrimination and the Protection of Minorities in Japan* was produced in response to a request made the previous year by the Economic and Social Council of the United Nations (aka EcoSoc). Twenty-eight-pages long, it was compiled by the Civil Liberties Bureau which had been created in 1947 within the MoJ. It set out for the first time in English an overview of the situation of the Ainu, Burakumin, and Korean residents. It appears to recognise them as minorities as defined by the UN even though the Japanese government would resist this view for the rest of the twentieth century (Senryōki no Buraku Mondai, 1991, 424–53).

So, in the immediate aftermath of the war, a movement of and for Burakumin had been re-created but it was struggling to attract broad support from those whose interests it sought to represent. Local governments in the Kansai area and west Japan revived some Dōwa projects that aimed to do something to mitigate the effects of dire poverty in the Buraku communities. However, they were desperately short of resources and were unable to attract any financial support or even interest from central government. At the end of the 1940s, central government too was subject to severe financial pressure and not in any position to respond positively to demands and requests from the NBLC or local governments for renewed funding for Dōwa projects. Moreover, the purge of leftists from positions of influence removed two of the most active advocates of the Buraku communities from their elected roles. Nevertheless, it did respond positively to the requests from the UN to report about its marginalised communities, a response which might have been the basis for further positive action as Japan became free from external control.

Dōwa policy in the early 1950s

Conservative domination over national politics was consolidated in 1955 with the formation of the Liberal Democratic Party, while the newly reunited JSP emerged as the key opposition party within what looked like developing into a two-party, parliamentary system of government. Left of centre political activity manifested itself not only in electoral politics but also in the extra-parliamentary opposition to the government's attempts to re-centralise control over the police and education systems that many saw as a worrying pre-cursor to rolling back the democratic reforms of the late 1940s. This extra-parliamentary protest culminated in the widespread street demonstrations of 1959–60 opposing ratification of the Security Treaty whose provisions had been revised following negotiations between PM Kishi and President Eisenhower. These campaigns had the support of not only left-wing political parties such as the JSP and JCP but also student groups, the union federations, and organisations such as the Buraku liberation movement.

At the start of the 1950s, the NBLC began to develop a strategy through which it sought to link protest against instances of discrimination to demands for the creation of local government projects that would eliminate the circumstances which underlay these prejudices. The pre-eminent example of how this might work was provided by the All Romance incident of 1951. A story entitled 'Tokushu Buraku' appeared in a pulp fiction magazine notionally set in a Buraku community in Kyoto. The title of the story was provocative enough but it presented a lurid account of living conditions amid black-marketeering, illegal sake brewing, crime, and violence. Indignation increased when it was discovered that the author was an official within the Kyoto city offices. The campaign then expanded to include criticism not only of the publisher but also of the municipal authority and included demands that more be spent on improving living conditions in the city's Buraku communities. One tangible outcome of the campaign was that the city's Dōwa budget increased 580% for the following financial year, 1952/3 (for more on this incident, see Amos 2017, 109; Kanai, 1991, 75–8). It probably helped that there had been a Dōwa Mondai Kyōgikai established within the city since 1946 and that its mayor was a member of the JCP which made him more sympathetic to the demands of the NBLC than most of his equivalents elsewhere.

Buraku living conditions in Kyoto were undeniably grim. A survey conducted in 1951 of eight communities in the city found that around two-thirds (57.4%) of the 3,360 buildings were over 30 years old and a third of them either needed major repair or were irreparable. Very few residents had direct access to water within their dwelling; 69% relied on shared access to a well or communal tap. Around 40% used some kind of communal kitchen and 58% a communal toilet. Whereas 75% of households in the city were spending over ¥12,000 a month on living expenses, only 8.7% of Buraku households did so. Between 1945 and 1950, 81.2% of marriages were endogenous (i.e. of Burakumin to other Burakumin). Absences from school were common: 6.4% and 28.9% of Buraku-based children were not attending primary and junior high schools respectively compared to 0.3% and 2.3% in the mainstream communities (Kanai, 1991, 71–5). There is no reason to think that the situation in Kyoto was exceptional.

While there is no evidence that the Occupation authorities impeded the development of Dōwa policy at the national level, neither did it do anything to positively promote Dōwa programmes. Still, once Japan regained formal independence on 28 April 1952, we can see the first moves towards the formulation of a national policy. While not explicitly mentioning Buraku issues, in June 1952 the Ministry of Education (MoE) issued advice expressing its regret at the continuance of discriminatory attitudes. This became the starting point for the development of a Dōwa education policy (Murakoshi et al., 1989, 55). The Ministry of Construction (MoC) conducted surveys of housing in Buraku communities of Kobe, Kyoto, and Osaka (Suginohara 746, 2006, 78). Horiki Kenzō of the Liberal Party became the chair of its Buraku Policy committee later that same year.[4] Between 1 and 10 January 1953, some members of the Health and Welfare committee of the House of Councillors visited Buraku communities in the Kantō, Kansai, and Chugoku regions.[5] There then followed the first post-war MHW budget provision for Dōwa projects comprising support for the construction of Rinpokan, community centres for Buraku communities, and public baths. However, the overall amount was quite small, ¥13.48m, less than that budgeted for Dōwa projects in Osaka prefecture (¥13.76m) (Kanai, 1991, 105–6). Meanwhile, the annual meetings of the Zendōtai repeated its demands for a better developed policy framework: an overall policy committee to coordinate the activities of all relevant ministries, committees in both houses of the Diet, and more funding for regional projects (Kanai, 1991, 98–9; Nara-ken, 2003, 100).

The purge order on Matsumoto was lifted in August 1951 and he recommenced political activity standing successfully for a seat in the national constituency at the HC election held in 1953. At this time, the JSP was formally divided into Left and Right with the key cleavage issue being policy towards the USA. Matsumoto stood well to the left. While continuing in his role as the chair of the NBLC, he was developing an international focus attending meetings associated with the peace movement in Europe and making visits to China in support of Sino-Japanese reconciliation. It was left to other JSP (Left) Diet members to take the initiative in demanding government develop its Dōwa policy, notably Tanaka Orinoshin, secretary general of the NCBL and later BLL, and Yagi Kazuo.[6] Both Yagi and Tanaka began to make the case within the party and Diet for the adoption of a strategy for Dōwa policy support.

The Buraku liberation movement had re-formed within a year of the end of the war. Thereafter, it held annual conferences, published a newspaper, set up a research centre in Kyoto, and established branches in most prefectures. However, despite the success of the All Romance incident, the leadership began to recognise by the middle of the 1950s that the movement was lacking momentum and initiated an internal debate about how to energise its activity. One basic issue was to clarify the nature of the Buraku problem and how it might be resolved.

Despite the successes of the Suiheisha movement in the pre-war period, the restrictions placed on freedoms of thought and publication had effectively prevented any serious research taking place on many historical issues and that of the origin of Buraku communities was no exception. This explains why it was a priority for the movement to establish its own research organisation, the Buraku Mondai Kenkyūsho in 1948. No-one still seriously proposed that Burakumin were racially different from mainstream Japanese even though the idea continued (and continues) to be entertained by many in Japan. But if the existence of Buraku communities was essentially a product of status discrimination, how did this relate to other features of contemporary Japanese society? Most particularly, was the solution to the Buraku problem possible within the structures of existing capitalist society or would it require fundamental social reform amounting to socialist revolution. We should remember at this point that most post-war social scientists in Japan subscribed to some form of Marxist social analysis and that most activists within the Buraku liberation movement were members or supporters of either the JSP or JCP as were their sympathisers outside it.[7]

The NCBL had managed at first to maintain a 'united front' composed of academic and activist supporters of both of the left of centre mainstream parties, non-aligned socialists, and liberals who were linked to former Yūwa activities such as Yamamoto Masao. Already centrists were starting to peel off by the mid-1950s but at the same time the division between the JCP group, hitherto dominant on the NCBL central committee, and a slightly more diverse group, perhaps most of whom were JSP supporters, began to come into the open and manifest itself in a debate that related theory to strategy.

To simplify a complex debate: on the one hand, there were people such as Kitahara Taisaku who argued that Burakumin and discrimination against them continued to exist because they were one of a number of remnants of feudal society which also included the emperor system that although no longer essential were used by the Japanese capitalist system to maintain its power. This was the position taken by the JCP whose supporters within the NCBL/BLL wanted it to function as a wing of the working-class movement. On the other hand, Inoue Kiyoshi, a Marxist historian at Kyoto university who worked with the NCBL and served on its central committee 1951–63, developed a 'trinity' liberation theory that explained the nature of the Buraku issue as being composed of elements of status discrimination (*mibun sabetsu*), residency/location, and trade/occupation. This theory not only explained the process of the historical emergence of Burakumin as a social phenomenon; it also suggested links with the contemporary situation since 'liberation' depended on the removal of material differences in residence and occupation in Buraku areas. Asada Zennosuke used these ideas as the foundation for his view that Buraku discrimination manifested itself in the economic and social inequalities that could be observed within their living conditions. These inequalities were qualitatively different to those experienced by other impoverished sectors of the proletariat who were unencumbered by status discrimination. Inoue's theory as interpreted by Asada supported the demands for material improvements (aka Dōwa projects). Indeed, 'the everyday economic demands of Burakumin themselves are a struggle feudal social relations' (Asada, 1979, 167–8). This position was criticised by the JCP group as exclusionary 'Buraku first-ism' which weakened solidarity with the rest of the working class.

As it emerged from the 1940s, the NBLC seems to have envisaged itself as a core leadership (Leninist?) organisation. However, as it tried to engage with Buraku communities, it consciously began to move towards developing as a mass movement. The culmination of this process was at the Tenth conference held in 1955 where it formally changed its name to the Buraku Liberation League (BLL) and adopted a completely revised platform that described the communities it represents as being trapped in a vicious circle of poverty and discrimination. It declared its core aim as the elimination of the 'semi-feudal' status relations which underpin the 'semi-feudal' discrimination. At the same time, it made specific demands for improvements in housing, communal facilities, roads, infrastructure, and education (Morooka II, 1981, 99–104). The new programme also committed the BLL to promote international cooperation opposing the divisive policies of imperialism, demanding the closure of US bases, and working with opposition to the re-militarisation of the country. So, the BLL sought targeted improvements for Buraku communities while at the same time recognising the need to collaborate with other progressive organisations nationally and internationally.

Analyses of mainstream politics in Japan often point to 1955 as being the 'year zero' of post-war politics and the political structure that lasted until 1993 as the '1955 system'. This was the year when the JSP re-united precipitating the formation of the LDP from the conservative Liberal and Democratic parties. It also saw the defeat of the ultra-leftist line within the JCP which paved the way for its re-adoption of the parliamentary path to socialism and involvement in local and national elections over the next decade. The BLL and its supporters began to press their demands for a national Dōwa policy within this new 'system'.

Towards a new Dōwa policy

After years when the topic seemed to have become almost taboo, there was a 'Buraku boom' in mass media attention at this point. It seems to have begun with BLL protests at the casual and discriminatory use of the phrase, *Tokushu Buraku*, in an Osaka edition of the *Asahi* newspaper in January 1956. In an apologetic response to this, later that year the newspaper ran a series of articles about the issue, the first time there had been such extensive coverage of the Buraku issue post-war. Over the following 12 months, national and regional newspapers as well as several of the heavyweight journals, including *Sekai*, *Chūō Kōron*, and *Fujin Kurabu*, carried articles about the issue. There were even programmes produced for NHK television and radio in 1957–8 (Kanai, 1991, 122–3).

This prompted and provided the context for the JSP to devise a Buraku strategy. In January 1957, Yagi Kazuo, with Matsumoto's support, set up a Special Committee on Buraku Liberation within the party's Policy Council. It met nine times over the following months and in early September produced a set of proposals which described the Buraku problem as being caused by the divisive policies of the ruling class which ultimately would only be resolved by the creation of a socialist society. However, for the short term, it proposed the creation of a Buraku Problem Solution Council (Buraku Mondai Kaiketsu Shingikai) composed of representatives of the Buraku communities, workers' and farmers' organisations, political parties, and relevant ministries charged with the task of producing a report for the PM Office recommending solutions to the problems faced by Burakumin in five areas: living environment, housing, education, employment, and agriculture/fishing (Kanai, 1991, 124–5). These were very similar to the proposals that had been formulated by the BLL and, it was hoped, being based on constitutional principles would be difficult for PM Kishi to object to.

Shortly afterwards, on 30 September, the JCP issued its first comment on the Buraku problem in the post-war period. It consisted of a single sentence, 'The party will campaign to correct the situation in which semi-feudal discriminatory treatment towards the Unliberated Buraku remains deep-rooted' (Kanai, 1991, 126).

At the end of 1957, the campaign moved up a gear as Asada Zennosuke, a leading member of the BLL central committee, visited Tokyo to talk to union leaders, senior bureaucrats, and politicians such as Miki Takeo, now head of the LDP Policy Affairs Council. That same December, the BLL's Twelfth conference urged its members to begin a campaign to request all local governments to establish Dōwa programmes and for central government to devise a national strategy. A conference was convened in Tokyo at the end of January 1958 demanding the establishment of a National Policy for Buraku Liberation that was attended by 420 delegates mainly from BLL groups but also including representatives of organisations such as labour unions and politicians such as Miki Takeo. In the days following the conference, BLL leaders held a series of meetings with the ministries that already had or were likely to formulate contributions to the Dōwa policy programmes. Their main demands were for a policy council to be set up in the Cabinet office, a committee to be established within the Diet and each ministry to take responsibility for devising Dōwa administrative measures relating to its area of competence.

Yagi questioned deputy PM Ishii Mitsujirō on 28 February 1958 in the HR Budget committee about the government's intentions. Ishii seemed to commit to the implementation of a comprehensive plan at the earliest opportunity. This promise was repeated by PM Kishi on 11 March (Kanai, 1991, 132; Suginohara 747, 2006, 78). Progress however was slow. On 8 October, a Dōwa Mondai Giin Kondankai (Dōwa Problem Diet members Discussion Group) was formed from LDP Diet members from both houses (HR 67, HC 21) chaired by the veteran Hoshijima Nirō.[8] It set up its organisational base in the offices of the Zendōtai. On 22 October, a Dōwa Mondai Kondankai was created within the Cabinet office to organise meetings of the *jimujikan* (most senior bureaucrats) from the PMO, MoF, MoE, MHW, MAFF, MITI, MoC, and what would shortly become the MHA. In January 1959, members of the LDP Kondankai held a conference jointly with the Zendōtai in Tokyo which set out a series of policy recommendations that were taken up by the LDP (Morooka III, 1982, 298). This led to the creation of a Dōwa policy sub-committee on 3 March within the LDP Policy Affairs Council (Seisaku Shingikai) jointly chaired by Horiki Kenzō and Akita Daisuke[9] but reportedly strongly influenced by ideas from Yamamoto Masao, formerly of the Yūwa movement. After four meetings, it produced a document whose diagnosis of the problem was remarkably similar to that of the JSP (and BLL): a vicious circle of impoverished living conditions, poor employment prospects, and inadequate education leading to a lowly social image was re-creating prejudice and discrimination among the majority population. It even suggested that the issue could be regarded as a 'feudal remnant' that should be eliminated from a democratic society. It suggested a programme which would break this cycle by improving employment, living conditions, economic prospects, and educational performance (Chiiki Kaizen Taisaku Kenkyūsho, 1986, 487–9).

So, finally, it seemed that the policy system had responded to the demands of extra-parliamentary groups (mainly the BLL) and local governments (Zendōtai) as channelled through both the opposition and ruling parties (JSP and LDP). However, the key demand for the establishment of a *shingikai* had not been accepted instead of which all that emerged was a half-hearted and poorly funded policy response.

In February 1960, a new 'Ten-Year Plan' was announced that would establish improvement projects in selected Buraku communities, the so-called 'model projects'. As Kanai points out, there has been hardly any research published about this programme and what there is only focuses on the first few years. What is clear is that nothing like the amount of money was spent compared to what was promised. Instead of the planned ¥3 billion per year (¥30 billion in total), in years 1, 2, and 3 spending was ¥400m, ¥600m, and ¥800m, respectively. Moreover, only a few communities benefited from the plan, looking at the first three years: 1960 – 16, 1961 – 27 (16 new), 1962 – 45 (26 new), in total just 58 districts, 1% of the total (Kanai, 1991, 144–5).

Just as this programme was being launched, in May 1960, a new organisation was created, the Zen Nihon Dōwakai. Preparations for its launch had been underway since the start of the year focused in areas where the pre-war Yūwa movement had had a strong base. It selected as its first chair Yanai Masao who had been an active supporter of the NCBL in Yamaguchi prefecture.[10] At its founding meeting, the Zen Nihon Dōwakai set out its opposition to the 'divisive' class struggle approach and suggested instead 'positive support for the integrating Dōwa policies which had been recently launched by the government for FY1960' (Kanai, 1991, 149). The Zen Nihon Dōwakai office was located in the same building as the LDP's headquarters leaving little room for doubt about its political allegiance. Moreover, it was said that the existence of a branch of the Dōwakai in a Buraku community was a necessary pre-condition for the provision of projects within the new Ten-Year Plan. On 11 October 1961, the minister at MHW announced its intention to foster the Dōwakai and not cooperate with the BLL (Morooka III, 1982, 306). For many in the BLL, this reminded them of the first version of a Ten-Year Plan launched in 1935 which became closely linked to the state mobilisation of the nation's resources in support of the war effort. The fact that Yamamoto Masao, formerly of the Yūwa movement, was a key advisor only added to this impression.

The fear that the Dōwa policy of 1960 was part of a broader attempt to create an authoritarian structure resembling that of the 1930s was perfectly understandable, given the parallel efforts being made to centralise state control over the police and education system and tie Japan more closely into a subordinate relationship with the USA. However, in retrospect, it is probably better to understand this as another example of the way in which the LDP worked closely with the bureaucracy to create a mesh of formal and informal, party political and bureaucratic relationships which would blur the boundary between ruling party, state, civil society, and local government. In 1958, the legislative framework had been put in place that would fill the gaps in the social welfare system but it did so *not* by creating a new structure at the national level but by building on the devolved framework that had been first set up in the late 1930s which placed primary responsibility for the administration of health care on the municipal authorities. What we can see in the processes that were creating this embryonic Dōwa policy were forces that could well have continued to be dominated by the combined conservative might of LDP plus bureaucracy that imposed a solution to the Buraku problem that suited them best.

Meanwhile, support for the Zen Nihon Dōwakai closely resembled a broader pattern of politics within the '1955 system' whereby the LDP took every opportunity to expand its 'circles of compensation'. Calder develops this concept to explain the creation of networks to link the bureaucracy to the political world to explain Japan's 'strategic capitalism' (Calder 1993). We can perhaps see the Dōwa policies of the late 1950s as an early attempt by the LDP to devise a strategy through which it might attract voters within the Buraku communities away from their support of the JSP.

By the end of the 1950s then LDP policymakers had created a Dōwa policy committee within what would shortly be re-named the Policy Affairs Research Council (PARC) and the bureaucrats had formed the Dōwa Renrakukai within the Cabinet office to coordinate policy in central government. The Zendōtai formed in the early 1950s represented the views of local administrators implementing Dōwa policies to the centre and it was their members who implemented policy decided in Tokyo. Meanwhile, the creation of the Zen Nihon Dōwakai was an attempt to develop links between those parts of Buraku civil society which did not support the JCP/JSP left-wing consensus to the LDP, thus completing the triangular policy structure of party, government and NGO that did not embrace the other key actor, the BLL. Moreover, through the creation of the Dōwakai, policymakers must have been confident that they could contain BLL influence through the manipulation of the *shingikai* process of which they had extensive experience. It is to that which we turn next.

Notes

1 This is apparently confirmed by the passage in the Dōtaishin, 1965, 'following the Occupation policies of the Allied army special administrative policies targeted at Dōwa districts were abolished…' (Dōwa Gyōseishi Henshū Iinkai, 252, 2002).

2 Kanai suggests that the idea that the US Occupation was ignorant about the Buraku issue and hostile to the continuation of Dōwa policy only developed during the early 1950s alongside the broader view that Japan had become subject to the exploitation and colonial control of American imperialism '…which had even prevented the meagre spending by the state on improvements of the living

environment of Burakumin'. From the platform adopted by the Tenth BLL conference in 1955 (Kanai, 2019, 23).

3 Kanamori was appointed a minister of State in the first cabinet of Shigeru Yoshida and played the key role in guiding the draft constitution through the process of consideration by the Diet. In the course of 114 days of debate during the spring and summer of 1946, Kanamori responded to over a thousand questions.

4 Horiki Kenzō, 1893–1974, had been Head of the General Affairs Railway Division, Ministry of Transport during the war, and was elected to the House of Councillors in 1950. He served as minister in the MHW in the first Kishi cabinet.

5 More specifically in Chiba, Saitama, Ibaraki, Kyoto, Nara, Wakayama, Hyōgo, Okayama, and Hiroshima (Kanai, 1991, 105).

6 Yagi Kazuo, 1911–76, after graduating from Tokyo University returned to Nara and joined the JSP becoming chair of the local party with Yoneda Tomi, his deputy. Elected to the LH in 1952, he convened the first meetings between the Left JSP and NCBL in 1953. Over the next two decades, he championed not only Dōwa policy but also pensions and welfare policies.

7 For a detailed account of the debate on the theory informing the liberation movement, see the five-volume work by S Morooka, *Sengo Buraku Kaihō Ronsōshi*, 1980–5.

8 Hoshijima Nirō, 1887–1980, first elected to the lower house of the Diet in 1920, was a member of the Rikken Kokumintō who supported liberal causes such as universal manhood and female suffrage. He opposed the passage of the Public Peace Police Act of 1925. He stood as a non-IRAA-endorsed candidate in 1942. After the war, he joined the Nihon Jiyūtō (Japan Liberal Party) and was a minister under Yoshida. He was a founding member of the Nihon Minshūtō in 1954 and served briefly as Speaker of the LH in 1958. He retired from politics in 1966.

9 Akita Daisuke, 1906–88, was the eldest son of a politician who had served prewar as Speaker of the lower house. He represented Tokushima in the lower house from 1946 losing his seat and retiring from politics in 1983. He served as deputy speaker during 1972–6 and served as a chair of Diet committees on education, labour and social welfare and foreign affairs. He was a minister at MHA in 1970–1 and MoJ in 1971.

10 Yanai had for a time worked closely with Matsumoto Jiichirō and at one point had been talked of as a potential successor. However, he was expelled from the movement in the early 1950s – accounts vary as to exactly why (see Amos, 2017, 111–2).

Bibliography

Amos T., (2017) 'Pathways to Buraku Liberation: Competing Images of Freedom in Early Postwar Japan', *The Journal of Northeast Asian History*, vol. 14, no. 2, 95–118.

Asada Z., (1979) *Sabetsu to Tatakai Tsuzukete* (The Struggle against Discrimination Continues), Tokyo: Asahi Shimbunsha.

Buraku Kaihō Kenkyūsho (ed.), (1991) *Shiryō: Senryōki no Buraku Mondai* (Documents on the Buraku Problem from the Occupation Period), Osaka: Buraku Kaihō Shuppansha.

Calder K. E., (1993) *Strategic Capitalism: Private Business and Public Purpose in Japanese Industrial Finance*, Princeton, NJ: Princeton University Press.

Chiiki Kaizen Taisaku Kenkyūsho (ed), (1986) *Chiiki Kaizen Taisaku Jigyō: sono chōsa to bunseki* (Regional Improvement Policy Projects: Surveys and Analysis), Tokyo: Gyōsei.

De Vos G. and Wagatsuma H. (eds), (1972) *Japan's Invisible Race, (revised edition)* Berkeley: University of California Press.

Dōwa Gyōseishi Henshū Iinkai (Dōwa Administration History Editorial Committee), (2002) *Dōwa Gyōseishi* (A History of Dōwa Administration), Tokyo: Sōmuchō Daijin Kanbō Chiiki Kaizen Taisakuhitsu.

Kanai K., (1991) *Dōwa Gyōsei: Sengo no Kiseki* (Dōwa Administration: the postwar path), Osaka: Buraku Kaihō Shuppansha.

Kanai K., (2019) *Senryōki to Buraku Mondai* (The Buraku Problem in the Occupation Period), Osaka: self-published.

Kurokawa M., (1999) *Ika to dōka no aida* (In between Alienation and Assimilation), Tokyo: Akashi Shoten.

Morooka S., (1980) *Sengo Buraku Kaihō Ronsōshi* (The Postwar Debates on Buraku Liberation), I Tokyo: Shashoku Shobo.

Morooka S., (1981) *Sengo Buraku Kaihō Ronsōshi* II Tokyo: Shashoku Shobo.

Morooka S., (1982) *Sengo Buraku Kaihō Ronsōshi* III Tokyo: Shashoku Shobo.

Murakoshi S., Watanabe T., Miwa Y., Umehara T., and Tomonaga K., (1989) *Buraku Kaihōshi* (A History of Buraku Liberation), Osaka: Kaihō Shuppansha.

Nara-ken (ed.), (2003) *Naraken Dōwa Gyōsei Jigyōshi* (A History of Dōwa Project Administration in Nara Prefecture), Nara-ken.

Neary I., (2010) *The Buraku Issue in Modern Japan: The Career of Matsumoto Jiichiro*, Abingdon: Routledge.

Suginohara J., (2006) 'Sengo Dōwa Gyōsei no Tenkai to Shihai Seisaku' (The Evolution of Postwar Dōwa Administration and Ruling Policies), *Jinken to Buraku Mondai*, Kyoto: Buraku Mondai Kenkyūjo,

No. 744, April 2006, pp. 74–9.No. 746, June 2006, pp. 71–80.No. 747, July, 2006, pp. 73–80.

Takemae E., (2002) *Inside GHQ: The Allied Occupation of Japan and Its Legacy*, London: Continuum.

5 From the *Shingikai* to the Special Measures Law – the formation of the Dōwa policy in the 1960s

In the previous chapter, we saw how, even without central government guidance, some local governments in those parts of the country where there were relatively high concentrations of Buraku communities had re-commenced Dōwa policy implementation in the late 1940s and that both the range of policies and amount of spending gradually increased across the late 1950s as the BLL became more active and economic growth increased the margins for local initiatives. Moreover, prefectural governments organised a coordinating council to exchange ideas about Dōwa policy practice and to lobby the government to provide funding. Central government was slow to respond. National politics was dominated by an ideological battle between conservatives and socialists which became institutionalised following the formation of the LDP and re-unification of the JSP in 1955. This peaked in what seemed like a serious crisis in governance in 1960 with the coincidence of a major confrontation between the representatives of labour and capital – the Miike struggle in the north Kyushu coalfield – and the massive demonstrations against the terms of the newly negotiated Security Treaty in streets of cities across the country but particularly in Tokyo. However, both of these issues had been defused by the end of the year and PM Ikeda Hayato led the LDP to success in a general election held in December getting more than twice as many Diet seats as the JSP (300:144) as well as twice the electoral support (58.1%:27.4%). The LDP suspended, temporarily at least, its ambition to revise the constitution. Political life then largely turned away from ideological issues and towards consolidating 'Japanese-style' capitalism and the 'Japanese-style' welfare state whose foundations had been put in place at the end of the 1950s.

The BLL had become closely identified with the JSP. Several of the movement's senior officials, for example, its chair and secretary-general, Matsumoto Jiichirō and Tanaka Orinoshin respectively, were also JSP Diet members. From the mid-1950s, the JSP had supported the BLL demands for a nationally coordinated Dōwa strategy even though it does not seem to have been very high among its priorities. Nevertheless, it was JSP Diet members who raised the issue in parliament, thus starting the process that would lead the Japanese state to devise and adopt a Dōwa policy. In the narrative

DOI: 10.4324/9781003127994-5

that forms the basis for this chapter, we will consider in some detail the policymaking process from the emergence of the demands to establish an advisory policy council in the late 1950s to the passage of a Special Measures Law in 1969 that was intended to put its policy recommendations into practice.

The decision to set up a Shingikai

Faced by the sustained demands for a national Dōwa strategy from the JSP, the BLL, the organisations representing local governments who were already implementing Dōwa projects (Zennihon Dōwa Taisaku Kyōgikai – Zendōtai) and even a substantial group of its own Diet members, the LDP-led government had made significant concessions in producing a 'Ten-Year Plan' funding exemplary projects which began in Spring 1960. However, the element that government seemed most reluctant to concede was the creation of an independent policy council (*shingikai*) to set out an overall vision that could inform a national Dōwa policy and provide the basis for detailed recommendations as to how it could be financed.

The most extensive examination of the role of *shingikai* in Japanese politics in English is by Frank J Schwartz who looked at the role they played in 1987–8 in the amendment of the Labour Standards Act, the legal framework that allowed the creation of financial futures markets and the changes made in the rice price support mechanism (Schwartz, 1998). The period we are concerned with is more than 25 years earlier than this but some of his general points apply. He discusses how they are used in various ways: to postpone policy decisions, sometimes indefinitely; to act as 'fairy cloaks', that is, to put off criticism and evade responsibility, or to sort out the conflict between rival ministries, or simply to legitimate administrative decisions through the involvement of apparently neutral outsiders. Or, just occasionally, that they are arenas which enable democratic involvement in the policymaking process. Murakawa Ichirō's overview of the Japanese policy process comments only briefly on the role of *shingikai*. He suggests that although they are formally established by and responsible to the Diet, they are usually selected from a limited number of reliable individuals who serve repeatedly, rely on the relevant ministry for data and documents, and often simply endorse the conclusions as required by the responsible ministry. In fact, he concludes that as far as the process of policymaking is concerned, most ministries regard *shingikai* as a waste of time (Murakawa, 1985, 210–1).

In the course of this chapter, we will be concerned to consider what role the Dōwa Taisaku Shingikai played in the formulation of Dōwa policy. It is not a principal purpose of this chapter but an outline of the impact of this *shingikai* will add to the literature on the role they have played in policymaking.

We begin by tracing the process that led from the initial proposal to establish a *shingikai* in the mid-1950s to its operation between 1960 and 1965.

We will then summarise the core aspects of its report before analysing how its recommendations were dealt with by elected politicians and ministries in the period 1965–69.

Dōwa Taisaku Shingikai – the proposal accepted

The creation of a council to make broad policy recommendations had been a central demand in the report on Buraku issues endorsed by the JSP in 1957/8. PM Kishi had promised a swift response to this in answer to a question from JSP member Yagi Kazuo in the Diet in March 1958 but no action was taken immediately. A set of proposals that came from the LDP committee in March 1959, while very similar to those of the JSP, noticeably did not include any support for a *shingikai.* However, undeterred, Yagi put forward a proposal to create a Buraku Kaihō Shingikai as a private member's bill in November 1959. In his proposal, the council would have been dominated by Diet members (8 HR, 5 HC) and its brief would have been based on Article 14 of the constitution which begins, 'All of the people are equal under the law...' The LDP was not happy with this. Kanai reports that there was a particular fear among the conservatives and bureaucrats that the presence of Diet members on the council would result in Matsumoto Jiichirō being able to dominate the proceedings (Kanai, 2009, 429). The JSP, however, only controlled around one-third of the seats in the lower house, so it was always unlikely that this bill would be enacted without the support of the ruling party.

Akita Daisuke acting on behalf of the Dōwa policy group within the LDP opened discussions with Yagi at the start of 1960 about how to take the proposal forward and this resulted in the deletion of the reference to Article 14 of the constitution, the replacement of 'Buraku Kaihō' (Buraku liberation) with 'Dōwa Taisaku' (assimilation policy) in its title, and a specification that it would have no more than 20 members of whom a majority were to be bureaucrats, one from each ministry concerned, eleven in all, plus up to nine 'persons of learning and experience', the standard formulation for lay members which usually meant either academics, reliable local politicians, or employees of what in the UK would be called Quangos – quasi-autonomous non-government organisations – many of whom were retired bureaucrats. This should have kept the committee firmly under bureaucratic control while allowing for some outside input. A cross-party group was set up in early 1960 and unanimously endorsed the creation of a Dōwa Taisaku Shingikai. The Cabinet Affairs committee (Naikaku Iinkai) of the HR accepted the draft bill on 17 May 1960. It was promulgated on 13 August with a time limit of two years and a budget of ¥1.1m.

The law established the Dōwa Taisaku Shingikai within the PMO and defined its tasks as being,

> ...to investigate the main elements for the resolution of the social and economic problems encountered in Dōwa districts and the establishment

> of the necessary comprehensive policies in order to resolve the Dōwa problem.
>
> And,
>
> …to submit a report and make proposals to the PM as appropriate.
>
> (Dōwa Gyōseishi Henshū Iinkai, 2002, 223)

Why did the LDP make this concession? There are several levels of possible explanation. First, during the first half of 1960, Japan was gripped by a political crisis so serious that some questioned its commitment to democratic practices. PM Kishi had negotiated revisions to the Security Treaty with the American president and signed them off on the White House lawn but he then had to return to Japan and have them approved by the Diet. The JSP and all on the left were opposed to them and took part in a series of massive street demonstrations from late 1959 into the summer of 1960. At one point in the summer of 1960, PM Kishi even considered mobilising the SDF to pacify the streets of Tokyo. The coalition of groups which organised these protests included large sections of the organised labour movement, student groups, and many other civil society organisations. The BLL was one of these and had been sending representatives to the preparatory meetings of the anti-Security Treaty organisation since February 1958. It encouraged local branches to join in protest activity, including the demonstrations of 1960 (Murakoshi et al., 1989, 84). Several commentators suggest that the more conciliatory line taken to the BLL in 1960 was aimed at weakening its commitment to the anti-Ampo campaigns and thus splitting the anti-Ampo coalition. Second, the concession reflects a change in broader policy concerns to place increased weight on social welfare policy creating the various elements that would become the Japanese-style welfare state. The National Health Insurance (NHI) system which made affordable health care available to all those who were not covered by employer-funded systems was introduced in 1958 and became fully operational in 1961. A 'safety net' type of pension system was introduced in parallel with this. This meant that as the economy grew rapidly across the rest of the 1960s, no sector of Japanese society felt completely left behind. The government was thus open to arguments based on ensuring the welfare of all. Third, and at a more abstract level, the changes taking place in Japan's political economy were thought of as manifestations of its 'modernity'. While there was much disagreement as to the origins of the Buraku communities and the nature of the persisting discrimination against them, there was wide agreement that their existence was not compatible with a 'modern' Japan. Something had to be done, but what? Maybe a *shingikai* could answer this question.

The selection of its members and proceedings

The first task was to select the nine lay members. Two people were chosen to represent the Buraku organisations: Yanai Masao of the Dōwakai and Kitahara Daisaku who was a member of the BLL central committee although for unexplained reasons his affiliation is often listed in the formal documentation as the Chūbu Nihon Shimbun. However, it seems to have been difficult to fill the other positions. Kanai commented in 1991 (and it would still be true in 2021) that the reason for the delay was that 'then as today there were many even among progressives who regarded the Buraku problem as "untouchable"' (Kanai, 1991, 160). It took until November 1961, 16 months from the time the act was passed to recruit the full complement of *shingikai* members. Apart from Yanai and Kitahara, there was an elected representative from local government, two academics with expertise in social welfare policy, two members of other *shingikai* in related areas (and former bureaucrats), an architect, and a journalist.[1]

First, we should note that the first chair of the Dōwa policy *shingikai*, Kimura Chujirō,[2] was the deputy chair of the Japan National Council of Social Welfare and continued to serve on the Dōtaikyō until May 1974. Also on the *shingikai* between 1960 and 1965 was Ogata Tadashi, committee member of the Shin Seikatsu Undō Kyōkai (New Life Campaign Association).[3] We do not know what influence they had on the report's recommendations or the implementation of policy but their presence on these councils suggests that its thinking was at least informed by the developments in social welfare policy elsewhere in government which, as we suggested earlier, was by 1962 starting to turn its attention to the problems faced by those living on incomes below the poverty line.

At the first session, Kitahara insisted that they should commission a thorough survey of the contemporary situation and the proposal was included in the budget for FY1962. A survey sub-committee was set up in May 1962 chaired by Isomura Eiichi and this provided an opportunity to invite several others to contribute their direct experience of the problem to the panel notably Yoneda Tomi and Nomoto Takeichi from the BLL, and Yamamoto Masao of the Dōwakai. Two separate surveys were commissioned. First, each prefecture was invited to report on the number of Buraku communities, their size in terms of households, and population as of 1 January 1963. This came to 4,160 communities in 407,479 households and a total population of 1,113,043. However, nine prefectures refused to respond: Hokkaido, Aomori, Iwate, Miyagi, Akita, Yamagata, Tokyo, Kanagawa, and Miyazaki. Hokkaido was only populated by the Japanese after the Meiji restoration and had no Buraku communities. Neither did Okinawa although at that time it was not under the jurisdiction of the Japanese government. The five prefectures of Tohoku and Miyazaki were reported in the 1935 survey to have a few Buraku communities, although all of them small. The most significant omissions from this survey were Tokyo and Kanagawa where the 1935 survey located 20 and 31 Buraku communities, respectively. In the second phase of the survey, sixteen communities were selected for a more detailed analysis chosen to represent different types of Buraku: urban communities in large and small municipalities, rural communities in both the suburbs and more remote agricultural and fishing communities, communities which depended on traditional Buraku industries (leather making, for instance) and those which relied on 'modern' industry (more detail in Noguchi and Ishimoto, 2014, 187–98).

In February 1963, three more sub-committees were set up to cover education, the living environment (chaired by Takayama), and the economy.[4] According to the reminiscences of Kitahara and Yamamoto, the bureaucrats knew very little about the issue and the academics were reluctant to say much, so most of the contributions came from those with direct experience in Buraku issues, the representatives from the BLL or Dōwakai (Kanai, 1991, 164; Morooka III, 1982, 333). The reports from each sub-committee were submitted to the full committee in May 1965 and subsequently published. However, it proved very difficult to get agreement on the final recommendations. Kitahara and Yanai acquired the reputation of speaking at great length, often for more than an hour, thereby dominating proceedings. Discussion about whether to include a sentence about the implementation of Dōwa policy 'as a duty of the state' is said to have lasted three days (Dōwa Gyōseishi Henshū Iinkai, 2002, 8). The chair threatened to resign three times as an agreement seemed impossible such that it seemed unlikely that they would be able to unanimously endorse the report by mid-August but the PMO refused to allow any further extension (Morooka III, 1982, 333–4). Finally, the report was signed off and presented to PM Sato almost exactly five years after the law establishing the *shingikai* had come into effect.

The report – Dōtaishin

The *shingikai* report, Dōwa Taisaku Shingikai Tōshin – Dōtaishin – was relatively short comprising only 43 pages as usually reproduced. It divides into three substantive sections: its analysis of the Buraku/Dōwa problem, a review of the development of Dōwa policy hitherto, and recommendations for policy henceforth. Its preamble defines the problem as 'an issue that concerns basic human rights that are guaranteed by the constitution and are connected to the universal principles of human freedom and equality'. It takes the view that the rapid resolution of this problem is 'the responsibility of the state and at the same time a task for the nation' (Full text Dōwa Gyōseishi Henshū Iinkai, 2002, 228–71).

The first section begins by explaining that the problem is one of discrimination against a group of Japanese citizens which has been created as a result of Japan's historical development and which has resulted in serious infringements of their basic human rights. It emphatically rejects any suggestion that they are not racially the same as other Japanese citizens. Although formally freed from status discrimination by an edict in August 1871, they are poor and remain on the margins of Japanese society. It points to the 'dual structure' of the Japanese economy and suggests that Buraku industries are located within the sectors that have not benefited from post-war growth.

This duality of the economic structure is reflected in the social structure which also is composed of one part that is characterised by modern civil society and the other where feudal status structures and patriarchal family relationships persist. Irrational beliefs and superstitions which form the basis of prejudices are strongly rooted in the latter social structures. It identifies both material and cultural (psychological) aspects to discrimination and argues that as they are inter-connected, policy must address both – both the ideas that prevent normal social relations such as access to education and marriage and also the material conditions that reproduce negative images such as inadequate housing, high levels of unemployment, and poverty. This is followed by a brief review of the survey data on both the material conditions within the communities and the attitudes of majority Japanese towards them.

The second part, reputed to be mainly the work of Kitahara Taisaku, briefly reviews the pre-war evolution of Yūwa policy, the contemporary Burakumin movements, and concludes with a summary of post-war policy. For the future, it recommends that the Dōwa issue should become part of the nation's basic policies such that all agencies of government should make the direct and indirect promotion of the elimination of Dōwa discrimination a fundamental priority. This, it argues, will require close collaboration between central and local governments to assist poorer regions and significant increases in central government funding of the Dōwa projects. It describes how this might happen, setting out the basic structure of five policy areas: improvement of the living environment, social welfare, industry and employment, education, and human rights. Careful consultation with the residents of the Dōwa communities will be needed to ensure that the plans accommodate their particular circumstances. While pre-war policy was based on the ideas of the Emancipation Declaration (*Kaihōrei/Senmin Haishirei*), this new policy is founded on the rights ideas set out in the constitution and thus is a basic obligation of the state.

This responsibility of the state to support Dōwa policy will continue as long as Buraku discrimination exists. To this end, three basic principles should inform each of the five policy areas. First, policies should seek to raise the social, economic, and cultural living standards in these communities such that differences with the neighbouring communities are eliminated while at the same time encouraging a spirit of self-reliance. Second, it will be necessary to eliminate the prejudices and discrimination against these communities through education within schools and society at large and the promotion of human rights activities so as to remove irrational beliefs and superstitions. Finally, the resolution of the social and economic problems of the Dōwa communities should be located in the context of the overall improvement of the living environment and the promotion of equal opportunity in employment.

Wherever possible, the report links its recommendations to specific articles of the constitution. So, for example, the section on social security is explicitly linked to articles 14 on equality and 25 on minimum standards of 'wholesome and cultured living'. The section on Dōwa education is linked to article 26 and the commitment to equality of educational opportunity as expressed in the 1948 Basic Law on Education.

The final section sets out six steps that will need to be taken to support the aims of the report:

- To pass legislation that will regularize the legal basis of the various projects that are being implemented as Dōwa policy,
- To create a policy council to unify and promote the various Dōwa policies across government,
- To strengthen the national financial structure to support the development of Dōwa projects that it will be the duty of local governments to implement,
- To set up a structure to enable special funding to be provided for government projects,
- To provide special funding for projects within Dōwa districts,
- To formulate a long-term plan for the basic resolution of the Dōwa problem considering the various aspects of living environment improvements, economy, employment, education etc.

(Kanai, 2018, 13)

Responses

The report was presented to the prime minister on 11 August 1965 and he announced his intention to set up an Interim Dōwa Problem Cabinet Council (Rinji Dōwa Mondai Kakuryo Kyōgikai) to consider the report and suggest policies. Narita Tomomi, the secretary-general of the JSP, met with the Chief Cabinet Secretary requesting full implementation. That same day, Matsumoto Jiichirō, the chair of the BLL, held a press conference at which he welcomed the report as a first step towards a comprehensive Dōwa policy, something which they had been campaigning for since 1957. However, he gave notice that there were some aspects that the BLL could not accept and that they would take a keen interest in the government's response (Asahi Shimbun, 12 August 1965). Meanwhile, *Akahata*, the JCP daily newspaper, while recognising that the report could result in some improvements, argued that there was a danger that it would promote 'Yūwa-ism' and anti-communism. It reminded its readers of the importance of prioritising the joint-struggle against the US imperialism and Japanese monopoly capitalism (Kanai, 1991, 179).

Two months later, the BLL held its 20th annual conference which welcomed the report's 'confirmation that the resolution of the Buraku problem was a responsibility of the state and its clear setting out of the basic approach of providing administrative guarantees for civil rights and freedom' (Kanai, 2018, 10). In the words of Tanaka Orinoshin, JSP Diet member and secretary to the BLL, 'No-one thinks that complete liberation will result from the report but we should systematically examine its content and work out how we can fight for its implementation and how we can improve on its inadequate aspects' (Kanai, 1991, 181).

Oga Masayuki, a leading Buraku activist from Osaka who played a key role in the city and national organisations, argues that the Dōtaishin was crucial in demolishing three arguments that had previously hindered the coordinated development of Dōwa policy at the national level:

- that Buraku discrimination did not really exist anymore, and even the traces that remain were being eradicated by the post-war process of democratisation;
- that even where some elements of discrimination still remained, it was a result of 'fate' or 'human nature' and thus not amenable to elimination by policies implemented by the state;
- that even if it were possible for policy intervention to have some impact, the best approach would be through 'general' policies to clear slums or enhance the education performance of all the socially and economically disadvantaged. To introduce targeted policies would risk generating feelings of 'reverse discrimination' and thus perpetuate the problem.

The report, he suggests, swept aside these arguments based on the evidence from the surveys that clearly demonstrated the extent to which Buraku communities were disadvantaged compared to the majority and even their neighbours, and the existence of deep-rooted prejudice within the mainstream community. This is despite nearly 20 years of commitment to democratic practice and rapid economic growth. The report discussed the existence of Buraku discrimination as contrary to both universal principles and the constitutionally guaranteed notions of liberty and equality that it was the duty of the state to do something about. Finally, Oga notes the way the report committed the state to take a lead in implementing a positive policy to improve living conditions and life chances as well as creating broad legal protection for human rights to make discrimination illegal and provide redress when it occurred (Oga 2015, interview 28 August 2015).

The administrative response to the report can be summarised fairly simply. On 17 August 1965, a cabinet committee was formed to coordinate the activities of the various ministries composed of a representative from each plus the PMO/Cabinet Office. Having delivered its report, the *shingikai* was dissolved but on 16 June 1966 a Dōwa Taisaku Kyōgikai (Dōwa Policy Council – Dōtaikyō) was formed consisting of up to 20 individuals appointed by the PM to '… investigate fundamental issues relating to the close coordination of the relevant administrative agencies for the promotion of Dōwa policy, including making recommendations to the PM or relevant ministries' (Dōwa Gyōseishi Henshū Iinkai, 2002, 273). The make-up of this council was very similar to that of its predecessor: ten ministerial representatives and ten lay members, six of whom had been on the *shingikai*. Of these latter, two were from the Zen Nihon Dōwakai, one of them Yanai Masao, the other Itouchi Tadashi at 40 the youngest member of the council, two from the BLL, Kitahara now with Yoneda Tomi as a full member. Yamamoto Masao was co-opted as a specialist member with Nomoto Takeichi from the BLL. In other words, four of the ten full lay members and two of the five special members had a Buraku background.[5]

On 25 February 1967, the Dōtaikyō published a draft long-term plan which proposed to introduce legislation by April 1969 noting that it would be necessary for the relevant ministries to coordinate their programmes but that it should be an underlying aim of policy to encourage the self-reliance of the residents of the Dōwa districts. A draft law was published in March 1968 which over the next 12 months was slightly amended to become the *Dōwa Jigyō Taisaku Tokubetsu Sochihō* as promulgated on 10 July 1969. Two days earlier, Cabinet had approved the Dōwa Policy Long-Term Plan which set out a timetable divided into two five-year sections. It thus took almost exactly four years between the presentations of the *shingikai* report to PM Satō to the start of the implementation of the law.

To explain why it took so long, we need to look more closely at the political process. Following the BLL conference held in early autumn 1965, members of the new central committee visited the offices of the relevant ministries demanding full implementation of the report. Fukuda Takeo, then CCS, explained that, although cabinet had not yet decided on its response, it was likely to include the passage of a Basic Law and provision for special financial arrangements to fund Dōwa projects (Kanai, 2018, 14). A special committee was formed within the BLL to sustain pressure on the government with the aim of having draft legislation presented in the next Diet session in the first half of 1966.

A 1,500-person conference convened on 28/9 January 1966 was comprised mainly of BLL members but also had representatives of the labour movement and local government officials. It urged the rapid implementation of the Dōtaishin proposals. A cross-party group of Diet members – LDP, JSP, DSP – was formed. As a practical suggestion, it was proposed that legislators might look to the Remote Islands Law as a possible model.[6] However, despite an apparent commitment to a two-stage process – Basic Law plus Special Measures – and to central government providing up to 90% of the costs of projects, no substantial progress was made and the Diet session ended in June without any legislation having been passed. One stumbling block seemed to be the name of the policy. Akita Daisuke, in particular, was opposed to the use of the word Dōwa. He also pointed out that while inhabitants of remote islands could be relied on to vote for the LDP, the BLL would almost inevitably become involved in the administration of the new Dōwa projects and their supporters mostly voted for the JSP or JCP (Kanai, 2018, 17).

The detailed development of policy seems to have taken place within the Dōtaikyō which met 13 times, somewhat irregularly, between July 1966 and March 1968. Although the membership was similar to that of the *shingikai*, it was more closely linked to the ruling party. The chair, Horiki Kenzō, had worked with PM Satō in the Railways Ministry during the war before being elected to the HC in 1950 serving in the first Kishi cabinet at MHW. His involvement in Dōwa policymaking started in 1952. He had been a leading member of the Dōwa Policy sub-committee of the LDP PARC when it was formed in 1959 but he did not stand for re-election in 1962. Another new recruit to the council was Hashimoto Masayuki who served as an LDP Diet member briefly during 1958–60 before being elected the governor of Yamaguchi. He too was close to Kishi and Satō.

Horiki was a more active chairman than his predecessor on the *shingikai* had been and the ministry representatives, now possibly better informed about the issue, played a more active role. A sub-group was formed in February 1967 of six members, including Kitahara, Yamamoto, and Isomura to draft the new law but still progress was slow. In May, another survey was proposed with the specific remit of assessing the tasks of the various ministries and in addition to the national survey, there was a more detailed survey of the specific problems being faced in 21 municipalities carried out between September and November (Noguchi and Ishimoto, 2014, 199–200). The results of these surveys fed into discussions held between November and March 1968. By this time, there were three sets of proposals: quite detailed suggestions from the BLL and Zen Nihon Dōwakai with a more minimal proposal from the chair, Horiki, and the LDP. The BLL proposals insisted on a clear commitment to the principles of equality of opportunity and demanded legislation that would make discrimination illegal. At the same time, it was concerned that the LDP would opt for just a *rinenhō* ('concept law') with no commitment to concrete improvements.[7] One specific disagreement was about who should qualify for support within the new system: the BLL wanted to keep the definition as wide as possible to include all residents of Buraku/Dōwa communities *as well as* descendants of Burakumin wherever they lived although it was unclear how this could be operationalised (Kanai, 2018, 41). In the spring of 1968, a cross-party committee[8] was set up in the HR but there remained opposition to the draft law within the LDP not only to its basic approach but also its title and the share of the cost to be paid by central government. The Dotaikyō submitted a proposal for a draft law in March (Dōwa Gyōseishi Henshū Iinkai, 2002, 284–5). At the end of May, CCS Fukuda promised to submit a bill to the autumn session of the Diet but nothing appeared. The BLL held another major conference in Tokyo in December attracting 5,000 people and, in response to questions in the HR, PM Satō promised to submit a bill to the spring session of the Diet. Yagi continued negotiations with the LDP on specific issues such as the financial burden to be borne by central government and the mechanism for the issuing of bonds by local government to finance the programmes. Finally, on 12 February, a bill was published in the official gazette, *Kanpo*. Even then it was not formally approved by cabinet until 11 April and took another two months to pass through both houses of the Diet being formally promulgated on 10 July 1969.

The outcome

The law itself was very short, just 11 clauses, two and a half pages long and entitled the Dōwa Taisaku Jigyō Tokubetsu Sochihō, The Special Measures Law for Dōwa Policy Projects . There is no particular significance to the usage 'Special Measures Law' which is commonly used in measures on a variety of issues from terrorism to influenza policy. The aim of the Dōwa policy is set out in the first clause,

> This law, in conformance with the Japanese constitutional principle of guaranteeing the enjoyment of basic human rights of all citizens, as well as clarifying the aims of the Dōwa policy projects to be carried out by the state and local governments in cooperation with communities where progress in the improvement of the living environment has been hindered for historical and social reasons (that is the 'target communities'), by taking the special measures necessary to achieve this target will nurture the economic growth, stabilise the living conditions of residents and improve the welfare of those in the target communities.

Clauses two, three, and four reiterate the importance of the reciprocal recognition of basic human rights among all citizens and the principle of cooperation between central and local governments. Article five talks about eliminating the various elements that have unfairly prevented the improvement of the living conditions of the residents of the target areas and article six lists seven specific areas of improvements that roughly correspond to the areas of responsibility of the seven major 'spending ministries': MoC, MHW, MAFF, MITI, MoL, MoE, plus the MoJ with a final sub-clause that covers all other measures that need to be done to carry out these aims. Clause seven sets out the principle that the state's burden should be two-thirds of the cost in most cases. Meanwhile, local governments must begin to follow the lead of state policy. The final clauses deal with technical details relating to finance and repeat the need for central and local cooperation. It will apply until 31 March 1979 (Dōwa Gyōseishi Henshū Iinkai, 2002, 307–9).

Two days earlier, a Dōwa Policy Long-term Plan had been published which determined that implementation would be split into two five-year periods and discussed in some, but still not very great detail the basic parameters of Dōwa policy to be carried out by each of the seven ministries (Dōwa Gyōseishi Henshū Iinkai, 2002, 316–23).

It was far from what the BLL had wanted or indeed what Fukuda seemed to have promised in 1965. First, and most importantly, the 'special measures' were not located in the framework of a Basic Law. These are laws which set out the basic parameters within which policy will be developed in a specific administrative area. At the time of the publication of the Dōtaishin, there were only six covering such areas as education (1947), nuclear power (1955), and agriculture (1961). From the late 1960s onwards, the passage of a Basic Law has been used to indicate that the state has decided to take responsibility for a new policy area and to set out the basic framework of its approach. At this time, the MHW was considering policy towards the disabled which resulted in the passage of a Basic Law on the Disabled in 1970. In 1967, a Basic Law on the Environment was passed and then amended in 1970. In the following months, the Diet went on to approve the drastic amendment or fresh enactment of fourteen pieces of environmental legislation. Since this time, it has become more common to pass Basic Laws: as of 2016, 54 were on the books of which more than half had been passed since 1990. There is still no Basic Law on human rights or Buraku issues.

The BLL and its supporters in the JSP wanted something similar which would commit the government to the protection of basic human rights, create a framework for laws against discrimination in general as well as specific measures to support Dōwa programme policy. Yagi envisaged creating a mechanism that could be used to hold government to account but all that emerged was a Special Measures Law valid for ten years that authorised funding for improvements to be implemented by local governments (Kanai, 1991, 194).

As we will see, the BLL did not give up on the idea and renewed its campaign for a Basic Law on Buraku Liberation from the mid-1980s. One reason why the BLL was reluctant to commit too much energy at this point to demands for a Basic Law was their fear that the LDP would choose to *only* endorse this part of the report. That is, to commit simply to a law that would declare discrimination to be a 'bad thing' but provide no central government funding and/or leave responsibility for planning Dōwa projects to local government.

There was also an absence of enthusiasm among those on the policy council even among the representatives of the Burakumin themselves. Kitahara Taisaku had been one of the most vociferous advocates of the need for the state to take responsibility for the improvement of Buraku living conditions and is reputed to have spoken at great length about it in the *shingikai* discussions.[9] During the 1950s, he had been among those on the BLL central committee who had subscribed to the view that full emancipation from prejudice and discrimination would only be possible following a socialist restructuring of society but in the shorter term, the state should be persuaded to make some special provision. However, in the course of the 1960s, he seems to have changed his position following his observations of the rapid economic development being experienced by Japan. Morooka talks of his 'glorification' of modernisation theory[10] (Morooka III, 1982, 353). One interpretation of the results of the two surveys carried out of Buraku conditions in 1963 and 1967 was that rather than the 'immiseration' of the proletariat that seemed to be predicted by Marxism, the rapid progress of capitalism was improving the lives of Burakumin as the benefits of modernisation 'trickled down' to them. Put in Marxist terms, as fundamental changes were taking place in the economic 'base', it was inevitable that change would occur in the 'superstructure' of ideas and one aspect of that would be the withering away of feudal remnants, such as prejudices against Burakumin. Kitahara was content to support the funding of Dōwa projects that would alleviate historic social and economic backwardness but not legislation against discrimination.

Meanwhile, Yamamoto Masao, who is recognised as being one of the 'brains' behind the Zen Nihon Dōwakai, took a similar position if from a quite different ideological stance. In 1962, he produced a detailed critique of the BLL Marxist analysis adopted two years earlier totally rejecting their class-based analysis and arguing that the Buraku problem can be considered without reference to 'capitalism' or 'socialism' but rather from a 'humanistic perspective'. He argued that discrimination was simply a 'bad custom' that could be resolved within Japan's liberal democracy. He recognised the existence of a vicious cycle that linked poverty and discrimination and which could only be broken by government-funded improvements but he suggested that the 'blame', if any, should be ascribed to at Japanese society, not its government. This view also envisaged discrimination being eliminated from Japanese society through the Dōwa policy programmes without the need for legislation to deter it (Morooka III, 1982, 305–10). This line of thinking was taken up by Isomura Eichi.

The BLL greeted the passage of the SML as 'a milestone on the road to liberation' since it created a 'legal basis for campaigns to achieve demands for the improvement of everyday life' (Morooka IV, 1984, 209) even if it had failed to get the commitment to eliminate discrimination that it had sought. Not only was there no Basic Law, there was no part of central government – a specialist bureau, *kyoku*, or agency, *chō* – charged with the responsibility to develop or administer Dōwa policy unlike, for example, 25 years later when the government set up the Headquarters for the Promotion of Gender Equality within the Cabinet Office that would in 2001 become the Gender Equality Bureau (*Danjo Kyōdō Sankakukyoku*). There was no obligation to report progress to the Diet and it was not clear that sufficient funding would or could be provided to ensure the projects would have any impact. Those less optimistic about future economic growth, such as Fujitani Toshio of the Buraku Mondai Kenkyūsho, doubted whether it could ever be fully funded since to do so would consume too large a proportion of the social welfare budget (Morooka III, 1982, 353). Matsumoto Jiichirō had worried about what impact the full funding of the Dōtaishin recommendations might have on the movement saying in November 1965, 'An SML contains the danger that it will corrupt the liberation movement. People will throw all caution and conscience away in pursuit of the money and the movement will be ruined' (Kanai, 2018, 26 quoting Uesugi Saichirō, see Buraku Kaihō Chūō Honbu, 2002, 193).

The JCP-oriented grouping within the BLL initially announced its conditional acceptance of the law. They disliked the fact that it was time-limited and argued that programmes should be devised from within Buraku communities rather than being imposed on them from outside. However, they soon became more critical arguing that Dōwa policy was designed to split the movement by encouraging rightist reformism within the Buraku which would increase the influence of the LDP (Kanai, 2018, 60–1). It accused the BLL of being uncritical of the Dōwa legislation and of lacking connection with other parts of the working-class movement (Morooka IV, 1984, 212). Within a few years, the JCP supporting group would organise a faction within the BLL that later in the 1970s would depart to create a rival organisation.

Concluding comments

Why did the LDP pass a law that many of its Diet members disliked? Several factors might contribute to an explanation. First, just as in the period 1959/60, the later 1960s was a period of political crises in which there were massive demonstrations on the streets and campuses of Tokyo and other major cities in protest about the renewal of the Security Treaty and the war in Vietnam among other things. These measures may have been in part designed to weaken that anti-government coalition (Kanai, 2018, 53). Second, in a major speech in November 1964, PM Satō had committed himself to develop a high-grade welfare state. He may have felt at that point constrained by critics within his party but having won a third term as leader of the LDP, and thus PM, in 1968, he probably felt free to push forward with an unpopular piece of legislation. Third, the provision of special measures to address the needs of this particular group fitted in well with PM Satō's plans to develop a high-grade welfare system through the improvement of housing, living environment and social capital, as expressed, for example, in a speech he made in the Diet on 21 November 1964 (Kanai, 2018, 4). Finally, by emphasising that Dōwa project initiatives should come from and be implemented by local governments, the SML could be presented as having the characteristics of a regional promotion law that particularly emphasised infrastructure improvements. By the late 1960s, dwindling support for the LDP was allowing JSP-led opposition coalitions to take control of many municipalities. The JSP hoped that these local successes could be translated into support for its parliamentary candidates. The 'model projects' that had been launched in 1960 were often funded in areas where the LDP was influential. No doubt, LDP Diet members could see how the SML could be used to shore up their electoral bases which were threatened by opposition party electoral cooperation.

Schwartz argues that the ministries could use *shingikai* to mitigate demands for basic reforms by keeping the process of policymaking under bureaucratic control. The in-built majority of active bureaucrats supported by the retirees from the bureaucracy and ex-LDP politicians might have ensured that the Dōwa Taisaku Shingikai produce a feeble report defined by the policy preferences of the ruling party/bureaucracy. This tallies with the description of *shingikai* activity by Murakawa. However, as we have seen, from the early phase of the creation of the report, *shingikai* members with a Buraku background were able to exercise considerable influence. Kitahara commented in 1979,

> The first meetings of the *shingikai* were like seminars for the officials from each ministry. They knew nothing about the Dōwa problem. Meetings were held once a month but those who expressed any opinions were the full time or co-opted members from the movement groups, either BLL or *Dōwakai*. The other lay members of the council hardly said anything. And the officials from the ministry took the attitude of 'being told'...
>
> (Quoted by Kanai, 1991, 164)

And Isomura commented in 1993 that representatives on the committee from the movement groups did not understand what the role of the administrators was, so they earnestly insisted on all of their long-standing demands. In other words, in the face of the ignorance of the administrators and the reticence of the other lay members of the council to express an opinion, the representatives of the Buraku communities were able to exert a powerful influence. Not content to rely on data from the PMO and assisted by Isomura Eichi, a leading urban sociologist, they demanded and then shaped the terms of the surveys carried out in 1963. Yagi had tried to have the *shingikai* brief incorporate references to the constitution but this was over-ruled by the LDP. Nevertheless, as we have seen, some quite specific references to constitutional commitments were a conspicuous part of the final report. Further, their robust advocacy of a positive, what one might call 'affirmative action' policy *avant la lettre*, also influenced the content of the 1965 report. The 'construction' of the Dōwa problem in the Dōtaishin, then, was very strongly influenced by the Burakumin on the *shingikai* which probably explains why it went much further in its recommendations than either bureaucracy or ruling party had expected.

However, if the process of creating a *shingikai* and it then writing a report was certainly not the 'waste of time' that Murakawa suggests, once the report had been delivered, the Dōtaikyō, although re-constituted with many who had served on the *shingikai*, was put under a chair much closer to the leadership of the LDP and containing several other LDP and bureaucratic OBs. Moreover, the representatives of the bureaucracy were now better 'educated' about the Buraku issue and less susceptible to having the policy agenda highjacked by the movement representatives. In any case, some of them, Kitahara in particular, were moving towards positions compatible with if not necessarily based on the same ideological premises as the bureaucrats.

As a result, the negotiations of the terms of the implementation of Dōwa policy did not end in the outcome the movement wanted and seemed at times to have been promised. Rather, government insisted on an interpretation of the Buraku problem that was amenable to administrative intervention and which could articulate with the broader developments in social welfare policy that were taking place within MHW, housing policy within MoC, and education policy within MoE. Moreover, to anticipate our narrative a little, it is no coincidence that the acceleration of funding for Dōwa policy programmes really began to take off in 1972–3 at the same time as PM Tanaka Kakuei was announcing his plans to remodel the Japanese archipelago (*Nihon Rettō Kaizōron*) and the re-launch of social welfare policies in which he designated as the 'First Year of Welfare' – *Fukushi Gannen*.

The most generous interpretation of this is that the focus of policymakers and movement activists was on the alleviation of the dire poverty that was being experienced by many residents of Buraku communities as a result of which there was no more than minimal attention to rights issues. It suited the LDP to opt for a time-limited SML which had a focus on infrastructural measures that it might be able to use to suit its own interests and avoid the creation of standards or mechanisms that might be used to hold it to account. The content of the Dōwa policies made possible by this statutory framework was something that was up for negotiation between central and local governments in response to the demands being made on them by Buraku communities articulated by both national organisations and local networks. It is to how that worked out that we next turn our attention.

Notes

1 The full list of the *shingikai* members is Isomura Eichi (professor, social welfare policy, Tokyo Metropolitan University), Itō Noboru (editorial board, *Asahi Shimbun*), Ishimi Motohide (governor of Ehime prefecture), Ogata Tadashi (Employment Stability Council), Kitahara Taisaku (BLL), Kimura Chujirō, chair (formerly permanent vice-minister MHW, National Social Welfare Council), Takayama Eika (Professor, Dept Architecture, Tokyo University), Tanabe Shigeko (Professor, Dept of Law, specialist in family law and the only woman on the council, Senshū University), Yanai Masao (chair, Zen Nihon Dōwakai).

2 Kimura Chujirō, 1907–78, was a MHW OB having worked there until 1957 following graduation from Tokyo University in 1930. After retirement, he was appointed the head of various social work colleges and from 1976 was the head of the Social Welfare Research Institute.

3 This was a state-funded organisation established in 1955 which oversaw the activities of the burgeoning improvement societies throughout Japan having inherited the modernising mission and language of the pre-war campaigns. It brought together conservative and progressive forces with an agenda that *inter alia* included the promotion of public morality, the rationalisation of savings and

household accounts, improvements in the customs of daily life, improvements in health and sanitation, the defeat of superstitious customs, and family planning (Garon, 1994, 358–9).

4 Yoneda was a member of all four panels. Yamamoto served on the survey, living conditions, and education panels.

5 More detail on the council's membership, Kanai, 2018, 22–3.

6 Enacted in 1953, the Remote Islands Development Act was initially limited to ten years with the aim to 'eliminate backwardness' in remote islands. However, it has been renewed for further ten-year periods ever since. Between 1953 and 2004, a total of ¥44,153B had been spent on a variety of projects all of which in some way were aimed at addressing the 'malignant cycle of poverty'. There are 261 designated islands whose population declined from 920,000 to 470,000 in 2000. See Kuwahara, 2012, 1.

7 A *rinenhō* is a conceptual law that establishes a principle rather than creating institutions or penalties for action or inaction.

8 Its membership was LDP 5, JSP 3, DSP 1, Kōmeitō 1.

9 For example, at the initial plenary sessions of the *shingikai* held until May 1962 when the sub-committees were set up, Kitahara would speak for between one and a half to two hours. Yanagi was only slightly less vociferous. According to Isomura,

> The two of them would talk for a total of around 3 hours. They spoke about their hard past and difficult living conditions and no-one could ask questions or do anything about it. That was why we proposed to conduct a survey into these conditions…
>
> (Sōmuchō, 1993, 7–8)

10 Suzuki Ryō also mentions how Kitahara was at this time strongly influenced by modernisation theory especially Rostow's views on the role of infrastructural change (Suzuki, 2010, 233).

Bibliography

Asahi Shimbun, 12 August 1965.

Buraku Kaihō Chūō Honbu (ed.) (2003) *Uesugi Saichirō Den* (Biography of Uesugi Saichirō), Osaka: Kaihō Shuppansha.

Dōwa Gyōseishi Henshū Iinkai (Dōwa Administration History Editorial Committee), (2002) *Dōwa Gyōseishi* (A History of Dōwa Administration), Tokyo: Sōmuchō Daijin Kanbō Chiiki Kaizen Taisakuhitsu.

Garon S., (1994) 'Rethinking Modernization and Modernity in Japanese History: A Focus on State-Society Relations', *The Journal of Asian Studies*, vol. 53, no. 2, 346–66.

Kanai K., (1991) *Dōwa Gyōsei: Sengo no Kiseki* (Dōwa Administration: The Postwar Path), Osaka: Buraku Kaihō Shuppansha.

Kanai K., (2009) 'Sengo Dōwa Gyōsei to Yamamoto Masao' (Postwar Dōwa Administration), in Osaka Jinken Hakubutsukan (ed), *Kingendai no Buraku Mondai to Yamamoto Masao* (The Modern Buraku Problem and Yamamoto Masao), Osaka: Kaihō Shuppansha, 408-434.

Kanai K., (2018) *Tokusōhō Jidai no Makuhirake* (The Opening of the SML Era), Osaka: self-published.

Kuwahara S., (2012) 'The Development of Small Islands in Japan: An Historical Perspective', *Journal of Marine and Island Cultures*, vol. 1, 38–45.

Morooka S., (1982) *Sengo Buraku Kaihō Ronsōshi* III, Tokyo: Shashoku Shobo.

Morooka S., (1984) *Sengo Buraku Kaihō Ronsōshi* IV, Tokyo: Shashoku Shobo.

Murakawa I., (1985) *Nihon no Seisaku Kettei Katei* (Japan's Policymaking Process), Tokyo: Gyōsei.

Murakoshi S., Watanabe T., Miwa Y., Umehara T., and Tomonaga K., (1989) *Buraku Kaihōshi* (A History of Buraku Liberation), Osaka: Kaihō Shuppansha.

Noguchi M. and Ishimoto K., (2014) *Buraku Jittai Chōsa no Shoshiteki Kenkyū* (A Bibliographical Study of Surveys in Buraku Conditions), Kyoto: Sekai Jinken Mondai Kenkyū Sentaa.

Oga M., (2015), *Naikaku Dōwa Taisaku Shingikai Tōshin 50 nen - Tōshin no Igi to Konnichi* (Fiftieth Anniversary of the Cabinet Commission of Enquiry on Dōwa Policy – Its Significance for Today), Osaka: Kaihō Shuppan.

Schwartz F. J., (1998) *Advice and Consent: The Politics of Consultation in Japan*, Cambridge: Cambridge University Press.

Sōmuchō Chōkan Kanbō Chiiki Kaizen Taisakuhitsu, (1993) *Dōwa Gyōsei Shihanseiki no Ayumi* (A Quarter Century of Dōwa Administration), Tokyo: Chūō Hōki Shuppan.

Suzuki R., (2010) *Nihon Shakai no Hendō to Dōwa Gyōsei no Dōkō* (Changes in Japanese Society and Trends in Dōwa Administration) in Buraku Mondai Kenkyūsho, *Buraku Mondai Kaiketsu Katei no Kenkyū* (Studies on the Process of the Resolution of the Buraku Problem), Kyoto: Buraku Mondai Kenkyūsho Shuppanbu.

6 Implementation I

The Dōwa policy process at the national level

As we saw in the previous chapter, during the 1960s the Japanese government commissioned a report on Buraku discrimination, the Dōtaishin, which offered a much more radical diagnosis and solution to the problem than many in the administration can have anticipated. Forceful advocates on the *shingikai* such as Kitahara Taisaku supported by academic liberals such as Isomura Eichi insisted on the report being based on the most recent research and ensured that it proposed a wide range of measures founded on constitutional principles. Most importantly, they insisted that it was the duty of the state to take action. But if it went further than the conservatives might have liked, its recommendations were not inconsistent with the trends of the times. Domestically, Ikeda Hayato, the prime minister between 1960 and 1965, embarked on his period in power by committing his government to an 'income doubling plan' to ensure that benefits of rapid economic growth spread across the whole nation. Already at the end of the 1950s, laws on pensions and health care insurance had been introduced that resulted in European standards of social welfare being in place by the mid-1960s. Attention then turned to what, if anything, the state might do to assist the poorest sections of society and we can perhaps regard the Dōtaishin as addressing the issues being faced by one sub-set of this group.

Ikeda's successor, Satō Eisaku, welcomed the report and committed himself and his party to its implementation. But the question was how, and for some, whether it could be implemented. At least, one researcher on Buraku issues doubted that the social welfare budget was sufficient to support the extensive plans proposed by the Dōtaishin. The main theme of this chapter is to set out how the state responded to the ambitions of the 1965 report in terms of the evolution of Dōwa policy across the final third of the twentieth century.

A political debate about the most appropriate response to the Dōtaishin took place as the bureaucracy was framing its strategy. The Dōtaikyō issued its suggestions in Dōwa Policy Long-Term Strategy on 23 February 1967 which set out the bare bones of how the policy would be organised: in two five-year sections within the appropriate ministries each of which was given responsibility for typically two or three policy areas with the coordination of

DOI: 10.4324/9781003127994-6

Dōwa policy to be implemented both across ministries and with non-Dōwa policies within a ministry (Dōwa Gyōseishi Henshū Iinkai, 2002, 275–81). It set out a programme for consultation with the ministries aiming to start the first five years of the Ten-Year Plan in April 1969. This target date was missed. Not until July 1969 were the 'Long Term Plan' (LTP) and the SML passed. The LTP described the basic Dōwa policy brief of each ministry and set out their particular planning objectives (Dōwa Gyōseishi Henshū Iinkai, 2002, 316–23). We will look in a little more detail at the role played by each ministry in the next chapter.

The BLL, despite the strong support from the JSP, had failed in its attempts to persuade the government to introduce a Basic Law or in some other way to legally embed the commitment made in the Dōtaishin to ending discrimination and prejudice. All that was introduced in 1969 was a time-limited Special Measures Law. Neither the BLL nor the JSP gave up on this campaign and across subsequent decades they would combine their demands for extensions to the SML with a campaign for firmer legal commitment to the principle of opposing discrimination and prejudice and the promotion of human rights.

In the pages that follow, we will take an overview of the policy process from the start of the SML until its termination in 2002 focusing on how the Japanese government responded to the challenge of implementing the 'rapid resolution' of the 'various social and economic problems which concern Dōwa communities' which, in the words of the Dōtaishin, is 'the responsibility of the state'. Chapter 7 will look at what the different ministries spent their money on and then Chapter 8 will consider how a sample of three local administrations formulated their policies and channelled the funding being provided by central and local governments. This chapter will trace how the Dōwa project policy (Dōwa Jigyō Taisaku) developed at the national level from the early 1970s until the late 1990s in the process of interaction between the ruling party, the bureaucracy, and the representatives of the Buraku communities. For convenience, we will divide our narrative into three periods, 1969–82, 1983–8, and 1989–2002.

Phase I 1969–82

Establishment of the Dōwa project policy (Dōwa Jigyō Taisaku)

As outlined in the previous chapter, the Dōwa Taisaku Kyōgikai (Dōwa Policy Council, Dōtaikyō) was established in the summer of 1966 as the successor to the Dōwa Taisaku Shingikai with the remit of providing advice to the PMO on the development of Dōwa policy. Its make-up was similar to that of the Dōwa policy *shingikai*. Overall, there were to be no more than twenty members: ten bureaucrats representing their ministry and another ten 'people of learning and experience'. Among the latter group, there were four representatives of the Buraku movements, two each from the BLL and

Zen Nihon Dōwakai on the main panel plus one from each group among the five advisers who served on the specialist sub-committees. Until May 1972, its chair was Horiki Kenzō,[1] a former LDP member of the Diet and known to be close to the PM, Satō Eisaku. He was replaced by Isomura Eichi, then president of Tōyō University and previously a professor of social policy at Tokyo Metropolitan University. He had been a founder member of the *shingikai* and would serve as the chair until December 1992.[2]

The Dōtaikyō had provided a series of recommendations to government during the late 1960s on the implementation of the Dōtaishin proposals, for example, on a long-term plan in February 1967, and it continued to play an advisory role once the projects began operation. In March 1971, it set up three specialist sub-committees: on the living environment and social welfare, industry and employment, and education and human rights. They each produced extensive reports – On the Promotion of Dōwa Policy Administration (*Dōwa Gyōsei Suishinjō no Tōmen no Shomondai ni tsuite*, August 1971, summarised Dōwa Gyōseishi Henshū Iinkai, 2002, 286–8) and On Dōwa Education and its administration (*Dōwa Kyōiku ni kansuru Tōmen no Shidō Shishin narabi ni Dōwa Kyoiku Gyōsei ni Taisuru Yōbō Jiko ni suite*, March 1972, summarised Dōwa Gyōseishi Henshū Iinkai, 2002, 289–92). In December 1972, members of the Dōtaikyō made visits to 15 Buraku communities and produced a set of recommendations about items for inclusion in the following year's budget. Then, with the second five-year term due to start in FY1974/5, in July 1973, it produced a report on policy promotion (Dōwa Gyōseishi Henshū Iinkai, 2002, 296–8) and another in February 1974 on long-term planning (Dōwa Gyōseishi Henshū Iinkai, 2002, 299).

Meanwhile within government, there was a separate policymaking strand. Despite the long-term plan having been agreed in 1969, central government did not consider itself well prepared to formulate or implement specific sets of policies. So another survey was carried out in June 1971 with a specific remit to look at those communities where there had previously been no Dōwa policy. It also focused on projects that could be supported by the MHW, MAFF, the SME Bureau in MITI, and the MoL (Noguchi and Ishimoto, 2014, 221). The results of this survey were accepted in June 1972 by the Provisional Dōwa Mondai Cabinet Council (Rinji Dōwa Mondai Kakuryo Kaigi) that was taking the lead role in policy implementation. In May 1973, this cabinet committee proposed policies for the second five-year term due to start of the following spring when a Dōwa Taisakuhitsu (Dōwa Policy Office) would be created within the PMO. Finally, a permanent coordinating mechanism was set up within central government.

In mid-December 1973, the *Asahi* newspaper ran an editorial on Dōwa policy in which it noted the increase in the amount of the Dōwa budget as the policy was about to enter its second quinquennium. It suggested that a careful analysis of the policy's impact was needed while at the same time quoting data that suggested continuing discrimination and poverty existed within Buraku communities: over 30% of Buraku housing was inadequate compared to only 3–4% in the mainstream population, their dependence on day labour remained high, and there was continuing evidence of status investigations (Asahi Shimbun, 11 December 1973).

Meanwhile, the tensions that had been building up with the BLL between the mainstream group and the JCP supporters moved inexorably towards a split. The JCP had lost its control over the BLL central committee in 1965. After the death of Matsumoto Jiichirō in 1966 and the selection of Asada Zennosuke to replace him, personal antagonism between Asada and Kitahara Taisaku along with ideological disputes and arguments over how to distribute Dōwa funding made division within the Buraku movement almost inevitable. A JCP-led fraction – the Buraku Kaihō Dōmei Seijōka Zenkoku Renraku Kaigi (National Coordinating Committee for the Rectification of the Buraku Liberation League, Seijōkaren) – was formed in 1969 which criticised the current BLL central committee as being a 'Buraku-exclusionary, anti-Communist, violent special interest group' and announced its aim to 'reform' the BLL. When their attempts at reform from within were deemed unsuccessful, they broke away to create a rival group, the Zenkoku Buraku Kaihō Undō Rengōkai – Zenkairen in March 1976. There were a number of major 'flashpoints' in this rivalry. Two occurred in and around high schools in the Osaka area in Yata in 1969 and Yōka 1974, and there were series of disputes that spilled over into the mainstream of local politics in Tokyo in the late 1960s and 1970s (see Neary 1986; Pharr 1990; Rohlen 1976).

Asada Zennosuke, chair of the BLL, and Sakaki Toshio, central committee member of the JCP, were interviewed by the Mainichi newspaper early in 1975 and their answers were serialised daily between 14 February and 19 March. Asada was critical of the JCP and the Seijōkaren which he describes as an organisation 'subordinate' to it. Out of the many points that he makes, I will highlight two. First, his view of the role of Burakumin within contemporary society in which he argues that they serve as an 'industrial reserve army'[3] (Mainichi Shimbun, 15 February 1975). That is, a group within contemporary Japan that endures chronic unemployment and is willing to work for low wages, thus pulling down the overall level of pay and living conditions for all workers in Japan. Buraku discrimination is therefore a product of and contributes to the functioning of contemporary Japanese society, not merely an anachronistic relic of its feudal past. Second, he emphasises the aim of the BLL to have the recommendations of the 1965 report fully implemented through Dōwa projects and justifies the role of the BLL in their administration arguing that, for example, it is important to ensure that non-Burakumin are not given loans from Dōwa funds. More controversially, he suggests that those Burakumin who do not publicly acknowledge their Buraku background, as was often the case in Tokyo, should not be eligible for such loans. Moreover, he continues, it is reasonable to require those wanting such loans to attend study classes to ensure that they understand their obligation to repay the money. And where, as in Kyoto, *kairyō jūtaku* ('improved housing') has been built, only those Burakumin who have been living in the Buraku community (even if their place of origin is outside the city) should be eligible to be rehoused there, while non-Burakumin should have their right to housing guaranteed but be rehoused in general public housing – the principle of *zokuchi zokujin* (Mainichi Shimbun, 26 February 1975). It is appropriate, he argues, that the BLL decides – certifies – who should qualify for the loans and new housing and who provides the 'study classes'.

The JCP response to this was that the Meiji restoration had been incomplete so that many feudal aspects remained within Japan's social and political system. Buraku communities and discrimination against them are examples of this but they are gradually being overcome. Sakaki challenges the 'industrial reserve army' thesis (without mentioning it by name) suggesting that unemployment is not as widespread within Buraku communities as Asada insists and that there are clear class divisions within Buraku communities. For example, Asada himself owns several companies. There are examples of Buraku employers who have not permitted the formation of unions, so it is not correct to equate all Burakumin with the working class nor to regard the BLL campaigns as equal to 'class struggle' (Mainichi Shimbun, 6 March 1975). While agreeing with the 1965 report on the need to eliminate discrimination from employment and marriage, it should not be exaggerated (as Asada arguably was want to do). Sakaki warns against making excessive demands on local governments for Dōwa funding. He argues that the provision of 'super-deluxe' primary schools in Buraku communities, while in other areas of Osaka there are over two hundred aged and dilapidated schools, fans the flames of feelings of 'reverse discrimination'. Moreover, he alleges that the 'Asada faction' receives a 0.2–0.7% rebate (i.e. 'kickback') on Dōwa building projects that in some cases is as high as 5% (Mainichi Shimbun, 13 March 1975). He is very critical of the way the Asada faction dominates the distribution of Dōwa project benefits through the '*Madoguchi Ippon*' (Single Window) strategy which he claims promotes 'exclusionism'. While not opposed in principle to the idea that there needs to be some vetting of the applicants, he wants the process to be open to representatives from the BLL, Seijōkaren, Dōwakai, and teachers rather than being dominated by the BLL 'Asada faction', as he argues it is now (Mainichi Shimbun, 15 March 1975).

There is no independent account of the development of the Buraku movements across the late twentieth century in either Japanese or English. Moreover, it is not the purpose of this work to provide one. Although the LDP supported Zen Nihon Dōwakai and (later) the Zenkoku Jiyū Dōwakai worked with the left-leaning BLL in campaigns to extend Dōwa policy, no such cooperation was possible with the JCP supporting Seijōkaren which transformed into the Zenkairen. The positions of the BLL and Zenkairen would evolve over the decades but most of the issues that divided them were discussed in this series of article published in the mid-1970s. In the account that follows, we will allude at times to the increasingly bitter dispute that by the 1980s prevented even normal conversations taking place between members of these two rival groups, let alone any collaboration. It is a situation that has continued with rare exceptions into the twenty-first century.

An extension beyond ten years?

As Table 7.1 demonstrates, the amount of money spent on Dōwa projects increased rapidly during the first half of the 1970s. We will comment in more detail in subsequent chapters about how it was spent at the national level and by certain local governments over the 33 years of the projects but in 1977/8 it was by no means certain how or even whether the Dōwa policy might be extended.

In May 1976, the Dōtaikyō published its opinion on the progress of the Dōwa administration (Dōwa Gyōseishi Henshū Iinkai, 2002, 302–4) taking an overview of the first seven years of Dōwa policy implementation. It concluded that there was evidence of social and economic inequality, many hundred Dōwa communities had still not benefited from Dōwa policies, and more consideration needed to be given to the extent of understanding of and cooperation with Dōwa policies among the general population. In October, the BLL began a campaign demanding that the SML be extended (Asahi Shimbun, 27 October 1976).

As the SML approached its tenth, and potentially final, year, the Dōtaikyō began to receive petitions from individual local governments and the Zendōtai that it be extended. Outside government, the groups representing Buraku communities were arguing strongly for extension. The BLL had grown rapidly as more money had become available for improvement projects and membership of a Buraku organisation was one criterion used in many areas to certify eligibility for access to Dōwa project funding. At its 32nd conference held in March 1977, its leaders, while sympathetic to complaints that Dōwa policy was a burden on local governments who were not being fully supported by central government, argued that there was still much that remained to be done (Kanai, 1991, 238). Both the Zenkairen and Zen Nihon Dōwakai supported the campaign for the SML extension and the government announced its aim to present its plans during the next Diet session (Asahi Shimbun, 2 November 1977). Progress, however, was slow.

In February 1978, the Dōtaikyō in its draft report urged that 'The SML provides an important basis for the elimination of discrimination and so its extension is necessary' (Kanai, 1991, 239). To which PM Fukuda responded a month later that he intended to react 'positively'. Later, the Zenkairen would argue against the further provision of Dōwa funding but at its 7th conference held in March 1978, they resolved to support demands for the extension of the programmes while demanding the 'democratisation' of Dōwa administration which was a veiled reference to the *Madoguchi Ippon* policy and their desire to have other groups, especially itself, included among those who made decisions about access to Dōwa benefits.

The JSP announced that it supported a 'simple' five-year extension. The Dōtaikyō issued a report in May suggesting that serious problems remained unresolved in Buraku communities but without recommending any specific extension (Dōwa Gyōseishi Henshū Iinkai, 2002, 305–6). With all the members of the Dōtaikyō having served their two-year term, it was dissolved at that point not to be revived until 1981. A Dōwa policy sub-committee was formed within the HR Cabinet standing committee meeting which in June also suggested a five-year extension to the SML but after discussions within the Dōwa sub-committee of PARC, the LDP instead proposed just two years (Suginohara 754, 2007, 70). Finally, cross-party talks took place on 18 October at which a compromise was agreed to extend the law by three years. The BLL was unhappy with this but the JSP persuaded them to agree, fearful that the alternative would be that the SML would be allowed to expire. A short bill was passed through both houses over the next couple of days. It simply extended the date of the SML termination by three years and concluded by exhorting local governments to do all they can to put necessary measures in place. It was formally promulgated on 13 November. The timing of this bill ensured that provision for Dōwa funding could be included in the budget proposals that were being drawn up at that point for FY1979/80.

An editorial in the *Asahi* newspaper on 24 October applauded the decision to proceed with the extension pointing out that even the JCP had noted the continuance of discrimination in marriage, employment, and residence. It pointed out though that the remaining problems could not be resolved in just three years. Moreover, it noted that Isomura had argued for not just an extension to the existing law but the creation of a more fundamental or Basic Law that addressed either Dōwa or broader human rights protections (Asahi Shimbun, 24 October 1978).

What next?

This extension was so short that almost as soon as the new law was implemented, a debate began about what to do next. There was widespread support for a broadening of the terms of the legislation. As the *Asahi* had noted in October 1978, Isomura, chair of the now apparently defunct Dōtaikyō, was already in favour of such an approach.

The BLL began its campaign for a further extension of the SML following its 35th conference in March 1980. It now wanted not just to extend the existing law but to develop a legislative framework that would endorse Dōwa policy at the same time as extending the state's commitment to the basic principles of non-discrimination and developing understanding and protection of human rights standards among the wider population as proposed in the final section of the Dōtaishin (Kanai, 1991, 243). These ideas seem to have influenced the development of JSP policy. In December 1980, it produced a draft bill that would have gone much further than simply extending the SML by establishing a comprehensive planning process that would, for example, ensure consultation with those neighbouring the Buraku community in order to mitigate any envy or resentment at their 'special treatment'. It would have placed restrictions on discriminatory activity, in particular the work of private investigators, and would have encouraged the 'correct understanding' of the issue through school-based and social education (Murakoshi et al., 1989, 229–30).

A campaign demanding extension of the SML began at the start of 1981 and the BLL convened a conference in the Shūgiin Kaikan within the Diet building to which it invited 130 representatives of political parties, labour unions, bureaucrats, major companies, and religious groups. They set up a campaign committee (Asahi Shimbun, 10 February 1981). Not long after this, Isomura wrote an article for the *Asahi* newspaper in which he pointed out that the SML would only run for one more year and the government seemed not to understand the importance of the issue. He repeated criticisms that he had made two years earlier that the government was not taking the Dōtaikyō seriously, only using it when it suited their purposes. More positively, he proposed that rather than simply extending the SML, a completely new law should be produced – a position very similar to that being taken by the BLL (Asahi Shimbun, 7 April, 3 March 1981).

Then, the Zen Nihon Dōwakai on 25 June 1981 endorsed a set of proposals that included not only renewing the SML framework but also expanding funding for Dōwa education, support for economic development in Buraku communities and for human rights protection (Murakoshi et al., 1989, 233).

Changes to the Dōtaikyō

As we have seen, the Dōtaikyō and its predecessor, the Dōwa policy *shingikai* had both contained a significant number of representatives of the Buraku communities evenly balanced between the BLL and Zen Nihon Dōwakai. As the cracks appeared within the BLL during the early 1970s, Kitahara Taisaku had moved over to the JCP-supporting fraction. He remained on the Dōtaikyō until 1974, meaning that until that point the three strands of Burakumin opinion were presented on the council. When he was replaced in 1974, a promise was made to have a Zenkairen member on the council but this was never fulfilled (Asahi Shimbun, 13 June 1981). We noted in passing above that in June 1978, the authorised terms of the Dōtaikyō members expired and for three years it did not meet. When it was reconvened in June 1981, its membership was very different.

With the SML extension agreed, the media lost interest in the Dōwa issue. For example, while the *Asahi* newspaper had followed the debate on SML extension quite closely with 19 articles appearing in 1978, there were just two in 1979 and only one in 1980. In February 1979, the *Asahi* commented on the failure of government to re-establish the Dōtaikyō. One reason seems to have been an impasse that had been reached because the Zenkairen, formed in 1976, demanded representation on the Dōtaikyō. The BLL and Zen Nihon

Dōwakai opposed this as did the opposition parties who supported them – the JSP and LDP, respectively. Meanwhile, the PMO argued that if the Zenkairen were to get a seat, other groups would demand representation and there were at least 30 groups that could make a claim. This of course was nonsense. The Zenkairen estimated that it had support from around one-third of all Buraku activists making it second in size to the BLL. Only the Zen Nihon Dōwakai had anything like this national presence. However, the excuse was sufficient to stall any attempt to re-establish the council (Asahi Shimbun, 26 Feb 1979, 13 June 1980).

The PMO's solution to this problem when the Dōtaikyō was recreated in the summer of 1981 was not to include any representatives of Buraku organisations (or indeed any women). In fact, as far as one can tell, until its final dissolution in 1996 – there would be no Buraku origin individuals on the Dōtaikyō. When revived in June 1981, apart from the ten ministry representatives, it contained five university professors, three elected politicians, and two quango heads – one with a specialism in social welfare, the other the head of the League of Civil Liberties Commissioners.[4] Elements of continuity were provided by Isomura who continued in the chair and Yamamoto Noboru, a sociologist from Osaka, who had been on one of the sub-committees before 1978 and was promoted to the full panel.

Once reconvened, it was tasked to formulate budget proposals by the end of July and then to discuss options for Dōwa policy after the expiry of the SML which was due at the end of March the following year (Asahi Shimbun, 13 June 1981). It met six times over eight weeks in the summer of 1981 before presenting an interim report to the PMO on the future of Dōwa policy after the expiry of the current SML. This noted the improvements that had taken place in the communities' living environment and high school attendance but pointed to the continuing evidence of discrimination which suggested that more effort was needed to develop human rights education/*keihatsu* (Kanai, 1991, 245). It basically suggested that Dōwa policy continue to be funded at existing levels (Asahi Shimbun, 19 August 1981).

Already, in a parallel process, an LDP Dōwa Policy Committee chaired by Maeda Isao[5] had been set up in Spring 1980 within the PARC. It created a sub-committee that held discussions with the various ministries, local governments, and movement groups. Its report, produced in August 1981, proposed that a new law be passed to support Dōwa projects and that provision for funding be included in the budget for FY1982. There were some in the LDP who had opposed extension in 1978 only to be persuaded to support it on the basis that it would be the 'last time'. Many in the LDP continued strongly to oppose any extension. This report argued for both a change of name and a review of the content of policy to emphasise the reduction in the material disparities between neighbouring communities, Buraku and non-Buraku. In place of 'Dōwa', which some argued had discriminatory connotations, the policy should be referred to as 'Chiiki Kaizen' (regional improvement) which carried no negative nuance. They wanted a review of the eight projects listed in clause six of the original SML which had formed the basis of the plans devised in each ministry (Asahi Shimbun, 13 August 1981; Kanai, 1991, 244).

A consensus seemed to be emerging in favour of extension. Despite the background of fierce rivalry and ideological differences between the three Buraku organisations, Isomura managed to convene a round table discussion at the start of November 1981with senior representatives from each of them. To briefly summarise their positions: Oka Akira (Zenkairen) wanted the early end of the SML and policy based on the constitution to reduce the isolation of Buraku communities; Uesugi Saichirō (BLL) argued for the continuing need for Dōwa policy to ensure Buraku employment, education opportunities and *keihatsu*, the need to initiate policy in areas where there had so far been none, and the need for a law on discrimination; Isomura agreed with this arguing for a move from emphasis on projects to basic principles. An editorial in the *Asahi* newspaper thought that this round table discussion marked a turning point in inter-group relations which hitherto had been marked by mutual recriminations. Sadly, this proved not to be the case.

It had been hoped to enact new legislation during the autumn Diet session. When this had not happened, mainly it seemed because the government was insisting on waiting for the Dōtaikyō final report, on 27 November, the penultimate day of the Diet session, a one-line resolution was passed by the LH affirming that 'Financial and legal provision is necessary for the Dōwa problem' which had the support of all parties (Chiiki Kaizen Taisaku Kenkyūsho, 1986, 613; Dōwa Gyōseishi Henshū Iinkai, 2002, 30).

The Dōtaikyō report was finally delivered on 10 December and began by noting the recent ratification of the international covenants on human rights (Civil and Political Rights, and Economic, Social and Cultural Rights) in 1979 and CEDAW in 1980. This had been a key concern of Isomura over the previous two years as expressed in his op-ed pieces in the *Asahi* newspaper in which he bemoaned the fact that the government and Diet were reluctant to ratify the international human rights covenants, to develop Dōwa policies and more general policies towards human rights within Japan (Asahi Shimbun, 7 April 1979, 2 December 1980). The report commented on the progress made by the Dōwa programmes in education, industry, and issue awareness (*keihatsu*) but pointed to evidence of continued discrimination and the need to extend funding of existing projects and develop new ones particularly in smaller communities. More specifically, it suggested that attention be paid to the financial burden on local government, issues relating to both the context and management of projects, the existence of discrimination encountered by children, and the demands being made at the local government level by movement groups. Finally, it noted the criticisms being made of Dōwa policy by the general public but urged government to work with the movement organisations (Chiiki Kaizen Taisaku Kenkyūsho, 1986, 610–3; Dōwa Gyōseishi Henshū Iinkai, 2002, 331–2).

An extension on these terms was not what either the BLL or the JSP had wanted but the JSP leadership feared that if these recommendations were not accepted, there was a real possibility that the SML would not be extended at all. An *Asahi* editorial comment on 11 December noted the 'fading colour' of the SML as the memories of the Dōtaishin fade and the diminished independence of the Dōtaikyō whose most recent report had done little more than smooth the way for the adoption of the LDP draft proposals. What, it asked, was the long-term plan? Discrimination would not be eliminated in three or five years, so what then?

When the text of the new law was published in early January 1982, it initially only proposed a three-year extension. Lobbying by the opposition parties and local governments resulted in it being extended to five when it was presented to the cabinet for approval on 16 February. It started its passage through the Diet the following week. An attempt at amendment by the JCP was rejected and the law was finally passed on 31 March becoming effective the following day.

In many ways, the new law simply enabled existing projects to continue but there were some changes. It specifically required those implementing projects to 'endeavour' to operate them fairly so as to enhance the integration of the 'target areas' with their neighbours. This was related to three issues. First, in some areas such as the Chikuhō area of northern Kyushu, there was widespread poverty and unemployment caused by the rapid closure of coal mines during the 1960s. Buraku communities there were seen to be getting preferential treatment, considered by some to amount to 'reverse discrimination'. Second, there was sometimes a problem of unimaginative provision of infrastructure projects which, for example, only improved roads up to the boundary of the Buraku community which not only made its location more obvious but also further aroused discontent among the neighbours whose roads had not been improved. Finally, we should note that the passage of this law started the process of the restriction of the scope of Dōwa projects. The SML of 1969 had designated seven types of projects that were eligible for Dōwa funding but also spoke in clause 6 of 'arrangements necessary to achieve the aims of the previous clauses' which gave some scope for interpretation. The new law as defined by the cabinet order is more precise and relates the Chiiki Kaizen projects to pre-existing legislation such as projects to build or improve public housing to the 1951 Public Housing Act or the provision of vocational training facilities to the 1969 Vocational Training Act (Dōwa Gyōseishi Henshū Iinkai, 2002, 354–60).

A review of the first phase of the policy process

But to return to the Dōwa policy process. By the end of this first period, a pattern had started to emerge. There had been the formalisation of the coordination of policy within government in 1974 with the creation of the Dōwa Taisakuhitsu in the PMO. There was a gradual expansion of the range of Dōwa projects being funded by the various ministries as they interpreted their briefs as set out in the 1969 LTP. The number of projects across the ministries increased from 39 to 100 and the budgets increased rapidly (see Table 7.1 and Figure 7.1 in the next chapter and in the Appendix Table A.1 and Figure A.1).

The Dōtaikyō provided some input into this decision-making process. It was composed of representatives of all the main Dōwa spending ministries plus the MoF as well as representatives of the two organisations with roots in the Buraku communities, representatives of some local governments plus, as is usual on Japanese government advisory bodies, a couple of university professors and some retired bureaucrats ('OBs') now rebranded with their post-*amakudari* destination.

In parallel with this, there was a sub-committee of the LDP main policy-making body, the PARC, convened from time to time which took a special interest in Dōwa policy. This had first been created in the late 1950s at the time when the government was being persuaded to fund a nationally led policy and set up the *shingikai.* It does not seem to have had a full-time existence but rather was recreated when needed, for example, in 1968–9 when the responses to the Dōtaishin were being debated and thereafter when there were demands for an extension of the SML, i.e. in 1978 and 1980–1. At the level of the Diet, since policy was formulated within the PMO, it was subject to the overview of the cabinet committees in both houses where from time to time a sub-committee on Dōwa policy was created.

Outside the state structure were the campaigning organisations: the BLL, the Zen Nihon Dōwakai, and, from 1976, the Zenkairen. The former two were represented on the Dōtaikyō and linked to the JSP and LDP, respectively. Meanwhile, other groups in society such as religious groups and labour unions could become involved in the policy process by taking part in the conferences periodically convened by the BLL to recruit broad societal support for the Dōwa-related policies they were advocating. The Dōtaikyō would also from time to time take evidence from such groups.

Finally, there were the local governments who were on the front-line of policy implementation. On the one hand, they were dealing with the demands being made by local communities and the branches of the national level NGOs and we will consider how some of them formulated their policy responses in a later chapter. Some of the bigger local governments such as the Tokyo Metropolitan Government (TMG) and Osaka city and prefecture could contact government departments or address the Dōtaikyō directly. On the other hand, smaller authorities could influence demands for Dōwa policy made through the councils of prefectural governors, city or municipal mayors. They were also represented on the Dōtaikyō, or through the Zen Nihon Dōwa Taisaku Kyōgikai (Zendōtai) that held annual meetings which aggregated the demands and opinions of Dōwa policy administrators from local governments across the country. Adapting the representation of this process from a model by Mizuuchi (1998), we can map the Dōwa policy process up to 1981 as follows (Figure 6.1).

Two more general points about this. First, there is something quite normal about this policy process: it involves the LDP/PARC, a *shingikai* rather than the Diet is the main arena for policy deliberation where the bureaucracy can dominate but there is also Diet committee involvement. Second, it amounted to a minimal response to the Dōtaishin proposals in terms of the

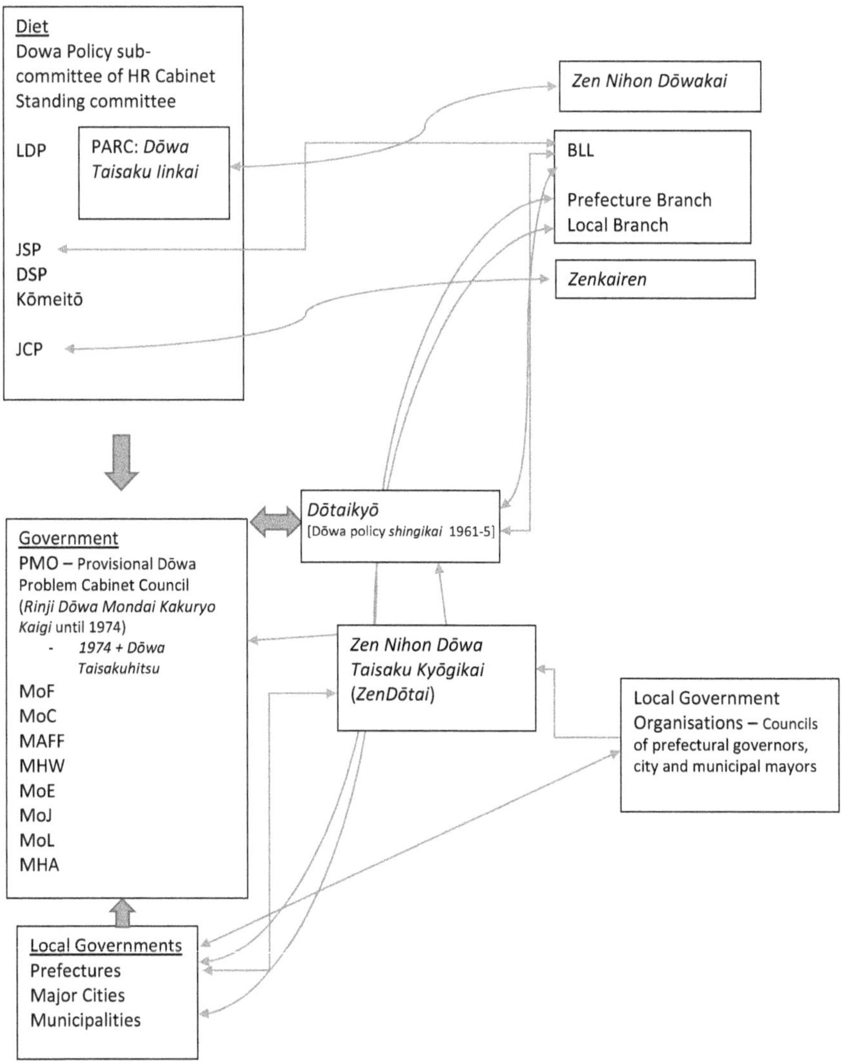

Figure 6.1 Dōwa policy map 1969–82.

machinery of government that was created to administer what developed quite quickly into a major expenditure stream. Apart from the *shingikai*, only a small policy 'office' was set up to deal with the Dōwa policy and that only from 1974. The rest was done through the ministries and local government administrations, placing a particularly heavy burden on the latter.

A digression on discrimination and how it was carried out

At this point, I want to digress slightly from our core focus on Dōwa policy to consider a dimension of policy towards Buraku communities that prompted a parallel set of legal changes.

Given that there were no racial, ethnic, or religious features that distinguished Burakumin from other Japanese, ultimately discrimination was based on the test of 'common knowledge'. You were a Burakumin if other people thought you were and you may have accepted that definition. It was possible to 'prove' that someone was of 'Buraku heritage' by demonstrating that s/he had been born in a Buraku community with at least one Burakumin parent defined as someone whose forebears could be traced back to the *eta, hinin* or one of the other marginalised groups of the Edo period (more detail about Buraku history can be found in Teraki and Kurokawa, 2019). Some Burakumin have taken, and do take, pride in their descent from families that have resisted societal attempts to define them as marginal Japanese during and since the Edo period (see, for example, Kadooka 2005). Some prominent leaders of the Buraku movements who have protested against discrimination have triumphed personally in spite of or sometimes even because of their encounters with obstructions based on prejudices. Matsumoto Jiichirō was an example of an individual who across his lifetime enjoyed economic and political success despite the fact that his Buraku background was well known. He led the BLL until his death in 1966 and does not seem to have been interested in supporting a campaign that would have made it more difficult to determine an individual's family's former status.

During the 1950s and after, rapid industrialisation had been made possible *inter alia* by mass migration from rural areas to the cities such that it became difficult to know much about the background of a neighbour or fellow worker. But many people still held prejudices about Burakumin such that they would prefer not to work alongside them and would try to prevent one marrying into their family. If there was any doubt about a person's background, it was not unusual for a company or prospective in-law to employ an investigator to check them out (Hayashida, 1975). This was relatively easy since the family registers – *koseki* – were openly accessible and using these you could trace an individual's family back to the first modern registers created by local governments in 1872 which often would clearly indicate whether a family had belonged to one of the marginalised communities of the Edo period (Krogness 2008). The *koseki* law was amended over the years but the principle of open access to it was re-affirmed in 1898.

The Suiheisha in 1923 and 1927 demanded the revision or total abolition of the *koseki* system but to no avail. However, in the late 1960s, the BLL took up the campaign to restrict public access to these records. In 1968, access to the 1872 *koseki* was restricted and from 1974, it became possible to deny requests to inspect the *koseki* if there was 'a risk of discriminatory usage'. Finally, in 1976 the Diet passed a partial amendment to the Civil Code that closed *koseki* records to all but a small number of, mainly legal, professionals and even then, it was possible to refuse access if it was suspected to be for 'unjust purposes', including '...discriminatory behaviour, using *koseki* items as clues to investigate if someone has a Dōwa background' (Krogness, 2008, 305).

These changes were consistent with the Dōtaishin recommendations in 1965 and represent a victory for the BLL campaign. However, just as the reforms were being implemented, evidence emerged that there was still a demand for this kind of information which, if it was no longer easily available from public sources, the private sector would provide.

At the end of 1975, BLL activists were anonymously informed that *chimei sōkan* – address lists – were being offered for sale by private investigators. These listed the current names being used for wards in each municipality and matched them to the Buraku communities identified by the Yūwa survey compiled in 1935. Their discovery led the BLL to launch campaigns demanding that major companies take more pro-active measures to eliminate discrimination. The purchase of these books was condemned by the Osaka Civil Liberties Bureau in 1976 as an 'exceedingly pernicious violation of human rights' but there continued to be evidence that companies were buying these lists even after the initial campaign. The CLC bureau within the MoJ reported on 3 December 1976 that it had received reports of 27 companies having bought copies of these books which had clear implications for equal opportunity in employment (Chiiki Kaizen Taisaku Kenkyūsho, 1986, 611). There were said to have been at least seven editions of these lists which were purchased by several hundred companies and at least one university (Upham, 1980, 65).

The significance of this for our broader theme is that the revelations of the existence of these *chimei sōkan* demonstrated that discrimination continued to exist in contemporary Japanese society and it shows how quickly new methods were devised to circumvent changes in the regulation of *koseki*. This is a continuing theme. There are examples well into the twenty-first century of the ways in which individuals determined to identify a person's status origins were able to evade or subvert this regulation.

Phase II 1982–87

Further extension?

While the size of the overall Dōwa budget was building up rapidly over the course of the 1970s – from ¥11,893m in 1970 to ¥252,482m in 1980 – the key question in the early 1980s was how long the policy could or should continue. A pattern of Dōwa spending had been established across the first 13 years and this would be maintained across the 1980s as is clear from Table 7.1 and Figure 7.1 in Chapter 7 (and Table A.2 and Figure A.2 in the Appendix). The programmes had been extended for five years 1982–7, but as the *Asahi* editors had commented in late 1981, what then? No-one, with the possible exception of some in the JCP, thought that all the issues relating to Buraku discrimination and prejudice would be resolved by 1987.

As the Zenkairen never tired of pointing out, the rapid increase in the amounts of money made available for Dōwa projects was accompanied by accusations of corrupt practices and fraudulent use of Dōwa funding throughout the 1980s and beyond. This was a particular problem since although the money ultimately came from the central government ministries, it was used to fund projects that were defined and administered by local government officials who were open to all kinds of pressures. Yanai Masao, the leader of the Zen Nihon Dōwakai, was implicated the inappropriate use of funds to construct a shopping centre in Yamaguchi and forced to resign from that organisation and the Dōtaikyō. In 1981, the Kokura Times newspaper reported on the sale of a plot of land in Yahata in 1978–9 which generated profits of more than ¥270m for senior members of the local BLL. This triggered newspaper reports of 20 similar cases over the next months involving the BLL and the Zen Nihon Dowakai, including Yanai's successor as the head, Matsuo Masanobu (Suginohara 754, 2007, 72).

Shortly after a similar scandal in Kyoto said to involve ¥300m resulted in seven people being arrested between 1985 and 1986. Suginohara suggests that the increase in fraudulent use being made on Dōwa projects followed the imposition of restrictions on the *sōkaiya*[6] which meant that organised crime groups – *yakuza* – had to find new sources of income (Suginohara 757, 2007, 75).

The second set of scandals in Kita-Kyushu resulted in an investigation into the city's Dōwa policy administration being led by Isomura who produced a report in October 1983. This criticised the loose controls over the Dōwa budgets and the attitude that the more money was spent, the more progress was made towards problem resolution. It noted that 80% of the local Buraku population were members of the BLL, so involving it in Dōwa administration had the advantage of smoothing the implementation process but it also meant that very few 'outsiders' were involved. Isomura was particularly concerned by the opacity of the Dōwa administration and recommended opening it up. His report argued that three principles should be used to guide the reformed policy: 'respect human rights', 'neighbourhood solidarity', and 'self-reliance, self-control'.[7]

The office providing coordination within central government was re-designated the Chiiki Kaizen Taisakuhitsu. Its advisory council was renamed the Chiiki Taisaku Kyōgikai (Chitaikyō). Already when the Dōwa Taisaku Kyōgikai had been recreated in 1981 though still chaired by Isomura, it contained no representatives from Buraku communities. Their places were taken by three more university professors and another local government politician. This would be the make-up of the council until it was finally abolished in 1996 (Dōwa Gyōseishi Henshū Iinkai, 2002, 337). Stripped of the representatives of the Buraku communities, its main role now was less about policy creation than ensuring coordination between the national level agencies involved in Dōwa administration, the LDP, and local governments.

A minor administrative reform took place in July 1984 transferring the Chiiki Kaizen Taisakuhitsu from the MHW to Sōmuchō when the latter was re-structured. However, at the level of policy implementation, there was very little change despite the language of the 1982 law which encouraged re-assessment of Dōwa projects. Funding continued to increase and indeed, the mid-1980s was the peak of Dōwa funding (see Table 7.1 and Figure 7.1).

The 1965 Dōtaishin had distinguished between the material and attitudinal aspects of discrimination and prejudice. Hitherto most attention had been paid to improvements to 'hard' projects such as infrastructure and housing. Now it turned to the 'soft' non-material issues. The Chitaikyo's first meeting in July 1982 suggested giving priority to *keihatsu*, a word not easy to translate into English – dictionaries suggest various meanings from enlightenment to public awareness – education in the widest sense: from Dōwa education in primary and high schools to lectures in community centres and at university, short courses in the workplace and for central and local government administrators, and campaigns to oppose discrimination in all areas of society. After 17 meetings, an 11-page report on *keihatsu* was published by the Chitaikyō in June 1984.

It begins with a section on its aims which are, 'as well as overcoming the mistaken consciousness of feudal status discrimination among the Japanese public, to cultivate a spirit of autonomy and independence among the residents of Dōwa districts' (Dōwa Gyōseishi Henshū Iinkai, 2002, 192). The report is divided into sections on method, content, and division of responsibility, including the role which can be played by schools and administrators. It concludes with comments about the need to ensure the 'free exchange of ideas' – no doubt a reference to the increasing hostility between the two wings of the Buraku movement but also to a heightened degree of intolerance among BLL activists to anything that they perceived as 'discrimination' whether at the level of an individual or an organisation. This had reached the level where publishers of newspapers or books would avoid any mention of the Dōwa or Buraku issues rather than risk bringing down the wrath of BLL activists. Second, and related, the report comments on the widespread problem of fraudulent (*ese*) Dōwa groups. There were reports of individuals approaching company managers claiming that its employees had committed discrimination of some kind and that therefore the company should compensate those affected by an apology, the purchase books or magazines, and/or paying the protesting group to provide training courses to the company's employees. The publications and courses were often bogus and the groups making the demands connected to organised crime. They were able to capitalise on the reputation of the BLL for its intolerance of discrimination to persuade people to pay up. A committee on *ese Dōwa* activity was set up within government in September 1986 and the following month a survey of the extent of such activity was carried out. How to develop effective *keihatsu* policies and how to prevent *ese Dōwa* activities were important strands of Dōwa policy for the next 20 years and beyond.

Following the Dōtaikyō report on *keihatsu*, Sōmuchō decided that it needed to commission another survey to assess levels of prejudice and discrimination. It was carried out in November 1985 (Summary of the survey results Dōwa Gyōseishi Henshū Iinkai, 2002, 780–804). This was then considered by a committee formed within Sōmuchō which produced quite a detailed (18 pages) circular on *keihatsu* that was circulated to all prefectures in 1987 (Dōwa Gyōseishi Henshū Iinkai, 2002, 434–52).

On the margins of the main infrastructural projects, there were often relatively small amounts of funding made available to support research on Buraku issues. For example, in 1974 as the Dōwa projects began to be implemented in Fukuoka prefecture, the Fukuoka Buraku Kaihōshi Kenkyūkai (Fukuoka Buraku Liberation History Research Council) was established and a similar if smaller group in Nagasaki in 1979, the Nagasaki-ken Burakushi Kenkyūsho. Meanwhile, both wings of the national movements still had their own research institutions based in Osaka and Kyoto which found ways of accessing funding to support their research groups which often developed close connections with local universities. This was the context for the creation of the Chiiki Taisaku Kenkyūsho in April 1985 by the LDP. The nominal chair was Horiuchi Toshio[8] who at the time was a member of the HC but the institute was led by Shinboku Shigeki with a 14-member steering committee all of whom were serving LDP Diet members (Asahi Shimbun, 20 April 1985). Its main achievement was the publication of a compilation of documents on the development of the Dōwa policy, *Chiiki Kaizen Taisaku – sono chōsa to bunseki* (Regional Improvement Policies – survey and analysis) in 1986. This does not in fact contain a great deal of analysis but it was important as the first attempt to bring together data from the various surveys and texts of the laws and regulations related to the previous 16 years of Dōwa policy implementation. It provided background data to decisions about what should happen when the current Dōwa project legislation was due to expire in March 1987. The main function of this research institute was to provide input to the LDP's Dōwa/Chiiki Kaizen policy committee and generate a narrative about the Dōwa policies that was more sympathetic to the government/ruling party's policies than those produced by the other research groups (Kanai, 1991, 256).

The *Asahi* newspaper sponsored another round table discussion (*zadankai*) on 28 October 1985 to which it invited Isomura of the Chitaikyō, Horiuchi of the LDP Dōwa policy committee, and Kumashiro Akihiko,[9] the head of the Chiiki Kaizen office within the Sōmuchō. Much of their discussion covered the usual ground emphasising the need to give priority to *keihatsu* activity. Isomura insisted that an extension to the law was necessary. Horiuchi argued that education was the key to the resolution of the problem. Most interestingly, and in what is the only overt discussion of the problem that I have come across, Isomura points out how the representatives of the two movement organisations, the BLL and the Zen Nihon Dōwakai, had been on the Dōwa policy *shingikai* and Dōtaikyō and their views had contributed to the consensus about policy which had filtered down to the local level. The implication is that he would like to have them on the Chitaikyō as he had previously mentioned in newspaper interviews. Horiuchi seems to agree. Kumashiro simply refers to the report in June 1984 which emphasised the need for the free expression of ideas. Is this an oblique way of suggesting that the tension between the BLL and Zenkairen would make their presence on the same committee impossible? (Asahi Shimbun, 29 October 1985) Or was he indicating that there was no interest in the bureaucracy in engaging in serious discussion within the Dōtaikyō? Interestingly almost exactly four years earlier, when a similar *zadankai* on Dōwa policy had been convened by the *Asahi* newspaper, it was attended by representatives of the three organisations – BLL, Zenkairen, and Zen Nihon Dōwakai – chaired by Isomura which seems to have managed a civilised exchange of opinions. Had inter-group relations deteriorated so badly? Or does this also reflect the way that discussion about Dōwa policy was now under the sole control of bureaucrats and LDP politicians with representatives of the Buraku communities having been excluded from the policymaking arena.

In January 1986 with just over a year to go before the existing SML expired, Isomura established a study group of eight[10] to assess the results of policy so far and make suggestions for the future. Using the data gathered in the survey carried out in late 1985, after 13 meetings, they produced an interim report presented to the full council (the sub-committee, the governors of Ehime and Wakayama and a municipal mayor from Fukuoka, and the representatives of ten ministries) in August. The tone of the report is set by its prefatory note that, since the time of the Dōtaishin, the circumstances of many Buraku communities had changed as a result of well-funded projects implemented by local governments while a number of completely new issues had arisen: how to create an environment in which the free exchange of ideas was possible, how to ensure the administrative integrity of administration, and how to deal with the *ese-Dōwa* groups.

The Chitaikyō then held hearings during the autumn with representatives of local government and Burakumin groups before putting together a final report 'Regional Improvements Henceforth' (Kongo ni okeru Chiiki Kaizen Taisaku ni Tsuite (Iken Gushin)) which was presented to PM Nakasone on 11 December 1986 (Dōwa Gyōseishi Henshū Iinkai, 2002, 42, text of report 397–409; Kanai, 1991, 266–7; Suginohara 758, 2007, 74–5). It endorsed the idea that the Dōwa projects should be extended but suggested that the new law should focus on finance and proposed that, following a review of the existing projects, wherever possible they should cease to be 'specially' funded and be incorporated into 'general' (*ippan*) projects. Programmes that furnished grants to individuals or individual families should in principle be terminated or limited to ones that promote self-reliance. The regulations that gave some Buraku residents exemption for paying certain taxes should be re-examined, perhaps abolished (Dōwa Gyōseishi Henshū Iinkai, 2002, 43).

Meanwhile, the BLL had established a campaign committee on 25 May 1985 in support of a Basic Law on Buraku Liberation (Asahi Shimbun, 25 May 1985). This was to have four components: a 'declarative' element – which clarified the Dōtaishin statement that the resolution of the Buraku issue was the responsibility of the state; a 'project element' which supported funding for both 'hard' infrastructural improvements and 'soft' educational policies; an educative '*keihatsu*' element that committed the state to the promotion of human rights; and, finally, a 'regulatory' element directed at legal controls to prevent discrimination in employment and status investigations. This of course was not the first time that the BLL had tried to have opposition to Buraku discrimination legally embedded. Efforts to do this can be traced back to 1966 and along the way they received support from many sides, including Isomura Eichi (see, for example, Asahi Shimbun, 1 December 1983). The nominal head of the campaign committee was the leader of the Honganji Jōdōshinshū Buddhist sect and it was also backed by the JSP, the DSP, and the Zenkoku Jiyū Dōwakai (Suginohara 757, 2007, 78; 760, 2007, 77). Their petition was signed by 6.7 million people, including 286 (55%) members of the HR and 119 (47%) of the HC. However, it was ignored by the LDP leadership which following Nakasone's convincing victory in the double election of July 1986 was firmly back in charge of the policy agenda.

The Zenkairen and JCP were opposed to the Basic Law proposals arguing that as the differences between Dōwa communities and their neighbours were narrowing, government should move towards bringing the Dōwa projects to an end. It supported demands for an extension to the SML but this should be for a maximum of five years and should be the last such extension. Those projects supported should focus on employment, industry, education, and *keihatsu*, that is, the major infrastructure projects should be phased out (Asahi Shimbun, 26 September 1985).

The reputation of the Zen Nihon Dōwakai had been seriously damaged by the series of corruption scandals at the end of the 1970s involving its chairman, Yanai Masao, that led to his resignation from the organisation. In 1985, several branches mainly from Shikoku left the organisation and in July 1986 they convened a conference that was attended by 2,000 activists to create the Zen Nihon Jiyū Dōwakai taking a position characterised by opposition to both '*ese-Dōwa*' and 'class struggle'. By May 1987, it was claiming a membership of 40,000, most of whom were thought to be LDP supporters.[11]

Horiuchi Toshio, in his role as the chair of the LDP's Dōwa/Chiiki Kaizen Policy sub-committee, announced in September 1985 his opposition to the BLL's Basic Law proposals on the basis, first, that to make discrimination illegal would require a legal definition and that there was a danger that doing so could have the perverse consequence of preserving it. Second, that it would run counter to the Dōtaishin principle that the elimination of discrimination was the 'duty of the people'. This conveniently ignored the other principle set out in the same sentence that it was also the 'obligation of the state'. Horiuchi issued instructions to all members of the LDP that they should resist being persuaded to sign petitions or in any other way support the BLL campaign for a Basic Law (Suginohara 757, 2007, 80). At the time, there was a strong feeling within the LDP that the law should not be extended at all and indeed Horiuchi announced in October 1985 that it was unlikely. However, on 1 November, a sub-committee of the Diet Cabinet Standing Committee was set up to consider Buraku/Dōwa policy.

From the start of 1986, the LDP Chiiki Kaizen Taisaku Tokubetsu Iinkai chaired by Horiuchi held a series of meetings to consider what, if anything, should replace the 1982 law. It consisted of Horiuchi, seven deputy chairs and 29 core members but it is reported that other LDP Diet members attended the nine meetings and took part in the sometimes heated discussions. As a whole, the committee expressed its concern about a number of issues, including *ese Dōwa* projects (was some kind of coordinating council needed to deal with this problem?), the issue of neutrality in Dōwa education projects (was it being used to recruit pupils into political and social movements?), and the tax concessions being given to individuals and groups. These points were brought together in a *Horiuchi Memo* adopted by the HR on 19 November (Dōwa Gyōseishi Henshū Iinkai, 2002, 426–7).

A *zadankai* was hosted by the *Asahi* newspaper on 23 December to hear responses to the report. Horiuchi welcomed the proposal to create a new law but pointed out that only a small number of Buraku communities would need infrastructural projects – 200 out of 4,600. Challenged by Isomura, he accepted that not all of his party supported extension of the law but suggested that the 'opinion' (Iken Gushin) of the Chitaikyō would make his task of persuading them easier. Kumashiro from the Sōmuchō noted how different the situation is now compared to the mid-1960s, the time of the Dōtaishin report, but suggested that discrimination is taking on new forms. He expressed concern about the problem of Dōwa policy engendering welfare dependence and supported the demand for the abolition of personal grants on that basis. While Horiuchi supported the *kyūdan* tactic, Kumashiro was keener to stress his fear that it often went 'too far'. Isomura tried to persuade his colleagues that new thinking is required for Dōwa policy to locate it in the context of the 'welfare state' (*fukushi kokka*) and the international era of human rights. Both Horiuchi and Isomura urged the mass media to be more courageous in reporting Dōwa issues – Horiuchi noted that they had not even mentioned the *Iken Gushin* (Asahi Shimbun, 23 December 1986).

A project team had been created within Horiuchi's committee to review the plans for various Dōwa policies and its recommendations fed into the decisions being made for the budget of FY1987. The key points from these sessions were included in the Framework Plan for Chiiki Kaizen (Kongo no Chiiki Kaizen Taisaku ni Kansuru Daikō) adopted by the Sōmuchō on 27 December 1986 and endorsed by a cabinet resolution. It suggested a fundamental review of what was being funded. Continued funding should only be given to a limited number of projects that were absolutely necessary and aimed to develop self-reliance. Personal grants should in principle be eliminated; the independence of the Dōwa administration should be guaranteed. The new focus was to be on finance and promoting the transfer of projects from 'special' to 'general'. The policy was renamed and henceforth would formally be Chiiki Kaizen Taisaku Tokutei Jigyō – Regional Improvement Policy Designated Projects. This was to be the final extension (Dōwa Gyōseishi Henshū Iinkai, 2002, 428).

On 13 January 1987, a circular was sent to all local government officers responsible for Dōwa/Chiiki Kaizen policy ordering them to sort through the policies as defined in 1982 designating which should be continued and which not (Dōwa Gyōseishi Henshū Iinkai, 2002, 429–33). Some 28 of the 82 types of projects were to be suspended or were made 'general', 20 projects continued but only following serious revisions leaving just 34 project categories unchanged (Dōwa Gyōseishi Henshū Iinkai, 2002, 429–33; Kanai, 1991, 267–8). Overall, these reforms proposed reducing the Dōwa budget by 13.4% for FY1987 compared to the previous year. There was to be more focus on *keihatsu.* The funding used to support high school attendance could henceforth also be used to support university students on both two- and four-year programmes; more was to be provided for vocational training and training to improve management and technology within Buraku-based SMEs.

These changes were being planned in advance of steps being taken to draft a new law. In January, Sōmuchō produced a draft bill for consideration in the Diet which on 10 February was approved by the LDP committee and endorsed by Cabinet on 13th when it passed to the Diet Cabinet Affairs committee. It was not finally approved by the HR until 25 March and the HC the following day. At both stages, the JCP attempted to amend the bill but failed and it was finally passed with just days to spare before the new law commenced operation on 1 April.

It begins by specifying that it is mainly about defining the special arrangements for financial administration of the projects. In early March, Kumashiro Akihiko, then head of the Chitaikyō office in the Sōmuchō, answered questions about the next phase of Dōwa policy for the *Asahi* newspaper. He notes that the new bill omits all reference to the constitutional principles which protect basic human rights that the 1982 law had mentioned in two places (clauses 1 and 3). The aim was to continue the projects in the 'target areas', 'improving the living environment, promoting industry, stabilising employment, encouraging education, strengthening human rights protection and enhancing social welfare' (from paragraph 2) but preparing the way for the transfer of responsibility for these improvements from projects supported by 'special' funding to those which are part of general support for welfare. Despite the movements' (mainly the BLL) assertions that there were up to 1,000 communities that had not been formally recognised, no more districts will be designated as Dōwa communities and therefore eligible for Dōwa project funds. They have had 18 years to do so. Most Dōwa projects that funded major infrastructural improvements were complete and those that provided individuals with payments would be reduced, or where possible even completely eliminated, but where they remained only Burakumin living within designated Dōwa communities would be eligible to receive them. He suggested that local authorities should be stricter in their supervision of funds used to subsidise movement organisations. The local tax exemptions granted to some residents and companies in Dōwa areas should be reviewed.

Overall, this new law suggests a tightening up of control over Dōwa funding and a firm commitment to ending the policy within five years. An editorial published in the same edition of the *Asahi* newspaper again asked: So what will happen in five years time? Will discrimination have disappeared by then? If policy ceases at the national level, will it then continue under the control of, and somehow funded by, local governments? (Asahi Shimbun, 7 March 1987).

Summary of what was going on here

Over these five years, the BLL developed a national campaign in support of their demands for a Buraku Liberation Basic Law which marked a significant elaboration of the principles they had been advocating since the late 1960s. This campaign had been endorsed by a petition signed by seven million people, including more than half of both houses of the Diet, all the opposition parties apart from the JCP. Isomura personally seems to have been well-disposed to the idea of introducing a Basic Law from as early as 1980 as part of a much broader commitment by the government to the protection of fundamental human rights as were being elaborated internationally and linked to the idea of a Japanese-style welfare state. He would reiterate his support for locating Dōwa policy in a wider context of legal institutionalisation of protection of human rights but he was unable to prevail over the bureaucrats on the Chitaikyō and LDP politicians. Articles by him and reports quoting him in the *Asahi* newspaper show him frustrated by the way in which the Chitaikyō was not permitted to play the role of providing independent advice to government. The LDP seems to have been divided about this, the JCP were fundamentally opposed to it and there was no enthusiasm for these ideas within the bureaucracy. PM Nakasone made it clear both that he would not support the Basic Law proposals and that this should be the last extension of the SML arrangements (Asahi Shimbun, 6 February, 7 March 1987).

The result was that not only were the proposals for a new Basic Law completely disregarded but the law that was eventually passed was little more than an administrative ordinance that enabled the continuation of Dōwa/Chiiki Kaizen projects. Even the most basic reference to constitutionally protected human rights was eliminated. Overall, we can see from the early 1980s the routinisation of the formulation of Chiiki Kaizen/Dōwa policy as well as a reduction in the ambition of its content. The most obvious aspect of this was the decision not to re-appoint any members of the movement organisations when the advisory council was re-constituted in the summer of 1981 despite protests from the movements themselves and criticism of this decision by Isomura. This was, to say the least, unusual: a council on gender policy that had only male members or on diversity issues that contained only representatives of the majority community would not be regarded as legitimate in most states. On the one hand, the degree of bitterness that poisoned the relations between the Zenkairen and BLL may have made sessions difficult had they both been represented but on the other hand, as Isomura was to say on a couple of occasions, if both of them had had to work together on the council that might have produced greater consensus about policy which, in turn, might have lubricated relations between groups at the local level.

With the representatives of the various parts of the Buraku community only being able to take part in the policy process when they were invited to appear before or provide information to the Chiiki Kaizen sub-committee of the LDP's PARC or the Chitaikyō, there emerged a tri-partite elite decision-making structure composed of elements of the ruling party, existing bureaucrats plus some OBs plus a sprinkling of outsiders: representatives of local government (two prefectural governors and one town mayor), a couple of professors, and a journalist.

It is perhaps indicative of the changing role of this council that the reports that it produced from 1981 onwards were significantly shorter than those produced in the previous decade. While the documents of the Dōtaikyō in the 1970s would often run to two or three hundred pages, those of the Chitaikyō were usually ten pages or fewer. The transfer of the Chiiki Kaizen office from the PMO – the core of the policymaking process – to the Sōmuchō which was a repository for miscellaneous parts of the administration also demonstrates how Dōwa policy had become routinised and no longer as central as it had been to the policy process (Figure 6.2).

This was part of the pattern in which the LDP and the bureaucracy resisted the attempts of the BLL and opposition parties, mainly the JSP, to redefine the aims of Dōwa policy during the 1980s as not being **only** about making infrastructural improvements, raising educational levels, and improving employment opportunities but also related to the promotion and protection of human rights in Japanese society as a whole. To use the language which we introduced in an earlier chapter, the social construction of the 'Buraku problem' was from the early 1980s increasingly placed under

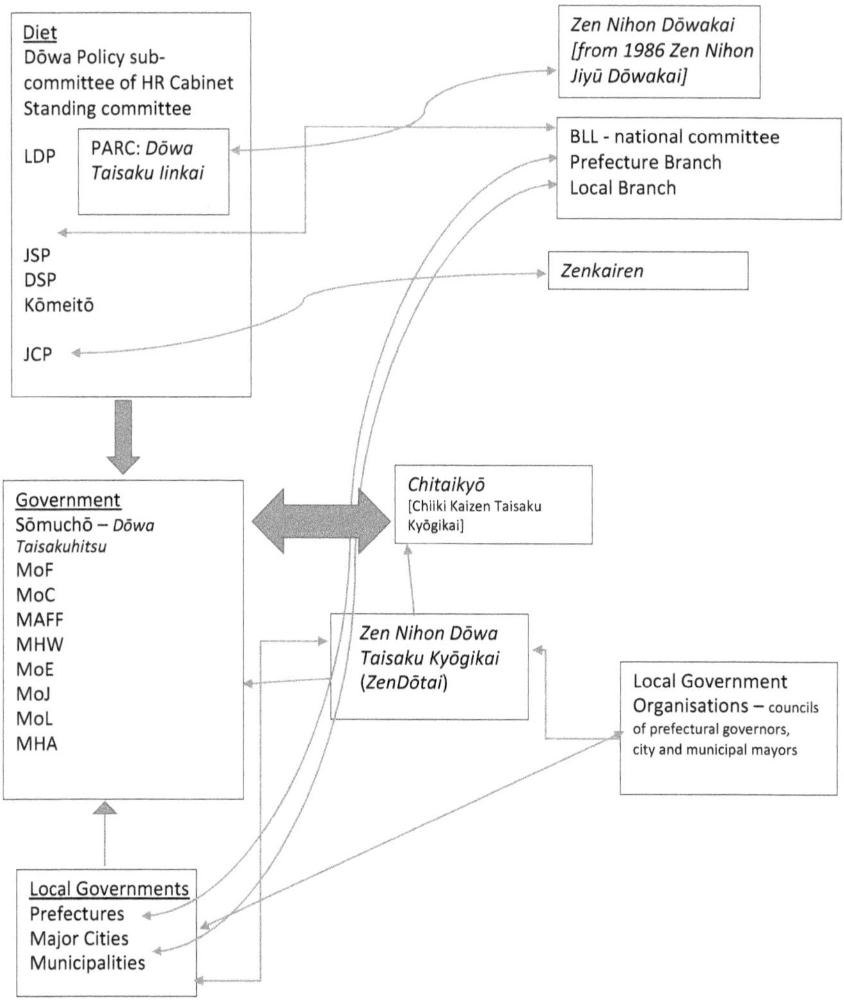

Figure 6.2 Dōwa policy map 1982–97.

the control of liberals and conservatives who defined it as being one which could be resolved through the application of appropriate amounts capital to redress historical backwardness. Since those projects could be quantified quite easily, it would also be possible to decide when the policy was complete. In this context, I think we can see the decision to establish a research institute under the wing of the LDP as an attempt to ensure that the mostly left-wing Buraku liberation study groups did not monopolise the literature on Buraku studies.

As Japan approached the end of the 1980s, the Dōwa policies and the process behind them had been in existence for nearly 20 years. They were becoming embedded into the policy framework. The changes to the membership of the Dōtaikyō, then renamed the Chitaikyo, placed the movement groups at arms-length. The precise reasons for this are unclear and were left unspecified but the rivalry between the BLL and Zenkairen wings of the liberation movement was becoming increasingly bitter and the Dōwakai had been discredited by the incrimination of its leaders in cases of serious fraud. Changes were also taking place within the BLL; its leaders began to recognise that significant improvements had taken place in their living environment but their members were still encountering everyday discrimination. Their response to this was to re-emphasise the need for the Japanese state to commit itself to the protection and promotion of the human rights of residents in Buraku communities. This had been recommended in the final section of the 1965 report, had formed part of the requests of the BLL 1966–9 but in the end set aside by the LDP leadership. In 1989, the LDP suffered an embarrassing defeat in the HoC elections. The JSP appeared to be on the verge of a revival in its fortunes. If this were to happen, the prospects for the passage of a Buraku Liberation Basic Law might still be on the cards.

Phase III Dōwa policy development in the 1990s – towards termination

The 1990s had the potential to be a decade of transformation. Indeed, Kingston argues that behind the anguish about it being a 'lost decade' caused by the slow or no annual increase in GDP, some quite remarkable changes took place (Kingston, 2004). Certainly, the international situation changed dramatically with the collapse of the Soviet Union and elimination of Russian control over many of its former satellite states. For the time being, at least it no longer posed a military threat to the 'west' or Japan. Within Japan, the LDP lost its grip over the policy process in 1993 and only returned to power in coalition first with the JSP and later with the Kōmeitō. Each of these contextual changes would have an impact directly or indirectly on the evolution of Dōwa policy.

Overall, the pattern across the 1990s was for there to be a gradual reduction in the budgets provided for Dowa projects and the scope and ambition of those projects. As is documented in Table 7.1 and Figure 7.1 (and the material presented in the Appendix, Tables A.4–A.5 and Figures A.4–A.5), the Dōwa budget was drastically reduced as the MHW and MAFF, previously key players, practically ceased all Dowa-linked activity.

At the same time, across the 1990s, there were signs that the Japanese government was being persuaded to take human rights more seriously. In the post-Cold War world, Japan ratified several major human rights conventions: on children (1994), on the elimination of racial discrimination (1995), and on the abolition of torture (1999). Its reports produced as part of its commitments made in these and similar international human rights treaties became less perfunctory and its diplomats began to engage seriously with the UN's human rights committees. Moreover, there were changes made to legislation on maternity leave, the environment and disability, stronger legislation to encourage gender equality, less restrictive regulation of the resident Korean communities, the abolition of the discriminatory and anachronistic Leprosy Law, and the abolition of the Aboriginal Protection Law as part of a more positive policy towards Ainu communities (more discussion in Neary 2002).

However, as Kumashiro had made clear in his interview with the *Asahi* newspaper in March 1987 just before the extension to the SML was passed in the Diet, the overall plan for the Dōwa policy was that projects would be reduced in size and scope leading to the transfer of the whole programme to the general budget over the five-year period ending in 1992. Two new themes were starting to emerge that would be added to the Dōwa policy agenda. First, a central liaison council to monitor '*ese-Dōwa*' activity was created within government in June 1987 composed of representatives of all concerned ministries coordinated by the Sōmuchō. The initial meeting quoted a MoJ report that 22% of companies had experienced some such threat (Asahi Shimbun, 13 June 1987).

The second issue was what should be done about those Buraku communities that for whatever reason had not been designated as Dōwa areas. Kumashiro had been quite clear that no new areas would be designated but the BLL argued that there were perhaps as many as a thousand such communities. Although the BLL did not resist the overall trend towards a reduction of Dōwa policy, they did make the recognition of new areas a key new demand. In this, they were assisted by a decision of the Niigata district court in January 1988 which supported an appeal against the refusal of a village office to accept the application for a loan under the Dōwa project SME programme because the community inhabited by the applicants was not formally registered as a Dōwa district. The judge argued that the community had had the 'stable improvement of its living environment impeded for historical and social reasons' so whether it was designated or not was irrelevant (Asahi Shimbun, 27 January, 3 June 1988). This seemed to suggest that the Dōwa policy was being, or at least could be, guided by constitutional principles rather than a narrow, administrative interpretation of the Dōwa legislation.

The BLL campaign to recognise more 'undesignated' communities many of which were quite small – mostly fewer than 50 households – continued across the 1990s. Their investigations found a town in Gumma prefecture which had listed nine Buraku communities in its 1967 survey but denied their existence after 1969 largely on the urging of wealthier members of these communities who urged a 'let sleeping dogs lie' approach (Asahi Shimbun, 17 May 1987). How to deal with Buraku communities who did not want the attention that 'improvements' would attract was a dilemma for the movement. Moreover, although the leader of the BLL, Uesugi Saichirō, accepted that in areas where the local government had been seriously committed to the Dōwa projects, more than 80% of the 'hard' projects had been completed, not all authorities had been so positively involved, and so there were projects that remained incomplete, communities where more needed to be done. The impact of the slowdown in economic growth nationally made the arguments that neither central nor local government could afford to fund Dōwa projects at the previous high levels more plausible. However, in fact, overall social security spending continued to increase across the decade and there were several high-cost, non-Dōwa-related infrastructural projects undertaken.

Still, there was little resistance to the notion that Dōwa spending could be reduced, even from within the BLL. It was starting to alter its approach characterising its history as having had three periods: from the formation of the Suiheisha in 1922 to the renaming of the movement in 1955, from 1955 to 1988 where the focus had been on demands to have a policy council convened and then to ensure that its recommendations were implemented, followed by the somewhat less successful campaign to demand a Basic Law on Buraku Liberation; and now, the third era, when both the movement and state were internationalising their perspectives, the state with its ratification of international instruments and the BLL through increased engagement with the international human rights frameworks. By 1994, Oga Masayuki of the BLL theory committee was arguing that,

> With the end of the cold war the international situation has changed. It is time for the movement to give priority to values common to humanity such as human rights and the environment rather than a class struggle perspective. We must also change our approach from being centred on [Dōwa] projects.
>
> (quoted in Asahi Shimbun, 25 February 1994)

The BLL had presented evidence to the UN human rights committees based in Geneva about the situation of Burakumin during the 1970s and 1980s but it had had to do so by invitation from one of the organisations which had consultative status. One important milestone for the movement was the Second World Conference against Racism organised by the United Nations (UN) in Geneva in 1983. With the help of Ben Whitaker, Executive Director of the Minority Rights Group, the BLL was able to give a presentation to the assembly – the first time the issue of Buraku discrimination was formally discussed within a UN body. During the 1980s, it decided to create a group that would give it direct access.

This was the background to the launch of the International Movement against All forms of Discrimination and Racism (IMADR) in 1988 that aimed to development transnational solidarity between minority communities giving priority to empowerment, solidarity, and advocacy (Hankins, 2014, 188–9). It requested consultative status with the UN Economic and Social Council (EcoSoc) in January 1989. This was supported by the Zenkoku Jiyū Dōwakai which called it 'a plus for the promotion of human rights within and outside Japan' but opposed by the Zenkairen who gave evidence to EcoSoc that the BLL had itself committed discriminatory acts (Asahi Shimbun, 15 January, 4 February 1989). EcoSoc deferred making a decision at this point on the basis that IMADR had only been in existence for a year and then again in 1991 but finally in 1993 consultative status was granted and IMADR established a permanent office in Geneva. One of its top priorities was to have Japan ratify the UN Convention on the Elimination of All forms of Racial Discrimination (CERD) which was achieved in 1995. It then used meetings of the committee of CERD as a forum in which to argue the case that Buraku discrimination is 'discrimination based on descent' and thus under the purview of the CERD. This is still not accepted by the Japanese government (for more discussion about this, see Hankins, 2014, 167, 174–5 and Tsutsui, 2018, 183–98).

In July 1987, when he was re-appointed as the chair of the Chitaikyō, Isomura had argued for a 'new start' in thinking about Dōwa issues that took on a 'global perspective' (Asahi Shimbun, 30 July 1987). However apart from activity relating to policies on *ese-Dōwa* activity not much happened for the next few years.

With the SML due to expire at the end of March the following year, in the first half of 1991 there was a cluster of meetings and conferences held to consider the future of Dōwa policy:

> 27 February Dōwa Mondai no Genjō o Kangaeru Renraku Kaigi (Liaison Council to Consider the Current state of the Dōwa Problem) – convened by the BLL and Zenkoku Jiyū Dōwakai and attended by representatives of the Zenkoku Jiyū Dōwakai Kenkyū Kyōgikai, Zenkoku Rinpokan Renraku Kyōgikai, Buraku Kaihō Kenkyūsho, Chiiki Kaizen Taisaku Kenkyūsho and 200 representatives of all the political parties except the JCP
>
> 19 March Conference of the Zendōtai – the local government organisation
>
> 21 May Meeting of the national mayors' association's Dōwa Taisaku Tokubetsu Iinkai (Special Committee on Dōwa Policy)
>
> 12 July Conference on Dōwa Taisaku Hōteki Sochi (Legal Measures for the Dōwa Policy) – attended by 1400 people including many governors and deputy governors from 36 prefectures, 9 cities and 290 municipalities.
>
> (Asahi Shimbun, 13 July, 1991)

The positions taken by each of these conferences was slightly different but there was an emerging consensus that discrimination still existed and that there were both 'hard' and 'soft' Dōwa projects that would not be complete by the time the current law expired (March 1992). So, it continued to be important to strengthen human rights protection and eliminate the non-material differences that existed.

The BLL was persevering with its campaign for a Basic Law. In 1990–1, it tried to bring together a coalition of groups within the UH, now no longer controlled by the LDP following the 1989 election, in support of its campaign for both the passage of the law and the extension of the Dōwa projects. It launched a petition which sought to attract ten million signatures. The proposal even seems to have had some support among LDP Diet members to the extent that the party leadership in February 1991 had to repeat its request to them not to sign the petition or attend meetings called in support of the campaign (Suginohara 759, 2007, 77).

At the same time, a fairly familiar pattern was emerging. In December 1990, the Chitaikyō, which had not met since July 1989, reconvened with Isomura still in the chair with eight out of the ten lay members being the same. They met more or less monthly over the next year. In July, Isomura made a public comment that government should include Dōwa projects into its budget plans for the next financial year which suggests that there was a real possibility that central government money might not have been forthcoming. Their final report to PM Miyazawa issued on 11 December 1991 argued that it was not yet appropriate to end all of the Dōwa projects (Kongo no Dōwa Chiiki Kaizen Taisaku ni tsuite, Dōwa Gyōseishi Henshū Iinkai, 2002, 453–9). It did however comment on the need for administrative independence, the promotion of self-reliance, the elimination of *ese Dōwa* activity, and the creation of a climate in which the free exchange of ideas was possible as a means to generate a national consensus on Dōwa policy (Asahi Shimbun, 11 December 1991; Dōwa Gyōseishi Henshū Iinkai, 2002, 56).

Meanwhile within the LDP, the Chiiki Kaizen Taisaku committee (a sub-committee of the PARC) resumed its meetings chaired by Maeda Isao, its previous chair Horiuchi having lost his seat in the HC election of 1989. It set out its approach towards 'Chiiki Kaizen' in a one-page document published on 18 December 1991 urging the rapid conclusion of existing material projects and/or their transfer to 'general' policy, a positive emphasis on non-material policies such as the promotion of employment, industry, and education, and the further development of 'appropriate administration' ('Kongo no Chiiki Kaizen ni suite', Dōwa Gyōseishi Henshū Iinkai, 2002, 481). This reinforced the recommendations of the Chitaikyō and two days later the Sōmuchō produced a slightly longer report, two pages long (Dōwa Gyōseishi Henshū Iinkai, 2002, 57, 482–3; Suginohara 760, 2007, 75). These reports emphasised that only those projects for which there was a clear need should be funded, for example, in areas where the local authority had been slow to engage with the national Dōwa programme. Elsewhere, projects should be transferred from special support to general budgets as soon as possible. So, for example, support for a Buraku kindergarten should come from the local government's pre-school budget not from 'special' Dōwa funding. They urged that the new law should have a clear expiry date and that a comprehensive survey be carried out to assess the impact of Dōwa policy so far and, one suspects, to justify the termination of the programme.

So, even while recommending extension, the report was also urging the reduction of the scope of Dōwa programmes. A review was carried out of Dōwa policy at the national level and ten of the 55 projects were removed from the 'special' category. When the Dōwa budget for FY1992 was settled on 28 December, it was overall 20.3% less than that of the previous year although there was an *increase* of 12.4% to support *keihatsu* projects run by the Sōmuchō, MoJ, and MoL. Cabinet approved the extension of the SML on 14 February but the bill passed slowly through the Diet not finally being approved until 27 March with the support of most of the LDP and most of the opposition parties, having survived attempts by the JCP to amend it. The LDP was insistent once more that this should be the very final extension, whereas the JSP were arguing in support of a broader human rights Basic Law (Asahi Shimbun, 14 February 1992).

It was not a new law but a partial amendment to the law of 1987 extending it to 1997. Once again, the expectation seems to have been that this would be the final extension. No new areas were designated for the receipt of funding but it was recognised that where a community had been late to adopt Dōwa policy, there would be some projects outstanding. As in previous years, emphasis was given to developing 'soft', *keihatsu* projects and to how the 'hard' infrastructure projects could be transferred to general policy implementation.

In September 1992 at a conference on Buraku research, the BLL announced that it would not be asking for any further extension of the Dōwa projects but its leader, Uesugi Saichirō, did commit his organisation once more to a campaign to ensure that a Basic Law on Buraku Liberation would be in place by 1997 when the current Dōwa legislation expired. In parallel, BLL branches were demanding that local governments should establish ordinances that made it illegal to conduct background investigations for the purpose of discrimination. This would later result in 10 prefectures and 621 municipalities passing regulations aiming at the elimination of Buraku discrimination and all other forms of discrimination by 2000 (Onishi, 2009, 693). Also in 1992 the BLL's right of centre rival, the Zenkoku Jiyū Dōwakai, at its 9th conference passed a proposal for a Basic Law on Human Rights. The JCP connected organisations wanted nothing to do with either of these proposals but apart from them it did seem that a consensus of sorts was emerging.

It will be remembered that the LDP fell out of power in the summer of 1993 after an election that had been precipitated by the defection of a group of Diet members prominently led by Ozawa Ichirō. The resulting cabinet was made up of representatives of all the opposition parties except the JCP with the largest number of seats being held by the JSP. Following the short premiership of Hosokawa Morihiro, and even shorter period in power of Hata Tsutomu, to almost everyone's surprise, the LDP returned to government in June 1994 within a coalition agreed between the LDP, Sakigake Shintō, and the JSP in which Murayama Tomiichi, the JSP leader, became PM.

The BLL had had a close relationship with the JSP since the 1950s when its chairman, Matsumoto Jiichirō, was a leading member on the left wing of the party. However, from the start of the 1990s, the BLL began to move away from supporting the JSP. One reason was that the JSP had been slow to support its campaign for a Basic Law and ratification of the CERD while at the same time the BLL leadership was shifting away from its 'class struggle' line. In the 1992 UH election, for example, in Wakayama prefecture the local BLL group supported not the JSP candidate but the incumbent LDP Diet member, Maeda Isao, who had favoured a five-year extension to the Dōwa policy and been chair of the PARC Dōwa policy sub-committee (Asahi Shimbun, 24 October 1994). In 1993, the BLL started a process to develop a new theory for the movement's 'third era' and set up sub-committees to look at existing discrimination, Dōwa education policy, and attitudes to Dōwa policy (Onishi, 2009, 710). At its 51st conference held in March 1994, the BLL announced that in response to the end of the '1955 party political system' it would no longer give automatic support to the JSP but rather recommend support for candidates based on the attitude they took on such issues as the Basic Law. It also announced that it would embark on a course of 'self-criticism' to re-think its basic aims. In particular, it wanted to reconsider its slogan often used up to that point of 'liberation the end, [Dōwa] projects the means' which was used to justify the focus on making demands for material improvements. The BLL claimed 160,000 members but realised that it would need to adapt if it were to maintain such levels of support (Asahi Shimbun, 5, 23, 25 February 1994). Then at its May 1995 conference, it announced that it would shift from a class-based perspective to one that talked of building a democratic society within which 'human rights were established within autonomy and co-existence' to be brought about by broadening solidarity with other citizens.

This internal review was completed in 1997 with the adoption of a new programme which 'recognised the prospects for Buraku liberation within a democratic society' and a movement focused on opposing the undemocratic *ie* system and discrimination while supporting peace movements and a concern with the environment (Suginohara 761, 2007, 65–6). The new platform softened its class struggle line emphasising instead 'human rights, welfare and the environment'. It recognised the improvements that had taken place over the previous 30 years. 'Formerly there were big disparities between Buraku and non-Buraku communities but now younger people have been better educated and earn higher incomes so that there is social stratification and diversity within Buraku communities'. Instead of the focus on a class struggle view of history and an emphasis on material disparities as the basis of discrimination, the new document points to the 'culture of discrimination – undemocratic systems, irrational superstitions and beliefs, *ie* awareness and hierarchical values, and notions of pollution (*kegare*)' as well as committing to 'opposing the family register (*koseki*) and emperor systems which strengthen status awareness'. The new document talks about the 'eradication of discriminatory attitudes and contributing to the enhanced dissemination of human rights awareness'.

On the one hand, these changes brought the BLL closer to that of the central government position which was reducing its stress on the material element of Dōwa policy at the same time as reflecting trends within the international human rights movement. They were aware that this new stance had significant implications for the future. Oga Masayuki, the main theoretician within the BLL, was also aware that the movement and Burakumin now needed to address the prospect of the elimination of discrimination and prejudice, albeit distant as yet.

> Burakumin do not have a legal existence. Burakumin are not a race. An Ainu liberated from discrimination is still a member of the Ainu race and a liberated black person is still black. But what does a liberated Burakumin become?
>
> (all quotes from Asahi Shimbun, 29 March 1996)

This question would become increasingly pressing in the twenty-first century.

PM Murayama was constrained in what he could achieve by the need to keep the LDP on board; however, he did try to advance his own agenda, for example, to reach some final agreement about compensation for those whose health had been damaged by the industrial pollution of Minamata bay and to push forward human rights protection. Some in the BLL felt that this was an opportunity to get their Basic Law on to the statute book (Onishi, 2009, 694). In April 1995, a draft for a Buraku Problem Basic Law was presented to the HR legislative bureau but not proceeded with. The JSP had resolved to take the bill forward even without the support of the other parties but the Diet session concluded without it having been considered. Exactly why this opportunity was missed is unclear but we should remember that in the first half of 1995, the JSP was already crumbling and would fall apart over the next 12 months. Second, the coalition government was facing a series of acute crises, notably the Kobe earthquake in January and the Aum Shinrikyo sarin attack on the Tokyo underground in March so that there was less 'bandwidth' than usual to devote to the creative resolution of chronic problems. Then at the start of 1996, Murayama was replaced as PM by Hashimoto Ryutarō and, although his cabinet continued to contain members of what remained of the JSP, he was able to impose his own policy priorities which did not include a Buraku or Human Rights Basic Law.

During the period of the LDP/Sakigake/JSP coalition government, the role that had been played by the PARC and its sub-committees in formulating policy and liaising between Diet politicians and bureaucrats was taken over by a number of 'project teams' composed of Diet members belonging to the LDP, JSP, and Shintō Sakigake. Accordingly, a *Jinken to Sabetsu ni Kansuru* (Human Rights and Discrimination) Project Team was formed in December 1994 (membership LDP 3, JSP 3, Sakigake 2) which met twice a month – a total of 31 times – across 1994–6 chaired by Yamaguchi Tsuruo, a member of the right wing of the JSP.[12] It published an interim report in June 1995 in which it noted the much-delayed ratification of the CERD and the Planning for the UN Decade of Human Rights Education by the PMO. Another report entitled 'Basic Approach for Policy Aiming at the Rapid Resolution of the Dōwa Problem' appeared in draft on 20 December 1995 and was finalised in March 1996.

The continued existence of the Chitaikyō had been authorised in late March 1992 at the same time as the partial amendment of the Dōwa legislation. It was re-constituted in March 1993 with some incremental changes to its lay membership of which the most important was the replacement of its chair, Isomura Eichi, who by this point was aged 89, by Miyazaki Shigeki, chancellor of Meiji University who had a background in international law. It commissioned three major surveys of conditions and attitudes that were carried out in 1993. It also established a sub-committee to consider how the projects might be transferred to the mainstream budget, the development of *keihatsu* projects and appropriate administration of any future projects.

The 1993 surveys

The Chitaikyō commissioned surveys 'to measure the impact of the regional improvement policies so far implemented, to understand the situation within the Dōwa districts and the attitudes of the population towards them'. To do this, three surveys were commissioned. The first examined the situation in each district that had implemented Dōwa policies. The second employed researchers to survey living conditions in one in five of the Dōwa-related households and the third looked at public attitudes of both the Dōwa residents and the general public. The results were published in March 1995 in three reports each of over 200 pages and summarised in a report from the Chitaikyō sub-committee dated 8 June 1995 (Dōwa Gyōseishi Henshū Iinkai, 2002, 805–947). This was the most comprehensive attempt to summarise the situation of Burakumin and their communities at the same time as trying to capture the attitudes of the mainstream community in a way that enabled comparison with those within Buraku communities.

To pick out some of the key points from the survey of Buraku households:

- The proportion of 'elderly households' was much higher than the national average (as in a 1992 survey) – 18.1% compared to 11.8% – moreover, it had almost doubled since the previous survey in 1985. This led to speculation that it was caused by an exit of younger people leaving their communities which was not compensated by an equivalent immigration. Poverty measured by rates of receipt of welfare payments or exemption from resident tax payment was high at 25.8% compared to a national average of 15.9%.

- Health standards measured by time spent in hospital were poor – 1.8% spent more than 15 days in hospital compared to a national rate of 0.3% – and the difference was particularly high in the over 70s: 7.5% compared to 1.4%
- There was clear evidence of different patterns of employment but the differences between those in their 20s were fewer than those in their 50s in terms of a blue-collar/white-collar divide and size of company. (Noguchi and Ishimoto, 2014, 294).

The attitude survey revealed some significant differences in the way discrimination was perceived. Around 25% of the non-Buraku sample claimed not to know about the existence of Buraku areas (Dōwa Gyōseishi Henshū Iinkai 2002, 929). There were still around 10% of people who thought that discrimination was a result of racial difference (Dōwa Gyōseishi Henshū Iinkai, 2002, 932). On attitudes to marriage: 33.8% of the Dōwa district sample felt that it should only concern the two individuals, 60.5% agreed that while family and other opinions should not be ignored, the wishes of the couple should be respected, 3.8% agreed that while the views of the couple should be respected, those of family and friends should take precedence, and 1.0% thought that family views should predominate. The responses from non-Dōwa districts were 11.2%, 81.4%, 5.9%, and 0.8%, respectively.

The third survey asked local governments or schools to supply basic data on the size and circumstances of Buraku communities which it compared not simply to national level averages but to data drawn from the same locale. So, for example, it found a rate of dependence on public assistance to be 5.2% compared to a figure of only 0.8% in neighbouring communities. Long-term absence from junior high schools was 4.5% in Buraku districts, but only 2.5% elsewhere, while the average rate of advancement to high schools for Buraku children was 91.8% compared to 96.2% for children in the same local government areas (for further commentary on the surveys, see Noguchi and Ishimoto, 2014, 292–310).

The amount of data generated by these surveys was such that it defies simple summary. In many respects, the simple message was: much improvement has taken place, but more needs to be done.

The Iken Gushin

In parallel with these surveys, the Chitaikyō sub-committee between October 1993 and July 1994 held a series of hearings on a range of topics mainly with the ministries but also with representatives of the movement organisations and their research bodies (Dōwa Gyōseishi Henshū Iinkai, 2002, 487–8). Having received the report from the LDP/JSP/Sakigake 'Project

Team' mentioned above on 16 June 1995, it issued a statement of its 'Basic Approach' on 18 December on what to do when the current version of the SML came to an end in March 1997. The two key phrases quoted frequently in subsequent reports were that the 'main aims have been achieved' (*ōmune mokuteki o tassei shita*) but there 'needs to be just one more push' (*ittei no kufu ga hitsuyō*).

Consultation with local government representatives over the first months of 1996 heard that there were regions such as Fukuoka and Nara where planned work could not be completed by the end of March 1997. These were followed by a meeting of the full Chitaikyō in March 1996. The attitudes of the three Buraku groups were summarised as follows:

- The BLL remained concerned about the communities that had not been formally designated and where disparities remained, it was still campaigning for a Basic Law and emphasising the need for improved education and *keihatsu*.
- The right of centre Zenkoku Jiyū Dōwakai was not opposed to the transfer of funding of Dōwa projects to the general budget but agreed with the BLL that disparities still existed that cannot be addressed by general policies and that some kind of Basic Law on human rights was required to support human rights education and community building.
- Zenkairen argued that most disparities had been resolved. Rather than fund 'special' projects, social welfare overall should be improved and it opposed human rights education on the grounds that it was likely to threaten freedom of thought.

(Asahi Shimbun, 26 March 1996)

Meanwhile in the political arena, what remained of the JSP/SDP continued to support the BLL demands for a Basic Law. The centrist opposition party, Shinshintō, had set up a Dōwa policy project team which seemed to support more legal measures, while the LDP and Sakigake were reported as not yet having formulated their positions (Asahi Shimbun, 29 March 1996).

The formulation of the Chitaikyō 'opinion' (*Iken Gushin*) 'On the Future Measures for the Rapid Resolution of the Dōwa Problem' (*Dōwa Mondai no Sōki Kaiketsu ni Muketa Kongo no Hōsaku no Arikata ni suite*) was thus the result of a process of several years discussion within the committee having heard representations from local governments and the movement organisations and engagement with the politicians on the 'project teams'. It was presented to the PM on 17 May 1996. There had been several previous *Iken Gushin* on Dōwa policy but this was the last. From that time until the time of this writing, many activists have regarded the Iken Gushin of 1996 as a definitive statement of government policy at the end of the Dōwa policy equivalent to a second Dōtaishin. We will therefore discuss it in a little more detail.

It is composed of four parts: a review of the basic approach, a summary of the policy process thus far and the current situation, the prospects for the resolution of the Dōwa problem, and the direction of main policies in the future. It locates the current discussion in the context of the post-Cold War, a time when Japan has become part of the international human rights treaty system having recently ratified the CERD in 1995. However, it notes that 50 years after the end of the Pacific War and 25 years after the start of a national Dōwa policy, the issue remains unresolved. However, as the Dōtaishin pointed out, the Dōwa issue is not a problem of the past but a current human rights issue.

Section 2 starts with a very brief review of the evolution of Dōwa policy from the first MHW budget in 1953 up to the major surveys carried out in 1993 and then summarises the current situation using data from those surveys: the age of residents of Buraku communities is now older than average as younger people have moved out, inter-marriage has increased but discrimination at the point of marriage continues to be a, if not the, most serious human rights violation. Living conditions within Buraku communities, housing, roads, and infrastructure such as sewage systems have been greatly improved to the extent that there are few if any differences with their neighbouring communities even if they are often both below national levels. The education gap in terms of high school attendance has narrowed to a few percentage points but there remains a big gap in access to higher education. Measures of employment stability show that it is increasing. Around 30% of Dōwa community residents report having experienced discrimination although very few formally report it. In conclusion, most of the material gaps have been filled although some issues remain in education and employment and there remains work to be done to further eliminate prejudices and discrimination.

Third, the Iken Gushin notes how the policies implemented so far have done much to break the vicious circle whereby poverty justified prejudices and discrimination created the circumstances that then recreated poverty. Most of the 'hard' projects have been completed but there remains more to be done in the area of *keihatsu* and to eliminate accusations of 'reverse discrimination'. In terms of the future, policy directions needed to focus on the removal of differences in education and employment through the implementation of 'general' policies which are informed by human rights ideas. The report continued to insist that the fact that the SML-funded programmes are coming to an end does *not* signal that the Buraku problem has been 'solved' and that therefore nothing further needs to be done. On the contrary, it repeats the point originally made in the Dōtaishin that as long as discrimination remains, it will be the duty of the state to deal with it.

Japan was one of a small number of countries to take an active part in the UN Decade of Human Rights Education 1995–2004 and this was linked to its commitment to enhance *keihatsu* policies to oppose discrimination. At that moment, the system to promote human rights and provide redress in cases of violations was not robust nor easily accessible, so the report argues that the creation of such a system should be a priority. Indeed, the Iken Gushin comments that, 'It is no exaggeration to say that a country's human rights redress system is indicative of its attitude to human rights' (Dōwa Gyōseishi Henshū Iinkai, 2002, 501). It suggested that the SML should be extended to deal with a small number of Dōwa projects in Buraku communities, but they should be transferred as soon as possible from special funding into general projects. Finally, the Iken Gushin re-states the importance of ensuring the independence of project administration, a focus on self-reliance, the elimination of *ese-Dōwa*, and the creation of an atmosphere in which there is free exchange of ideas to deepen correct understanding of the issue (Dōwa Gyōseishi Henshū Iinkai, 2002, 493–506).

The Iken Gushin was submitted to PM Hashimoto on 18 May. Nakanishi Sekisuke, minister at the Sōmuchō, promised to consider the report seriously.[13] The LDP/Sakigake/SDP 'Project Team' now led by Ishii Kōki[14] agreed on the need for some further extension of the projects and measures to support the elimination of discrimination. Its response to the Iken Gushin was worked out over the summer and included recommending giving priority to Dōwa education and support for *keihatsu*, creating a legal framework to deal with human rights violations, and establishing a legal basis for a few improvement projects that would continue for a maximum of five years. The LDP side wanted just 15 projects to be continued, the SDP/DPJ suggested 37. On 26 July, the Cabinet endorsed just 15, which gives a clear indication of who was in charge (Dōwa Gyōseishi Henshū Iinkai, 2002, 508–12). Nevertheless, the *Iken Gushin* was welcomed by the BLL at its conference held in September 1996 as evidence of the government's commitment to a legal basis to deal with discrimination and provide redress in cases of human rights violations.

The final years

The result of the 1996 election left no party with a majority but the LDP was by far the largest party with 239 seats and the successor to JSP, the SDP, reduced to only 15 seats. The left of centre Democratic Party of Japan, the party which would replace the JSP as the main opposition party in the twenty-first century, only got 52. Thus, there was no effective opposition to the LDP. The BLL had optimistically concluded that the introduction of a Basic Law was close when its conference met in September 1996 but by the end of the year all that had been put on to the statute books was a Law to Promote Measures to Protect Human Rights and a cabinet agreement on 3 December to set up a *shingikai* to consider new measures for human rights protection.

Thereafter, the policy process can be divided into two streams. There was a series of measures introduced between 1997 and 2002 that amounted to the running down and tidying up of the remaining Dōwa policy projects in preparation for the termination of the SML on 31 March 2002. Meanwhile, and in parallel, there was the evolution of the Dōwa/Chiiki Kaizen policy framework into something which promised to address human rights issues more broadly.

If we take the latter theme first: the Human Rights Policy Promotion Law (Jinken Hogo Shisaku Suishinhō) of December 1996 led to the creation of the *Jinken Hogo Shisaku Suishinkai* in March 1997, a *shingikai* charged with the promotion of a more general human rights policy and in particular with making suggestions for the development of human rights education within two years and a human rights violation redress mechanism within five. It owed its existence to the 1996 Iken Gushin and the subsequent recommendations of the Project Team on Human Rights and Discrimination. It defined its remit as including gender, HIV, sexual orientation, foreigners resident in Japan as well as Dōwa issues and produced its first report in 1999 on the promotion of human rights in schools, public institutions, and through the mass media (Dōwa Gyōseishi Henshū Iinkai, 2002, 69–70). This amounts to the 'generalisation' of the desire that the various incarnations of the Chitaikyō had expressed to promote *keihatsu*, human rights education in a broad sense. Also, in 1996, Cabinet ordered a review of the work of the Chiiki Kaizen Keihatsu Sentaa (established 1987) that resulted in its transformation into the Jinken Kyōiku Keihatsu Suishin Sentaa (Center for Human Rights Education and Training) on 1 April 1997. Its first head was Miyazaki Shigeki, until 31 March that year chair of the Chitaikyō. He served in that position until 2006.[15]

In 2001, the *shingikai* made some suggestions on the formation of a permanent commission to promote human rights protection and redress for human rights violations (Dōwa Gyōseishi Henshū Iinkai, 2002, 557–9). Following the suggestion in the Iken Gushin about the importance of creating a human rights enforcement mechanism, it emphasised that it should be independent of the government. It looked as though these proposals might have a chance of being implemented when in 2002 a discussion group on human rights was created from members of the LDP and Kōmeitō chaired by Nonaka Hiromu, someone who had succeeded in rising through the ranks of the LDP despite having never hidden his Buraku background. This process of the proposals of a *shingikai*-like body being endorsed by a group of elected politicians was starting to look similar to that which had led to the various extensions of the SML. It did indeed make some serious proposals for the creation of a human rights commission but they were never taken forward. Since then, further proposals for a human rights commission have been put forward from time to time but so far without any results (Croydon, 2017).

Meanwhile, funding for the 15 Dōwa projects (only nine of them for 'hard' projects) had been built into the Budget for FY1997. A partial revision of the 1992 law was agreed by cabinet on 7 February 1997 and passed through the 140th Diet on 28 March authorising funding for the Chiiki Kaizen projects for a final five-year period. The Dōwa/Chiiki Kaizen budgets for the Sōmuchō, MoJ, MAFF, and MHA were cut completely but the MoE budgets only reduced from ¥8,748m to ¥5,557m p.a. across the five years (total ¥34,152m). The MITI budget remained broadly unchanged at just over ¥9,000m per year and the MoC budget was reduced from ¥42,468m to

¥19,101m across the final years; a total of ¥146,494m, which though significantly less than the peak years of the 1980s, was still more than twice the size of its spending in the first five years of Dōwa spending (¥69,739m) (more detail in the next chapter).

The Chitaikyō ceased to exist as of 1 April 1997 and it looked as though the SML really would come to an end in March 2002. This was by no means certain though since every previous time that the SML had been extended, it had been accompanied by statements to the effect that this would be the last extension and then the Chitaikyō or its equivalent had been revived. However, in January 2001, the Sōmushō[16] issued a statement explaining why the Dōwa policy would not be further extended. First, it argued that the living conditions within the 'target areas' had been substantially improved by the projects implemented over the previous 30 years. This had reduced differences between Buraku communities and their neighbours such that the circular relationship between poverty and prejudice/discrimination had been broken. Second, it was argued that there could be no certainty that continuing the special projects would further contribute towards eliminating prejudice. This seems to be a veiled reference to the accusations of 'reverse discrimination' and the 'envy' (*netami*) still present in the mainstream population in certain areas. Finally, the Sōmushō argued that it had become increasingly difficult to administer Dōwa projects especially in urban areas due to people with Buraku heritage moving out and those without such a background moving in. This seems to be a restatement of previous concerns about the difficulty of administering projects 'fairly', that is, in a way which did not require the intercession of movement representatives to identify who should receive benefits (Dōwa Gyōseishi Henshū Iinkai, 2002, 78–9). One way round this difficulty might have been to change the definition of who was eligible but by this time one suspects that the brief of those responsible for the policy in the Sōmushō was to justify the termination of the Dowa programme, not its extension and certainly not to find new definitions of the problem.

The LDP maintained a Special Committee on Regional Improvement Policy (Chiiki Kaizen Taisaku) within the PARC (chair: Iwasaki Junzō) and on 20 June 2001 it reported on the school grants system and the transfer of funding for housing projects to general budgets. The following week, a cross-party discussion group composed of representatives of parties in the ruling coalition (LDP, Kōmeitō and the Conservative Party) considered the views of the LDP committee and made a submission to the CCS, Fukuda Yasuo, and Sōmushō minister, Katayama Toranosuke, with three sets of recommendations about a new system for human rights promotion, on funding for the high school grant support system to be operated through prefectures, and transitional measures to support small-scale housing improvement projects after 2002 (Dōwa Gyōseishi Henshū Iinkai, 2002, 80–1). The latter recommendation looks like provision being made for the undesignated Buraku communities that had concerned the BLL from the late

1980s. After September 2001, the LDP Special Committee on Regional Improvement Policy now chaired by Kumashiro Akihiko continued discussion about the developing human rights administration.

National funding for all of the material projects came to an end in March 2002 but funding continued for the scheme that supported young people at high school through a new organisational structure. From April 2002, being a Dōwa community was no longer in itself a sufficient reason for it to benefit for infrastructural improvements; it was now down to the municipality or prefecture to decide on its own priorities. The 'office' originally set up as the Dōwa Taisakuhitsu within the PMO in 1984 and later renamed the Chiiki Kaizen Taisakuhitsu within the Sōmuchō ceased to exist on 31 March 2002. The Jinken Keihatsu Chūō Shochō Renraku Kyogikai (Central Liaison Council for Human Rights Education) in the MoJ continued to exist as a coordinating body for the exchange of information about education on human rights protection within the structure of central government (Dōwa Gyōseishi Henshū Iinkai, 2002, 84–5). Meanwhile, the government commitment to address the *ese-Dōwa* problem was renewed with the revision of the brief of the '*ese-Dōwa* Activity Policy Liaison Council' in March 2002.

On 29 March 2002, the Sōmushō published the following statement:

> The government has positively promoted various related measures over a period of thirty-three years since 1969 for the rapid resolution of the Dōwa problem centred on special measures funded through the SML that was established in three stages. With the expiry at the end of March of the final special law [...], the special measures which targeted Dōwa communities and Dōwa related people will come to an end.
>
> Dōwa related measures embraced the conclusions of the Dōtaishin of 1965 and were implemented with the aim of rapidly improving the poor economic circumstances and living environment of the Dōwa districts and by these policies planned to resolve the Dōwa problem, that is to eliminate Buraku discrimination.
>
> Following many years of effort by central and local governments the circumstances in which the very poor living environment recreated discrimination have been greatly improved and education aimed at the elimination of discriminatory attitudes has been encouraged in original and creative ways. As a result of these great changes in the circumstances surrounding Dōwa districts the central government has terminated all special policies. Henceforth the districts which have benefited from special measures will be eligible for the implementation of suitable and appropriate policies as necessary on the same basis as other districts.
>
> Furthermore, it is our intention to take measures necessary to promote in a comprehensive manner the protection of human rights in a number of ways through the establishment of a new system and to set out a basic plan to promote human rights education.

> We would like to express our gratitude and respect for the assistance and cooperation from all who have been involved with the policy so far including the local authorities.
>
> (Dōwa Gyōseishi Henshū Iinkai, 2002, 83–4)

Conclusion

Dōwa policy then at the national level did not so much stop as gradually fade away, becoming transformed into a generalised but ultimately weak commitment to human rights promotion and protection. The decade of the 1990s had held the potential at its start to see the transformation of rights policy in Japan from being focused on Buraku issues to becoming a firm and broad commitment to human rights protection and promotion in line with international norms. There was support for that across the party-political spectrum and within the Dōwa policymaking framework: from Isomura through to the Zenkoku Jiyū Dōwa groups and the BLL. By 2002, this potential remained unfulfilled. What had happened instead was that as the scope of Dōwa material projects was tapered down so in parallel was the breadth of commitment to consolidating human rights policy. The more expansive, liberal approach to rights issues promoted in the 1996 Iken Gushin can be accounted for by the influence of non-LDP representatives who served on the 'project team' and in government posts during the brief period 1994–7. Once the LDP resumed control of the policy process, enthusiasm for human rights ebbed.

A pattern emerged by which the SML was incrementally extended from the initial ten-year period to continue in the end for a total of 33 years. In the year prior to expiration of the SML, the movement groups would take a position, invariably recommending extension; the Dōwa/Chiiki Kaizen Kyōgikai would meet several times before issuing a report usually in the December in the year before expiry, sometimes also commissioning a survey to provide background to their recommendations; in parallel with this, the Dōwa policy group within the LDP would convene a series of meetings that would organise support for the extension of Dōwa programmes sometimes trying to set parameters on what the new programme should contain. This would result in a bill endorsed by cabinet in the first few weeks of the following year which would pass through both houses of the Diet with the support of all the parties with the exception of the JCP which would argue for major revision or rejection of the proposal.

During the first ten years, 1969–78, the process was open to input from the opposition parties, especially the JSP, and from the movement groups, notably the BLL and Zen Nihon Dōwakai. However, when the Chiiki Kyōgikai was reconvened in 1981 after a gap of three years, the representatives of the Buraku communities were excluded and thereafter could make no direct input into the policy process, rather having to wait until invited to make a submission. From this point onwards, decision making was routinised and the scope of Dōwa policy incrementally reduced. No significant changes were made in either content or the philosophy which informed Dōwa policy although the overall size of the Dōwa budget gradually decreased from a peak in the early 1980s. This was not because there were no new suggestions. Indeed, the BLL from the early 1980s in its suggestions for a Basic Law on Buraku Liberation proposed a series of ways in which policy could have been re-imagined so that it would have embedded the Dōwa programmes into a structure that committed Japan to the protection and promotion of the human rights of residents of Buraku communities as well as the propagation of human rights ideas within Japanese society more generally. Instead, Dōwa policy was envisioned as an administrative process with ends clearly defined such that it was possible to argue in the early years of twenty-first century that its task had been completed. One marker of this is the length of the reports produced by the policy council which in the 1970s had stretched to several hundred pages but by the 1990s were no more than a perfunctory couple.

The only deviation from the pattern took place in the middle of the 1990s at a point when a renewed commitment to the international human rights framework coincided with the prime ministership of Murayama Tomiichi of the JSP and the creation under him of a Human Rights and Discrimination policy 'project team' which included non-LDP Diet members. Even so, the LDP retained ultimate control over the process so that although the Iken Gushin of 1996 went further than it might have liked, it did not form the basis for either SML extension beyond 2002 or a new policy that committed the state to human rights through creation of a new administrative apparatus.

However, there was nothing to prevent local governments from continuing to devise and fund their own Dōwa projects, apart from the criticism from the JCP-linked groups. They just would no longer be able to access state subsidies for them. We will discuss some of these post-SML projects in the section on regional Dōwa policy implementation, Chapter 8, following a résumé of the roles played by each of the main ministries in the next chapter.

Notes

1 For more details on Horiki, see Chapter 5, p. 16.
2 For biographical details of Isomura Eichi, see Chapter 1, pp. 12–3.
3 'The industrial reserve army, during the periods of stagnation and average prosperity, weighs down the active army of workers; during the periods of over-production and feverish activity, it puts a curb on their pretensions'. K Marx, Capital Vol 1, Penguin Books, 1976, 792.
4 Full list of the membership: Isomura Eichi, Irisawa Wataru (Yokohama National University, ex-MoC, Professor of Town Planning), Uemura Hajime (Head, Welfare and Medical Service Agency), Kariya Shirō (Governor of Wakayama, 1975–95), Kitagawa Yoshio (Mayor, Neyagawa-shi, Osaka, 1970–83), Satō Kunio (Head, National Civil Liberties Commissioners Council), Shiraichi Haruki

(Governor of Ehime 1971–87, LDP/Tanaka faction), Yamauchi Kazuo (Gakushuin University, Law Dept, ex-Cabinet Legislation Bureau), Yamamoto Noboru (Osaka City University, Dept Sociology, research on urban sociology and Buraku issues), Yokoshima Akira (Utsunomiya University, Educational Psychology, author of two books on Buraku discrimination, 1984, 1992).

5 Maeda Isao, 1943–2016, was a law graduate of Keiō University. His father, Kazuo, had been elected to the HC from Wakayama prefecture in 1956 and following his death in 1978 Isao stood as an LDP candidate in the by-election. He was subsequently re-elected on three more occasions serving as the Minister of Justice for 13 months during 1994–6. He was defeated by a Liberal Party candidate in 1998 and never returned to the national political stage.

6 *Sōkaiya*, are specialised racketeers, associated with the *yakuza*. They blackmail companies by threatening to publicly humiliate their management, usually in their annual general meeting (*sōkai*). Alternatively, they demand payments to prevent others from embarrassing the company by disrupting the annual meetings.

7 Interestingly, the same page of the *Asahi* newspaper which carried the report about the Kita-Kyushu case carried a summary of the appeal by Tanaka Kakuei against his sentence for involvement in the Lockheed scandal (Asahi Shimbun, 21 October 1983).

8 Horiuchi Toshio, 1918–2009, was elected three times to the post of mayor of Tenri-shi, Nara prefecture and then to the HC in 1976 where he represented the LDP until 1989. He was the chair of the HC Education committee during 1982–3 and served briefly as the Minister of the Environment during 1987–8.

9 Kumashiro Akihiko, b 1940, graduate of Dept of Law, Tokyo University, joined the MHA in 1963 and took a master's degree at Wisconsin University in 1970 later moving to MHW. He retired from MHW in 1993 to stand for the HR in Okayama 1 as an LDP candidate. He opposed Koizumi's post office privatisation policy and lost his seat in the election of August 2005. He became active in local politics in 2011 and at the time of writing was a member of the Okayama city council.

10 Isomura plus the four university professors (town planning, administrative law, sociology, and educational psychology) the then senior vice minister at the Sōmuchō plus two other members of the full Chitaikyō who were former bureaucrats. Dōwa Gyōseishi Henshū Iinkai (2002, 396).

11 For comparison, it is estimated that in 1989 the BLL had around 300,000 members and the Zenkairen 80,000.

12 Yamaguchi Tsuruo 1925–2015, originally a primary school teacher, was one of the architects of the JSP/LDP coalition and rewarded with the cabinet post of head of Sōmuchō June 1994–August 1995.

13 Nakanishi Sekisuke, 1926- , LDP Diet member for Fukuoka 1976–2003, was born in Tagawa-gun, Kawara machi. His appointment was welcomed by local politicians as being good for the prospects of SML extension.

14 Ishii Kōki, 1940–2002, a Diet member from 1993 first in Horikawa's New Party but in 1996 he joined the DPJ and won a reputation for investigating corrupt practice within government. He was murdered in 2002.

15 The Jinken Kyōiku Keihatsu Suishin Sentaa located in Tokyo continues to exist (as of 2021). It operates a human rights library and convenes conferences on such topics as Corporate Social Responsibility and Human Rights and seminars on *ese-Dōwa* issues with the support of the MoJ Human Rights bureau.

16 What was previously the Management and Coordination Agency (Sōmuchō) was up-graded to ministerial status in the reforms of 2001 to become the Sōmushō with the English name of Ministry of Internal Affairs and Communications.

Bibliography

Asahi Shimbun various dates.

Chiiki Kaizen Taisaku Kenkyūsho (ed), (1986) *Chiiki Kaizen Taisaku Jigyō: sono chōsa to bunseki* (Regional Improvement Policy Projects: surveys and analysis), Tokyo: Gyōsei.

Croydon S., (2017) 'Progress or Prevarication?: The Move Toward the Establishment of a Human Rights Commission in Japan', *Human Rights Quarterly*, vol. 39, no. 2, 369–92.

Dōwa Gyōseishi Henshū Iinkai (Dōwa Administration History Editorial Committee), (2002) *Dōwa Gyōseishi* (A History of Dōwa Administration), Tokyo: Sōmuchō Daijin Kanbō Chiiki Kaizen Taisakuhitsu.

Hankins J. D., (2014) *Working Skin, Making Leather, Making a Multicultural Japan*, Berkeley: University of California Press.

Hayashida C. T., (1975) 'The Koshinjo and Tanteisha', *Journal of Asian and African Studies*, vol. 10, no. 3–4, 198–208.

Kadooka N., (2005) *Hajimete no Burakumondai* (Introduction to Buraku Issues), Tokyo: Bunshun Shinshō.

Kanai K., (1991) *Dōwa Gyōsei: Sengo no Kiseki* (Dōwa Administration: the postwar path), Osaka: Buraku Kaihō Shuppansha.

Kingston J., (2004) *Japan's Quiet Transformation: Social Change and Civil Society in the Twenty-first Century*, London: RoutledgeCurzon.

Krogness K. J., (2008) *The Koseki System and 'Koseki Consciousness': An Exploration of the Development and Functions of the Modern Japanese Household Registration System and How It Influences Social Life*, PhD Dissertation, University of Copenhagen, Institute of Cross-Cultural and Regional Studies, Japanese Section.

Mainichi Shimbun, *Sabetsu no Jittai* (The Reality of Discrimination – interview with Asada Zennosuke), 14 February to 1 March1975.

Mainichi Shimbun, *Sabetsu e no Kenkai* (A View on Discrimination – interview with Sakaki Toshio) 2 to 19 March 1975.

Marx K., (1976) *Capital Vol 1*, Harmondsworth: Penguin Books.

Mizuuchi T., (1998) 'Private Struggles, Public Supports: renovating Japanese Minority Community, Buraku', *Osaka Shiritsu Daigaku, Dōwa Mondai Kenkyū*, vol. 20, 29–43.

Murakoshi S., Watanabe T., Miwa Y., Umehara T., and Tomonaga K., (1989) *Buraku Kaihōshi* [A History of Buraku Liberation], Osaka: Kaihō Shuppansha.

Neary I., (1986) 'Socialist and Communist Party Attitudes towards Discrimination against Japan's *Burakumin*', *Political Studies*, vol. XXXIV, no 4, 556–74.

Neary I., (2002) *Human Rights in Japan, South Korea and Taiwan*, Abingdon: Routledge.

Noguchi M. and Ishimoto K., (2014) *Buraku Jittai Chōsa no Shoshiteki Kenkyū* (A Bibliographical Study of Surveys in Buraku Conditions), Kyoto: Sekai Jinken Mondai Kenkyū Sentaa.

Onishi Y., (2009) 'Buraku Kaihō Undō' (The Buraku Liberation Movement), in Osaka Shakai Undō Kyōkai (ed) *Osaka Shakai Rōdō Undōshi* [A History of the Social and Workers Movements in Osaka], Osaka: Osaka Shakai Undō Kyōkai, pp. 692–706.

Pharr S., (1990) *Losing Face: Status Politics in Japan*, Berkeley: University of California Press.

Rohlen T. P., (1976) 'Violence at Yoka High School: The Implications for Japanese Coalition Politics of the Confrontation between the Communist Party and the Buraku Liberation League', *Asian Survey*, vol. 16, no. 7, 682–99.

Suginohara J., 'Sengo Dōwa Gyōsei no Tenkai to Shihai Seisaku' (The Evolution of Postwar Dōwa Administration and Ruling Policies), *Jinken to Buraku Mondai*, Kyoto: Buraku Mondai Kenkyūjo,

No. 754, January 2007, pp. 69–78.

No. 757, March 2007, pp. 75–80.

No.758, April 2007, pp. 73–80.

No 759, May 2007, pp. 72–77.

No 760, June 2007, pp. 74–80.

Teraki N. and Kurokawa M., (2019) *A History of Discriminated Buraku Communities in Japan*, trans. Ian Neary, Folkeston: Renaissance Books.

Tsutsui K., (2018) *Rights Make Might: Global Human Rights and Minority Social Movements in Japan*, Oxford: Oxford Scholarship On Line.

Upham F., (1980) 'Ten Years of Affirmative Action for Japanese Burakumin: A Preliminary Report on the Law on Special Measures for Dōwa Projects', *Law in Japan*, vol. 13, 39–73.

7 Implementation II

Spending on Dōwa policy projects by the main ministries

In some states, the launch of a policy supported by a constellation of programmes would be the occasion for the creation of an agency or institution dedicated to the solution of the newly identified problem. Or, at the very least, given that it was clear that the Dōwa issue was not amenable to resolution through the efforts of a single ministry or agency, a first priority would be to establish a powerful coordinating mechanism. This did not happen. As Upham noted, '…the central government has never chosen to exercise any significant role in the formulation of *dōwa* policy' (Upham, 1980, 47). Instead, in a continuation of the pattern already established, individual Dōwa projects were administered within Buraku communities and supervised by local government officers with only the broad pattern of Dōwa policy spending decided at the national level within the separate ministries.

In the words of clause 8 of the SML,

> Local authorities must endeavour to provide the necessary facilities in conformity with national measures.

Thus, responsibility for Dōwa policy implementation was pushed downwards.

Why the government adopted this approach is not clear and does not seem to have been explicitly discussed. It may be that it was felt that the Dōwa issue was a problem that really could be resolved within not much more than ten years so that no elaborate policy mechanism was necessary. Indeed, to adopt a view taken by the Zenkairen later in the century, it may have been thought that to create a permanent institution would risk embedding the issue into the framework of government in a way that would hinder rather than help the rapid resolution of the problem. Or, it may simply be that they did not anticipate that the Dōwa policy budget would grow as rapidly as it did from the mid-1970s.

However, it is also consistent with a broader pattern in which very little change took place within the overall pattern of government between the early 1950s and the restructuring of the central government in 2001. Apart from the upgrading of the Agency for Local Autonomy to ministerial

DOI: 10.4324/9781003127994-7

status in 1960, until 2001 most additions to the machinery of the state were achieved through the creation of a new agency that was then located within the PMO. We saw this with the Economic Planning Agency (1953), the Self Defence Agency (1954), and the Environment Agency (1971) among others.

No Dōwa Policy Agency was ever proposed. Instead, Dōwa policy was promoted and coordinated through the Dōwa Taisaku Kyōgikai set up in 1966 composed of senior members of the related ministries and ten 'people of expertise' plus, in the first instance, a sub-committee of the cabinet. The latter was replaced in 1974 by a Dōwa Policy Office (Dōwa Taisakushitsu) located in the PMO, later re-named the Regional Improvement Policy office (Chiiki Kaizen Taisakushitsu) in 1982. Its institutional location was transferred to the Sōmuchō when that agency was reorganised and strengthened in 1985. The 'office' remained there until it was dismantled in March 2002 marking the end of the final phase of the SML.

In the previous chapter, we traced the political process that guided the development of Dōwa policy between the late 1960s up to the start of the twenty-first century. In this chapter, we will be concerned rather to look at the administrative process and what kind of projects the Dōwa funding was spent on. In other words, to answer the question: what was the outcome of the demands that the Japanese state should enact a Dōwa policy? We will largely concern ourselves here with the national level of Dōwa policy and look at some examples of local Dōwa policy administration in the following chapter.

Initial policy evolution

As we saw in Chapter 5, some ministries began to respond in a piecemeal way to requests from Buraku groups and local governments to support Dōwa projects during the 1950s. MHW was the first of these and set up a coordinating committee, Chihō Kaizen Kyōgikai, that operated during 1953–8. As first the JSP and then some members of the LDP began to articulate demands for a more coherent policy; a Dōwa policy agenda began to emerge. The initial governmental response to this was the creation of a discussion group at cabinet-level, the Dōwa Mondai Zadankai, on 17 October 1958 under the chairmanship of the deputy head of the Cabinet Secretariat composed of representatives from the MoJ, MoF, MoE, MHW, MAFF, MITI, MoC, and the Local Autonomy Agency. Each of these ministries would then go on to be represented on the *shingikai* that met between 1961 and 1965 and produced the Dōtaishin.

In March 1966, the PMO law was amended to establish the Dōwa Taisaku Kyōgikai to 'promote close relations between the administrative agencies' responsible for the promotion of Dōwa policies (Dōwa Gyōseishi Henshū Iinkai, 2002, 272). This was duly established by June the same year and in the following February, it produced a draft Long-Term Plan (LTP) for the implementation of Dōwa policy. This not only set out some of the basic administrative framework – that it should be a Ten-Year Programme divided into two five-year sections – but it also suggested that more surveys of current conditions were needed for the ministries to make their plans. It set out what it thought were the main areas to be addressed and suggested a division of ministerial responsibility. For example, the main pillars of policy on the living environment should be:

- Improving housing (MoC),
- Improving roads, drains, water provision, and town planning, including play areas (MHW, MOC), and
- Provision of facilities such as *Rinpokan*, nurseries, and social welfare facilities (MHW, MoE).

Education policy should be devised by the MHW/MoE/MoL and community policies by MHW, MoE, MAFF, and MoJ. Finally, economic policies were to be the responsibility of the MoL, MoE, and MHW in the areas of employment but MAFF and MoL for agricultural matters and the SME Agency and MHW for industrial issues. The 1967 draft also set out a timetable for the development of policy leading to the implementation of the plan in April 1969. This timetable was more or less adhered to.

Two days before the SML was formally promulgated on 8 July 1969, the Dōwa Policy LTP was approved by the Cabinet. Based on the 1967 policy draft, this set out the main policy areas to be owned by each of the key ministries – MoJ, MoE, MHW, MAFF, MITI, MoL, MoC – and outlined the kind of policies they would need to devise within these parameters each aiming at 'eliminating the various obstructions that prevent the improvement of the social and economic situation of the residents of Dōwa communities' (Dōwa Gyōseishi Henshū Iinkai, 2002, 317). So, while it is true that in the words of Frank Upham the SML promulgated on 10 July 1969 *itself* 'gave broad authority for government action while mandating virtually nothing', launching the Dōwa policy programmes was more than simply a 'political statement in statutory form' when taken together with the LTP which had been approved two days earlier (both quotes from Upham, 1987, 86). This was confirmed at the end of the month by a memorandum sent out to prefectural governors, mayors of scheduled cities, local education committees, and vice ministers in the eight ministries encouraging them to implement the Dōwa SML. Moreover, this was followed up by similar memos sent out in 1971, 1973, and 1975 (Dōwa Gyōseishi Henshū Iinkai, 2002, 327, 328, 329). These suggested that local governments should formulate projects to be funded by the central ministries either individually or in collaboration. We will return to the topic of the evolution of Dōwa policy at the local level in Chapter 8 but for the rest of this chapter, I want to say a little more about planning for and spending on Dōwa projects at the national level.

Development of the spending pattern

The overall patterns of spending are clear from Table 7.1 and Figures 7.1 and 7.2. They show how rapidly it increased during the mid- to late 1970s and then declined gradually from a peak in the mid-1980s. This expenditure was organised in two contrasting ways: thematically and by ministry. The available literature on Dōwa policy that emanates from the ministries devotes a great deal of space to the presentation of data showing exactly what these ministries spent their money on although many questions remain both unasked and unanswered, prominent among which are how did the individual ministries set their priorities? What kind of coordination existed between ministries particularly when they were both working on the same theme? And, what was the process through which the ministries made their case to the MoF to demand their share of the Dōwa cake? To answer such questions would require access to the decision-making processes inside each ministry which we simply do not have. The best we can do is to describe the main patterns in which the expenditure was organised firstly by looking at how spending was organised across the different periods and then how each ministry spent its money (Table 7.2; Figure 7.3).

Table 7.3 maps out the main responsibilities of Dōwa policy for each ministry across the period 1969–2002. This shows that the main policy areas follow the topics that were prioritised in the Dōtaishin – improvement to living conditions, improvements to social welfare, promotion of industry and employment, improvements to education, and promotion and protection of human rights – and then elaborated in the LTP published in summer 1969. These concerns provided the framework for Dōwa policy until the very final quinquennium, 1997–2001. Despite the debates that took place within the Dōtaikyō and Chitaikyō over the years, there was very little change in the kind of policies carried out by the various ministries or the division of responsibility between them.

The reports based on the 1993 surveys generated a bewildering amount of data on spending patterns. These are summarised in Tables 7.4 and 7.5 which show that more than half of all the Dōwa budget was spent in the Kinki region and suggest that around half of all Dōwa spending came from the municipalities. Moreover, despite the complaints expressed in evidence given to the Dōtaikyō and Chitaikyō over the 1980s and 1990s about the extent of the burden being imposed on municipalities, this burden gradually increased across the decades.

Between 1969 and 2002, Dōwa projects on average consumed around 4.1% of budgetary expenditure in those 1,094 municipalities which implemented them. However, the breakdown of municipal spending by regional block in Table 7.4 shows how there was wide regional variation from 7.2% in Shikoku to 1.1% in Kanto. Moreover, the data which shows Dōwa spending by prefecture suggests an even wider variation: 14.3%, 15.3%, 13.6% in Kōchi, Wakayama, and Nara but only 0.1%, 0.3%, and 0.4% in Nagasaki, Niigata,

Table 7.1 Total Dōwa Spending FY1953–2001 by Ministry

F/Year	**Sōmu**		**MoJ**		**MoE**		**MHW**		**MAFF**		**MITI**		**MoL**		**MoC**		**MHA**	**P**	**Total**
	¥m	*P*	*¥m*	*P*	*¥m*	*P*	*¥m*	*P*	*¥m*	*P*	*¥m*	*P*	*¥m*	*P*	*¥m*	*P*	*¥m*		
1953																			13
1954							12												12
1955							11												11
1956							12												12
1957							14												14
1958							24												24
1959					1		50												51
1960					5		134		22						238				399
1961	1				16		203		28						391				639
1962	4				16		263		46						439				822
1963	5				21		333		69				1		758				1187
1964	2				32		425		100				1		772				1332
1965	2				45		532		125				1		1143				1848
1966	2				77		687		163		13		17		2452				3411
1967	12				111		961		228		18		23		2688				4041
1968	5		1		152		1344		318		22		27		2118				3987
Sub-total Pre-SML	**33**		**1**		**476**		**5018**		**1099**		**53**		**70**		**11053**				**17803**
1969	5	1	1	1	213	9	1873	18	446	1	32	1	31	3	3616	5			6217
1970	6	1	2	2	338	9	3094	24	669	1	50	1	53	4	7681	7			11893
1971	43	2	4	2	506	9	4804	25	1836	3	105	3	72	4	13521	7			20891
1972	9	2	5	2	769	9	7054	26	2841	4	621	6	126	5	19946	8	35	1	31406
1973	15	3	8	2	1173	10	10399	26	4261	4	1372	7	250	6	24975	9	77	2	42530
1974	26	3	12	3	1771	10	14967	28	6180	5	2834	8	414	7	31197	11	112	2	57513
1975	84	4	52	5	2788	10	21245	28	8913	8	5149	9	740	8	43174	13	162	3	82307
1976	76	3	48	5	4001	10	27837	28	12451	8	8692	9	1183	8	53287	13	230	4	107805
1977	101	3	44	5	5374	10	35915	28	17695	11	13942	9	1542	10	64256	14	331	4	139200
1978	122	3	53	5	6676	10	45933	29	25361	11	19220	9	1932	11	84573	15	448	4	184318

1979	148	3	64	4	8033	10	56579	29	33278	11	24445	9	2419	12	100956	16	602	5	226524
1980	176	3	78	4	9366	10	62783	28	39302	11	25938	10	2895	12	111194	16	750	5	252482
1981	226	3	97	4	10551	10	70704	28	44240	11	28107	10	3315	13	121058	16	937	5	279235
Sub-total 1969–81	**1037**		**468**		**51559**		**363187**		**197473**		**130507**		**144972**		**679434**		**3684**		**1442321**
1982	268	1	115	2	10795	9	70459	11	43797	9	28229	5	3341	6	116599	11	928	1	274531
1983	314	1	128	2	10906	9	57861	11	36254	9	26255	5	3454	6	102387	11	834	1	238394
1984	359	1	142	2	11015	9	47460	11	33187	9	23797	5	3506	6	94660	11	726	1	214852
1985	407	1	155	2	11300	9	45516	11	31545	9	21355	5	3613	6	96065	11	653	1	210610
1986	452	1	168	2	11538	9	45549	11	31424	9	19412	5	3792	6	101548	11	607	1	214489
Sub-total 1982–6	**180000**		**708**		**55554**		**266845**		**176207**		**119048**		**17706**		**511259**		**3748**		**1152876**
1987	497	1	184	2	11541	9	44488	11	29176	9	13345	5	1033	6	90128	11	558	1	190949
1988	548	1	206	2	11677	9	37977	11	24812	9	11319	5	1062	6	91072	11	500	1	179173
1989	605	1	230	2	11894	9	37210	11	22078	9	10299	5	1122	6	80525	11	456	1	164419
1990	663	1	257	2	12043	9	36925	11	17746	9	10270	5	1174	6	71883	11	411	1	151372
1991	725	1	284	2	12243	9	38324	11	18390	9	10241	5	1230	6	74048	11	454	1	155940
1992	800	1	317	2	12297	7	33961	9	13089	7	10212	4	1261	5	58411	9	411	1	130761
1993	1207	1	351	2	12360	7	30042	9	12040	7	10190	4	1295	5	55919	9	362	1	123767
1994	994	1	387	2	12397	7	27756	9	11519	7	10189	4	1330	5	57389	9	350	1	122311
1995	1076	1	425	2	12211	7	24614	9	11567	7	10170	4	1368	5	58183	9	324	1	119938
1996	1181	1	465	2	12262	7	30072	9	10668	7	10156	4	1403	5	59615	9	193	1	126015
1997					8748	1	39	1	76	2	9461	2	899	2	42468	6			61691
1998					7455	1	32				9375	2	803	2	32989	5			50654
1999					6758	1	24	1			9290	2	724	2	31283	5			48079
2000					5904	1	16	1			9195	2	652	2	20653	5			36420
2001					5557	1	9	1			9096	2	583	2	19101	5			34345
Sub-total 1987–2002	**8296**		**3106**		**155347**		**341489**		**171161**		**152808**		**15939**		**843667**		**4019**		**1695834**
1969–2001	111135		4282		262457		971524		544840		402362		48617		2034360		11455		4291031
TOTAL	**11167**		**4283**		**262944**		**976544**		**545935**		**402415**		**48685**		**2045413**		**11455**		**4308830**

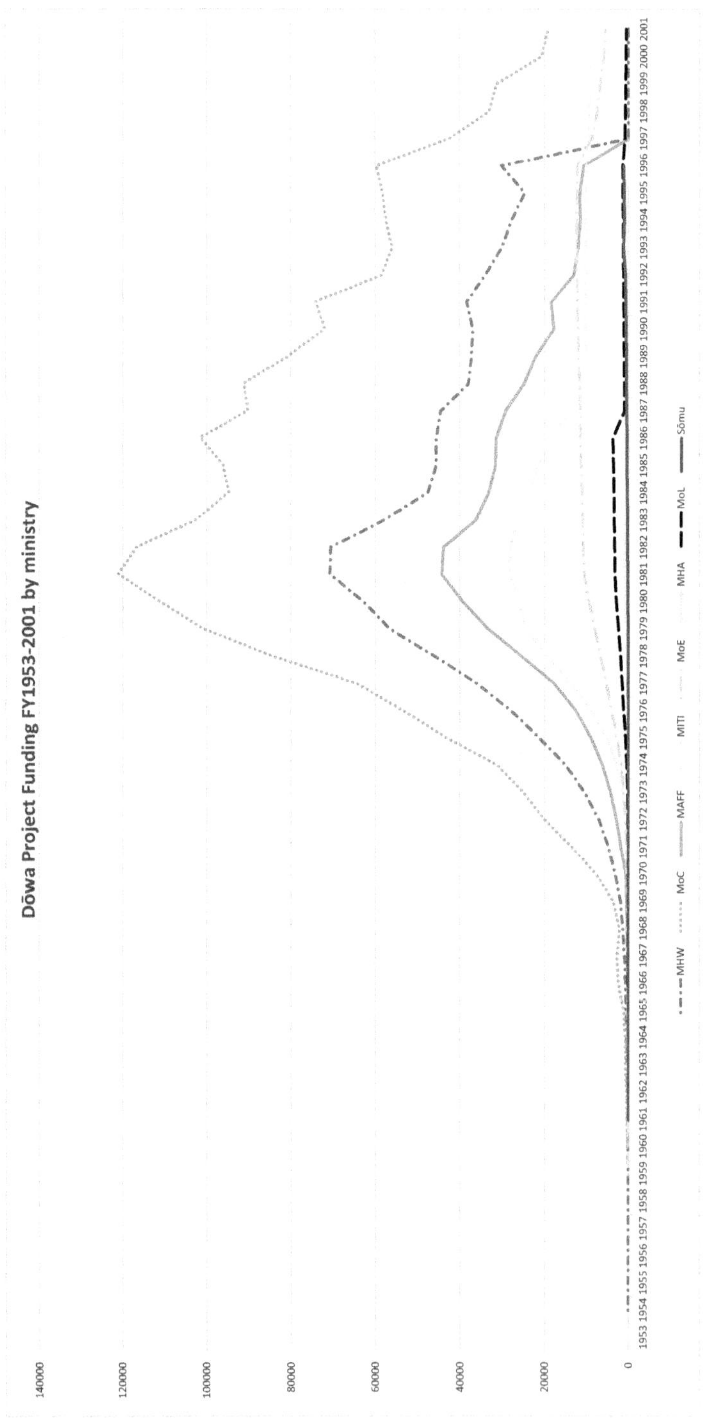

Figure 7.1 Dōwa project funding FY1953–2001 by ministry.

Table 7.2 Total Dōwa Policy Spending after 1969 – by Level of Government

	Total	*State*	*Prefecture (36)*	*Municipality (1094)*
TOTAL	13,363,304	3,691,578	2,794,849	6,876,877
1969–81	4,962,670	1,442,321	1,075,492	2,444,857
1982–6	3,781,961	1152876	776694	1,852,391
1987–92	3,370,635	841,853	678,772	1,850,010
1993–4	1,248,038	254,528	263,891	729,619

Unit: ¥ Million.
Dōwa Gyōseishi Henshū Iinkai (2002, 910).

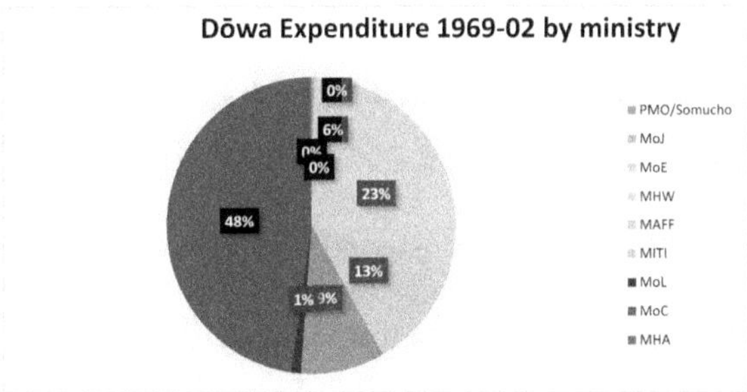

Figure 7.2 Pattern of Dōwa spending FY1969–2002 by ministry.

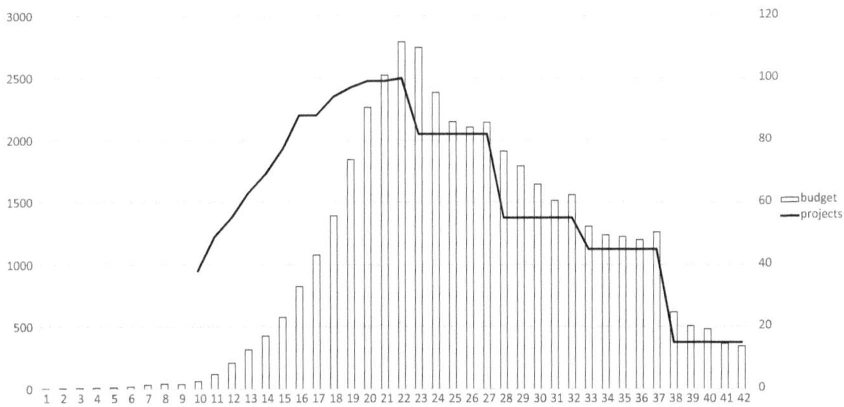

Figure 7.3 Total Dōwa spending and total projects FY1960–2001.

and Kanagawa (Dōwa Gyōseishi Henshū Iinkai, 2002, 909). The differences in the burden on prefectural budgets for the projects they took charge of are overall not so extreme but what stands out here is the relatively small proportion of the cost born by the state in the Kinki region only 12.4% at a time when in the rest of west Japan the state's share was around one-third. This reflects not only the presence of Dōwa communities in these prefectures but also the degree of political activity in those communities.

A careful examination of the tables contained in the Appendix will demonstrate that over the 33 years of the Dowa policy projects, there were some incremental changes made in the shares of the budgets consumed by each ministry and the nature of the projects administered by each of them. However, the broad patterns remained the same. In the following section, I will summarise the principal projects supervised by each ministry.

The Dōwa policy projects promoted by each ministry

Sōmuchō/PMO Total spend 1969–2002 ¥11,135m, less than 1%

We start with the Sōmuchō. It consumed one of the smallest Dōwa budgets across government but it took over responsibility for servicing the Dōwa policy council from the PMO when it was established in 1984. Thereafter, it played the main role in coordinating policy between ministries until 2002. It also took over responsibility for carrying out the national level surveys that provided data to inform both the deliberations of the policy councils and how the policy was formulated and implemented by each of the ministries.

As for Dōwa projects, Sōmuchō took over supervision of the training courses for central and local government bureaucrats that had started in 1976 and 1982, respectively. Contrary to the overall trend, from 1988 its Dōwa budget gradually increased as it benefited from the attention being paid to *keihatsu*: from ¥548m in 1988 to ¥1,181m in 1996. This was spent on general educational projects, including lectures, symposia, *keihatsu* festivals, advertising on TV, and the funding of the production of fourteen films, one each year between 1983 and 1996. It is not clear what happened to these films or who they were shown to.

No Dōwa-related projects were funded through this agency after 1997 when responsibility for *keihatsu* projects was transferred to the MoJ Human Rights Bureau (Dōwa Gyōseishi Henshū Iinkai, 2002, 129–34).

Ministry of Justice Total spend 1969–2002 ¥4,283m less than 1%

Dōwa projects within the MoJ were linked to the human rights protection activity within the Human Rights Bureau. Since its creation in the late 1940s, the MoJ had been responsible for the Civil Liberties Commissioners (CLC) system which had a broad remit of promoting human rights ideas and providing advice to those who felt their rights had been infringed through a network of volunteers who were appointed by each municipality

Table 7.3 Dōwa Policy Projects: Summary of Projects of Each Ministry 1969–2002

Ministry	*Proportion of total Dōwa spending*	*Main Dōwa project responsibilities*
Construction	47% ¥2,045,413m	Residential improvement projects in areas of inadequate housing and densely inhabited districts, projects to construct public housing, provision of roads and drainage systems
Health and Welfare	23% ¥976,544m	Provision of facilities to improve the living environment such as communal baths and workplaces, *Rinpokan* and kindergarten, projects that aim to improve public hygiene, provision of work through the construction of communal workshops to ensure equality of employment opportunity
Labour	1% ¥48,685m	Jurisdiction over projects concerning finding employment: employment guidance, introduction to jobs, provision of grants for employment training, creation of systems to support employment, promotion of employment training systems, deployment of Dōwa-specialist training advisors to public employment centres
Education	4% ¥262,944m	Projects to promote school attendance: grants for high school, university and junior college, grants to assist purchase of goods for school pupils. Promotion of Dōwa education in schools and society, provision of after-school education facilities
Agriculture Forestry and Fishing	13% ¥545,935m	Basic provision of facilities to modernise Buraku communities in rural, mountainous, and fishing communities
International Trade and Industry	9% ¥402,415m	Finance and financial advice for SMEs in Buraku communities [Mainly supervised by the Small and Medium Enterprise Agency 中小企業庁]
Justice	less than 1% ¥4,283m	Investigation of human rights infringements, human rights advice projects, public education
Home Affairs	less than 1% ¥11,455m	Administrative assistance for Dōwa projects carried out by local authorities, fire-fighting equipment
Sōmuchō	less than 1% ¥11,135m	Policy coordination, surveys, training for central and local government employees

Source: adapted from Uchida (2015, 3).

(see Neary, 1997). It was not a robust system and was largely dismissed by Buraku movement activists as ineffective.

From 1974, the MoJ began producing Dōwa-related promotional material; for example, in 1978 over a million leaflets were printed, funding was provided for TV commercials, and support given to meetings in community

Table 7.4 Dōwa Spending 1969–93 – Administered by Municipalities

	Dōwa budget (¥m)	*Material*	*Non-material*	*State*	*Prefecture*	*Municipality*	*Share of total budget*
TOTAL	10,318,012	58.4	41.6	22.6	10.8	66.6	4.1
Kanto	332,485	70.8	29.2	27.6	14.0	58.4	1.0
Chubu	716,752	67.1	32.9	27.0	13.1	59.9	2.1
Kinki	5,348,704	53.5	46.5	18.7	9.6	71.7	5.6
Chugoku	1,116,268	57.0	43.0	19.4	14.4	66.2	3.3
Shikoku	1,272,061	70.3	29.7	35.4	9.8	54.8	7.2
Kyushu	1,531,742	60.0	40.0	24.5	11.5	64.0	3.6
1969–81	3,826,068	67.8	32.2	24.4	11.7	63.9	5.7
1982–6	2,867,479	57.8	42.2	24.9	10.5	64.6	4.6
1987–91	2,616,704	49.7	50.3	18.9	10.4	70.7	3.1
1992–3	1,007,761	46.7	53.3	18.4	9.3	72.4	2.4

Source: Dōwa Gyōseishi Henshū Iinkai (2002, 908).

Table 7.5 Dōwa Spending 1969–93 – Administered by Prefectures

	Dōwa budget (¥m)	*Material*	*Non-material*	*State*	*Prefecture*	*Share of total budget*
TOTAL	3,562,363	37.0	63.0	21.5	78.5	0.9
Kanto	269,379	34.9	65.1	25.7	74.3	0.3
Chubu	291,033	34.0	66.0	20.4	79.6	0.3
Kinki	1,751,719	33.4	66.6	12.4	87.6	2.0
Chugoku	398,932	44.9	55.1	35.0	65.0	0.9
Shikoku	346,223	46.3	53.7	32.6	67.4	1.3
Kyushu	505,077	39.8	60.2	33.7	66.3	0.7
1969–81	1,327,768	45.9	54.1	19.0	81.0	1.2
1982–6	1,008,693	34.4	65.6	23.0	77.0	1.0
1987–91	888,445	29.4	70.6	23.6	76.4	0.7
1992–3	337,457	29.8	70.2	21.8	78.2	0.5

Source: Dōwa Gyōseishi Henshū Iinkai (2002, 908).

halls connected to the Human Rights week (which later became a month) held annually in most municipalities during July. From 1982 to 1996, there were over a thousand lectures and seminars held each year attended by a total of over 100,000 people. No additional funding was provided after 1997 so activity after this point must have been supported from within the budget of the Human Rights Bureau or left to local governments to support (Dōwa Gyōseishi Henshū Iinkai, 2002, 135–40).

Ministry of Education Total spend 1969–2002 ¥262,944m 4%

Dōwa education (*Dōwa Kyōiku*) has a history that can be traced back to the Yūwa policies of the 1930s both in the sense of the provision of education that targeted children from Buraku communities to combat their low academic achievement and issues related to low self-esteem but also education that aimed to dispel the prejudices held within the mainstream community. These activities were developed at a grassroots level in the 1950s by teachers supported by local education committees in most regions of Japan where there were Buraku communities. The MoE first became directly involved in the implementation of Dōwa policy in 1959 when it started to designate schools for research into Dōwa education and provided a small amount of money, just under one million yen, to support it.

Three principal concerns for MoE Dōwa policy were set out in the LTP in 1969:

- Leadership to eliminate prejudices and discrimination,
- the raising of educational and cultural standards of both children and adults in Dōwa communities, and
- put in place the facilities necessary to eliminate prejudicial attitudes and discriminatory circumstances.

(Dōwa Gyōseishi Henshū Iinkai, 2002, 317)

In March 1973, the Dōtaikyō produced a report on Dōwa education based on the principles in the Dōtaishin that it submitted to the MoE requesting the development of policy both within schools and for education in the wider community. It asked for the formulation of an LTP for the Dōwa education budget to provide additional teachers in classrooms, for research on Dōwa education, including the creation of teaching materials. It proposed grants to enable attendance at universities and suggested that plans be made to implement Dōwa programmes in higher education on the one hand and in kindergartens on the other (Dōwa Gyōseishi Henshū Iinkai, 2002, 289–92).

The improvement of educational attainment in Buraku communities was considered by activists and administrators alike to be crucial to promoting self-reliance. The strict rules that the MoE used to calculate the maximum number of teachers that could be employed in primary and junior schools were relaxed in the case of schools serving designated Dōwa districts and funding provided to appoint more teachers or classroom assistants than normal (Dōwa Gyōseishi Henshū Iinkai, 2002, 152).

Included in the MoE's Dōwa programme were several projects to support research on school-based Dōwa education policies and to provide specialist teacher training. This mainly focused on the compulsory sector (aged 6–15) but there were also attempts to connect up with nursery schools at one end and senior high schools at the other.

From the start of the SML era, it was considered important to increase the number of Buraku-origin children who continued their education in senior high schools and universities. As Upham noted, 'There is an elaborate and generous program of grants rewarding school attendance' (Upham, 1980, 49). These projects were designed to promote the improvement of levels of education 'in the target areas' and to promote social and economic self-reliance by increasing advancement into higher secondary education and above by providing one-off payments to buy products necessary for school attendance at enrolment (for example, school uniforms) and monthly grants for those attending high schools, specialist colleges, junior colleges, or universities.

Those who qualified for such support must firstly be, 'children of Dōwa related people who live in a target area', and secondly be from families that 'have low incomes such that it is difficult for them to afford for their children to attend school' (Dōwa Gyōseishi Henshū Iinkai, 2002, 142–3). Grants to support attendance at senior high schools began in 1966 when 2,730 pupils were provided with ¥1,500 each month. By 1973, 22,000 pupils were being given ¥4,000 per month. The following year, the amount provided for those attending private high schools was increased to ¥5,000. Gradually, the numbers receiving this funding and the public/private differential were increased such that by 1994, 23,650 and 9,200 young people were being supported at public sector and private sector high schools, respectively.

The programmes were extended to provide grants to enable university attendance in 1974 and by the end of the decade over a thousand students were receiving ¥21,000 monthly if they were at national universities and ¥32,000 if they were attending private universities. The value of these grants increased steadily. In 1978, one-off grants of ¥30,000 were provided to equip students for university life and in the 1980s around 3,300 students were receiving this each year. The equipment grants were converted into loans in 1982 and the monthly grants also became loans in 1987 but it was possible for the loan to be commuted in certain circumstances (and there were allegations from the Zenkairen that many people never repaid their loans). The programme was funded until FY 2001/2.

These programmes were operated either through prefectures or 'designated cities' with the state providing two-thirds of the funding. By 1996, the total cost of the programmes had grown to ¥9,885m with approximately two-thirds of the money spent on supporting senior high school attendance, the rest on higher education. Some of these programmes survived the expiration of the overall SML-funded schemes but most had been converted into means-tested schemes and became open to poor families from 2010 or thereabouts onwards.

A second set of MoE-based Dōwa projects focused on community-based adult education. One aspect of this was to fund the construction of buildings or rooms within buildings that could be used to enable the development of adult education in Dōwa districts. There was a substantial proportion of adults in some Buraku communities who in the late 1960s were barely literate, so some of this provided very basic lessons in reading and writing. The programme began modestly in 1962 with grants totalling only ¥8m for 10 buildings but at the peak of Dōwa spending – 1979–86 – around ¥1,500m was being spent on this policy supporting as many as 140–150 projects each year.

In 1967, just before the Dōwa education projects started, 66.8% of the total national cohort was going on to senior high school but only 30.0% of school children with a Dōwa background. By 1975, these figures were 91.9% and 87.5%, respectively, the 'performance gap' having been reduced from 36.8% to 4.4%. By 1998, the figures had changed to 96.8% and 92%, the 'gap' having grown slightly. Meanwhile in 1979, 37.4% of the national cohort entered higher education but only 14.2% of those with Buraku backgrounds did so. In 1985, the method used to calculate university attendance changed slightly and produced figures of 30.5% and 19.1%. Over the next decade, the grant programme made little impact on that gap – in 1998, the figures were 40.7% and 28.6%.

Of course, not all of these improvements in education achievement by Buraku children can be ascribed to Dōwa policy but by the mid-1990s the BLL recognised that the gap between Buraku and non-Buraku children had been substantially reduced. The topic of Dōwa education is one that has been extensively researched in Japan and has received some attention in the English literature too.[1] Despite the fact that it consumed only a small proportion of the total budget, it is the aspect of Dōwa policy that was best known outside the communities.

Ministry of Health and Welfare Total spend 1969–2002 ¥976,544m 23%

MHW was one of the three ministries that received the bulk of Dōwa funding across the 33 years – around one quarter of the total spend. It had been the lead ministry for the administration of Yūwa policy when created in 1938 from sections of the Home Ministry (Naimushō) and although all aspects of national level Yūwa policy ceased in 1945, MHW was the first ministry to revive Dōwa policy spending in 1953 when it provided funding for *Rinpokan* ('settlement houses', more below). Between 1953 and 1958, the MHW coordinated the inter-ministerial development of Dōwa policy through the *Chihō Kaizen Kyōgikai* and then between 1960 and 1968, it planned community improvements through the Model Projects Policy. From the mid-1950s, MHW became involved with projects to improve aspects of the infrastructure of Dōwa communities – communal bathing facilities from 1956 and provision of workshops from 1958. Many Buraku communities are located on low-lying land near rivers where drainage was a problem and the supply of potable water not guaranteed. MHW made a start with drainage, sewage, and water supply projects in the late 1950s although the amounts of money available were quite small. The limited Ten-Year Programme launched in 1960 coordinated a wide range of projects that included: provision or improvement of roads, sewage, drainage, communal baths, street lights, garbage disposal, crematoria, abattoirs, and communal workshops.

The draft LTP of 1967 was concerned more with the prioritising of policy areas than the responsibilities of ministries but it proposed MHW involvement in a range of policy areas from the more obvious ones of social welfare to road construction and physical infrastructure to aspects of educational and economic improvements (Dōwa Gyōseishi Henshū Iinkai, 2002, 278–80) The LTP in 1969 suggested four targets for the MHW: the improvement of hygiene, the provision and management of *Rinpokan*, the provision of large-scale communal workplaces to improve economic conditions, and the establishment of facilities to promote social welfare (Dōwa Gyōseishi Henshū Iinkai, 2002, 318). These aims were to be achieved by, firstly, a range of construction projects from roads, sewage, and drainage and bridges to communal bathing facilities, the provision of tap water, garbage disposal, and the moving of graveyards and creation of ossuaries. *Rinpokan* were to be built, as were large-scale communal workshops and facilities such as clinics, kindergarten, and social welfare facilities in collaboration with such groups as the *minsei iin* (Dōwa Gyōseishi Henshū Iinkai, 2002, 320–1). The pattern was not much different to what MHW was already spending on Dōwa projects but there were massive increases in the amount of money that became available: in 1967, the MHW budget for Dōwa projects was just less than ¥100m; by 1972, it was over ¥7,000m and peaked in 1980 at ¥70,000m.

Rinpokan ('settlement houses') are multi-functional community centres located in Dōwa districts that combine meeting rooms with study facilities for adults and children, kitchens to prepare food for celebratory meals or cooking lessons, clinics, and sometimes even bathing facilities. They trace their origin to the settlement movement in late nineteenth-century London which was inspired by the work of Arnold Toynbee. Toynbee Hall was established in the East End in 1884 by Samuel and Henrietta Barnett to alleviate local poverty. The first Rinpokan were established in Japan as part of the Yūwa policy in the late 1920s and 1930s but they continued to receive some inspiration from the international settlement movement. Post-war, MHW provided some funding for Rinpokan in 1953 and, responding to pressure from local branches of the BLL, some local governments built similar facilities within Buraku communities during the 1950s. It is estimated that in 1969 there were already 292 Rinpokan and fifteen years later there were 894, most of them constructed during the first years of the SML programme (Kanai 1991, 217). In 1971, a National Rinpokan Coordinating Council (Zenkoku Rinpokan Renraku Kyōgikai) was established and in 2015 had 828 members. The reduction in numbers reflected closures and amalgamations of facilities that took place after the termination of the SML.

What is most noticeable about MHW Dōwa policy activity is its range which goes well beyond social welfare provision to include building roads and bridges as well as clinics. This probably reflects the pioneering role it played in the development of Dōwa policy during the 1950s so that it was reluctant to allow rival ministries such as the MoC to encroach on its territory.

Most of the MHW-supported projects either ceased operation during the 1990s or were transferred to the general budget such that in the final five years there was just one, low-cost project remaining.

Ministry of Agriculture Forestry and Fisheries Total spend 1969–2002 ¥545,935m 13%

MAFF's Dōwa policy budgets were the third largest within government. It was a relatively late participant in Dōwa programme administration. Its first project only dates from 1960 with the implementation of the Dōwa Policy Projects in Agricultural, Forestry and Fishing Villages supported by a budget of ¥20m. These began as part of the Model Project schemes initiated in 1959/60 but they were developed as post-1969 Dōwa policy and some of them would continue until the penultimate phase of Dōwa policy in 1992–6.

The Dōtaikyō proposed in 1967 that MAFF become involved in the development of social policies and industrial promotion policies in particular, of course, farming, fishing, and forestry (Dōwa Gyōseishi Henshū Iinkai, 2002, 280). The LTP noted that the scale of Dōwa community landholdings and enterprises was much smaller than average and their productivity low so projects should be developed to 'modernise' their productive base (Dōwa Gyōseishi Henshū Iinkai, 2002, 318). This was translated into major capital projects that sought to improve the quality of cultivated land by better irrigation, the selective expansion of plots of land, disaster prevention measures particularly the prevention of flooding, and the provision of forest roads and port facilities. Facilities would be provided that allowed the expansion of the scale of operations – whether for farming, forestry, or fishing – and the provision of facilities to modernise the distribution of their products (Dōwa Gyōseishi Henshū Iinkai, 2002, 321–2).

Some of these projects amounted to no more than the provision of small loans for the purchase of modern farming machinery but there were also major capital projects to improve irrigation systems and upgrade rural roads, bridges and even port facilities which at the height of Dōwa policy in 1983 consumed about half of the MAFF Dōwa budget – ¥18,033m out of ¥36,254m.

A re-evaluation of MAFF's programmes was undertaken in 1986 but this resulted in only one project being discontinued – which provided support for meat distribution – although the control of some projects was transferred into general administration. The review of Dōwa projects that took place in 1991 resulted in the transfer of many MAFF-funded projects into the mainstream budget and by the final phase, 1997–2001, only a loans programme and a system to provide advice on agricultural administration remained with a total budget of around ¥75m (Dōwa Gyōseishi Henshū Iinkai, 2002, 164–72).

Ministry of International Trade and Industry Total spend 1969–2002 ¥402,415m 9%

MITI, mainly through the Small- and Medium-Size Enterprise Bureau (SME), was one of the smaller players in the overall Dōwa administration consuming less than 9% of total funds over the whole period but it continued to be active right until 2002.

The 1969 LTP noted that many Buraku communities relied on traditional industries where the size of the enterprise was small and productivity low. The MITI/SME role in Dōwa policy therefore aimed to employ advisers from the local chambers of commerce to modernise their management and raise their technological level (Dōwa Gyōseishi Henshū Iinkai, 2002, 318). The bureau had been running similar projects since 1966 and this strand of policy would survive the various policy reviews to last until March 2002. It was the cheapest part of the policy package. The biggest item in terms of cost were the projects 'to provide long-term, zero-interest finance in order to rationalise management through the organisation of project co-operatives of SME managers in the target areas and plan the modernisation of their administrative base implementing cooperative projects and collective organisations' (Dōwa Gyōseishi Henshū Iinkai, 2002, 173). In any year, these projects would take up around 80–90% of the total MITI Dōwa spend. There was a third strand that also lasted through until the 1990s which provided advice on the development of new projects and designs.

MITI took a special interest in the development of the leather industry and had a 'desk' that specialised in this industry and a fund to help its development – *Hikaku Sangyō Shinko Taisaku Jigyō*. It is not clear how this was coordinated with the ministry's Dōwa policy or local leather industry promotion projects such as those in Osaka.

Ministry of Labour Total spend 1969–2002 ¥48,685m 1%

One theme within the Dōtaishin had been that the freedom of Burakumin to select their employment was hindered within contemporary Japan. Put another way, the under-employment of Burakumin caused by discrimination meant that they were not available to modern industry. So, although the amount of money channelled through the MoL was quite small the projects that it funded were a core part of the overall Dōwa objectives. MoL projects to promote employment in Dōwa areas began in 1963 and would continue until 1991 when they were merged with other projects that provided careers advice to school leavers and education and guidance to employers (Dōwa Gyōseishi Henshū Iinkai, 2002, 124, 127). The ministry was mentioned in several places in the 1967 Dotaikyō's draft LTP as having a role to play in education and employment policy in both urban and rural areas but in terms of cash spent it was not a major player. The 1969 LTP proposed the creation of an organisation to promote the employment of Buraku-origin workers so as to get school leavers into modern industry. Vocational training should be developed and measures put in place to broaden employment opportunities (Dōwa Gyōseishi Henshū Iinkai, 2002, 318).

The three elements of MoL Dōwa policy were employment promotion, employment stability and the elimination of discrimination in recruitment. The only detailed breakdown of spending is for the projects that lasted into the 1990s so it is hard to be sure where the bulk of the money was being spent at 'Peak Dōwa' in the mid-1980s. One project that began in 1970 and survived into the 1990s provided funding to enable younger workers to undertake occupational training. In 1985, it provided sums of ¥13,500 per person per month and had a total budget of ¥56m (Dōwa Gyōseishi Henshū Iinkai, 2002, 182). This looks similar to the MoE programme to encourage school attendance past the age of compulsory education. Overall, the sums of money spent on each project were relatively small, only ¥602,000 in the early 1960s and never more than ¥4 million in the mid-1980s.

More significant were the projects that provided training for individuals in 'unstable occupations' such as day labouring. In 1985 when the *per diem* was ¥2,900 the budget for this project was ¥448.8m = 154,758 days = 860 six-month periods. These grants were converted into loans in 1987. In 1994 the amount provided had increased to around ¥4,290 per day and those who qualified could also claim up to ¥42,500 per month to cover travel expenses. In total this consumed ¥570m about one-third of the MoL Dōwa budget of ¥1,330m. The programme was merged into the general training programmes provided by the MoL in 1997.

The MoL's Dōwa budget was cut by over a third with the reorganisation of Dōwa policy in 1986–7: from ¥3,791m in 1986 to ¥1,033m in 1987. Spending remained stable until 1994 but only four projects survived the revisions that year and they were consolidated into just one programme in 1997.

In 1968, the MoL produced a memo on the elimination of discrimination in recruitment and across the 1970s it supported various local governments' attempts to introduce a 'standard application form' (tōitsu ōbo shorui). This aimed to ensure that companies asked job applicants to provide only the information they needed to enable them to make a fair selection. It was feared, especially following the revelation of the existence of 'Buraku Lists' (*chimei sōkan*) in 1975, that companies were asking applicants to supply information that could be used to discriminate against those from Buraku communities or with Buraku 'heritage'. The campaign to persuade companies to adopt the 'standard form' continued until 2002. In the long term, this might have been the most significant of the MoL's Dōwa initiatives.

Ministry of Construction Total spend 1969–2002 ¥2,045,413m 47%

In most of the 33 years of Dōwa policy spending, over half went to the MoC. It began in 1960 with projects to improve housing that may have been part of the 'Model Projects' Ten-Year Plan. Later in the decade, the replacement of inadequate housing was discussed at length by the Dōtaikyō which proposed a housing and town planning strategy that would include the provision of buildings, roads, and other infrastructure 'in response to requests from prefectures and municipalities' (Dōwa Gyōseishi Henshū Iinkai, 2002, 323).

The LTP set out two overall goals for the MoC: to replace and improve the housing of residents in Dōwa communities and to effect improvements to all other aspects of their built environment, including roads and sewage (Dōwa Gyōseishi Henshū Iinkai, 2002, 318). From the start of the Dōwa SML in 1969, all the MoC projects that it shared with the MHW were administered as part of the 'Projects concerning the improvement of living conditions'. However, building new housing or making improvements to existing housing were at the heart of MoC policy, for example, taking up:

1971 ¥9,000m out of ¥13,520m
1985 ¥61,476m out of ¥96,065m
1997 ¥39,035m out of ¥59,615m

There were several different schemes often with very tight criteria. For example, the main project provided funding in 'target areas' where there were more than 50 houses considered 'defective' and/or where more than 80% of housing in the area was 'defective', where the housing density was over 80 per hectare and where the total area was 0.15 hectare or more (Dōwa Gyōseishi Henshū Iinkai, 2002, 188). Later schemes were devised to benefit small communities and there were separate schemes to construct community facilities such as parks, roads, sewage facilities, and earthworks to mitigate flood damage. In the mid-1980s, MoC was involved in nineteen national Dōwa projects but five of these closed down at the end of 1986.

There are two slightly unusual features of MoC Dōwa policy. Firstly, none of its projects used either Dōwa or Chiiki Kaizen in their titles. This may be a hangover from the 1960s when MoC officials argued against the need for a special Dōwa policy since their problems could be taken care of through a general slum clearance policy. Secondly, its policy planning process seems not to coincide with the rest of the Dōwa decision process in that the first plans ran from 1960, the projects to improve housing in small communities started in 1970 and a third on publicly owned housing began in 1984.

The 1993 survey reported that 'The material environment of Dōwa communities – housing, roads, etc., has been improved and overall there are no differences between the target communities and their neighbours' (Dōwa Gyōseishi Henshū Iinkai, 2002, 186). Mizuuchi and Jeon, in one of the very few specialist assessments of Dōwa policy, give a very positive evaluation of the Dōwa programme in general arguing that 'the worst slum-like elements of the Buraku have been overcome physically and living standards and education standards have been improved…'. Looking specifically at housing, they note that,

> 65,000 public housing units were rebuilt after the demolition of houses in a physically deteriorated condition, and 60,000 public housing units were newly provided for Buraku people. There were 72,000 cases of loan

> extensions for newly-purchased houses, and 98,000 cases of loan extensions for the repair of houses. To sum up all the cases: 295,000 households were newly provided or rehabilitated, nearly equal to the total number of Buraku people (sic) in Japan.[2]
>
> (Mizuuchi and Jeon 2010, 2–4)

However, as the SML was approaching expiration, there was a growing realisation that the housing construction that had taken place in the 1970s left many communities with a legacy of concrete buildings that were starting to decay. Moreover, as the 1993 survey had shown, since their incomes remained lower than average with a high degree of reliance on social welfare it was unlikely that they would be able to upgrade their living environments without some outside support. This would be an issue for local governments in the twenty-first century.

Ministry of Home Affairs Total spend 1969–2002 ¥11,455m less than 1%

The MHA was not mentioned in any of the preparatory reports or plans on Dōwa policy and it did not receive any Dōwa funding until 1972. Its role mostly derived from its obligation to administer fire-fighting services. This was a high-profile issue in many urban areas as the high density of housing in Buraku communities resulted in very narrow streets down which conventional fire appliances could not go. This was a complaint that arose during the 'All Romance' campaign in Kyoto and in the 1950s there were several incidents reported of houses in Buraku communities being destroyed because fire-fighters were unable to arrive in time or at all. MHA financed the installation of hydrants within Dōwa districts and the purchase and garaging of small fire-fighting appliances that were able to negotiate the narrow streets that often remained even following the housing improvements funded by the MoC.

Concluding comments

The most obvious trend across these three decades is the way the overall pattern of the spending was set in 1969 after which there were little more than incremental changes in the nature of projects being implemented even though there were quite massive fluctuations in the amounts of funding provided. This is true for both the overall division of labour between the ministries set out in the 1969 LTP and the kinds of projects undertaken by each ministry – at least as far as one can tell from the descriptions they provided. Moreover, these patterns seem to have been informed by the proposals for Dōwa projects that had been put forward by the BLL and JSP during the 1950s. A second characteristic is that there is a very clear division of responsibility at least at the national level. There is little evidence of the joint funding of projects although that might have taken place at the point of implementation within local government offices or the Dōwa districts themselves as in the case of Rinpokan construction.

As we saw in the previous chapter, there was a great deal of discussion in policy circles about the change of name of the policy from Dōwa Policy Projects (Dōwa Taisaku Jigyō) to Regional Improvement Policy Projects (Chiiki Kaizen Taisaku Jigyō) and yet the nature of the projects funded by each of the ministries remained largely unchanged. It was only after 1987, as the process of a gradual reduction in the overall number of projects was taking place, that we begin to see changes in how the projects are described (see Table 7.3 and Appendix). Then, moving into the 1990s, as the number of projects and overall expenditure was being reduced quite rapidly, we can see the absorption of projects into the 'general' budget although it is not always clear exactly what this means. For example, when a local government took responsibility for child care services in a Buraku community as part of its overall welfare responsibilities did that mean additional money was provided for that budget or that the existing budget had to be stretched to cover the broader responsibility? One suspects the latter.

Taking an overview of the spending on Dōwa policy projects three things stand out. First, is the role played by the MHW that went well beyond health and welfare as usually understood, second the massive role played by MoC, and third the way that the policy was coordinated (or possibly not). The first is probably best explained by the historical continuities that link the MHW to the various parts of the Home Ministry (Naimushō) that was responsible for Yūwa policy before 1938 and which prompted it to be the first ministry post-war to provide funding to improve living conditions in Buraku communities in 1953. From this point, it developed a range of policies that went well beyond its usual policy parameters, including funding various construction projects. It was, then, engaged with the delivery of funding for a broad range of projects well before the launch of any kind of national Dōwa policy that presumably it was reluctant to give up. The second feature of massive amounts of money being spent on construction projects by MHW, MAFF, and, of course, MoC is not only a feature of Dōwa policy spending but one, most probably **the,** characteristic feature of Japanese government spending over the period 1970 to the start of the twenty-first century. Commentaries on the special features and pathology of the 'construction state' began in the early 1980s – for example, Curtis and Ishikawa, 1983– and were taken up by critics such as McCormack in the 1990s and beyond.[3] This was undoubtedly stimulated by the 'Tanaka politics' of the 1970s and 1980s which, following the publication of the book entitled 'Remodelling the Japanese Archipelago' (*Nippon Rettō Kaizō-ron*) in 1972, led to a boom in construction. It is difficult to demonstrate any direct links in terms of policymaking between the massive projects building bridges between Honshu and Shikoku or parts of the Shinkansen network and Dōwa policy, but it is surely no coincidence that the MoC response to the passage of the SML was to join with local governments in planning major public works projects or that a major part of the MAFF-funded Dōwa projects were the hugely expensive irrigation and field consolidation schemes. Finally, although once again little has been written about the topic, the Dōwa policy area is unusual in that it was conducted by multiple ministries. Japanese ministries are notorious for being more concerned to protect their spheres of influence than to cooperate with other agencies. The fact that they were able to work together for more than 30 years on Dōwa policy is most unusual. Indeed, this cooperation is sometimes pointed to as a rare example within Japanese policy studies, arguably unique before the twenty-first century. And yet it was accomplished through the coordination provided by a small policy 'office' and a *shingikai* which met intermittently. So flimsy is this framework that one suspects that there was in practice very little coordination at the national level. However, the efforts of the ministries did need to come together at the local level where the projects were implemented and it is to some examples of local Dōwa administration that we turn next.

Notes

1 For example, Hawkins (1983), Hirasawa (1989, 1995), Bondy (2013).
2 This presumably should read 'Buraku households'.
3 See, for example, Curtis and Ishikawa *Doken Kokka Nippon* 1983, and McCormack *The Emptiness of Japanese Affluence*, 2001, especially chapter 1, The Construction State: the pathology of the *Doken Kokka*.

Bibliography

Bondy C., (2013) 'Centring and Marginalizing: The "Soft Middle" and Japanese Minority Education', *Asia Pacific Journal of Education*, vol. 34, no. 1, 1–14.

Curtis G. and Ishikawa M., (1983) *Doken Kokka Nippon* (Japan Construction State), Tokyo: Kobunsha.

Dōwa Gyōseishi Henshū Iinkai (Dōwa Administration History Editorial Committee), (2002) *Dōwa Gyōseishi* (A History of Dōwa Administration), Tokyo: Sōmuchō Daijin Kanbō Chiiki Kaizen Taisakuhitsu.

Hawkins J. N., (1983) 'Educational Demands and Institutional Response: Dōwa Education in Japan', *Comparative Education Review*, vol. 27, no. 2, 204–26.

Hirasawa Y., (1983) 'The Burakumin: Japan's Minority Population', *Integrated Education*, vol. 20, no. 6, 3–8.

Hirasawa Y., Nabeshima Y., Mori M., and Akashi I., (1995) *Dōwa Education: Educational Challenge: Toward a Discrimination-Free Japan.* Edited by Hirasawa Y and Nabeshima Y, Osaka: Kaihō Shuppansha.

Kanai K., (1991) *Dōwa Gyōsei: Sengo no Kiseki* (Dōwa Administration: The Postwar Path), Osaka: Buraku Kaihō Shuppansha.

McCormack G., (2001) *The Emptiness of Japanese Affluence*, London: Routledge.

Mizuuchi T. and Jeon H. G., (2010) 'The New Mode of Urban Renewal for the Former Outcaste Minority People and Areas in Japan', *Cities*, vol. 27, Supplement 1, June, 525–34.

Neary I., (1997) 'The Civil Liberties Commissioners System and the Protection of Human Rights in Japan', *Japan Forum*, vol. 9, no. 2, 217–32.

Upham F., (1980) 'Ten Years of Affirmative Action for Japanese Burakumin: A Preliminary Report on the Law on Special Measures for Dōwa Projects', *Law in Japan*, vol. 13, 39–73.

Upham F., (1987) *Law and Social Change in Postwar Japan*, Cambridge, MA: Harvard University Press.

8 Implementation III: how Dōwa policy was implemented locally

Examples from Osaka, Nara, and Fukuoka prefectures

We pointed out in Chapter 2 that because of fears that the Japanese state is growing too big, it is a characteristic feature of Japanese policymaking to try to keep the centre of government small. Moreover, we saw in the previous chapter that Dōwa policy was no exception to this in that although the amounts of money and variety of projects implemented as part of Dōwa policy were quite large, the administrative structures created at the national level to monitor, coordinate, and promote spending on Dōwa projects were kept to a minimum. At the centre, there was just an advisory council; the Dōwa Taisaku Kyōgikai, formed in March 1966, renamed the Chiiki Kaizen Taisaku Kyōgikai in 1982, and from 1974, the Dōwa Taisakuhitsu located in the PMO, renamed the Chiiki Kaizen Taisakuhitsu in 1982, and transferred to the Sōmuchō in 1984. Most of the detail of the project planning and administration was worked out between the funding departments, notably the MoC, MAFF and MHW, and the appropriate departments and bureaus within the local government units. This placed much of the responsibility for the initiation of policy onto local actors: politicians, activists, and administrators.

Given that more than one thousand local government units administered some form of Dōwa policy between 1969 and 2002, it is difficult to provide an overall view of how policy worked at the rice-roots level. In any case, there are very few accounts or analyses of the formation and evolution of policy at this level. However, to omit all reference to how policy worked where it had a direct impact on people's lives would be to ignore an important dimension of the Dōwa policymaking process. Moreover, much of the controversy about the impact and implementation of Dōwa policy can only be understood by reference to activity at the local level.

This chapter will explore some aspects of how that worked by looking at the practice of Dōwa policy in three areas: Osaka prefecture and city, Nara prefecture, and a small city located in the Chikuhō area in Fukuoka prefecture. The selection of these case studies was largely prescribed by the availability of data but it does allow us to demonstrate how the sets of policies decided centrally were interpreted locally. Material in the public domain enables us to portray the development of policy in Osaka and Nara with some

DOI: 10.4324/9781003127994-8

confidence even though there are some problems with relying on a relatively small range of sources. The inclusion of the city in Chikuhō was largely serendipitous but the area was singled out for mention in the Dōtaikyō report of May 1976 as an area where many Dōwa residents faced long-term employment and where local governments faced serious financial problems such that it would be necessary to devise long-term and comprehensive strategies with all the related agencies (Dōwa Gyōseishi Henshū Iinkai, 2002, 303; see also Kobayakawa, 2020, 8).

In each case, I will briefly summarise the situation up to the end of the occupation, then look at the formulation of policy before 1965, up to 1991, during the 1990s and then after 2002. The aim is not to provide a comprehensive account of the Dōwa policy implementation in each area but rather to pick out themes and examples that demonstrate how the policies sketched out by the Dōtaikyō sitting in Tokyo were implemented, emphasising variation in practice and the ways in which local groups tried to influence the policy process.

As Table 8.1 shows, most Dōwa policy projects – well over 90% in terms of expenditure – were implemented at the level of local government and were financed through if not always completely by the local administrative authority. Moreover, as already suggested in Chapter 4, in many areas, the provision of special or additional facilities for Buraku communities predated the development of policy at the national level as local governments were persuaded by representatives of their Buraku communities to invest in improving local facilities. This was a piecemeal approach and the resources available to municipalities were severely constrained until the period of rapid economic growth in the 1960s when local taxes began to generate income that they could use at their discretion. It was during this time that structures and standard operating procedures were created to administer Dōwa policies that, when fresh financing was provided in the early 1970s, were adopted for the local delivery of Dōwa projects.

However before considering how the Dōwa funding was spent in these three different areas, let us take an overview of how spending was organised according to levels.

Broad patterns of Dōwa spending

One thing that becomes immediately apparent from Table 8.1 is that, despite the commitment in the legislation of 1969 that the national government would bear up to two-thirds of the cost of these projects, overall the state's share of the total cost of Dōwa projects whether implemented by the prefecture or municipality was only slightly more than 20%. This seems to have continued across the three decades of the programmes' implementation despite the fact that the reports of the Dōwa policy advisory council would almost routinely complain that the burden on municipalities was too high. The relatively large amount of prefectural support for non-capital projects

Table 8.1 Dōwa Projects Summary – Spending by Local Governments 1969–93

Projects organised by:	*Number of units*	*Total spend* **[on Dōwa]**	*Share of capital projects*	*Share of non-capital projects*	*State share*	*Pref share*	*Town/ city share*	*Total budget [all]*	*Share of total budget on Dōwa projects (%)*
Municipality	1064	10,318 **A**	58.4	41.6	22.6 [of A]	10.8 [of A]	66.6 [of A]	225,523	4.0
Prefecture	36	3562 **B**	37.0	63.0	21.5 [of B]	78.5 [of B]		409,500	0.9

Unit: ¥B.

Sources: Mizuuchi and Jeon (2010), Dōwa Gyōseishi Henshū Iinkai (2002, 908).

Table 8.2 Date of the Establishment of a Prefectural Dōwa Policy Office

Before 1968	Mie (1962) Hyogo (1964) **Osaka** (1966) Wakayama (1967) Yamaguchi (1967) Shiga (1968) **Fukuoka** (1968)
1969–73	**Nara** (1969) Tokushima (1969) Tottori (1969) Tokyo (1969) Fukui (1970) Hiroshima (1970) Kyoto (1970) Kagawa (1970) Nagano (1971) Kochi (1971) Saitama (1972) Gumma (1973)
	Gifu (1973) Saga (1973)
1974–78	Okayama (1974) Kumamoto (1974) Tochigi (1975) Aichi (1975) Shimane (1975) Chiba (1975) Kagoshima (1975) Nagasaki (1976) Ibaragi (1977) Miyazaki (1977) Oita (1977)
1979+	Yamanashi (1979) Ishikawa (1981)
None as of 1991	Kanagawa Niigata Toyama

Kanai (1991, 224).

reflects the fact that they have the responsibility for certain local government services particularly those linked to education within their territory.

The degree of variation in the responses of different prefectures can be illustrated by a glance at Table 8.2 which lists the dates when they established their Dōwa policy office. These were important as they formed the focus for the coordination of policy across the various sectors of the prefectural administration and conducted negotiations with the municipal Dōwa communities and the organisations representing them. Highlighted in bold are the three prefectural authorities whose Dōwa policies we will examine in more detail in the chapter.

Dōwa policy in Osaka prefecture and city

Throughout the twentieth century, Osaka prefecture was the location of the second largest number of Buraku households; only neighbouring Hyōgo prefecture had more. Its importance to any account of Dōwa policy though lies not so much in the size of its Buraku population or the amount of money spent on them but rather that the city and prefecture were regarded as playing a pioneering role in developing the so-called 'Osaka method' of implementing Dōwa policy and because the headquarters of the BLL was located in Osaka.

There is evidence of the existence of marginal and discriminated communities existing in Osaka from the seventeenth century. During the late Edo period, the large *kawata* community of Watanabe-mura located to the south of the Osaka city limits was charged with a range of official duties, including disposing of human corpses and animal carcasses, and administering punishments. Over time, the village had emerged as the most important centre for the production of leather goods in western Japan with skins being shipped to it from Fukuoka and even imported via Tsushima from the Korean peninsula.[1] Its population included a group of influential merchants who supervised the distribution of leather goods across the country (Tsukada, 2012, 6).

In 1887, Watanabe village was officially renamed Nishihama-chō and was incorporated into the city ten years later. Its population increased rapidly due to an influx of migrants from former outcaste communities across Japan, in particular the Kinki region, and it expanded outwards into neighbouring districts as a gathering place for the urban lower class. By 1920, it had grown into what probably was the nation's largest urban outcaste community with a population of 16,000. While there was a group of the descendants of wealthy leather wholesalers who had handled the circulation of leather during the early modern period, the immigration from outcaste communities in the region and the growing number of poor people transformed the area into a slum whose residents encountered a range of social problems, including discrimination at school (Saga, 2012, 67).

Attempts made at the start of the century to promote Yūwa-style improvements led by members of the wealthy ruling stratum under the direction of the police and local officials were regarded sceptically by many impoverished residents of the district. The Rice Riots swept through Osaka with over 230,000 people reported to have taken part, including many Burakumin. This formed the backdrop to the development of radical groups representing urban workers, tenant farmers, and Burakumin (Hanes, 2012, 84). While the Suiheisha developed quite quickly in Osaka city and prefecture following its formation in 1922, the Yūwa movement evolved more slowly. By 1928, a body had been created at the *gun* level called the Kōdōkai, with a branch in each community. From the mid-1920s, some money was provided for Yūwa projects to improve housing and to fund trachoma clinics (eight in all).[2] In 1934, the Osaka prefectural budget for Yūwa projects was still quite small at ¥99,000, compared to ¥200,000 being spent in Hyōgo and ¥120,000 in Fukuoka (Osaka Dōwa Jigyō Gojūnenshi, 2001, 28).

The 1935 Yūwa national survey showed that there were 55 Buraku communities in Osaka city, seven of which had populations of more than 1,000 people and in the rest of the prefecture there were another 51, 17 of which housed more than 1,000 people. They made up 2.42% of the total population. In Osaka prefecture, 43 municipalities were host to at least one Buraku community. These were relatively large communities, around four times the national average size whose population had increased quite substantially as a result of the continuing immigration (Table 8.3).

The fact that many of the residents of these communities had not been born there may explain why there was a drop in their recorded population in 1948 reflecting the way people across Japan fled from urban areas to escape the US bombing.

Table 8.3 Buraku Population Resident in Osaka Prefecture

1921	48,000
1929	63,000
1935	104,375[a]
1948	86,868

Sources: Osaka Dōwa Jigyō Gojūnenshi (2001, 25–7).
a Zenkoku Buraku Chōsa 1935.

Dōwa policy in Osaka 1950–70

After the war, Osaka prefecture was one of the first local governments in the country to provide money for Dōwa improvement projects setting aside just over ¥2m in the budget for FY1947 (Osaka Dōwa Jigyō Gojūnenshi, 2001, 28). In June 1947, a Kinki Dōwa Jigyō Kyōkai was set up to coordinate projects across the region and asked in the name of its six prefectural governors for central government support for the development of a Dōwa Project Five-Year Plan. This group would become core of the Nishi Nihon Dōwa Taisaku Kyōgikai in 1949 that was subsequently renamed the Zenkoku Dōwa Taisaku Kyōgikai (Zendōtai) in 1951.

In September 1948, the Osaka prefectural council set up a Buraku Mondai Kyōgikai which suggested the creation of three separate bodies: one for the distribution of Dōwa funding, one for social scientific and policy research, and one for the resolution of incidents of discrimination (Osaka Dōwa Jigyō Gojūnenshi, 2001, 22). Locally, unemployment within Buraku communities was running at 25% and their traditional industries were in crisis. The local branches of the NCBL began to demand the early re-launch of Yūwa/Dōwa projects to provide employment assistance, treatment for trachoma, and improvements to housing to prevent the recurrence of the disease. However, reflecting on the way that the Yūwa projects had been used during wartime to enhance control over their communities, the various demands that were being made for more active Dōwa policy all emphasised the need for the new improvement projects to be under democratic control.

In Osaka, this resulted in plans to create an organisation that was independent of the liberation movement (called the NCBL at the time) but would nevertheless provide a democratic input into the process of Dōwa policy-related decision making and its implementation. The outcome was the formation of the Osaka-fu Dōwa Jigyo Sokushin Kyōgikai (Osaka Prefecture Council for the Promotion of Dōwa Projects – Fudōkyō) and in December 1951 a similar body was formed in Osaka city in 1953 – Shidōkyō (Morooka, 1985, 168). Fudōkyō defined its aims as 'promoting Dōwa projects in Osaka prefecture, promoting occupational stability, improvement in living conditions and otherwise improving culture'. It sought to act as an intermediary between the Buraku movement, the Buraku communities, and the Dōwa administration with a committee made up of representatives from each Buraku community in the prefecture and an office located within the Osaka prefectural building. Later in the 1950s, it would set up specialist committees on welfare, education, and project administration (Osaka Dōwa Jigyō Gojūnenshi, 2001, 61). It liaised with other organisations such as members of the prefectural assembly who had formed the Dōwa Sokushin Giin Renmei – but it was the Fudōkyō, for example, that proposed a set of 110 projects in 1954 comprising 65 improvements to infrastructure, 17 in education, and 16 relating to employment (Osaka Dōwa Jigyō Gojūnenshi, 2001, 52). It lobbied for more funding for Buraku improvement while also arguing that,

> Ours are not usual requests for projects that say 'we are poor so we want assistance', like a movement of beggars. Rather we are a movement that by combining our power, removing barriers by our own efforts and working together builds people and communities. When we ask the authorities for projects to provide assistance we do not expect them to be carried out by the authorities alone. They should raise the awareness of the masses in the communities, strengthen their participation and bring them into deeper co-operation.
>
> (Osaka Dōwa Jigyō Gojūnenshi, 2001, 88)

Pre-war 'Yūwa-ism' was seen to be the way whereby the Japanese state had utilised improvement policies to mobilise Buraku masses behind the war effort. The engagement of the Buraku masses in the formation of Dōwa policy through the Osaka-fu/shi Dōsokkyō was envisaged as a way of ensuring not only the improvement in the quantity and quality of Dōwa projects but also their democratisation. As one activist recalled, even in the 1950s, it was clear that the 'Buraku Problem' was not only about poverty and poor housing although that had to be dealt with first. Even where he was living (Hinode, Osaka), his family of six occupied in a six-mat room, got their water from a shared pump, used a common toilet, and the housing was liable to flooding, but there was no feeling that this was the result of administrative discrimination (institutional discrimination?). Rather, even in Hinode, there was a 'let sleeping dogs lie' (*neta ko okosuna*) attitude that favoured avoiding protest for fear that this might attract unwanted attention. So, for him, the issue was how to ensure improvements to the community at the same time as building up the liberation movement. A three-way division of labour resulted whereby the BLL provided overall political leadership, the local government the administration of the Dōwa projects, and the Fu/shi Dōsokkyō committees acted as a 'third sector' to channel requests for specific improvements and provide local supervision of their implementation (interview with Morooka, 1985, 170; Oga, 2002, 1; Oga Masayuki, 2015).

It formalised this role in 1957 successfully applying to the governor for registration as a non-profit foundation (Osaka Dōwa Jigyō Gojūnenshi, 2001, 90).

There was a significant increase in the Osaka prefecture budget for Dōwa projects the year following the creation of the Fudōsokkyō: from ¥3,256m (1952) to ¥13,756m (1953), most of it in the welfare section. In 1957, Fudōsokkyō made demands for more funding for education and housing projects (Osaka Dōwa Jigyō Gojūnenshi, 2001, 91) and there was another step change in Dōwa funding in 1958–9 when total funding increased from ¥21,146m to ¥43,378m with more money being channelled through the construction and education bureaus. In 1958, a Dōwa Kaikan (the local name for a Rinpokan) was opened near Momotani station and the Fudōsokkyō offices moved into it. This became a base for the movement, a location for some welfare activity and even some research.

In parallel with developments at the national level where politicians were beginning to advocate the formulation of a more comprehensive Dōwa policy, in Osaka the Fudōsokkyō presented petitions to the prefectural government in December 1958 and August 1959 urging the adoption of a five-year plan that would include a wide range of projects (Osaka Dōwa Jigyō Gojūnenshi, 2001, 94). It presented evidence in support of these claims which revealed enduring poverty in the Buraku communities. It demonstrated how around 30% of workers were in 'unstable' employment, 9.4% working as day-labourers; dependence on social welfare in Osaka city was 3% in Dōwa areas (compared to 1.0% in the city as a whole) and 6% in the prefecture's Buraku communities (0.9% outside them) (Osaka Dōwa Jigyō Gojūnenshi, 2001, 114).

During the early 1960s, provision for the Dōwa budget continued to increase: from ¥46m in 1959 to ¥100m 1960 and ¥263m 1962. There were renewed demands for low-rent housing but policy also included new provision for infrastructure, economic support, and education. While the BLL only gave a cautious, qualified welcome to the Dōtaishin in 1965, the Fudōsokkyō soon became involved in a campaign for its full implementation. The prefecture set up its own Dōwa policy committee in 1966 and, following the prospect of new funding, the commerce and agriculture sections of the bureaucracy also began to take an interest in Dōwa policy.

So, in the mid-1960s when central government was moving towards formulating a Dōwa policy, Osaka prefecture had already been implementing one for 15 years at a cumulative total cost of ¥1,022,012m of which around a third had, one way or another, come from central government. It included projects to improve the living environment, build public housing, renew, or create infrastructural facilities such as clinics, sewage and water systems, public baths, and roads. In addition, there was funding for education to support teachers in the classroom, to enable attendance at school and university, and to educate the wider public. Meanwhile, the Fudōsokkyō occupied an intermediate position between the BLL, the local administrators, and Buraku communities and had become involved in both the lobbying for and aspects of the administration of Dōwa projects. This meant that members of the BLL, as members of the Fudōsokkyō committees, were involved in the allocation of some of the benefits produced by Dōwa projects, such as housing, which it distributed with a preference for those who were active in the movement (Morooka V, 1985, 172). There is no doubt that the lines separating these groups were becoming blurred.

Osaka prefecture and the implementation of the SML, 1969–82

As we have seen, Osaka prefecture had been supporting Dōwa projects across the 1950s and 1960s with limited resources most of which funded projects on road maintenance, drains, communal baths, and Rinpokan. From the mid-1960s, the prefectural Dōwa budget increased steadily (Table 8.4):

The prefecture and city established a Dōwa Taisakubu and Dōwa Taisakuhitsu in October and December 1966, respectively, to plan their responses to the Dōtaishin. In October 1968 and October 1969, the Dōwa policy councils of the city and prefecture presented their mayor and governor with proposals for the development of local Dōwa policy. These local government plans were more positive than those at the national level about the need to eliminate prejudice and discrimination and placed emphasis on respecting the wishes of Buraku communities so as to enhance their autonomy.

But it was not clear how the prefectural or city *Dōsokkyō* fitted into this planning process. In 1967, it tried to define its position:

> Dōsokkyō organises the Buraku masses but it is not a movement group which campaigns for complete liberation... nor is it a body that lobbies on behalf of its claimants. Rather it is a consultative body that enquires how to promote Dōwa projects so that they enhance Buraku liberation to make optimal use of the Dōwa funds and projects and make clear the educational elements in the projects.
>
> (Quoted in Osaka Dōwa Jigyō Gojūnenshi, 2001, 170)

As the range of Dōwa activity increased in the 1970s and the amounts of money grew, there was an increased scope for Dōsokkyō committees at the city and prefectural levels to play a supportive or advisory role in the

Table 8.4 Osaka Prefecture Dōwa Project Allocations, Late 1960s

1965	¥799m
1966	¥1,080m
1967	¥1,990m
1968	¥2,894m

(Osaka Dōwa Jigyō Gojūnenshi, 2001, 392)

Table 8.5 Osaka Prefecture Dōwa Project Allocations: First Five Years of the SML

1969	¥6,652m
1970	¥9,642m
1971	¥11,422m
1972	¥18,806m
1973	¥21,838m

Osaka Dōwa Jigyō Gojūnenshi (2001, 393).

surveys, management of housing, or development of programmes, for instance, to assist SME promotion.

The passage of the SML at the national level did not see the immediate increase in the amounts of Dōwa funding by Osaka prefecture or city that one might have expected. It was only in 1972 that the provision really starts to accelerate. By the end of the first five-year period of SML implementation, the Dōwa budget stood at ¥21,838m and would continue to exceed ¥20,000m for most of the next 20 years (Osaka Dōwa Jigyō Gojūnenshi, 2001, 393).

The bulk of Dōwa project funding was spent on construction projects that benefited the communities as a whole but there were also a range of programmes that paid cash directly to Buraku households. Upham gives an overview of the system of financial grants provided in the mid-1970s by Osaka city to families eligible for Dōwa payments: biannual grants, ¥11,000 in mid-summer and ¥12,000 at year end; on marriage ¥75,000 and birth of a child ¥215,000; grants enabling school attendance from day care to high school; fees for universities plus an annual attendance grant with similar provision for those enrolled in vocational training. He estimated that a family with two children could receive as much as ¥400,000 annually. This did not include indirect payments such as subsidised rents or low interest loans. Most were provided regardless of income (Upham, 1980, 49). Osaka city was perhaps a little more generous than most local authorities but the range of payments was similar wherever Dōwa policy was implemented (Table 8.5).

The JCP and Dōwa policy

However, barely had this new phase of Dōwa policy begun than it became engulfed in controversy and conflict which was particularly intense in Osaka. Criticism of Dōwa policy came mainly from the JCP which was a significant player in local politics. Both the JCP and the JSP had supported Kuroda Ryōichi in his successful campaign to become governor in 1971 but by 1975, the JCP was his sole party sponsor and at least part of the reason for this change in strategy by the JSP was down to disagreements about Dōwa policy.

The BLL and the *Dōsokkyō* in both Osaka prefecture and city insisted that Dōwa policy should not become 'Yūwa-ist' by which they meant that it should not be used by central or local governments to reward Buraku élites for compliance with their policies or by local élites to build up their political and economic power bases within Buraku communities – which is how the pre-war Yūwa policies were perceived to have evolved. Moreover, from the time of the formation of the Suiheisha in 1922, it had been part of the movement's ideology that, 'We ...shall achieve total liberation by our own efforts'. Its founding declaration explicitly rejected relying on charity or the efforts of others and sought instead 'to emancipate ourselves by promoting respect for our human dignity'. This was interpreted to mean that Dōwa funding should not make residents of Buraku communities the passive recipients of state aid but rather be used to encourage them to take an active role in freeing themselves from their discriminatory circumstances. This fear that too much social welfare creates welfare dependency and a class of the indigent poor is shared by both conservative politicians and some progressives.

However, we must remember that left of centre politics was dominated by Marxist ideas of various stripes and the Buraku liberation movement was no exception. In the eyes of JCP activists, there was a concern that Dōwa policy might be implemented in a way that undermined the solidarity of the Buraku-based working class. The JCP took the line across the 1950s that the Buraku problem could not be solved independently of the emancipation of the working class as a whole. So, to treat the Buraku problem as an isolated issue, in particular to single out their communities for special treatment, would divide the working class. It was, they argued, an example of rightist reformism.

The exact relationship of the Buraku communities to the class structure of contemporary Japan was an issue that exercised many Marxist theorists of the time and this is not the place to discuss it in depth.[3] Simply put, the JCP argued that rather than demanding special treatment through the Dōwa programme, the BLL should work with other parts of the proletarian movement, not only labour unions but also, for example, the organisations representing Koreans resident in Japan, to demand the provision of facilities that all low-income households would have access to in a way that would enhance working-class solidarity.

There was one aspect of Dōwa administration that its JCP critics took particular exception to as being a source of community division – the *Madoguchi Ippon* strategy which we will translate as the 'Single Window'. As we have seen, there was no objective element that could be used to identify someone as being of Buraku background. Moreover, the letter of the Special Measures Law did not provide much help defining who might be eligible for the benefits that it made available since in its key article five, it spoke only of those communities and their residents whose 'economic development has been impeded by historical and social reasons'. So how could local government decide which communities and within them which households should have their roads improved or get access to new housing or benefit from the grants to enable school attendance? In Kyoto, the local government accepted the word of applicants that they were indeed of Buraku origin on the grounds that the degree of discrimination was such that no mainstream Japanese person would fraudulently so identify themselves. In 1965 it adopted the so-called *zokuchi/zokujin* policy which allowed benefits only to be provided to Buraku people in Buraku communities (Upham 1980, 55 n 54; Yamamoto, 2020, 154). This strategy was associated with Asada Zennosuke who became a leader of the BLL in 1966 following the death of Matsumoto Jiichirō. The BLL tried to draw an analogy between nationality and Buraku status as a qualification for the receipt of state benefits such as welfare. However, the location of Buraku communities even in urban areas had changed since the Tokugawa period and there had been extensive degrees of migration both into and out of them. So although in many places the test of 'common knowledge' could identify Buraku boundaries with some precision, it might not help decide uncontrovertibly where Buraku 'really' were.

Migration into these communities made identifying the recipients of individual Dōwa benefits difficult too. From the late 1960s, the BLL had campaigned to restrict access to the *koseki* records. As a result from 1976 local administrators could not refer to them for routine purposes. How then were they to decide where and who should benefit from the Dōwa programmes? One possibility might have been for them to devise maps of the local Buraku communities and/or registers of the families in them who were direct descendants of the marginal communities of the Edo era. However, the BLL feared that this would simply create another set of records that could be used for discriminatory purposes. In some places, the local Rinpokan created lists of households in the locality who were eligible to benefit from the programmes they administered. Sometimes, this meant that it was representatives of the BLL who were responsible for certifying eligibility for Dōwa funds. However, Mizuuchi shows that the BLL did not monopolise this role and, for example, that in several towns in in Wakayama prefecture, the Zenkairen was as influential as the BLL and in one 'JCP assembly members acted as intermediaries between local government and the Zenkairen'. In one small city where a quarter of the population were Buraku residents, neither of the major national organisations were involved in the negotiations about Dōwa projects (Mizuuchi, 1998, 42).

In Osaka, it was the prefectural or city Dōsokkyō committee that negotiated with local government about the Dōwa projects and often controlled access to Dōwa funding by certifying who in a Dōwa community was of Buraku heritage. Based on his fieldwork conducted in the mid-1970s, Upham explained that to access any of the Dōwa programmes' benefits, a prospective recipient had to first apply to the community Dōsokkyō which would normally forward the application to the appropriate part of the local administration – construction section for housing, education section for a scholarship, etc. It would occasionally use its discretion to give priority access to (say) housing to those who had fought most actively in the campaigns to improve the living conditions in their community. Activists such as Oga argued that the Single Window strategy was about strengthening Buraku solidarity, and placing Dōwa policy under democratic control. It was not necessary to be a member of the BLL to be eligible for benefits but simply to be active within the local community (Morooka V, 1985, 184).

This was relatively uncontroversial until the late 1960s when the JCP faction first formed a splinter group which sought to 'reform' the BLL and then in 1976 broke away entirely from it. From that point, the JCP criticism was not just a theoretical point about the way Dōwa policy weakened solidarity within the working-class movement but more concretely it also claimed that the BLL used its control of the 'Single Window' to ensure that only those supporting the mainstream BLL got access to Dōwa benefits. This they argued was unfair, undemocratic, and unconstitutional (Osaka Dōwa Jigyō Gojūnenshi, 2001, 218–9). Claimants who objected to the role played by the BLL in Dōwa administration supported by the JCP or its affiliates launched court cases in dozens of different districts during the 1970s. The one that attracted most attention was brought to the Osaka High Court and merits further attention.

The case concerned an application for Dōwa-related pregnancy benefits that in 1972 the plaintiff submitted to her local branch of the Osaka Welfare Office without Dōsokkyō endorsement. The city refused to consider it on the grounds that it was 'incomplete'. She asked the court to declare this (in) action illegal on the grounds that it was unfair and contrary to article 10 of the Local Autonomy Law which granted equally right of access to the activities of all residents to the function of local government and constitutionally guaranteed freedoms of thought and association.

There were two strands to her argument. First, that requiring the endorsement by Dōsokkyō of a claim for Dōwa benefits amounted to 'illegally delegating...official duties to a private institution'. And, second, that getting Dōsokkyō endorsement required their judging her to be of 'Buraku origin' and having a 'desire for Buraku liberation'. Her lawyers claimed that the first was a violation of the SML because identifying a Burakumin was likely to increase discrimination. Moreover, the second criterion being abstract and vague lent itself either to arbitrary judgements by the Dōsokkyō or amounted in practice to requiring membership of the BLL or one of its affiliates which was a violation of the freedoms guaranteed by the constitution.

The court's opinion first expressed in 1979 and then confirmed later in the 1980s allowed both sides to claim some measure of victory. The role of Dōsokkyō in the process of administering Dōwa programmes was recognised as enabling the city to deal with applications quickly and efficiently. Moreover, the criterion of a 'desire for liberation' was accepted as 'necessary to prevent a return to the paternalistic and humiliating type of Dōwa programs of the past'. However, the court ruled that it was not appropriate for the Dōsokkyō to have a final say in the denial of benefits and, recognising that the Dōsokkyo was dominated by the BLL, it acknowledged that it was difficult for those in the plaintiff's position, i.e. a member of a group militantly opposed to the BLL, to get the required endorsement. Therefore, the court argued that the city must 'provide a second avenue for an applicant who has been refused an endorsement' (both quotes from Upham, 1980, 61).

The BLL feared that this might lead to a proliferation of groups playing some kind of an intermediary role between Burakumin and local government. This does not seem to have happened. Although there were a few places which adopted the 'Osaka-method' of having a third-party organisation like the Dōsokkyō play a role in the Dōwa programme administration, there were many other places where groups affiliated to the BLL or otherwise representing the local Buraku community were involved in both the process of formulating and transmitting demands to the local administration and making sure that the benefits were distributed fairly to those eligible to receive them.

Putting the relationship of the JCP argument to Marxist theory aside, there was some evidence that over the 1950s and 1960s, there had been a degree of cooperation emerging between Burakumin and non-Burakumin within these communities and that demanding improvements only to Buraku communal facilities undermined this. Indeed, it threatened to recreate a 'line' that potentially reinforced isolation of the Buraku. On the other hand, it should also be noted that in some areas of Osaka, the Dōsokkyō from the early 1970s had sought to develop joint struggles with both the local Zainichi Korean communities and other working-class democratic movements (Osaka Dōwa Jigyō Gojūnenshi, 2001, 206).

Another aspect of JCP criticism of Dōwa policy, which was linked to its potentially divisive consequences, was that Dōwa programmes were too generous. They argued, for example, that although Burakumin only made up 2% of the population of Osaka prefecture, Dōwa projects were consuming 9% of the prefectural budget and that by the mid-1970s in some parts of the prefecture, Dōwa projects were consuming half of the available funds (Osaka Dōwa Jigyō Gojūnenshi, 2001, 220). 'Dōwa excess' (*Dōwa torisugi*), they said, was responsible for the crisis in local government finance and driving the feelings of 'envy' (*netami*) that were reinforcing existing prejudices about Buraku communities (see also interview with Sakaki Toshio of the JCP, Mainichi newspaper 7 March 1975, quoted in Chapter 6).

The Fudōsokkyō rebutted these claims point by point showing, for example, that the hospital established by Dōwa funding did not exclusively serve Burakumin but that 80% of its patients came from the wider community. Moreover, it argued that many of the critics' claims exaggerated local government support and underestimated the degree of central government subsidy (Morooka V, 1985, 196–200; Osaka Dōwa Jigyō Gojūnenshi, 2001, 220–1). They further argued that if implementation of Dōwa policy was creating problems for local government finance, this was because central government was not providing the subsidies promised in the SML.

However, the broader points in the JCP allegations resonated with local communities. From the start of the implementation of the SML and at least from the mid-1970s, there was criticism that the Dōwa projects were providing Burakumin with 'unfair' advantages compared to their non-Buraku neighbours creating local jealousies which exacerbated feelings of prejudice. This went beyond local ill feeling and had consequences for local and indeed national politics (see Amos, 2020; Neary 1986).

******

While the overall parameters of Dōwa policy were set out for the prefecture and city by the early 1970s, many municipalities were slow to respond, so the Fudōsokkyō set about encouraging communities to make budget requests in the autumn of each year linking their specific demands to the overall plans and then monitoring the progress of projects in their area. This became particularly important as the amount being spent on infrastructure projects grew. For example, the amount spent on Dōwa programme-funded public works across the prefecture increased from ¥60m in 1968 to ¥620m by 1970 and ¥1,188m by 1973 and the increases in the budget of the Construction and Town Planning section from ¥1,361m to ¥2,343m to ¥3,748m over the same period (Osaka Dōwa Jigyō Gojūnenshi, 2001, 393). As we saw in the previous chapter, the major projects concerned improving roads and bridges, upgrading housing, and providing sewage and drainage. But there were other projects funded by the MoL or MITI SME agency which in Osaka supported the creation of the Leather Research Institute in May 1972 and a Leather Division was set up within the prefectural Technological Research Institute. In 1973, a Buraku Leather Industry Federation was formed to encourage the modernisation of the industry in the face of internationalisation and the growing competition from 'monopoly capital' (Osaka Dōwa Jigyō Gojūnenshi, 2001, 230).

In 1975, the Dōwa budget in the prefecture reached ¥28,649m, peak Dōwa spending of the whole 33-year period. As Table 8.6 illustrates, it decreased gradually if unevenly thereafter.

In the second half of the 1970s, the Dōsokkyō was approaching its 25th anniversary at the same time as the SML-funded Dōwa programme was entering its second five-year phase. It renewed its commitment to preventing Dōwa projects becoming either examples of state benevolence or simple welfare policies. Its stated aim was to ensure that the projects contributed to

Table 8.6 Osaka Prefecture Dōwa Project Allocations: Decline at the End of the 1970s

1975	100
1976	77.3
1977	86.4
1978	76.9
1979	81.5
1980	80.1

Osaka Dōwa Jigyō Gojūnenshi (2001, 250).

Buraku liberation whether or not the recipients were members of the BLL. It claimed that it did not give privileged access to Dōwa funding to BLL members but neither did it allow funds to be used to support Buraku 'bosses' or the BLL leadership. Rather, it sought simply to ensure the democratic management of Dōwa funding (Osaka Dōwa Jigyō Gojūnenshi, 2001, 237–9). It argued that the strategy distributed Dōwa funding regardless of BLL membership and contributed to solidarity with the Buraku communities and the resolution of Buraku issues (Osaka Dōwa Jigyō Gojūnenshi, 2001, 250–1).

However, there were doubts about what impact these Dōwa programmes were having. In 1982, a survey of conditions in Osaka was carried out by a group supported by the Dōsokkyō, the BLL, and the Buraku Liberation Research Institute (BLRI). It demonstrated that Burakumin were still highly reliant on public housing, were more likely than their neighbours to be unemployed or in unstable jobs, still lagged behind in terms of educational attainment, and still were experiencing discrimination. So, they concluded, after more than a decade of SML administration of the Dōwa projects, there was clear evidence of unresolved problems (Table 8.7).

Table 8.7 Summary of Results of 1982 Survey, Osaka Prefecture

25,900 households, 82,756 population 3.2 people per household

Housing:

- those resident in publicly owned housing (prefecture or municipality) 59.2%, privately rented 11.6%,
- owner occupier 26.2% [compared to 43.3% in Osaka-fu, and 59.2% nationally]
- housing that does not meet national minimum (space) standards: 31.5% [compared to 24.1% Osaka-fu, and 14.8% nationally]

Income:

Annual take home pay ¥273,000 (including Dōwa programme benefits) [prefectural average ¥380,000]

Employment:

- 53.5% usually in work	[66.3% Osaka-fu]
- 18.1% in unstable employment	[7.06% Osaka-fu]
- 17.1% completely unemployed	[Osaka-fu 3.3%]

[Some evidence of improvement in extent of professional employment since 1973, from 3.9% to 13.3% and in service industries, from 5.4% to 11.9%]

Educational achievement:

Still lagging some 20 years behind national average. Only 67.3% reported they had no difficulty reading and writing.

Discrimination:

40.4% of the sample reported direct experience of discrimination: 22.5% in marriage, 18.5% in the neighbourhood, 12.1% at school, 3.7% at work.

49.5% of marriages since 1980 are with non-Buraku partners but in half the cases they do not keep in touch with their parents.

n = 67,210.

Osaka Dōwa Jigyō Gojūnenshi (2001, 267–71).

In 1984, the Osaka-fu Dōwa Taisaku Shingikai, chaired by Yamamoto Noboru, a sociologist from Osaka City University who was also a member of the national level Chitaikyō, presented the governor with a report that suggested the next phase of Dōwa policy should address further infrastructural improvements, educational reform, and enhancement of employment opportunities. It endorsed the role of the Dōsokkyō as a promotional and cooperative structure that could lead by reflecting the general will of the residents of the communities and thereby provide democratic oversight. It continued to see itself having an important role mediating between the movement and the project administration.

Dōsokkyō had extended its reach across the prefecture so that it had committees in 42 of the 48 Buraku communities. In part as a result of its agitation, in March 1985, the prefectural assembly made it unlawful to commission an investigation into an individual's background for the purposes of discrimination. This was a pioneering move that would be followed by other local authorities in subsequent years. In a related policy, the prefecture and city decided to establish a museum of human rights history to be located near to Osaka's largest Buraku community and the location of the city's leather industry. It would become known as Osaka Jinken Rekishi Shiryōkan or *Liberty Osaka* for short (Osaka Dōwa Jigyō Gojūnenshi, 2001, 276).

In the mid-1980s then, at what would turn out to be the mid-point in the evolution of Dōwa policy under the SML, there was a massive amount being invested in Dōwa projects across the prefecture and city, a high level of interest in human rights alongside some lingering doubts about how effective Dōwa programmes were at reducing prejudice and eliminating the material basis for discrimination.

Dōwa policy in Osaka from the mid-1980s to the end of the SML

Figure 8.1 clearly shows that 1973–96 was the period which saw the bulk of Dōwa project spending in a number of senses. The early 1970s was the period when SML funding consumed the greatest portion of the prefectural budget but in Osaka, as in most areas of Japan, it was after 1975 when the large-scale, transformative infrastructural projects were implemented. However, precisely because of the high profile of many of these projects, Dōwa policy began to attract increased criticism from neighbouring communities that there was now some kind of 'reverse discrimination' in operation which was disadvantaging mainstream citizens. Then in response to and arguably taking advantage of this situation, it was also the peak period for the national debate between various parts of the Buraku movement divided as it now was between the BLL mainstream based in Osaka, the JCP-oriented Zenkairen based in Kyoto, and the conservative Zen Nihon Dōwakai whose main office was in Tokyo. The main thrust of the Zenkairen argument at this point was that even if there had been good reasons to provide special funding for Buraku communities, that time was now past and most of the 'special projects' should be brought to a close with some of the remaining schemes –

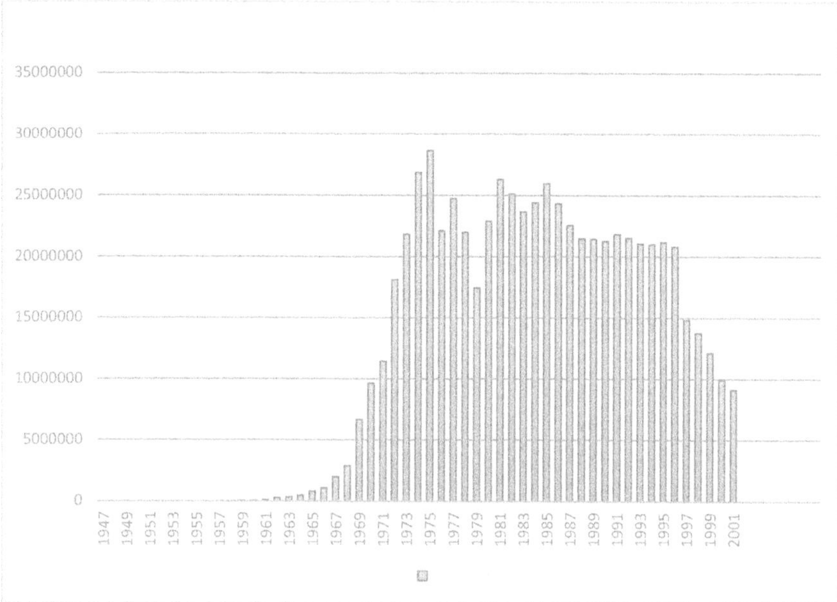

Figure 8.1 Dōwa policy-related expenditure in Osaka prefecture, 1947–2002.

providing school and university scholarships, for example – being opened up to all applicants from low-income households. The latter argument was supported by allegations that there was a high degree of mis-use and corruption in the administration of Dōwa projects which was channelling taxpayers' money into the pockets of people who were either community élites and/or involved in organised crime, or both.

At the national level, the Chitaikyō in December 1986 set out guidelines for the re-examination of Dōwa policies at the local level. Where possible, the 'special' policies should end and be replaced by 'general' policies. Where targets had been met and outstanding needs were few, Dōwa projects should cease. As a matter of principle, the schemes which gave assistance to individuals and families of the kind that Upham had documented in the mid-1970s should close. Overall, this amounted to planning for the termination of Dōwa policy. The next extension, the report argued, should be the last. Advice to governors issued on 1 April 1987 urged them to examine the full range of Dōwa policies and ensure that the criteria used to identify those individuals and households eligible for payments were 'appropriate and fair', 'objective' and that where projects were extended care should be taken to avoid the creation of big differences between Dōwa areas and their neighbours.

The immediate impact of this in Osaka was that they abolished 13 'soft' projects, i.e. non-infrastructure projects, and support for *Jidōkan* (children's centres) was cut from 50% to 33% (Osaka Dōwa Jigyō Gojūnenshi, 2001, 285). The prefectural Dōwa Taisaku Shingikai produced a report for the governor with eight key points that included the target of completing the material projects within five years, abolishing those judged ineffective, ensuring that funded projects enable self-reliance, and continuing to promote *keihatsu* – rights awareness projects.

Meanwhile, the BLL was shifting its position. In 1988, it began considering what it might mean to enter its 'third phase' when its focus would still be opposing discrimination but now in an international context. Locally, the Dōsokkyō committees continued to play an important role as the promoter of Dōwa projects within Buraku communities but, in line with the new policy, it sought to place less emphasis on the distribution of goods while still working with low-income groups within the communities in *machizukuri* (urban renewal) projects of various kinds. Consistent with this, the prefecture produced its *Dōwachiku Sōgō Fukushi Keikaku* (Comprehensive Welfare Plan for Dōwa areas) in May 1988 (Osaka Dōwa Jigyō Gojūnenshi, 2001, 287). This suggested a broad conception of welfare that included plans for both health care and employment. Another report on the provision of lifelong education noted the need for Kaihō Kaikan – Liberation Halls, a local name for Rinpokan – to provide adult training not only for social workers active in Buraku communities but also for those serving the aged and disabled (Osaka Dōwa Jigyō Gojūnenshi, 2001, 288). Nevertheless, although the documentation produced at the time talked pessimistically about budget reductions and change of focus, between 1987 and 1991, the prefectural Dōwa budget only fell very slowly year on year and actually increased by 2.6% in 1991 (Osaka Dōwa Jigyō Gojūnenshi, 2001, 291).

Another extensive survey was carried out in 1990 that covered over 34,000 households in 48 communities across Osaka prefecture. To pick out some of its key points: it concluded that household incomes were still relatively low, only 80% of the local average (although up from 70% in 1971) which they explained by reference to the continuing higher reliance of day-labour or similarly unstable employment – 8.8% compared to 5.3% – and high levels of social security dependence – 12.5% compared to 0.94%. Around a third (31.7%) of Buraku residents surveyed had experienced discrimination as had about a fifth (19.3%) of the non-Burakumin residents of the communities. In the prefecture as a whole, 32.6% of Buraku dwellers were not of Buraku origin and in Osaka city it was slightly higher, 41.2%. Overall, educational performance in school was equivalent to the mainstream but 20% of parents were concerned about the impact of discrimination of their children's education and the rates of admission of higher education remained about 20 years behind the mainstream (Osaka Dōwa Jigyō Gojūnenshi, 2001, 292–8).

The Dōsokkyō activities at the start of the 1990s aimed to encourage the opening up of access to Dōwa projects. In 1992, for example, their plans incorporated consideration of the problems faced by Koreans resident in

Osaka (*Zainichi Chōsen/Kankokujin*). The following year, they decided to promote the use of Kaihō Kaikan for education projects made available to neighbouring communities. In 1995, 'Dōsokkyō method' that gave it the much-criticised ability to control the 'Single Window' to access Dōwa project benefits was seriously questioned and in Osaka city, the Dōsokkyō consultation system was ended.

The prefectural position had been set out in a 1995 document, 'Basic Directions for Osaka Dōwa Administration', which re-affirmed that Dōwa policy would be needed while discrimination existed and there would continue to be 'the need for efforts to eliminate those elements that give rise to discrimination' (Osaka Dōwa Jigyō Gojūnenshi, 2001, 322). Overall, in the final half of the 1990s, Osaka's local governments began to move from a sole focus on Dōwa towards a broader focus on human rights issues. This included concrete plans for the coordination of activity in Buraku communities with plans for *machizukuri* – urban renewal. Overall, Dōwa spending gradually dropped: 1996 saw a 40% reduction in the prefectural budget. In December 1998 and then in April 2000, both the city and prefecture adopted new sets of ordinances that framed policy in terms of 'Building a Society which Respects Human Rights' (Onishi, 2009, 698).

Two trends can be observed on approaching the end of the 1990s. There was a growing consensus that the task of the improvement of basic facilities and infrastructure was now complete but there remained unresolved issues in employment, education, and marriage. Reflecting the views in the Iken Gushin of 1996, the Buraku issue was seen no longer as simply a domestic concern but rather part of Japan's international obligations in the sense that Dōwa problems were not issues of the past but of respect for human rights in the present and future. In this spirit, the BLL at its conference held in April 1998 adopted a number of new points, including taking a lead in the new era for human rights to promote political engagement and encourage participation in new joint projects in the fields of education or welfare. In parallel with this, Osaka prefecture passed regulations in November 1998 concerning human rights promotion and protection (Osaka Dōwa Jigyō Gojūnenshi, 2001, 332–3). The second trend towards a broader emphasis on human rights connected with demands made initially in 2000 that Japan should ratify the ILO convention C111 'concerning discrimination in respect of employment and occupation'. Japan remains one of only 12 countries which have not ratified it at the time of writing (although significantly another is the USA).

The Dōsokkyō began to change its approach. While continuing to assert that 'Liberation is the goal, Dōwa projects the means', it began to suggest a change of emphasis from dealing with the *results* of discrimination to the *causes* of discrimination which was not necessarily incompatible with the absorption of Dōwa projects into more general welfare or infrastructural projects. Within this process, the Dōsokkyō continued to play a role representing the ideas of residents in their discussions with local bureaucrats to ensure that the projects funded operated in their interests.

Another major survey was conducted in Osaka prefecture between November 1999 and May 2000 which formed the basis of a report published the following year on policies and procedures to be taken when the Special Measures Law expired. Over 85% reported being aware of the Buraku problem; rates of welfare dependence remained relatively high – Dōwa areas 8.9%, rest of Osaka prefecture 2.6% – with the figures for unemployment being 9.7% male (6.6%) and 8.2% female (5.6%) (Osaka Dōwa Jigyō Gojūnenshi, 2001, 353). One-third of Burakumin surveyed had encountered discrimination, half of them in the previous ten years.

The response of the Osaka Prefecture Dōwa Policy Council to this was a report of September 2001 that noted how many social problems were concentrated in Buraku areas. It proposed that major projects and overall policy should focus on three aims: to eliminate discrimination and foster human rights, to ensure that remaining Dōwa policy supports self-reliance, and to encourage the free exchange of ideas across the communities. It emphasised, however, that Buraku discrimination still existed and problems remained within Buraku communities so that Dōwa policy would need to continue even if only within the human rights policies supported by local government.

Osaka Dōwa policy in the twenty-first century

The position taken in the Iken Gushin of 1996 was that although the Dōwa SML would shortly come to an end, this did not mean that the problem was solved but rather that a new approach would be required that focused on human rights. And, as we saw in the account of policy at the national level in Chapter 6, towards the end of the 1990s there seemed to be reasons for optimism that this approach might yield some results if government pursued the line then being taken.

In Osaka, consistent with this decision to re-focus on human rights, in 2002 the prefectural Dōsokkyō was transformed into the Osaka-fu Jinken Kyōkai (Osaka Prefecture Human Rights Council). Over the next decades, it sought to provide support and advice on a broad range of human rights issues, including the organisation of training courses for local government employees. As well as Dōwa policies, it addresses a wide range of issues, including gender equality, children's rights, the elderly, HIV, Hansen's disease, the homeless, and LGBT+ issues (Oga, 2002, 8–9).

Dōwa policy projects in the prefecture were wound down quite quickly after 2002 and the expiration of the SML. However, debate continued about the situation within the Buraku communities of Osaka: whether discrimination continued to exist and what, if anything, central or local government could do to address these problems. To a certain extent, the different approaches divide on 'party' lines. That is to say that the research that comes out of the Buraku Mondai Kenkyūjo, whose members have been critical of the BLL approach and were sceptical of the value of the Dōwa policy programmes particularly in its last ten years, starts from the premise that the 'problem' has been 'solved'. Those connected with the BLL, while not necessarily contradicting this view, take a more nuanced position. To illustrate the range of opinion on the present situation, let me briefly summarise three pieces of research on the situation in Osaka.

Kōno Takeo, in an essay published in 2010, concludes that the Buraku problem as such has been solved and that if there remain any outstanding issues, they are the result of the neo-liberal policies that have been introduced since the start of the century which removed many of the safety nets within the welfare system. Using data from a survey carried out in 2000, he suggests that 61.6% of Buraku residents live in public housing much of which, around 80%, was built in the period 1961–80. It is therefore old, in need of refurbishment, but rents are low. The flow of people in and out of these communities is high such that at any one time, 8–11% of the Dōwa housing (*kairyō jūtaku*) is unoccupied (Kōno, 2010, 98). He suggests that over the decades of Dōwa policy implementation, it acted as a 'poverty pump' by which he seems to mean that those who thrived in the late twentieth century whether benefiting from Dōwa policies or simply by their own efforts moved out of the Buraku communities, whereas those with poor and unstable economic circumstances moved in. Particularly since 2007 with the opening of *kairyō jūtaku* to all, not just Burakumin or members of the BLL, migration into Dōwa districts has increased. He suggests that in this process, these 'immigrants' are bringing their poverty with them into the (former) Buraku communities rather than the fact of residence in those communities being the cause of that poverty, as measured, for example, by dependence on social welfare. This can be dealt with by 'general' welfare or housing policies; Dōwa-specific policies are not required (Kōno, 2010, 118).

Noting that there has been no reliable data on Dōwa communities produced in this century, Uchida Ryushi uses data from the 2005 and 2010 censuses to assess social change in the Dōwa districts. His analysis looked at 'socially excluded' areas of Osaka prefecture as a whole which he defines according to six criteria linked to household, education, and employment (Uchida 2015). He found that the population of Dōwa districts dropped from 92,436 to 79,411 between 2000 and 2010 but at the same time 25,413 people have moved in suggesting total emigration of around 38,438 – more than one-third (Uchida, 2015, 7). Of current residents, around two-thirds (65.6%) were there five years previously but only 2% are known to have come from outside Osaka prefecture, 9.9% came from within the same municipality, 3.2% from other municipalities in the prefecture, but the background of 16.5% was unknown. Some of his data on housing confirms Kōno's conclusions in that while only 6.3% of Osaka's general population live in public housing (*kōei jūtaku*), the figure was 40.7% in Dōwa communities and 45.5% for 'socially excluded areas'. Uchida looked in detail at the patterns of family structure, household size, education, and employment patterns. In summary, he found that levels of educational achievement remained low for

Buraku residents even after 40 years of the SML programmes which might have been expected to have had an impact by 2010 on people in middle age, and that there is a clear link between education and employment.

Shima Kazuhiro used not only data from the 2005 and 2010 censuses but also the 2008 Survey on Housing and Land Statistics and the 2012 Basic Survey on Employment to examine the formation of class structures in Osaka city. He begins by demonstrating that incomes in the 12 Dōwa areas are low, unemployment high and that they contain more single parent families and older people. However, he points out that it is not only people in Dōwa areas who are poor and, while they are poorer than average residents of Osaka city, there are considerable income differentials between them. He looks in some detail at the patterns of emigration from the districts: most are children aged 5–14, adults aged 30–40 (their parents?), and those aged over 70. Conversely, those aged 40–70 tend to stay put. The numbers moving out of public housing are high among all ages and the absolute number of residents in public housing dropped between 2005 and 2010. There is a relatively high level of immigration of younger people. This creates two distinct groups: younger 'immigrants' in their 20s and a stable older group aged 40–70. He asks if this is leading to a reduction in the 'specialness' of the identity of these communities. The absence of data does not permit any analysis of those who move out but overall he concludes that the social status of those who move in is higher than those already resident in the Dōwa areas. Migration then is changing the class characteristics of the formerly 'impoverished' Buraku. However, this is only aggregate data and he points to degrees of class difference that continue to exist within Buraku communities (Shima, 2015).

The number of people moving out of public housing is high among all age groups and the absolute number of residents in public housing dropped between 2005 and 2010. The social class of those resident in public housing is low but so is that of those who move into such accommodation. So, he asks, is the low social status of those resident in and who move into public housing a characteristic of Dōwa areas? Or is it a characteristic of people who live in public housing? In other words, is this a problem of recreating poverty in a district that has a lot of public housing rather than a problem of Buraku poverty in a Dōwa district?

He presents evidence of a relatively rapid turnover of residents in the private rental sector and his detailed study of four Dōwa districts in Osaka city suggested that those who move into private rented accommodation tend to be in white-collar occupations (skilled office or sales workers) with permanent contracts. So, there may be some evidence of the old (Dōwa) identity of these areas disappearing, or at least changing, but there remains the possibility of them retaining an 'impoverished core' that remains relatively isolated within the public housing where some of the elements of Buraku discrimination are being recreated – low status, low paid occupations, and a location with a 'poor reputation' (Shima, 2015).

However, it should be repeated that there is great variation between Dōwa areas nowadays, even in regard to public housing. Although the average figure for residence in public housing in Dōwa areas is around 40% (compared to only 5.8% for Osaka prefecture as a whole), it ranges between 0% and 99% across different communities. Similarly rates of unemployment in Dōwa districts are on average 13.5% (compared to Osaka-fu 8.0%) but ranged between 4.5% and 26.2% (Uchida, 2015, 16).

To move on to a different topic: the attitudes of Osaka residents to human rights. A survey carried out in 2010 was compared to similar ones conducted in 2000 and 2005. Given a list of possible reasons for avoiding marriage with someone either for oneself or for one's child, which also included occupation, educational background, and nationality, 20.6% ticked Dōwa district resident for themselves and 21.2% for their children compared to 20.2% in 2005 and 18.1% in 2000 – this compares to responses about education 13.7% (17.9% for a child), occupation 26.4% (35.0% for a child), and nationality 25.2% (26.7% for a child). The 2010 survey also found that many more people than in 2005 would avoid living in a property in a Dōwa district or where the local primary school enrolled pupils from a Dōwa district: 61.4% compared to 28.2%. The same survey asked respondents to predict whether discrimination in marriage and employment would disappear in the near future and found that there was significantly less optimism than in 2005 (Kamibara 2012).

What conclusions, however tentative, can we reach from this about the impact of Dōwa policy in Osaka? Certainly, the majority – over 90% – of the local community were aware of the 'Buraku Question' and 20% were prepared to admit that they would avoid a 'Dōwa marriage'. One suspects that this underestimates feeling about the issue since if Dōwa education at school and *keihatsu* programmes did nothing else, they will have made people aware that they should not hold prejudices or at least admit to them. This suggests that there is a need for more education and perhaps moral leadership by the state in stating categorically that discrimination is not acceptable. This might happen if government were to take seriously the commitments made in the 2016 law against Buraku discrimination.

However, there is the intriguing suggestion in the work of both Uchida and Shima that the problem is no longer just about the (former) Dōwa districts but rather focuses on residents in public housing. So while the identities of Buraku communities and their boundaries with the mainstream are being eroded by migration in and out, the public housing within them is still seen as the location where people on low incomes and with low status reside. Prejudices against these people are related to and reinforced by older discriminatory ideas which originate in the twentieth century and earlier. The solution to this problem would be one that addressed the low quality of public housing in Osaka as a whole, not just in Dōwa communities. Interestingly, this is a solution which resonates with the proposals that have come from the JCP and its supporters since the 1990s.

The presence of several large Buraku communities and the BLL's research organisation in Osaka has made it the area that is most frequently referred to when examples are sought of the effectiveness or otherwise of Dōwa policy. This is mainly because there is relatively little attention paid to the implementation of Dōwa policy elsewhere in Japan. In the next two sections of this chapter, we will seek to partially remedy this by providing summaries of the evolution of Dōwa policy first in Nara prefecture which is also in the Kansai region and then in one part of Fukuoka where the context of Dōwa policy is quite different.

Dōwa policy in Nara prefecture

From pre-war to the end of the occupation

According to the 1935 survey, Nara prefecture had 49 municipalities which hosted 77 Buraku communities with a total of 37,444 residents, 6.6% of the total population.[4] Most were relatively small with only nine having more than a thousand residents. There were four Buraku in Nara city, two significantly larger than the others: in terms of households: 203, 125, 45, and 53. The same survey lists virtually all of the prefecture's Buraku communities as relying on day-labour as their primary or secondary source of income.

Histories of the outcaste communities in Nara city and prefecture demonstrate the existence of communities of *kawaramono* – 'riverside folk' – at least as far back as the thirteenth century (Teraki and Kurokawa, 2019, 30). How far there is any continuity between those communities and those of the medieval period and then between them and the Tokugawa period is debated by historians but we can say without doubt that many if not most of the Buraku communities that existed in the twentieth century had roots that go back before the establishment of the Tokugawa regime. And there were several of them comprising households which produced leather goods (Nara-ken, 2003, 3).

The population of urban Buraku increased rapidly from the mid-nineteenth century. The larger Buraku community in Nara city reportedly consisted of 21 households with 105 members in 1850 but had grown to 171 and 807 by 1917. This would more than double again by 1950 with 1,447 people being recorded in 397 households that year (Nara-shi, 1983, 623). The leather industry continued to be important post-war: in the same Buraku, 18.8% of households reported involvement in some aspect of leather making in 1959 (Nara-shi, 1983, 650).

Attempts to 'improve' Buraku communities began early in Nara prefecture. The Matsukata deflation policies of the early 1880s had a major impact on all Buraku communities but those in Nara city that were more dependent on the leather industry fared worse than average. The wealthier members of these communities tried to encourage their fellow residents to make themselves more acceptable to the mainstream by improving their living conditions and education standards. In some Buraku communities, committees were set up to encourage school attendance and as many as 20 such groups had been created by 1909. These were the forerunners of local Yūwa committees and around this time the prefectural government funded a series of projects designed to improve everything from toilets to morals (Nara-ken, 2003, 20). Meanwhile, as mentioned in Chapter 3, there were those such as Matsui Shōgorō who had against all the odds acquired a university education but returned to the area determined to not only encourage his colleagues to improve themselves but also to urge majority society to overcome its prejudices and accept Burakumin as fellow citizens of the empire.

An organisation of and mainly for Burakumin, the Yamato Dōshikai, began in Nara city in 1912 founded and funded by Matsui. It held meetings protesting about discrimination and, through its journal *Meiji no Hikari*, it campaigned against the prejudices held by people within the prefecture and more widely. In parallel with its activities, Nara prefecture devised and implemented new improvement policies from 1912 which, for example, merged the separate schools for Buraku children with their mainstream neighbours and set up clinics to treat trachoma which was affecting up to half the population of some communities (Nara-ken, 2003, 29).

In 1920, the prefecture set a budget of ¥7,000 for Yūwa projects to be spent on roads, sewage, and public baths, half coming from central government and half from the prefecture (Nara-ken, 2003, 34). Then, following the formation of the Suiheisha in 1922 mainly as the result of the organisational initiatives of activists native to Nara prefecture, local authorities encouraged the revival of the Yamato Dōshikai with the new name, Yamato Yūwakai. It made periodic requests for the better funding for 'regional improvement' (*chihō kaizen*) in the prefecture and in 1925 it became part of the central Yūwa Kyōkai under Home Ministry (Naimushō) control.

This led to better coordination of the Yūwa strategy. There was some provision of facilities – for example, funding for the improvement of 12 bath houses (*sentō*) and related projects (total cost ¥24,746 of which the prefecture provided half), and support for trachoma clinics in 37 Buraku (total cost ¥3,500, again half from the prefecture). From 1928, 3 November was designated as 'Yūwa Day' – an occasion when posters would be put up, leaflets distributed, and meetings held in schools urging an end to discrimination. In the mid-1930s in anticipation of the Ten-Year Plan, a survey was undertaken of Buraku communities in the prefecture. On the basis of this, they proposed a local version of the plan which included improvement projects in 82 communities across 48 municipalities in the prefecture. There were plans, for example, to build 16 Rinpokan, embark on 73 building improvement projects on 2,866 houses, and build 35 communal work places and 36 communal baths. In FY1936, Yūwa projects began in Nara prefecture at a total cost in the first year of ¥71,287 of which around 38.6% came from the state, 26.3% from the prefecture, and 35% from the municipalities (Nara-ken,

2003, 50–1). According to the plan, every Buraku community would benefit from some kind of Yūwa activity.

The mobilisation of the economy to support the war in 1937 had a deep impact on the leather industry which had remained important within Nara's Buraku communities. Central regulation of the industry from 1938 caused a significant reduction in the number of companies and employees (Nara-ken, 2003, 52–3). In 1939, the Yūwa plan was revised to include finance for 'urban community facilities', to improve living conditions in slums, assist the management of Rinpokan, and provide assistance for those who moved out of the Buraku communities. In 1941, the Yūwa movement in Nara was restructured to create a Daiwa Kiitsukai within which former Suiheisha leaders worked alongside Yūwa administrators. Yūwa project money continued to flow until 1944 supporting improvements to roads, infrastructure, and trachoma clinics with around 80% of funding coming from the state (Nara-shi, 1983, 725–6).

From the late 1940s to 1965

In October 1946, a meeting of the Dōwa Jigyō Kondankai was held in Kyoto with representatives from seven prefectures, Nara being one of them. Nara prefecture supported 41 Dōwa projects in FY 1948 at a cost of just over ¥2m – mainly the provision of roads, bridges, sewage/drinking water, and bath houses with the amount of subsidy for each project varying between 8% and 50% of the total cost (Nara-ken, 2003, 67). The Buraku communities in Nara city still relied on the leather industry, while outside the city they were mainly farmers each with only small plots of land meaning that very few benefited from the post-war land reform. Poverty remained endemic. In 1955, the two largest Buraku communities of Nara city reported rates of reliance on public assistance of 28.8% and 22.3%, while the average for the city was 12.8% (Nara-shi, 1983, 685).

The NCBL spread quickly across Nara as it attempted to establish a presence in each community. Meanwhile, the older generation of Suiheisha activists, who had collaborated with the Yūwa organisations during wartime, created the Muikakai, a group that met on the sixth of every other month to try to build links between the Dōwa administration and their communities. Administration of Dōwa policy in Nara was re-envigorated in 1949 when the local NCBL reacted to an incident of discrimination by demanding the resignation of the governor, the dismissal of the official concerned, and a thorough set of policies addressing Buraku issues. The first two demands were rejected but they did punish the official, establish a research organisation,[5] and set up a Dōwa policy committee within the Public Welfare office of the prefectural administration. In 1951, a local survey of Buraku communities in the prefecture's 46 municipalities was followed by the division of the prefecture into eight blocks for the purposes of Dōwa project administration. In FY1952, a prefectural Dōwa Taisaku Kyōgikai (Dōwa Policy

Council – Ken Dōtaikyō) was established. It was to have a maximum size of 30 and be composed of the chairs of the prefectural assembly committees on health, welfare, education, and the local economy plus appointees from educational institutions in Nara and Buraku movement organisations. It had four sub-committees – welfare, education, industry/economy, and environment improvement and met for the first time on 13 June 1952 (Nara-ken, 2003, 77–82; Nara-shi, 1983, 714).

Yoshimura Kiyotarō had been the first chairman of the pre-war Yūwa education research committee and he resumed his activity post-war producing a key document 'On Dōwa Education' in which he argued that Dōwa education was about 'raising people of character who would respect basic human rights and form the basis of a democratic, free, civilised society' (Nara-ken, 2003, 87). However, a serious practical problem was still how to reduce the long-term absences from school of Buraku children. A survey in 1946 found that 20% of Buraku children but only 5% of mainstream children were absent from school for more than ten days each year. In 1952, a local Dōwa Policy Education Policy Research group was formed to guide policy over the 1950s. It held conferences annually and in 1954 produced a manual on Dōwa education with a new edition being produced annually thereafter. A long-term strategy was developed to create lead teachers with a special responsibility to promote attendance – 14 junior high schools had such teachers by 1958. Meanwhile, in an attempt to fill the gaps left by non-attendance in childhood, evening classes were provided by some schools from 1950 onwards and by 1956 were available in schools in 11 Buraku across the prefecture. In 1957, there was ¥780,000 provided to promote school attendance which rose to ¥1m in 1958. From 1960, grants became available to enable senior high school attendance. These measures did not entirely eliminate the differences between the educational attainment of Buraku children and the mainstream but they narrowed the gap. Between 1960 and 1972, a series of textbooks for use in 'Dōwa Education' entitled '*Nakama*' were prepared for all levels of schooling, including adult education (Nara-ken, 2003, 92).

There were various ways devised to incorporate representatives of Buraku communities into the policy process. In Nara city as early as 1951, a Dōwa Policy Promotion Council had been established with representatives from each of seven communities. This cooperated with the prefectural organisation from the mid-1950s. Nine members of the Muikakai met the governor in March 1953 and later that same day he had meetings with the local branch of the NCBL to discuss the Dōwa policy budget. Meanwhile, groups were being formed in each Buraku community to liaise with the prefectural and municipal Dōwa policy organisations to propose and coordinate the formulation of programmes. The prefecture set up a council formed of representatives from each Buraku community (two from those with over 300 households). While the NCBL sent representatives, such as Yoneda Tomi and Sakamoto Seichirō, to these bodies, it remained suspicious of the possible 'Yūwa-ist' and 'reactionary' nature of these policies.

By 1954, Nara prefecture was spending about ¥7m each year on Dōwa projects. For example, a Rinpokan was constructed in the largest Buraku in Nara city funded jointly by state, prefecture, and municipality, 50:25:25 (Nara-shi, 1983, 716–7). Another priority area was to ensure treatment for trachoma initially in those areas with the highest rates of infection. Nevertheless, until the early 1960s, the prefectural Dōwa budget was quite small, at most ¥15m or around 0.1% of the total of which in most years half was spent on infrastructure, 10–20% on the research centre, and, particularly 1952–4, around 25% on trachoma prevention. At the city level too, treatment of trachoma had a high priority. In 1956, it took on the burden of maintaining the Rinpokan.

In October 1957, a coordinating committee was formed under the leadership of the BLL to campaign against discrimination, encourage the development of Dōwa policy locally, and fight for the democratisation of Buraku communities. The prefectural level Dōtaikyō was re-organised in July 1957 and from early the following year, it began to demand more positive Dōwa policy for education and environment improvement. However, Yoneda Tomi who attended this founding meeting complained that these meetings were doing little to improve conditions, people attending them had no interest in the issues, and rather they fostered discrimination. The small amounts of money were having little impact on anyone's problems.

Around this time, Yagi Kazuo, a JSP Diet member elected eight times in total from Nara prefecture, was leading his party's campaign for the creation of a Buraku policy at the national level. Within the Nara prefectural assembly, the JSP group put forward a series of demands in December 1957 and January 1958 for improvements to local Dōwa policy. These included a training programme in skills such as painting, building, and nine other trades, and an industry promotion programme to improve the quality of leather goods and agricultural practice.

Between 1961 and 1962, prefectural support for Dōwa programmes underwent a step change increasing from ¥14m to ¥56m as it took on policies to provide training for teachers and to improve housing. By 1965, the cost of these projects had doubled to reach ¥110m by which time it was taking up 0.5% of the total budget. The increase in the Dōwa budget in Nara city is similarly dramatic going up from just over ¥5m in 1960 to ¥92m just before the passage of the SML in 1969. The main reason for this increase was the adoption of housing construction projects which by 1968 had built 1,700 Dōwa housing units across the prefecture (Nara-shi, 1983, 727–9).

In January 1965, well before the Dōtaishin was published, the prefectural Dōtaikyō produced a resolution on Buraku policy which called for more spending on the living environment, promoting industry and education. So, just as in Osaka between 1950 and 1965, both prefectural and municipal levels of government in Nara had devised a Dōwa policy and created an administration to implement it. However, unlike in Osaka, structures had been created within both municipal and prefectural levels to represent the interests of the local Buraku communities without the need for a 'third sector' organisation.

Dōwa policy in Nara 1965–87

The immediate response of the prefectural and municipal assemblies to the Dōtaishin in September 1965 was unanimously to approve a motion calling for its 'positive and complete implementation' (Nara-ken, 2003, 120; Nara-shi, 1983, 816). The next step was to establish a Dōwa Policy office within the prefectural building to provide research for the concrete development of policy implementation. However, as in Osaka, the first couple of years did not see much increase in the Dōwa budget (Table 8.8).

By 1972 though, it had increased to consume 2.27% of the prefectural budget, up from 0.54% in 1967. It would reach over 6.13% by 1982 and stay at that level until 1988.

The scale of many projects was quite different to those in Osaka reflecting the smaller size of the Buraku communities. For example, between 1970 and 1977, Nara prefecture cooperated with the MoC's 'smaller community improvement projects' which targeted Dōwa communities 'with over 15 houses of which 50% or more were designated as defective': 724 houses were demolished and 944 constructed in 13 communities across the prefecture during 1970–77. From 1972, loans were made available at 6.2% interest (6% from 1973) to enable the acquisition of land for housing or community improvement projects. Grants of up to ¥2m were available for municipalities to support old people's homes or ¥2.4m in the case of child care facilities. There was a special project to provide additional day nursery places within Buraku areas. In 1975, kindergarten with places for over 60 Buraku-origin children became eligible for this support and an additional 19 teachers were provided. The following year, the threshold was lowered to 40 children and 15 more teachers were funded. From August 1976, proposals were launched aiming to enhance both the quality of care and the qualifications of the carers. Some ten years later in May 1986, these policies were further developed in a policy document, 'Basic Principles for Dōwa Day Nurseries', as the Nara administration was preparing for the new phase of Dōwa project policy (Nara-ken 2003, 129–33).

Table 8.8 Nara Prefecture Dōwa Project Allocations 1967–72

1967	¥177m
1968	¥317m
1969	¥411m
1970	¥600m
1971	¥1046m
1972	¥1692m

Nara-shi (1983, 727).

There was a wide range of other projects. Nara's leather industry had been adversely affected by the combined impact of the 'dollar shock' of 1971 on the ¥/$ exchange rate and the reduction of taxes on imported baseball gloves which were sold at prices well below those produced domestically. In 1972, two projects were launched to provide capital for SMEs to modernise their production with over ¥70m made available in the first year. There were also projects designed to modernise farm management, projects to give career advice to graduates of junior and senior high schools and vocational training schools (Nara-ken, 2003, 137). In Nara city, a five-year project resulted in the demolition of old buildings in Nishinosaka machi and their replacement with seven- and nine-storey apartment blocks, a total of 164 dwellings with workshops on the ground floors (Nara-ken, 2003, 138).

Finally, there were attempts to spread the anti-discrimination message. These activities at first focused on a single day, 10 July, but from 1972, it was extended to a week in July during which the CLCs in the prefecture, the BLL, and 17 other organisations cooperated with local education committees to hold events in schools and community centres. It was further extended to last the whole of July from 1974.

The immediate impact of these policies was mixed. The national Dōwa survey in 1971 identified 60,949 people and 16,941 households as eligible for Dōwa benefits in 78 communities spread across 9 cities, 10 towns, and 8 villages in Nara prefecture. Compared to 1967, white-collar employment had increased and reliance on unemployment assistance was down. However, the overall reliance on social welfare was up slightly – 5.6–6.1% – as were long-term absences from primary school – 2.1–2.5% (Nara-ken, 2003, 142).

Reflecting the re-organisation of policymaking at the national level, in 1974 a Dōwa Policy Office (*Dōwa Seisakuka*) was created within the Nara prefectural administration to coordinate policy and in March 1975 a comprehensive strategy was launched for the second phase of the ten-year plan. This combined a set of general aims, such as the need to increase the awareness of the Dōwa issue among administrators, with specific plans to encourage the production of high-value leather items such as skiwear. A *Kaihō Sentaa* (Liberation Centre, aka Rinpokan) was completed in 1978 in Nara city that was used as a base for Dōwa lectures and training sessions. Following evidence that at least one local company had purchased a copy of a *chimei sōkan*, in 1977 a council was created to promote Dōwa employment by supporting training schemes which would reduce discrimination. This led, among other things, to a symposium on 'Dōwa Issues and Corporate Social Responsibility' (Nara-ken, 2003, 148).

In the second half of the 1970s, the BLL began a campaign locally to have the SML extended and Dōwa projects enhanced. The Nara Dōtaikyō in May 1978 produced a report that urged a return to the spirit of the 1965 Dōtaishin report and an extension to the SML. In October 1978, a Comprehensive Plan for Dōwa Policies in Nara was adopted at the same time as a discussion was taking place about the direction of national Dōwa policy.

The Dōtaikyō at the national level endorsed demands for an extension of the SML by three years from April 1979 but no sooner had the new period begun, there were requests for further extension. In September 1980, the prefectural assembly passed a resolution noting that most of the major projects were incomplete. The Nara Dōtaikyō supported this position and on 17 January 1981 requested both the strengthening and extension of the SML for a further period. This was followed up by a visit of representatives of the prefectural assembly to Tokyo to petition the PMO and both houses of the Diet about extending the Dōwa project finances. Similar demands were made by chairs of the national Council of Mayors (8 April) and the Council of Governors (20 July). They supported the report of the national level Dōtaikyō announced in December 1981 which recommended the extension of Dōwa project legislation for a further five years albeit under the new name of Regional Improvement Policy (Chiiki Kaizen Taisaku) (Nara-ken, 2003, 152–6). This enabled the continuation of the various projects to improve the infrastructure and to launch a new house building programme (Nara-ken, 2003, 156).

As the five years of Chiiki Kaizen Taisaku were coming to an end, the Nara Dōwa policy community once more made the case for a further extension. In June 1984, the prefectural assembly supported the BLL campaign for a Basic Law on Buraku Liberation, a survey on current Buraku conditions and the ratification of UN treaties on human rights. The following year, a JSP prefectural assemblyman pointed out that delays in the implementation of some Dōwa projects meant that they would not be completed by 1987, the end of the current phase of Dōwa legislation. The governor agreed that it was important to extend the policy and in January 1986 the Nara Dōtaikyō urged the state to commit to resolving the remaining issues. These local voices pushed the national level policy process resulting in the recommendation to create a new Dōwa-related law which was passed by the Diet in March 1987.

Nara Dōwa Policy – from the late 1980s to the early twenty-first century

Local reaction in Nara to the passage of the extension to the SML came in a document produced in May 1987 which welcomed its focus on financial issues, noted the importance of reducing provision where the need was low and the renewed ambition to implement policy so as to increase self-reliance within the Dōwa communities. Over the next few years in addition to continuing projects that improved infrastructure and housing, two new strands of policy sought to encourage the adoption of equal opportunity employment practices and, from 1990, to improve facilities in the meat industry, something that had been discussed since 1973 (Nara-ken, 2003, 164–6).

In line with national policy recommendations, Dōwa policy administrators in Nara began to address issues surrounding *keihatsu* – the portmanteau term that includes all kinds of measures that aim to change attitudes towards the Dōwa issue from education in schools, to adult education, as well as campaigns in the wider community aiming to reduce prejudices. Reports based on surveys of attitudes in the mainstream communities suggested that although the material conditions in most Dōwa districts had significantly improved, discrimination remained. The local Dōtaikyō proposed policies to deepen awareness of the history of the local Buraku communities, measures aimed to develop understanding of and cooperation with Dōwa projects and to raise overall awareness of human rights issues. In 1988, Nara prefecture set up an office in each municipality to promote *keihatsu* (Nara-ken, 2003, 164–8).

As the next deadline for the SML approached, there were renewed demands for an extension. The Nara Dōtaikyō put in its request for an extension on 17 January 1991 which was followed on 28 February by questions in the prefectural assembly about the state of Dōwa projects locally. The governor replied that several major projects remained incomplete and a further round of support from both local and national governments was necessary. This pressure from local governments was recognised at the national level when the Chitaikyō suggested in its report produced in December 1991 that the number of Dōwa projects be reduced but concluded that it was still not appropriate to make all these projects 'general', i.e. open to all and not funded by Dōwa money. The SML was extended for another five years (Dōwa Gyōseishi Henshū Iinkai, 2002, 453).

However, there was a distinct change of emphasis from this point. The BLL at its conference in 1992 announced the start of a transition into a 'third era' when the movement's focus should shift away from Dōwa policy towards an emphasis on peace, human rights, and the environment. Meanwhile, the Nara Dōtaikyō in December that year resolved that its aim would be to complete the outstanding projects but change the focus of its campaigns against discrimination from being simply about Dōwa issues to broader human rights promotion and protection.

One outcome of this was the adoption in March 1997 of prefectural policies aiming to end discrimination and promote respect for human dignity which embraced issues of gender and disability as well as Dōwa policy (Nara-ken, 2003, 172–6). All of this was consistent with the Iken Gushin of the previous year which both committed the state to human rights promotion in the long term and to a final five-year extension to the SML. However, the *Asahi* newspaper reported in March 1996 that there were estimated to be ¥5–60B of incomplete projects in Nara and the prefectural Dōwa policy office argued that, 'With the financial state of the municipalities being so weak, without central government support it will be impossible to complete the projects' (Asahi Shimbun, 26 March 1996).

In 1997, the Nara Dōtaikyō committed the prefecture to continuing with its Dōwa projects that enhanced the independence and livelihood stability of the residents of the Buraku communities while promoting exchanges with mainstream communities so as to eliminate prejudice. It re-iterated national policy that the end of the SML would not signal that all problems had been resolved but that henceforth the focus would be on broader issues of human rights, including the Dōwa policy. Following this, a Human Rights education (jinken kyōiku) project was created in 2000 and in the following year, the names of all the various prefectural and municipal committees were changed from 'Dōwa…' to 'Jinken…' (Nara-ken, 2003, 197–201). All 'Dōwa' projects came to an end in Nara in March 2002.

After the SML in Nara

Our main source of information on Buraku/Dōwa communities in Nara after 2002 comes from Ioka Yasutoki's analysis of data from the censuses of 2000 and 2010 concerning 16 of the 82 districts in Nara where Dōwa policy had been administered before 2002.[6]

Across the prefecture as a whole, the population declined slightly to 97% of its 2000 level while that of the Dōwa districts dropped to 88%. The number of households declined much less, and indeed increased in some areas, for example, in one of the districts in Nara city it went up by 11%. But overall the number of households in the Buraku areas was 3% down on 2000. Looking at the age profiles, there were significantly fewer children and considerably more older people (65+) in the Dōwa districts. The figures are particularly dramatic for the two districts in Nara city where the proportion of children which had been 9.3% and 9.4% in 2000 had dropped to 5.2% and 2.8% by 2010, while the figures for the city as a whole were 14.4% in 2000 and 12.6% ten years later (Ioka, 2014, 10). At the other end of the age range, the number of older people was very high: again just looking at two communities in Nara city, 25.4% and 33.7% compared to 9.6% in the city mainstream and many of these were living alone which may account for the reduction in the size of population but not the number of households. The data did not suggest such big differences for the prefecture as a whole but even so the average number of older people in the Dōwa districts was 14.3% compared for 9.0% for the prefecture overall and 9.1% for the municipalities in which the Dōwa districts are located.

There were big differences in the data about the length of time people had been living in their current residence. In some areas, the gap between the Buraku and non-Buraku areas was small but across the prefecture as a whole Burakumin were likely to have lived in their current dwelling longer and in the two districts in Nara city the number of people who had lived there for over 20 years was almost double the average, 53.5% and 60.8%, compared to 29.6%. This may reflect something about the continuing discrimination, or at least fear of discrimination, that residents might encounter if they tried to find somewhere else to live. It also suggests that the high proportion of older people living in these areas is not due to immigration into these areas.

Past patterns of education continued to cast a shadow over the Buraku communities. The data show that, measured in terms of level of education, the proportion of Buraku residents who had graduated from high school was broadly comparable with those of mainstream communities but relatively few had experience of tertiary education. This could, of course, reflect the fact that those who did go to university moved out but also that there was no compensating immigration as presumably occurred in the mainstream communities. Overall, the data showed that university had been the final educational institution for 22.3% of the mainstream community but only 9.6% of those in the Buraku districts. This may continue to have some relevance for these communities as a survey from 2009 showed that those parents with low levels of education experience had lower expectations for their children.

Finally, employment. The rates of unemployment across the prefecture were about twice as high in Buraku communities compared to the mainstream: 14.0% compared to 7.4%. However, this does hide quite considerable variations across the prefecture with some places having rates of over 20% and elsewhere as low as 7.4%. It is also related to age. Overall rates of unemployment of those aged 50 or over are all high although particularly so in Buraku communities. As for the nature of employment, the gradual drop in reliance on light manufacturing which had been over 70% in 1971 had reduced to 30.2% in 2000 and further to 21.6% by 2010. This in part is due to the contraction of, almost disappearance of, the leather industry locally with nothing to take its place.

Nara prefecture set up a Human Rights Promotion office in 2004 following the adoption of a Basic plan earlier that year. The *Naraken Jinken Shisaku ni Kansuru Kihon Keikaku* has been revised twice since then, most recently in 2020 (Nara-ken, 2020). The current version will run until 2029 and lists 17 categories of human rights topics that lie within its remit with the elimination of Buraku discrimination at the top of the list. It periodically surveys the attitudes to human rights among the residents of the prefecture, on one occasion in 2012 focusing on the attitudes of young people. The most recent survey conducted in 2018 repeated questions on choice of residence and marriage. Asked about selecting somewhere to live when a Buraku/Dōwa district is nearby, 18.8% reported that they would definitely and 34.5% would probably avoid it. This compares with responses about areas characterised by low incomes, 18.5%:36.9%; where many foreigners live, 16.3%/34.9%; near facilities for the disabled, 4.9%/17.6%; and near children's nurseries, 2.9%/7.5% (Nara-ken 2020, 19). On the key issue of marriage, 16.8% reported that they would ask their child to re-consider marrying someone from a Dōwa area, a figure that is almost unchanged over the last ten years. But there is less concern shown about this than the other potential options such as the potential spouse being a resident Korean 25.3%, Brazil-origin Japanese 21.2%, in a wheelchair 31.4%, or having a history of mental health problems 63.6% (Nara-ken 2018, 22).

In 2019, the prefecture adopted a by-law on the elimination of Buraku discrimination which references both the constitution and the 2016 law and commits itself to its elimination in cooperation with the state and municipalities.

What to conclude from this Ioka's analysis and the survey results? Even today, the (former) Buraku communities do not relate to the mainstream on equal terms. If so, we might have expected that the levels of those with a university education would be much closer. People who leave for university are not coming back and other people with university education are not taking their place. At the very least, this suggests that 'place' continues to be an important part of the mix. The average age of Buraku residents is increasing but this does not seem to be older people on reduced incomes moving in to the relatively cheaper (and often inferior) housing in the Buraku but rather that those already there do not move out while younger people (even without higher education?) do. Having said that, there was a large range in the raw data that we have not been able to represent here and there may be more going on. It is another example of an area where more research is needed if we are to answer questions about whether the Buraku Question has been resolved by Dōwa policy and, if not, what more could be done.

Meanwhile, Nara prefecture has adopted a pro-active policy on human rights promotion since 2002 which has concern for Buraku discrimination at its core. The periodic surveys have produced a wealth of statistical data which leads to the conclusion that prejudices about Dōwa communities and their residents remain even if they are less prevalent that those held about other marginal groups in contemporary Japan.

Fukuoka prefecture: Dōwa project policy in Q city

Buraku communities in the Kansai region, which includes Osaka and Nara, have histories which can be traced back well into the Tokugawa period and earlier even if they experienced rapid growth after the mid-nineteenth century. Many of them retained an association with the leather industry as one of the defining features of their marginal status even when their main source of income was farming. Then in the twentieth century, they were the location of the movements which resisted the emergence of a societal definition of their communities as being outside 'normal' society from the time of the formation of the 'improvement' (*kaizen*) groups of the late nineteenth century, to the Suiheisha from the 1920s and then the BLL from the 1950s. Much of the research on Buraku issues has tended to focus on this area and the work on Dōwa policy is no exception. However, in the final section of this chapter on regional case studies, I want to shift the focus away from Kansai and towards Kyushu and, moreover, to look not at the prefectural level of Dōwa policymaking but at how it was managed in one small city.

Buraku communities in Fukuoka prefecture in the twentieth century were characterised by a large number of quite small settlements. The 1935 survey found 170 municipalities with one or more Buraku community, a total of 475 Buraku and a total population of 71,913. Overall, they formed 2.6% of the total population although they were (and still are) unevenly distributed with more Buraku communities to be found in the northern, more industrialised parts of the prefecture than in the south and west. The 1993 survey identified 606 communities across 72 municipalities with 305,051 residents of whom 111,784 were regarded as 'Dōwa-related', 36.6% (Dōwa Gyōseishi Henshū Iinkai, 2003, 819). The difference in the number of local government units can be accounted for by local government consolidation but the larger number of Dōwa communities, which is consistent with other post-war surveys (the 1985 survey reported 617 communities), suggests that the 1935 survey was insufficiently thorough. Many municipalities in the prefecture have five, ten, or more small Buraku communities within their boundaries. The analysis below will focus on one city, located on the Chikuhō coalfield that for present purposes we will refer to as Q city[7] and which recognises 20 Buraku communities. We begin with a brief summary of the historical context of Buraku communities in the area which explains some of the differences in the implementation of Dōwa policy.

Background

The area covered by the Chikuhō coalfield stretches from Soeda on the border with Oita prefecture northwards as far as Nōgata which neighbours Kita Kyushu city.[8] All this area was part of Kokura han which merged with Fukuoka han and a few smaller feudal domains in 1876 (Eason, 2012). There were few, if any *eta, hinin* or similar communities in Kokura han at the start of the Edo period and the terms *kawata* and *eta* only appear in local documents in the late seventeenth century. The first discriminatory legal regulations were issued in 1728 and separate *koseki* drawn up in 1732 (Asō, 2010, 1; Q-shi III, 1979, 1013–4). The region was badly affected by the Kyōhō famine of the 1730s which resulted in the death of up to one-third of the population after which landless peasants and poor urban dwellers were encouraged to move into the area to farm land left uncultivated. These either were, or were treated as, marginal groups. Most of them relied on farming as a livelihood but a small number engaged in the disposal of dead cows and horses whose hides were despatched outside the area for manufacture into leather goods, some being sent to wholesalers in Osaka through the port in the town of Kokura. Over the next hundred years, restrictions would be periodically reinforced, for example, in 1853 when members of these communities were forbidden to enter Shinto shrines or wear certain articles of clothing (Q-shi III, 1979, 1023).

Coal was mined locally in the mid-Edo period but only in very small quantities and mostly for local use. However, in the aftermath of the Kyōhō famine of the 1730s, some impoverished farmers turned to mining coal out of desperation and it became known as 'a "famine industry" inaugurating a long legacy of discrimination against miners' (Phipps, 2015, 119). Those who migrated into the area to mine coal were not permitted to move into the main farming villages even though they would often cultivate some land. As a result, the size of the discriminated population grew. Coal mining was placed under the control of the domainal authorities in Kokura in 1788 and the area became the country's foremost coal producer. However, the mines were small and mining was a seasonal occupation that was only possible at times of the year when there had been little rain. The role marginal communities played in this development was largely confined to the transport of coal to the coast by river barge or to their manning of the mine drainage systems.

Towards the middle of the nineteenth century, demand grew for coal to be used in the manufacture of salt along the Inland Sea; then, industrialisation from the start of the Meiji period increased the demand for coal (Asō, 2010, 3; Q-shi III, 1979, 1036). The Japan Mining Law of 1873 led to a chaotic period during which local entrepreneurs established some small mines in response to this demand but outcrops close to the surface were soon exhausted, while the development of the richer seams deeper down required more advanced and expensive technology that included the use of steam pumps. The industry developed rapidly in the 1890s with the simultaneous development of port facilities at Moji that could export the coal to elsewhere in Japan as well as to places across East Asia, a railway system that could transport the coal cheaply and in large quantities to Moji, and the provision of capital that funded the application of Western technology to sink deep mines and keep them dry. The latter came both from zaibatsu companies such as Sumitomo, Mitsui, and Mitsubishi but also local businessmen (*chihō zaibatsu*) such as Asō Takichi, Yasukawa Keiichirō, and Kaijima Tasuke (Phipps, 2015, 124–5).

The size of the local population was insufficient to provide labour for these new mines stimulating a wave of migration into the area from the rest of Japan and even in the 1890s from Korea. However, there was resistance to working alongside Burakumin and many of the older prejudices about coal mining continued to isolate mining communities. Meanwhile, the replacement of the barges by railways and steam pumps for the traditional drainage systems deprived Burakumin of their former occupations so that they tended to find work in the smaller pits where the pay was less and the work more dangerous. As new mines were sunk and migrants moved into the area, some would end up living in Buraku communities, so the number of Buraku communities increased and each one grew bigger (Q-shi III, 1979, 1035–6). A survey conducted in the mid-1920s suggested that 20% of those employed in the Chikuhō coal mines were Burakumin. However, demand for coal was cyclical and periodically would dry up resulting in long periods of unemployment for the miners and severe poverty for their families.

In the late nineteenth century, there do not seem to have been any separate schools set up just for Buraku children in Chikuhō as happened in the Kansai region probably because the communities were too small to sustain a school by themselves but there are many stories told by elderly Buraku residents of their first encounter with discrimination having taken place at primary school in the later nineteenth and early twentieth centuries. Having said that, overall attendance at primary schools in the area was anyway low – absences by compulsory education age children in 1896 ran at 42.8% mainly caused by poverty (Q shi III, 1979, 1027–8). When in 1908 the length of compulsory elementary education was extended from three to six years, many in the Buraku communities could not afford for their children to go creating a big gap in education achievement. But discrimination was not only at school. Matsumoto Kichinosuke born in a town in the Chikuhō area was refused work on the railways on leaving school because of discrimination, so he went to work in the coal mines but even there he was not allowed to use the same bath as other miners (Matsumoto, 1977, 26–31).

A Suiheisha branch, formed in the area in 1925, led protests about instances of discrimination and organised campaigns against institutionalised exclusion demanding, for example, the right to participate in local Shinto shrine-based festivals (*jinko*) (Q-shi III, 1979, 1052). In 1930, there are reported to have been 200 paid-up Suiheisha supporters in Q gun out of 4,350 in the prefecture as a whole (Q-shi III, 1979, 1056). Suiheisha activity continued sporadically into the 1930s.

Following the lead of the central state, Fukuoka prefecture in 1920 announced its commitment to a Buraku Improvement policy (*Buraku Kaizensaku*) which included improvements to roads and living conditions, construction of clinics, public halls, and communal baths, as well as provision of sewage and water facilities, and projects to encourage migration and working away from home (*dekasegi*). Prefectural funding would cover up to a half of the cost of each project (Q-shi III, 1979, 1057–8). There is only fragmentary documentary evidence about what this Yūwa policy achieved in the Chikuhō region. Some Yūwa projects took place in the 1930s but not much Yūwa money flowed down to the level of municipalities at this time, most being kept by the prefecture here as elsewhere across the country (Q-shi III, 1979, 1063).

Buraku communities and the coal industry in the Chikuhō district after 1945

Coal Priority Production legislation passed at the end of 1946 created a variety of incentives that stimulated the rapid regeneration of the coal industry. In the early 1950s, there were 290 active coal mines of various sizes in the Chikuhō region employing 120,000 people and producing around one-third of Japan's total coal output. Q city prospered and its population grew from 75,000 to around 100,000 people by 1955. However, when the Korean War boom came to an end, there were massive coal stockpiles, and supply far exceeded demand. In 1952, the first Temporary Coal Rationalisation Bill (TCRB) was passed which set production quotas for the next three years. At the same time, tariffs on oil imports were relaxed. Nationally, 90,000 miners lost their jobs between 1952 and 1954. Over the same period, the Chikuhō mining workforce dropped from 120,000 to 90,000 (Allen, 1994, 62–4).

During the second half of the decade, MITI launched policies to allow the import of cheap coal and to prepare the economy for a transition from coal to oil as the main energy source. As a result, between 1955 and 1959, another 75,000 people employed in the coal mining industry across the Chikuhō region lost their jobs. Smaller mines were particularly adversely affected.

In an attempt to mitigate some of the social impact of increasing unemployment, a strategy was formulated to fund municipal improvements to the sewers, roads, and provision of tap water. Electric power lines were laid to the *tanjū* (cheap housing provided for coal miner's families), and a programme of housing improvements began. The aim was to provide gainful employment for former coal miners on these public works projects although there turned out to be far too many for them all to be employed in the schemes. By 1959, unemployment had become endemic and 49.4% of all families in Q city were receiving welfare payments (Allen, 1994, 66–9). Most of the remaining coal mines shut down during the 1960s and the very last one closed its gates in 1976.

Data for 1975 suggests a total Dōwa population in Fukuoka prefecture of 132,870, 3% of the total, living in 605 Dōwa communities. This was the largest number of Buraku communities in any prefecture and the third biggest Burakumin population. The Buraku population as a proportion of the total population in the two major cities of Fukuoka and Kita-Kyushu was quite small −2.4% and 2%, respectively, with the total number of residents in Dōwa communities 25,302 and 19,356. However, while 23 municipalities mainly in the south of the prefecture were found to have no Dōwa communities within their boundaries, 74 (17 cities, 54 towns, and 3 villages) recorded at least one Dōwa community although some of them were very small (Fukuoka-ken, 1979).

However, seven municipalities in Fukuoka prefecture had a 'Dōwa population' in the 1970s that amounted to 20% or more of their residents, many of them located in Chikuhō, with one town recording 57.3%. A large proportion of the residents in these Buraku communities were or had been employed in the coal mining industry often in the smaller pits. Buraku communities in the 1960s in Q city and elsewhere in Chikuhō then encountered the twin problems of discrimination and the devastating economic and social impact of the pit closures. Conversely, this meant that they not only benefited from Dōwa policy provisions but also the various measures that were intended to mitigate the impact of the termination of the coal industry on local communities. The latter are referred to the *Sekitan Roppō* (or sometimes *Chikuhō Roppō*) and consisted of projects to address the environmental pollution caused by the coal mining and to mitigate the social impact of unemployment and various other social welfare measures. They are estimated to have been worth around ¥10,000m to the local governments of the Chikuhō region[9] (Nishi Nippon Shimbun accessed 25 March 2020).

This makes it more than usually difficult to assess the impact of the Dōwa policy in the region as the administration of the Dōwa policy was often coordinated with the policies that supplied special unemployment relief and social welfare measures for the regional economy that had been devastated by the mine closures.

Dōwa policies in Q city

Fukuoka prefecture was slower to develop Dōwa policies after the war in comparison to Osaka and Nara. Not until 1953 was a *Kankyō Kaizen Jigyō* (Environment Improvement Project) created for Dōwa communities by the Social Affairs section of the Public Welfare Bureau (Minseibu Shakaika). Later, Dōwa policy projects were set up within the Education Bureau in 1959, Agriculture/Construction Bureau 1960, Public Works Bureau 1962, and Employment Bureau 1963. Only in 1966 was any attempt made to coordinate these policies when a Dōwa Taisaku Kaigi (Dōwa Policy Council) was set up presumably to consider how to respond to the Dōtaishin. Then, in 1968, a Dōwa Policy office was created. A survey of Dōwa districts in the prefecture was conducted in 1969 which provided the data for the formation of a long-term plan for Dōwa policy and Dōwa education. At this point, each municipality devised its own plan that reflected its particular circumstances. Q city set up its *Dōwa Taisakuhitsu* (Dōwa Policy Office) only after the passage of the SML and produced a basic strategy two years later.

Two neighbouring mining towns merged in 1943 to create Q city. Since its formation, the city has elected seven men to be mayor, two of whom served for long periods: A from April 1955–April 1979 and his successor B who was in post from 1979 to 2002. During the 1950s, B had been a JSP Diet member and served on its social policy and labour policy committees. He initially took office as a mayor as one of the wave of JSP supported candidates who were elected in the late 1970s and 1980s and resulted in around one-third of the population of Japan living under a local government controlled by the opposition parties. In many areas, the LDP reasserted its control over local government from the later 1980s but B was able to consolidate cross-party support and served until he was in his late 80s, not stepping down until the year of the expiration of the SML. Significantly for our purposes, after his election, he became the chair of the Dōwa Policy committee of the National Municipal Mayors Council and was a member of the Chitaikyō between 1982 and 1992.

One of the two towns which became Q-shi was found by the 1935 census to have 14 Buraku communities, the other six with a combined population of 3,169. Most of them were quite small, only one with more than 100 households and three with less than ten. Table 8.4 presents a very basic statistical outline of the circumstances in the Dōwa communities of Q city some 50 years later, around 1980. The population of Q city then stood at just over 60,000 and within its boundaries there were 20 Dōwa communities of various sizes containing 8,002 Burakumin, 12.9% of the city population with an estimated 'mixture' rate of 69.9% although we might note that if we include all residents in the Buraku communities, the proportion would increase to 18.5%. The city had been adversely affected by the mine closures but the impact on Dōwa communities was more severe. If we take dependence on social welfare as one index of this we find that for the city as a whole it was 5.2% but for Burakumin in the Dōwa communities it was 11.6%. By comparison, the figures for Fukuoka prefecture as a whole were 3.8% but on average 21.3% for all its Dōwa communities. In other words, the situation in some of the smaller Dōwa communities in other municipalities of the Chikuhō coalfield was even worse than in Q city. In turn, this was much worse than the national average; estimates of welfare dependency in Dōwa communities nationally were around 7.6%. Having said that, the 1984 document also suggests significant differences even between the Buraku communities of Q city: their size varied between 93 and 1,088 people, the 'mixture' between 49% and 99% and welfare dependency between 1.1% and 13.5% (Q-shi 1984, 15) (Table 8.9).

The two key sources for our overview of Dōwa policy in this city are documents published in 1984 and 2002, respectively, that reviewed the evolution of Dōwa policy.[10] They both preface their comments with remarks about the difficulties caused by the closing down of the coal mining industry which is estimated to have provided direct or indirect employment for 70% of the working population in the early 1950s. The last coal mine within the city's boundaries closed down in 1970 and in that year the city set up a 'Special Committee' to formulate a comprehensive, Fifteen-Year Plan to promote the growth of a 'Green Industrial City'. It was formally adopted in March 1971 and aimed to regenerate the area in the aftermath of the pit closures while maintaining the population at around 80,000. Within this document, there was a '*Q-shi Dōwa Taisaku Jigyō Suishin Kihon Kōsō*' (Basic Vision for the Promotion of Dōwa Projects in Q city). Here, the city announced its ambition to go beyond the plans set out by the state 'taking into consideration the unique features of the city' in order to 'protect the living standards of the modern citizens of Dōwa communities'. There were seven Dōwa-specific items: the construction of Dōwa Kaikan (aka Rinpokan), the provision of facilities to improve the living environment, improvements to housing, enhancement of social welfare and health care, promotion of agriculture and SMEs, the provision of careers advice, and school and adult education (Q-shi, 2002, 5; Q-shi III, 1979, 1070).

The 1984 document comments that the city was in a very weak financial state. Its commitments under the various unemployment projects, social welfare spending, and *tanjū* improvement plans produced a normal budget 2.4 times larger than cities of a similar size, while the poverty of its constituent communities meant that its income from local taxes was around one-third average (Q-shi, 1984, 90). Under these circumstances, a local authority might have been tempted to focus on the broader issues within the community and set aside the demands of the marginal groups. And indeed the 1984 Q city document does suggest that this may have been the initial strategy.

Table 8.9 Buraku Communities in Q City

Area	*Households*	*Population*	*% of Total Q city population*	*% of Dōwa communities 'Dōwa related'*	*Welfare dependency (%)*
Whole Town	20,037	61,901			5.2
All Dōwa communities	3,656	11,445			8.5
'Dōwa related' households	2,507	8,002	12.9	69.9	11.6

Area	Households All	of which: Dōwa related	Population all	of which: Dōwa related	'Mix' (%)	Welfare dependency (%)
M	56	26	189	93	49.2	1.1
U	525	331	1559	1088	69.8	13.2
Ti	213	105	720	361	50.1	3.3
I	253	154	618	367	59.4	6.0
A	187	151	575	474	82.4	0.4
B	171	146	634	550	86.8	2.0
O	52	30	191	109	57.1	5.5
K	234	187	798	635	79.6	12.0
S	155	138	527	469	89.0	4.9
T	81	74	279	256	91.8	3.9
H	267	114	769	388	50.5	8.7
Y	192	168	540	474	87.8	13.5
C	115	104	413	380	92.0	7.4
W	59	57	213	211	99.1	7.1
D	72	67	287	270	94.1	13.3
M	43	39	158	144	91.1	10.4
G	179	98	625	342	54.7	11.9
N	329	224	1107	582	52.6	4.8
R	84	68	293	244	83.3	9.0
Z	389	226	950	565	59.5	12.9

Each community has been assigned a random letter but the letters in bold on this table represent the same community in Table 8.6.
Source: Q-shi Dōwa Taisaku Jigyō no Gaiyō (1984, 15).

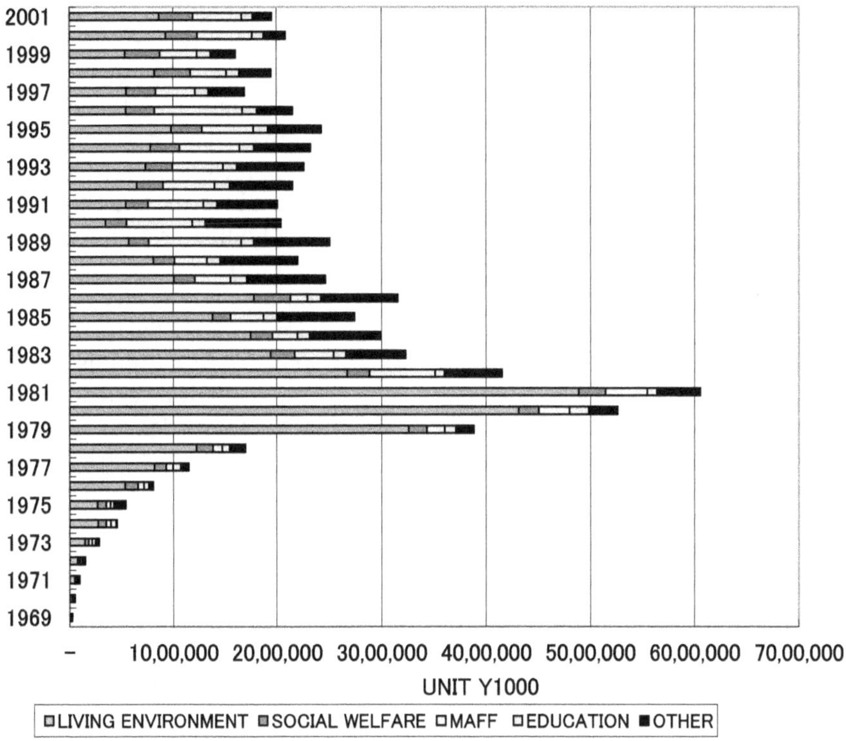

Figure 8.2 Dōwa spending in Q city 1969–2002.

As Figure 8.2 shows, the amounts provided for the Dōwa projects in the first few years were very small and nothing additional at all, for example, for primary schools until 1978.

What changed this seems to have been two incidents of discrimination. One of these which occurred in 1971 is described in some detail in the documents. It involved an engaged couple, one from a Buraku community, one not, both in their early 20s who were saving to buy a house when they encountered sustained opposition to their proposed marriage from the foster mother and sister of the young woman. She left for Tokyo. Her boyfriend attempted suicide. The issue was taken up by the local branch of the BLL and at least part of the responsibility for the incident was apportioned to, and seems to have been accepted by the local government (Q-shi, 1984, 108). From this point, the Q city authorities adopted a more active approach.

In November 1971, a Dōwa Policy office was established with five staff and a Dōwa policy unit was created within the Education section. The following year, a 'Dōwa policy coordinator' was appointed within each section and this was upgraded to become a 'Dōwa policy promoter' in 1978. In 1984, there were four Dōwa policy councils in the city administration: one conducting research on Dōwa education, one promoting Dōwa policy to the firms of the area, one which seems to be liaising with the BLL, the Buraku Kaihō Dōmei Q Shimin Kyōtō Kaigi (aka *Shikyō*), and one to ensure the progress of the Q city's Dōwa policy.

The Oil Shocks of the 1970s and resulting slow economic growth made the targets set in the 1971 Fifteen-Year Plan unattainable, so a second plan was adopted in 1981, initially to last for ten years, which included a set of Dōwa policies, substantially the same as those adopted in 1971 with the addition of a sixth item: 'the dissemination and improvement of human rights thought'. This plan too was set aside before completion and in 1988 a third plan was adopted to last for 13 years which talked of building a new Q city that was gentle on the environment and eliminated discrimination. This formed the background to demands from the local BLL and the city administration that the Dōwa policy, scheduled to come to an end in 1991, be extended for at least another five years. The mayor of Q city submitted evidence to central government that there were many projects planned to improve agricultural land and widen streets that could not be completed without state and prefectural support (Asahi Shimbun, 12 December 1991).

A new Ten-Year Plan was launched in 2001 noting the continued existence of discrimination despite all the efforts of the previous 30 years. It argued that there remained more to be done in terms of the 'hard' projects to improve the living environment but especially in regard to promoting human rights awareness. It concluded that, 'although there have been improvements in this area, there is still a big gap between what people say and how they act' (*honne to tatemae*) (Q-shi, 2002, 6–9). As the SML came to an end, there were negotiations between the representatives of the local BLL and council in 2002 about what, if anything, might replace it.

Policy formation and benefit distribution

How the Dōwa policy process worked at the local level is both very important and difficult to assess in most areas of Japan. However, in the case of Q city, we have access to minutes of meetings that took place in the final years of the SML which give some indication of how decisions were made. The key committee in the Dōwa policy process was composed of four members of the *Shikyō* the heads of the relevant bureaus of the city administration, and was chaired by the mayor. Reading the minutes of these meetings suggests a model of the policy process as shown in Figure 8.3.

A taste of how policy was determined locally emerges in the minutes of a meeting held in October 2000 as it anticipates the reduction in Dōwa project funding. The leader of the *Shikyō* group began with a review of the history of the Buraku liberation movement in the twentieth century starting with the formation of the Suiheisha in 1922 through to the creation of Dōwa policy and the SML and finishing with the question of what will happen when the current programmes come to an end. One might have thought that after 30 years of implementing Dōwa policy, this would be unnecessary but the *Shikyō* representatives had complained at other meetings that local administrators were poorly informed about the historical context of Dōwa policy. Next, the mayor described the legal and financial constraints of policymaking in the city. Not only was the SML being phased out within the next couple of years but so were the other programmes collectively known as the *Sekitan Roppō* that had supported the community over previous decades following the closure of the mines (see above n 10). In the near future, the city would lose access to several important income streams. Moreover, with the end of the SML and increased emphasis being placed on human rights, responsibility for Dōwa policy would shift from the Sōmuchō to the MoJ – implying perhaps that the prospects of further funding from central government for 'hard' projects were unlikely.

Next, there were reports from the section heads on the Dōwa projects under their control. A long report from the head of the Education Bureau reviewed the results of past programmes. He noted that there was evidence of continuing prejudice among children. However, while the gap in the academic performance of Buraku and non-Buraku children had narrowed over the period 1989–2001 (from 8% to 3.4%), progress from high school to university remained half that of mainstream students (34%:17%) although for that figure to have reached double digits was a success in itself. The programme had provided grants to assist attendance at high school and university for 6,722 people since 1983 and was supporting 172 at that point. This was followed by reports from the heads of the social welfare, construction, and economics bureaus. Common to all of them was their desire to deliver policy that would continue to address the issues being faced by people in the Dōwa communities. They suggested that these aims be included in the city's forthcoming Fourth Comprehensive Plan. The meeting finished with words from the leader of the *Shikyō* group.

Both at this and subsequent meetings, there was a consensus that simply because the SML was about to expire did not mean that the problems within Buraku communities had been resolved. The problem was how to fund future projects when national funding ceased and the local budget was so tight.

Although it does not seem to have been as controversial as in some parts of Osaka, or indeed elsewhere in Fukuoka prefecture, only the BLL was represented in the policy process. However, we noted earlier that mayor B had a reputation for cultivating a very broad support base that returned him to office for over 20 years. This may explain how he was able to reduce contention about this policy.

A Dōwa Policy meeting was held in December 2002 following the end of the nationally funded Dōwa programmes to discuss among other things how to select tenants for Dōwa housing. It noted that in the past, these decisions had been made on the recommendations of the 'related group' (*kankei dantai*) which is no doubt a coded reference to the BLL. Overall, the Dōwa housing policy was linked to the city's comprehensive plan to replace all the

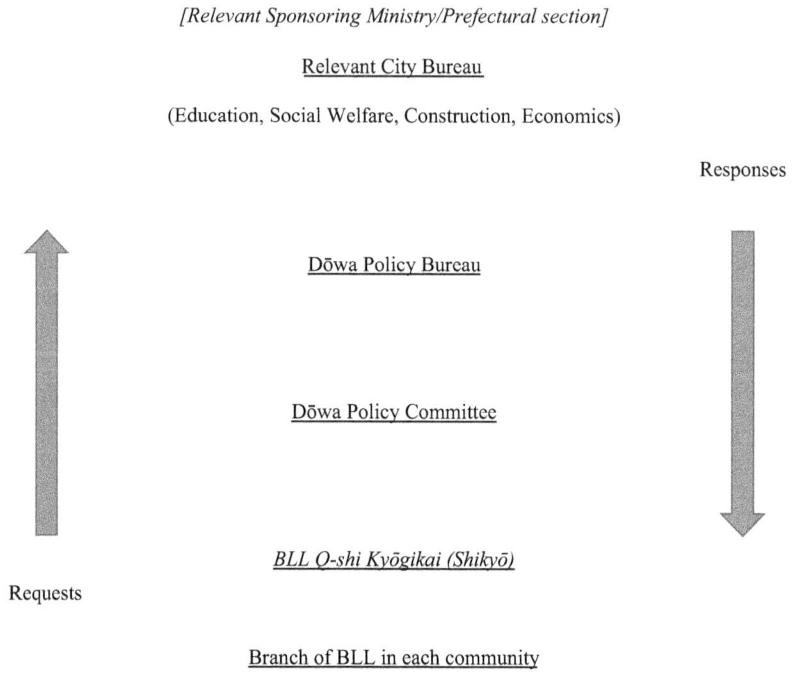

Figure 8.3 Dōwa policymaking in Q city.

remaining *tanjū* with decent housing, but where the new housing had been built in response to specific requests from Dōwa communities expressed though the BLL branch and funded by the Dōwa budget, it was considered reasonable that the BLL branch makes recommendations about who would take up the tenancies. However, it was argued that as the SML had come to an end, the previous definitions of 'special housing' were also ending, so it was up to the committee to decide how to deal with the allocation of tenancies. It was decided for the time being to continue with the old system but to set aside five units for allocation to families containing a disabled person (Q-shi December 2002).

Next, let us turn to briefly review what kind of projects Dōwa funding supported in this city and to complement the description of national schemes summarised in Chapter 7 whence much of the money came from to pay for them.

Dōwa spending in Q city

Figure 8.2 shows the overall pattern of Dōwa spending in Q city between FY1969–2001. Even more noticeably than in Nara and Osaka, the volume of spending in the early 1970s was low and only began to accelerate in the later 1970s and early 1980s. However, despite the rapid reduction in Dōwa

Table 8.10 Dōwa Spending in Q City by Bureau [Ministry]

Living environment	361	[MoC]
(Public Works, Construction and Housing Bureaus Doboku ka, Kenchiku Jūtakuka		
of which	94.5	housing
	160.6	Roads
	86.7	water/sewage
	16.6	Other
Social Welfare	64	[MHW]
(Dōwa Policy, Elderly Policy, Child Rearing Dōwa Taisaku、Kōrei Shinkaika、Jidō Hoikuka)		
Of which	9.0	Rinpokan
	45.9	nurseries (10.4 on buildings)
	9.1	Other
Agriculture and Forestry	107	[MAFF]
(Agricultural Administration- Nōseika)		
Commerce and Industry	2.1	[MITI]
Education	32.7	[MoE]
(Schools, Life-long Learning – Gakkō Kyōikuka Shōgai Gakushūka)		
Of which	6.5	schools
	26.2	other
Other	121	[MoL, MoJ, MHA]

Unit: ¥ 100m.
Source: Q-shi Internal Documents

project funding during the 1990s at the national level, Dōwa spending in Q city continued at high levels until the very end of the SML era.

This was supported by mayor B who was first elected in 1979. While we cannot say for certain that he was responsible for placing more emphasis on Dōwa spending, it seems likely as welfare had been one of his key interests while he served as a Diet member. As mentioned above, he became involved in Dōwa policy at the national level and he remained chair of the Q city Dōwa policy committee until the expiration of the SML.

Table 8.10 shows how the ¥68,300m spent on Dōwa projects in the city between 1969 and 2002 was allocated to five policy areas.

Living environment

Spending by the Public Works, Construction and Housing Bureaus (MoC) broke down into housing, sewage, roads, and other facilities (Table 8.11).

Housing

Between 1967 and 1987, the city built 406 units of public housing in ten apartment blocks *(danchi)* of various sizes for Dōwa communities at a cost

Table 8.11 Dōwa Housing Units Constructed in Q City

Community	*Structure*	*Date of construction*	*Number of dwellings*	*Of which*	
				General	*Dōwa*
U	Single or 2 storeys	1967–77	38	0	38
R	2 storeys	1972	18	0	18
E	2 storeys	1976	16	0	16
B	2 storeys	1977	14	0	14
K	2 storeys	1978	12	0	12
T	2 storeys	1970–4	66	0	66
D	3–5 storeys	1979	38	0	33
J	3–5 storeys	1985–7	94	50	44
N	5 storeys	1977–9	150	95	55
Q city	5 storeys	1979–81	223	113	110
Total	10 Dōwa Apartment Buildings		669	263	406

Source: Q city Internal Documents Dec 2002.

of ¥19,600m.[11] As Table 8.11 suggests, most were exclusively for Buraku residents but not in the three larger units. Unfortunately, the data available from different sources does not always use the same names for the Dōwa communities, so it is not possible to be certain of how these projects were funded in each case. However, the cost share in communities U, K, and D shows that the state was providing around two-thirds of the funding, the prefecture just under 10% with around 25% coming from municipal bonds.[12]

In addition, a further ¥66.8B (of a total of ¥94.5B) of 'soft' money was provided as loans for new building or building improvements by individuals or small companies. This seems to have been integrated into the overall city plan to replace all of the *tanjū* – low-grade housing provided by the mine owners for its employees which had been cheaply built and by the 1980s had deteriorated into slums. These improvement programmes began on a small scale in the late 1950s, started to focus on Dōwa communities in 1967 but by the mid-1980s, there was a rapid increase in the annual budget for 'new builds'. These schemes were reduced by about half after 1987 and the budget was a small fraction of its peak when it finally closed in 1996. At that point, most of the money was being provided by Q city.

Sewage

Between 1973 and 2002, ¥87.70m was spent on 514 separate sewage-related projects in Dōwa districts. These were part of the city's comprehensive plan to have all housing connected to mains sewage and water supply systems. However, it was a policy that was relatively slow to develop. There was nothing spent on sewage and water provision in the first few years, but by the end of the first period (1969–82), it amounted to around one quarter of the total spend. Funding came mainly through the MoC/Public Works bureau but there were some sewage-related projects funded by MAFF/Nōseibu.

Roads

Around ¥16,000m was spent on roads and bridges by the Public Works bureau/MoC over the 33 years of the SML. Usually, these were located within the Dōwa communities themselves. However, arguing that the creation of a major four-lane road would benefit the Dōwa communities as well as others in the vicinity, some Dōwa project money was contributed to the construction of the national highway that runs through the city. In addition, MAFF/Nōseibu organised ten projects to build or widen road access to and between rice fields at a cost of over ¥76m with funds coming from the state, the prefecture, and municipal bonds in almost equal proportions.

Other:

Parks: Eighteen small parks were created by the Children and Education bureau (*Jidō Kyoikuka*) at a cost of ¥2.600m paid for mainly by the prefecture and municipal bonds.

Ossuaries: (*Nōkotsudō* – buildings that serve as the final resting place of human remains) were built in 14 of the city's 20 Dōwa communities at a total cost of ¥1,600m with all the cost covered by the city and administered by the Dōwa Policy Division (*Dōwa Taisakuka*). In addition, a new crematorium was built in 1978 at a cost of ¥53m funded through the city Insurance and Pensions bureau – ¥6m from the state, ¥12.9m from municipal bonds, ¥33.8m of special state aid, and ¥2m from the city.

Social welfare

The biggest single item under the Social Welfare Dōwa budget was 'hard' funding to build nursery facilities and school buildings. Three nursery schools were constructed in Dōwa communities with the funds coming approximately half from the state, 20% from the prefecture, 20% from the city, and 12% by the issue of municipal bonds.[13] This building work was supplemented by a scheme that ran from 1974 to 2002 which paid both the fees for families whose children attended nursery school and to 'prepare' them for starting school. All the money for nursery school fees came from the city and was administered through the Children and Nursery division. In addition, in recognition of the importance of early years education, 'soft' funding enabled the employment of additional nursery assistants.

Another project that consumed both 'hard' and 'soft' money was the provision of Rinpokan. Three were constructed in Q city: one in the centre and one each to the east and west. The one in the east was originally constructed in 1961 but substantially rebuilt in 1986, two-thirds of funding coming from the city, the rest from the state. The central Rinpokan was newly built in 1975, half funded by the prefecture and most of the rest from municipal bonds. A kitchen was added in 1987 with the cost split half and half between the prefecture and the city. When it was substantially extended in 1998, around 75% of the funds came from the prefecture with the rest from the city. The Rinpokan to the east was newly built in 1981, funded almost 50:50 by the state and municipal bonds, and then substantially upgraded in 2000 with three quarters of the finance from the prefecture with the rest from municipal bonds. Altogether, the total cost of the Rinpokan building projects was ¥310m: ¥57m state, ¥105m prefecture, ¥81m municipal bonds, and ¥66m city.

From as early as 1965, funding was provided to support the running costs of Rinpokan. This started off quite small with a significant proportion coming from the state. However, it seems to have been one of the programmes cut in 1987 when state support dropped to zero. The difference was made up by the prefecture so that during the 1990s their administrative costs were shared by city and prefecture almost equally. Both funding for the building of the Rinpokan and their administration came through the Dōwa Policy Division.

During the mid-1990s, the *Shikyō* argued for the construction of a new Rinpokan in the north of the city claiming that there was insufficient provision of study space within that school catchment area. Building this Rinpokan was included in the list of incomplete Dōwa projects produced in 1993. *Shikyō* continued with this demand until as late as summer 2002 and it was considered carefully by successive Dōwa Policy committees. However, the city argued in public that the rationale behind Rinpokan policy had changed from being about improving conditions in the Dōwa area to creating stronger links with neighbouring communities and focusing on human rights issues, including the Dōwa issue, so its construction was no longer justified. In private, they argued that this demand was more about providing the local branch of the BLL with a convenient place to meet. In the end, it was not built.

Rinpokan provided a physical location for the implementation of such projects as the provision of additional care for the elderly, health care services for expectant mothers, afterschool activities for children, and sometimes meetings for the BLL and its related study groups. Indeed, this multi-functionality was reflected in the sources of funding. For example, funding for the Rinpokan to the west of the city came from three separate sources – MoE, MoC, and MHW. In some Rinpokan, there are signs showing which part of the building was funded by whom.

In addition, 'assembly halls' were constructed in 14 of the larger communities. Some had been originally built before the start of the SML, in one case as early as 1950. However, their construction continued across the 33 years with the final big project taking place in 1993. These did not attract money from the central state. In most cases, the cost was shared by prefecture and city either 50:50 or 66:33.

An interesting small scheme run between 1988 and 2000 by the Lifelong Learning Bureau provided literacy support to enable people to pass the theory part of the driving test as a way of increasing employment prospects. This was funded approximately 75:25 by the prefecture and city. Finally, between 1983 and 2002, the Old People and Disabilities bureau supported the formation and administration of Senior Citizen's Clubs with almost all of the finance coming from the prefecture.

Agricultural Administration (Nōseibu) and MAFF funding

Thirteen of the 20 Dōwa areas were regarded as primarily agricultural communities even though only 2% of the total Buraku population in the city were classified as full-time farmers. Many households owned and farmed land part-time and had done so even when their main income had come from mining. Average plot size in the city overall was small, a mere 50 *are* compared to an average for the prefecture of 89 *are* and nationally of 118 *are* (Q-shi, 1984, 38). Moreover, much of the land or the water beneath it had been polluted following decades of mining resulting in very low productivity. Nevertheless, MAFF was a major Dōwa funder in the city supporting a variety of projects to improve farm and forest roads, sewers, and water supplies for irrigation at a total cost of ¥6,500m. In one area, they realised that underground water was so polluted that it could not be pumped up to irrigate the fields. Instead, a complex project was funded that took water from the river into a small dam, pumped it from there to another dam on top of a nearby hill from where it flowed down through a series of pipes to water local paddy fields. Elsewhere, projects were funded to support enterprises such as growing chrysanthemums, raising *koi*, or fattening cattle. In addition, there were 43 projects funded between 1969 and 2002 modernising the agricultural infrastructure by providing modern farm machinery and garages in which to store them (Q-shi, 1984, 39–43).

Education projects (MoE)

A basic plan on Dōwa education had been agreed with the prefecture in 1970 but very little was spent on specific improvements to teaching in primary and junior high schools at the start of the SML. Almost nothing in the first ten years and overall only around 1% of the total Dōwa spend for the period 1969–81. At first, adult literacy was a major concern. It was discussed at length in the 1984 document and many primary and junior high school teachers volunteered to teach these classes. Adult literacy classes continued until around 1998.

From 1969 to 2002, a scheme was supported by the School Education Bureau (*Gakkō Kyōikuka*) to provide grants to encourage attendance at high schools and universities at a total cost of ¥506m peaking during the 1980s at over ¥25m pa, all provided from the city's budget. A slightly less well-funded scheme ran through the Dōwa Policy Bureau to support careers advice for junior high school graduates and attendance at technical colleges.

In the later phases of the Dōwa programmes, in Q city from 1988 onwards, with the increased national policy focus on education, more funding was provided for projects that targeted schools in or near to Buraku communities that aimed to enhance the educational achievement of Buraku children by, for example, providing additional teachers or classroom assistants. The city's education committee produced its own set of human rights textbooks.

In 1992, at a time when the size of Dōwa budgets was declining year on year, more money was allocated for the promotion of *keihatsu* – the awareness of human rights ideas and similar programmes and not only within schools. One result of this was that in 1992 Q city agreed to collaborate with other neighbouring municipalities to establish the *Q-Chiku Keihatsu Sentaa*. This had a number of functions, including the provision of human rights training to local government employees, organising *keihatsu* lectures, for example, in July and December, and carrying out surveys on discrimination and prejudice in the area. This was funded through the Lifelong Learning Bureau (Shōgai Gakushūka) in part by the city, two-thirds from the prefecture, none from the state.

Other

This includes the provision of fire-fighting facilities in each Dōwa community: both fire-fighting appliances (and garages for them) and hydrants. This had been a particular demand of the BLL because the narrow roads in many of the communities meant that they could not be accessed by normal-sized fire-fighting appliances. It was funded by the MHA through the city's General Affairs section (Sōmuka) with usually about half the money coming from the state and the rest from municipal bonds.

Between 1970 and 1981, the Commerce, Industry and Tourism bureau (*Shōkō Kankyōka*) was the channel for providing financial and tax advice to SMEs in the Dōwa communities – all funded by the city. There was also a scheme operated by the Taxation Bureau (*Zeimuka*) that provided rebates on or reductions in the amount of Property Tax paid by individual households 'because of the supply and demand situation'. When it was introduced in 1969, 543 households benefited from this – about ¥780 each. However, by the mid-1990s, there were over 2,000 cases each year and at its peak in 1998, 2,294 households were benefiting from it worth on average ¥17–18,000 each. If we remember that the 1975 survey of Q city found 2,500 households, this meant that practically every household was benefiting.

Q city – after the SML

In Q city, some Dōwa projects did continue after 2002. Local planners seem to have assumed that the SML would be extended once more – a not unreasonable assumption, given how many times it had been extended in the past. Some aspects of the *Sekitan Roppō* were extended for another five years not finally coming to an end until March 2007. A working group was set up and met in 2001–2 to consider what should happen to Dōwa policy in the city. It was decided that 20 projects should continue. The *Shikyō* was not happy with that decision and demanded the completion of 43 'unfinished' projects. These included a new bridge (rejected as the cost would be much more than the city could afford) and a new Rinpokan in the north (decision deferred once more).

The Dōwa Taisaku Iinkai in December 2002 produced a detailed plan to fund nine infrastructure projects in 2002–3; five pipework projects through the Agricultural Administration Section (*Nōseika*); and ¥165m of projects funded through the Public Works bureau for road and sewage improvements. About half of the funding for these projects came from the city with the rest from the prefecture and state. Four similar projects were funded the following year with about half from the city and the rest from prefecture and state, and two road improvement projects in 2003–4 jointly paid for by city and prefecture. Some welfare projects supported by the prefecture continued later in the decade. A document dated 2007 discusses 13 projects to provide health checks (*ningen dokku*) for older people and explained that 'child support' measures previously funded by the prefecture as Dōwa projects would be transferred to 'general' policies, in these cases, Old Peoples Welfare and Next Generation Promotion Support. All of this is small scale compared to the vast projects that were being funded during the 1970s and 1980s but their continuation does illustrate that not all Dōwa projects stopped in March 2002.

A 'rolling plan' for Dōwa projects was agreed by which the prefecture would provide some support for housing projects for five years at up to one-sixth of the cost. In 2006, the programmes to provide grants to enable Dōwa community-origin children to attend high school came to an end. At the same time, there was a discussion about the need to upgrade Dōwa housing but there was no further special funding available. Any improvements would thereafter have to come out of 'general' housing budgets.

In 2002, the Dōwa Policy bureau (*Dōwa Taisaku bu*) shrank to become the *Dōwa Taisaku-ka* and was absorbed into the *Shimin Seikatsubu* which also supervised the development of Gender Equality policies. Q city along with seven other municipalities in the area has continued to support the renamed *Q chiku Jinken Sentaa* (Q District Human Rights Centre) which now has a broader human rights remit. However, a document it produced in 2005 commented somewhat enigmatically, '"Fruit" is an abstract concept that does not exist, only oranges are real things. Similarly, "human rights" administration in general doesn't exist; what exist are concrete policies in response to Dōwa Issues, Women's issues, Old Peoples Issues etc.' So the problem is how to position the Dōwa issue within the city's human rights administration in the light of the prefectural and national plans and the requirements of the law. This was the local response to the promotion of human rights education at the national level which obliged local governments to cooperate with the state in the formulation and implementation of human rights education as appropriate to local conditions.

Conditions in Buraku communities in Q city after the SML

Data about living conditions in Dōwa communities in Q city in the twenty-first century is rather patchy mainly because, as already mentioned, there has been no systematic national survey of Buraku conditions carried out since 1993. Tsutsumi Keishirō used census data to assess the situation as of 2010. He shows how reliance on social welfare remained slightly higher among residents of Dōwa communities than their immediate neighbours and the mainstream community: 6.9%, 5.8%, and 4.7%, respectively (Tsutsumi, 2016, 17).

Unemployment rates were still higher among male residents of Dōwa communities although not of their female residents (Table 8.12).

Occupancy of public housing is not much different from their neighbours (Table 8.13). However, as might be expected, it is significantly higher for those with low household incomes (under ¥104,000 per month) although in this there is not much difference between Buraku and neighbouring non-Buraku households (Table 8.14).

Each of these sets of figures may be in part explicable by the demographic patterns that suggest that in Q city, as in many other parts of Japan outside

Table 8.12 Unemployment in Q City

	Dōwa (%)	*Neighbours (%)*	*Mainstream (%)*
Male	10.5	8.2	6.6
Female	3.1	3.5	3.9%

Source: Tsutsumi (2016, 26).

Table 8.13 Public Housing in Q City

Dōwa	*Neighbours*	*Mainstream*
8.9%	8.7%	5.4%

Table 8.14 Public Housing for Low-Income Households in Q City

Dōwa	*Neighbours*	*Mainstream*
31.7%	30.2%	16.7%

Source: Tsutsumi (2016, 20).

Table 8.15 Proportion of Elderly People (Aged 65+) in Q City

	Dōwa	*Neighbours*	*Mainstream*
2010	23.6	20.7	19.3
2015	25.8	21.5	15.4

Tsutsumi (2016, 15).

Table 8.16 School Absenteeism in Q City

	Buraku (%)	*Mainstream (%)*
Primary schools	1.7	1
Junior High Schools	5.6	4.4

Tsutsumi (2016, 39).

the major urban centres, there are proportionately fewer younger people, i.e. aged 5–14 and 35–54, and significantly more older people, 65+, although the differences are not as great as in Osaka and Nara (Table 8.15). In 2015, more elderly people in Dōwa districts were living alone in Q city than is common in the mainstream: 17.4% compared to 9.1%. Older people living alone have lower household incomes than those living with their relatives.

Finally, to look at education: the extent of absenteeism from school is overall small but there remains a slight gap between Buraku and mainstream communities (Table 8.16). The gap in numbers attending university has narrowed from 11.5% Buraku and 16.4% mainstream in 2000 to 17.0% and 17.3%, respectively, in 2015 (Tsutsumi, 2016, 40, 44).[14] However, both of these figures are very low compared to the national average where over 50% of senior high school students progress to university.

In June 2017, the *Q chiku Jinken Sentaa* carried out a survey to assess attitudes to 'human rights' among the citizens of Q city. This is something that has been repeated every five years and the overall conclusion was that not much has changed since the previous survey. In response to questions specifically about the Buraku issue, an impressive, if unsurprising, 94.6% admitted that they were aware of the issue. While 62% had an interest in human rights, only 39% felt that they were respected in the city. Asked about discrimination, just over 45% thought that it continued in marriage, 22% in employment, and 20% in living environment. Fourteen per cent of the respondents said that they had experience of discrimination or human rights infringements. Around 35% had heard of the law to promote the elimination of discrimination (*Q chiku Jinken Sentaa*, Jinken Mondai ni Kansuru Shimin Ishiki Chōsa, February 2018).

As in Nara, Q city endorsed the principles of the 2016 law to promote the elimination of Buraku discrimination by passing its own ordinance: a by-law in spring 2019 which came into effect on 1 April. As a result, in December that year, a committee was established to advise on policies to promote the elimination of Buraku discrimination in Q city, the *Buraku Sabetsu Kaishō Shingikai*. It is composed of twelve individuals, including representatives of two Buraku organisations (the BLL *Shikyō* and the local branch of the Zen Nihon Dōwakai) and the head of the *Q-chiku Jinken Sentaa*.

****

What does this discussion of Dōwa policy in one small city in the Chikuhō region tell us about Dōwa policy more generally? We have described policy implementation at the municipal level in some detail because it was at that level that individuals in Buraku communities came into direct contact with, and hopefully benefited from, the Dōwa policies.

However, the context was quite different to that in Osaka and Nara. First, there is no evidence that these Buraku communities had been formed much before the end of the Edo period and they had only a peripheral connection to the leather trade. Their earliest antecedents were probably those who were invited to farm land abandoned following the famines in the area during the Kyōhō period (1730s). Thereafter, residents of these communities played a marginal economic and social role that included involvement in coal mining as it began in the late eighteenth and early nineteenth centuries. As the industry grew rapidly in the late nineteenth century, their traditionally marginal role was reinforced as prejudice and discrimination made it difficult for them to find work anywhere other than in the smaller, least capital-intensive collieries, often referred to colloquially as 'badger holes' (*tanukibori*). The cyclical nature of demand for coal made it essential for them to hold on to some parcels of land, however small, to enable their families to survive periods of unemployment.

In the pre-war mines, 'gangmasters' were used to discipline the workforce. After the war, the management of human resources fell largely into the hands of *rōmu gakari* – labour overseers – who used harsh methods to prevent any attempt to form a labour organisation independent of the company union and to ensure that production targets were met. They played a particularly important role in the small- and medium-sized mines where their influence, power, and violent methods extended beyond the confines of the pits into the *tanjū* communities. Allen notes how a number of them joined the *yakuza* ranks as the mines closed down and he documents how their influence continued well into the 1990s (see, for example, Allen, 1994, 109). He suggests that at the time he was writing one such group had as many as 300 members and had 'had a pervasive and destructive influence on local issues since pre-war days'. This extended down to such quotidian matters as access to welfare payments, 'if a person who knew a senior man in the *yakuza* wanted to be on the dole, then it was arranged' (Allen, 1994, 253).

Given this, what is remarkable is not the extent of the connections between the implementation of Dōwa policy and organised crime groups – about which there are many rumours and unsubstantiated stories – but how few are reported. We will return to this in the next chapter.

In the detail about the way policy was decided, what is characteristic about this city is the role played by the *Shikyō* (*Buraku Kaihō Dōmei Q-shi Kyōgikai*). We only have access to documents from the 1990s but by that stage it was a partner in the process of deciding what projects should be funded presenting the local bureaucrats with lists of incomplete projects and, for example, conducting a prolonged if ultimately ineffective campaign to have a fourth Rinpokan built. Occasionally in the documents, there are references to the possibility of consultation with other groups in the city such as the *Shin Nihon Dōwakai Zenkoku Rengōkai* and the *Nihon Dōwa Rengōkai* but only *Shikyō* had a seat on the decision-making council.

Interpretation of the mass of fine detail of exactly how much money was spent on what is not always easy but there was obviously great variation in the way different schemes were funded. Although in some cases the share of funding between state, prefecture, municipality, and municipal bonds was fairly constant, in other cases the prefecture stepped in to fill the role vacated by the state. It was surprising to see how in some policy areas – for example, funding of attendance at university – so much, sometimes all, of the funding came from the city's general budget. Perhaps inevitably each new level of detail made available generates new sets of questions. For example, it would be interesting to know more about how the negotiations worked between the local administrators and their equivalents in the prefectural offices and ministries and whether the proportions of funding for different kinds of projects were standard across the country.

The various plans devised by the city authorities across the years have not stemmed the further decline of the area. Total population stood at 45,977 in 2020. Dependency on social welfare in the city continues at levels higher than most of the rest of Japan even if the situation is still not quite as bad as in some neighbouring towns. As Tsutsumi's figures suggest, at least as of 2010 there was not much difference between Buraku communities and their neighbours. However unless a more systematic survey is carried out, these estimates of local conditions are the only data we have.

However, if this partial data points to greater equality than 50 years ago, the evidence that comes from the local survey carried out in 2017 also suggests lingering discrimination. There was then plenty of justification for the decision to set up a council to consider how to eliminate Buraku discrimination although at the time of writing there is little evidence of its activity.

Comments on the regional case studies

The aim of this chapter has been to trace the development of Dōwa policy in three different parts of Japan before, during, and after the implementation of the SML. In doing so, I have sought to describe how policy was decided, how it was implemented, and suggest how these projects changed living conditions within these communities. What then can we conclude from the detailed studies of the implementation of Dōwa policy in these three parts of Japan? What do they have in common? What contrasts can we identify? What do they suggest about the overall nature and impact of Dōwa policy?

Variation at the rice-roots level?

It is worth repeating that Dōwa policy projects were implemented in over a thousand local government units across Japan (to be precise 1,112 municipalities and 36 prefectures) and yet there has been a detailed analysis of the background, content, and impact of those projects in only a handful of areas.[15] For whatever reason, even where local groups have been formed to study Buraku history, they invariably focus on the pre-war or pre-Meiji period. Ioka Yasutoki, who has examined the development of Dōwa policy in Nara prefecture, suggests that although there was considerable variation in the nature of Dōwa project implementation during the 1950s and 1960s, the formulation of a national level policy in the late 1960s resulted in a standardisation of both the content of Dōwa policy and its administration. We saw in Chapter 7 that the long-term plan approved by the cabinet in 1969 set out the guidelines for the development of Dōwa project policy by the eight related ministries and that they remained unchanged over the next 30 years.

However, the evidence from the surveys done in 1993 suggests that there was significant variation in how Dōwa funds were used if we compare different 'blocks'. For example, looking at the total Regional Improvement Project spending in 1991, overall 25.5% was spent on housing but it took up 33.4% of the spending in Shikoku while only 17.4% in Kyushu (Dōwa Gyōseishi Henshū Iinkai, 2002, 902). Similarly between 1969 and 1993, nationally the split between spending on material and non-material projects was 58.4%:41.6%, but 70.3:29.7 in Shikoku and 60:40 in Kyushu. If we consider the financial burden placed on different levels of government: nationally, the figures were 22.6:10.8:66.6 (state, prefecture, municipality), while in Shikoku it was 35.4:9.8:54.8 and in Kyushu 24.5, 10.5, 64 (Dōwa Gyōseishi Henshū Iinkai, 2002, 908). And, to take just one more set of figures, the proportion of the prefectural budget spent on Dōwa projects 1969–91 was 4.9% in Osaka prefecture, 15.3% in Nara, and 5% in Fukuoka (Dōwa Gyōseishi Henshū Iinkai, 2002, 909). It is not possible to unpack this data but it seems likely that the differences reflect both the living circumstances in different parts of the country and the effectiveness of the representatives of the Buraku communities to negotiate implementation of improvements. Despite a wealth of detailed information about expenditure in Q city, there is no clear indication about what the balance was overall between funding sources – state, prefecture, or city. Indeed, that information seems to have been deliberately obscured. The data only reveals the share of the cost between the three levels for particular projects. Moreover, with so little research about Dōwa policy administration at the municipal level, it is not possible to say whether Q city is typical.

Comparing the case studies

Nara prefecture was the birthplace of the Suiheisha, Osaka the location of the BLL headquarters. There is evidence of the existence of outcaste communities, including but not only of leatherworkers in both regions since the start of the Edo period with roots that go back much further into Japanese history. The prefectural authorities devised elaborate responses to the Yūwa policy initiatives in the 1920s and 1930s and were quick to revive Dōwa policy during the occupation. Things were quite different in Q city. There is no evidence of outcaste communities there at the start of the Edo period, let alone before then. While the social process that led to the formation of the Buraku communities is poorly understood, it was no doubt connected to the development of the coal mining industry. Although some Burakumin resident in the city took part in Suiheisha activity, Yūwa policy was not well developed and post-war Dōwa policy was slow to emerge. It was really only after the passage of the SML that it was incorporated into the plans to reconstruct the local political economy in the wake of the closure of the mining industry.

Often discussion of the Buraku problem and Dōwa policy is premised on a historical narrative which discusses the issue as related to deeply embedded 'feudal practice'. And yet as the Q city case demonstrates, the 'problem' is at least as much one that was derived from practices from the early modern period that were re-invented in the twentieth century. But if we can agree that Buraku discrimination in Q city is a problem rooted in Japan's modernisation not its feudal history, then this might suggest that this is also true elsewhere in Japan even where Buraku communities can be shown to have an ancient lineage. This supports the view often put forward by Kurokawa who makes the comparison between discrimination against Burakumin and women. That women were systematically disadvantaged in the period before 1868 and still in the twenty-first century can be readily demonstrated and this discrimination has persisted despite the massive transformation of political and economic structures and of the family system. However, the way misogyny manifests itself today is through contemporary structures. Addressing issues of gender equality then requires us to look at how those structures need to change. Similarly, if we conclude that discrimination against Burakumin persists, and the data from the various local surveys suggests that it does, then we need to consider what more needs to be done to address how it can be uprooted and not recreated by examining contemporary practice.

Top-down or bottom-up?

Previous studies such as those by Kanai and Suginohara have focused on the national level of policymaking, in particular the interaction between the BLL and the JSP with the LDP and structures of government. Clearly without the Dotaishin in 1965, the passage of the SML and its accompanying plan in 1969, the transformative amounts of money would not have been made available to local government. But, following the decision made not to create a central administrative agency, it was left to local governments and even the Dōwa communities within those local administrative areas to decide whether they wanted to benefit from the better funded policy and, if so, exactly what the new money should be spent on. In Osaka and Nara in the 1950s, the BLL was consulted as part of the process of formulation of Dōwa projects and this developed into a system that was elaborated from the early 1970s. In Q city, the more pressing concerns caused by the shut-down of the coal industry meant that attention did not turn to how the municipality could incorporate administration of Dōwa policy until the early 1970s. When it did, representatives of the BLL were included on the relevant committees and they were able to provide direct input of the wishes of the communities into the policy process. They did not always get their way as the failure of the campaign for a fourth Rinpokan showed.

It is hard to be sure how representative our three case studies are of the policy process. In each case, the mayor or governor at the start of the Dōwa policy programme was either a member of the JSP or supported by it and there was a significant cohort of JSP members on the local assembly. This no doubt facilitated the rapid implementation of Dōwa policy projects in these areas. It is not clear how this worked where the elected head of the local authority was not sympathetic to the JSP/BLL. This is yet another area where more research is required.

Where local representatives were incorporated into the Dōwa decision-making process, it enabled those decisions to be informed by local wishes and thus became a more democratic system than would have been created if Dōwa policy had been administered by a national level organisation.

After the Special Measures Law

From the late 1960s, central government began to take the initiative in formulating Dōwa policy even if most of the detailed administrative work was left to local governments. After over 30 years during which that policy was loosely coordinated at the centre and following the disbanding of the Chitaikyo in 1997, the responsibility for further initiatives reverted once more to those local governments. However, with the number of projects that needed to be administered shrinking quite quickly, the local Dōwa policy bureaus were reduced in size and absorbed into other structures sometimes with a new title that deleted reference to 'Dōwa' and spoke instead of 'Jinken' - human rights. Often, these changes were accompanied by solemn resolutions not to forget their commitment to promoting 'assimilation' but perhaps inevitably as these units extended their remit, the priority given to Buraku issues declined particularly in the absence of any national leadership.

With almost no central government finance and local taxes unable to provide funding as a substitute, Dōwa projects in our three areas soon ground to a halt. In some areas where a local government tried to continue to fund Dōwa projects, it was subject to strong criticism from a JCP member of the local assembly or successor to the Zenkairen,

Q city manage to support a handful of Dōwa projects for a few years with funding that came from Fukuoka prefecture and possibly through the *Sekitan Roppō* structures. Apart from that, the common pattern was for the remnants of Dōwa projects to be absorbed into a broader human rights strategy and for local government to adopt what was little more than a monitoring and exhortational role. They continued to conduct periodic surveys of attitudes while supporting human rights education in schools and *keihatsu* activities in the community. These surveys demonstrate how, at least in the areas we have examined, there remains a high level of awareness of the Dōwa issue even among those who claim to harbour no prejudices. In all three areas, there remain significant numbers of people who would, at the very least, still 'think twice' before agreeing to one of their children knowingly marrying someone from a Buraku community. Substantially more would avoid living in or near to one. Moreover, time does not seem to be diluting these feelings.

Research on the living conditions in these areas is fragmented and to my knowledge no-one has attempted to provide an overview. Ageing is a phenomenon whose diverse aspects can be seen across contemporary Japan. The evidence suggests that Dōwa district residents are on average older than their neighbours and the mainstream. The data from Nara suggests that this is because older people are more likely to remain in their communities, while younger people move out. Meanwhile, Uchida suggests that there is evidence in Osaka of older people moving into Dōwa districts attracted by the lower cost of housing. People aged 65 or over whether in work or not have less income than younger people, so it comes as no surprise that household incomes in Dōwa districts are low. So, the lower than average household incomes in Buraku communities may not be connected to discrimination in employment but rather be simply a result of the age profile. At the same time, it could be that those who do get good jobs are more likely to move out and those with similar jobs, status, and incomes do not move in to take their place. So, 'location' remains important. However, in the absence of broader-based and more sophisticated analyses, it is not possible definitively to answer questions about employment patterns.

Another topic that research at the local level could shed light on is the impact of the shift from the 'special measures' funding for infrastructural improvements to funding from the 'general' budget of the local government. In the late 1990s, many administrators and BLL activists became concerned about the need to upgrade or, better, demolish and replace the ageing concrete apartment blocks that had been built in the 1970s in the first wave of Dōwa housing. Following the termination of the SML, has this taken place? If so, have these projects been given more or less priority compared to the upgrading of other properties owned and administered by the local government? Similarly, where human rights education in schools and *kei-hatsu* activity continues in communities, how well is it funded, how extensive is it, and what impact is it having?

Finally, and perhaps most significantly, research at the local level particularly in places like Nara and Chikuhō that are outside the major conurbations could shed some light on whether those with Buraku backgrounds are more vulnerable to downturns in the economic cycle. The overall labour shortage which at times is said to be acting as a restraint on economic growth and requiring immigrant labour might suggest that there is no sense in which Japanese capitalism needs Buraku communities to act as an 'industrial reserve army'. However, the twenty-first century has seen a rapid increase in the proportion of the population employed on non-standard contracts. Are (former) Burakumin over-represented within that sector of the workforce?

Notes

1 During the first half of the nineteenth century, between 70,000 and 100,000 cow and horse hides were sent to Watanabe Village each year.

2 Trachoma is an infectious bacterial disease of the eye. It causes a roughening of the inner surface of the eyelids which leads to pain in the eyes, breakdown of the outer surface or cornea, and eventual blindness.

3 But see Morooka, *Sengo Buraku Kaihō Ronsōshi*, five volumes, 1980–5.

4 The most recent national survey in 1993 found 82 Buraku communities located in 29 municipalities with a population of 50,933 with a 'mixture ratio' of 87.7% (Dōwa Gyōseishi Henshū Iinkai, 2002, 819).

5 This was the Dōwa Mondai Kenkyūsho, forerunner of the Nara-ken Dōwa Mondai Kankei Shiryō Sentaa.

6 He could match the census data only to these 16 districts mainly because the others were so small that their data was included with that of the neighbouring community.

7 Concerned that I might expose some of these communities to discrimination, as far as possible I have anonymised all the sources that I refer to in this text relating to Dōwa policy at the municipal level.

8 The city of Kita Kyushu was created in 1963 by the merger of five municipalities (Moji, Kokura, Tobata, Yahata, and Wakamatsu) centred around the former feudal city of Kokura.

9 Strictly speaking, the term *Sekitan Roppō* refers to the laws introduced between 1952 and 1967 to deal with the immediate impact of coal mine closures but it has come to be used to refer to a larger package of measures implemented in the late twentieth century.

10 Q-shi Dōwa Taisaku Jigyō no Gaiyō, Q-shi 1984; Q-shi ni okeru Dōwa Taisaku Jigyō no Sōkatsu to Kongo no Arikata, Q-shi Dōwa Taisaku Kankei Jigyō Kentō Iinkai, March 2002.

11 For comparison, we might note that in 2001 Q shi owned 4,805 housing units, including those in the 406 Dōwa *danchi.*

12 The housing built in community U between 1969 and 1978 cost a total of ¥6,300m with funding coming from the state ¥3,700m, the prefecture ¥600m, the city ¥100m, and municipal bonds ¥1,700m. In K, the building between 1970 and 1981 cost in total ¥14,000m with ¥9,000m coming from the state, ¥1,300m from the prefecture, and ¥3,300m in the form of municipal bonds. One of the five

storey blocks in D costs ¥22,300m: ¥14,800m from the state, ¥1,600m from the prefecture, and ¥5,800m in municipal bonds.

13 The combined cost was ¥10,400m – ¥4,900m from the state, ¥2,000m from the prefecture, ¥1,200m from municipal bonds, and ¥2,200m from the city.

14 Note that this uses a different data set compared to that quoted on p. 75.

15 As this manuscript was being prepared for publication I learned of an addition to the literature on Dowa policy: *Shiga-ken no Dōwa Jigyōshi* published by the Shiga prefecture human rights centre.

Bibliography

Asahi Shimbun various dates.

Far Eastern Economic Review October 7, 1993.

Nishi Nippon Shimbun.

Allen M., (1994) *Undermining the Japanese Miracle: Work and Conflict in a Coalmining Community*, Cambridge: Cambridge University Press.

Amos T., (2020) 'Contested Liberation: The Japanese Communist Party, Human Rights Groups, and the New Anti-Discrimination Law', *Japan Forum*, vol. 32, no. 2, 220–43.

Asō T., (2010) *Tankō to Jinken* (Coal Mines and Human Rights), Lecture Handout.

Chūō Yūwa Jigyō Kyōkai, (1935) *Zenkoku Buraku Chōsa* (National Buraku Survey), Tokyo: Chūō Yūwa Jigyō Kyōkai.

Dōwa Gyōseishi Henshū Iinkai (Dōwa Administration History Editorial Committee), (2002) *Dōwa Gyōseishi* (A History of Dōwa Administration), Tokyo: Sōmuchō Daijin Kanbō Chiiki Kaizen Taisakuhitsu.

Eason P. V., (2012) *Forging Fukuoka: Locality and Development in Modern Japan*, Doctoral Dissertation, Princeton University.

Fukuoka-ken, (1979) *Dōwa Taisaku Suishinin Hikkei* (Manual for Members of the Dōwa Policy Promotion Committee), Fukuoka: Fukuoka-ken.

Hanes J. E., (2012) 'Progressivism for the Pacific World: Urban Social Policymaking in Modern Osaka', *City, Culture and Society*, vol. 3, 79–85.

Ioka Y., (2014) 'Kokusei Chōsa Shochiikishukei ni motozuku Nara-ken Dōwa Chiku no Henka to Genjo ni Kansuru Kōsatsu' (Reflections on the Changes in and Present Conditions of Dōwa Districts in Nara prefecture based on Data from the National Census), *Narajinken Buraku Kaihō Kenkyūsho Kiyo*, 32, April, 1–20.

Kamibara F., (2012) 'Osaka Fumin ni totte no Dōwa Mondai' (Residents of Osaka Prefecture and the Dōwa Problem), *Buraku Kaihō Kenkyū*, vol. 195, 59–74.

Kanai K., (1991) *Dōwa Gyōsei: Sengo no Kiseki* (Dōwa Administration, the postwar path), Osaka: Buraku Kaihō Shuppansha.

Kobayakawa A., (2020) 'Japan's Modernization and Discrimination: What are Buraku and Burakumin?' *Critical Sociology*, vol. 47, no. 1, 111–132.

Kōno T., (2010) 'Buraku Mondai Kaiketsu no Saishūkyokumen ga Tōmen shiteiru Mondaiten' (Problems Being Encountered in the Final Phase of the Resolution of the Buraku Problem), in Buraku Mondai Kenkyūsho (ed) *Buraku Mondai Kaiketsu Katei no Kenkyū* (Studies on the Process of the Resolution of the Buraku Problem), Vol. 1, Kyoto: Buraku Mondai Kenkyūsho Shuppanbu, pp. 93–121.

Matsumoto K., (1977) *Chikuhō ni Ikiru: Buraku Kaihō totomo ni Gojūnen* (Living in Chikuho: Fifty years with Buraku Liberation), Kyoto: Buraku Mondai Kenkyūsho.

Mizuuchi, T. (1998) 'Private Struggles, Public Supports: Renovating Japanese Minority Community, Buraku', *Dōwa Mondai Kenkyū*, Osaka Shiritsu Daigaku, vol. 20, 29-43.

Mizuuchi, T. and Jeon, H. G., (2010) 'The New Mode of Urban Renewal for the Former Outcaste Minority People and Areas in Japan', *Cities*, vol. 27, Supplement 1, June, 525–34.

Mori I., (2009) *Dōwa to Ginkō* (Dōwa and the Bank), Tokyo: Kōdansha.

Morooka S., (1985) *Sengo Buraku Kaihō Ronsōshi* V, Tokyo: Shashoku Shobo.

Nara-ken, (2003) *Naraken Dōwa Gyōsei Jigyōshi* (A History of Dōwa Administration Projects in Nara Prefecture), Nara: Nara-ken.

Nara-ken, (2018) *Jinken ni Kansuru Kenmin Ishiki Chōsa Hōkokushō* (Report on a Survey of Human Rights Awareness of the Residents of Nara Prefecture), Nara prefecture.

Nara-ken, (2020) *Naraken Jinken Shisaku no Kansuru Kihonkeikaku* (The Basic Plan Concerning Human Rights Policy in Nara Prefecture), Nara prefecture.

Nara-shi Dōwachiku Shiteki Chōsa Iinkai, (1983) *Nara no Burakushi* (A History Buraku in Nara), Nara-shi.

Neary I., (1986) 'Socialist and Communist Party Attitudes towards Discrimination against Japan's *Burakumin*', *Political Studies*, vol. XXXIV, no. 4, 556–74.

Oga M., (2002) *Shi Dōsokkyō 50nen no rekishi to Jinken Kyōkai e no Ikō* (Fifty Years of Dosokkyo History and the Transition to the Human Rights Association), lecture notes.

Oga M., (2015), *Naikaku Dōwa Taisaku Shingikai Tōshin 50 nen - Tōshin no Igi to Konnichi* (Fiftieth Anniversary of the Cabinet Commission of Enquiry on Dōwa Policy – Its Significance for Today), Osaka: Kaihō Shuppan.

Onishi Y., (2009) 'Buraku Kaihō Undō' (The Buraku Liberation Movement), in Osaka Shakai Undō Kyōkai (ed) *Osaka Shakai Rōdō Undōshi* (A History of the Social and Workers Movements in Osaka), Osaka: Osaka Shakai Undō Kyōkai, 692–706.

Osaka-fu Dōwa Jigyō Sokushin Kyōgikai (Osaka Prefecture Dōwa Projects Promotion Council), (2001) *Osaka Dōwa Jigyō Gojūnenshi* (A History of the Fifty Years of Dōwa Projects), Osaka: Osaka-fu Dōwa Jigyō Sokushin Kyōgikai.

Phipps C. L., (2015) *Empires on the Waterfront: Japan's Ports and Power 1858–1899*, Cambridge, MA: Harvard University Asia Center.

Q chiku Jinken Sentaa, (2018) *Jinken Mondai ni Kansuru Shimin Ishiki Chōsa* (Survey of Human Rights Awareness of Local Citizens), Q City Hall.

Q-shi, (1984) *Q-shi Dōwa Taisaku Jigyō no Gaiyō* (Outline of Dōwa Policy Projects in Q city), Q City Hall.

Q-shi Dōwa Taisaku Kankei Jigyō Kentō Iinkai (Dōwa Policy Related Projects Review Committee) (2002) *Q-shi ni okeru Dōwa Taisaku Jigyō no Sōkatsu to Kongo no Arikata* (Summary of Dōwa Policy Projects in Q city and the Next Steps), Q City Hall.

Q-shi shi Hensan Iinkai (Q City History Editorial Committee), (1979) *Q-shi shi* (A History of Q City) Vol. III, Q City Hall.

Saga A., (2012) 'Urban Lower-Class Society in Modern Osaka', *City, Culture and Society*, vol. 3, 65–71.

Shiga-ken Jinken Sentaa (2021) *Shiga-ken no Dōwa Jigyōshi* (A History of Dowa Projects in Shiga prefecture), Otsu-shi: Shiga-ken Jinken Sentaa.

Shima K., (2015) *Osakashinai 12 Dōwachiku no 'Shakai Kaisō'teki Ichi o Hakaru* (Measuring the 'Social Class' Position of 12 Dōwa Districts in Osaka City), Notes from presentation, Osaka, 29 November 2015.

Teraki N. and Kurokawa M., (2019) *A History of Discriminated Buraku Communities in Japan*, trans. Ian Neary) Folkeston: Renaissance Books.

Tsukada T., (2012) 'The Urban History of Osaka', *City, Culture and Society*, vol. 3, 1–8.

Tsutsumi K., (2016) *Rinpokan Jinken Kadai Toaku Chōsa*, Fukuoka: Fukuoka-ken.

Uchida R., (2015) *Osakafu ni Okeru Dōwachiku no Jittai Toaku to Shakai Haijō Chiiki Sekishutsu no Kokoromi* (An Attempt to Distinguish Between the Conditions in the Dōwa Districts and Socially Excluded Districts of Osaka Prefecture), Notes from a presentation, Osaka, 29 November 2015.

Upham F., (1980) 'Ten Years of Affirmative Action for Japanese Burakumin: A Preliminary Report on the Law on Special Measures for Dōwa Projects', *Law in Japan*, vol. 13, 39–73.

Yamamoto T., (2020) *Jūmin Undō to Gyōsei Kenryoku no Esunogurafi* (An Ethnography of Residents Movement and Administrative Power), Kyoto: Kōyō Shobō.

9 Corrupt practices? A comment on *yakuza* involvement

Those who have some acquaintance with Buraku issues and Dōwa policy administration may feel frustrated that the preceding accounts of the implementation of Dōwa projects at both national and local levels have only dealt parenthetically with the repeated accusations that have been made across the years that significant amounts of Dōwa funding were wasted on unnecessary projects or been channelled into the hands of Buraku bosses with links to organised crime (*yakuza*) and/or the BLL. One reason for this is that the available accounts on Dōwa projects rely on data either from movement sources or from local governments neither of which are eager to draw attention to an activity that may have allowed waste, fraud, or corruption. One is forced therefore to rely on reports from newspapers which are rarely thorough or able to contextualise the events described or even necessarily report their outcome. Those accounts that do allege or claim to document examples of corrupt practice rarely do so in a systematic way so that it is difficult to assess the veracity of their claims, their extent, or to work out how surprised we should be that some corrupt practice existed.[1]

To take this second point first: we noted earlier Kingston's comments in 2004 about the perversities of the 'construction state' where legal requirements favouring local firms meant that the construction industry became composed of many thousands of small construction companies. These rules, in place since 1966, have, he says, 'been a mechanism for influence peddling, bid-rigging, price gouging, bribes and under-the-table contributions to political funds' (Kingston, 2004, 124). Given the many thousand public works projects that comprised the Dōwa programmes even in a single city, it comes as no surprise to learn that some of them involved scams. It is impossible to work out if public works in Dōwa communities were more (or less?) likely to involve corrupt practice of some sort. There is no data enabling comparison between its incidence in construction projects in Buraku and non-Buraku areas.

The impression is sometimes given that the BLL was particularly vulnerable to fostering and benefitting from corrupt practice. This may in part be a function of its size – it has consistently been twice the size of its JCP-affiliated rival, the Zenkairen, whose membership was about the same as the

DOI: 10.4324/9781003127994-9

centrist Jiyū Dōwakai although all three have been in steep decline since the 1990s. So, if any malpractice were to be identified, it is twice as likely to have involved the BLL. Since the 1980s, the Zenkairen and its successors have argued that the BLL, dominated by the 'Asada faction', promoted successive extensions of Dōwa policy not only because of its ideologically misguided 'Buraku-first-ism' but also because it benefitted materially from Dōwa projects. As early as 1975, Sakaki Toshio of the JCP suggested in an article in the Mainichi Shimbun that in Osaka, the local BLL branches received 0.2–0.7% rebate (i.e. 'kickback') on Dōwa building projects that in some cases was as high as 5% (Mainichi Shimbun, 13 March 1975).[2] Such allegations have been repeated numerous times in books and newspaper articles and periodically major scandals have arisen which have given the impression that corrupt practice was endemic within Dōwa project administration.

There is an assumption that because it is 'known' (although again without any firm evidence) that organised crime groups (*yakuza*) have tended to recruit young men disproportionately from marginalised groups such as Buraku and Zainichi Korean communities, the construction projects conducted within them have involved corrupt practices involving local *yakuza*. This may be correct but there is also scope here for prejudices to overestimate its significance. There is no reason to believe that the involvement of organised crime in the building projects that took place in Q city, for example, was greater in the Dōwa infrastructure projects than in other construction funded by the *Sekitan Roppō* that took place in the rest of the city although no-one would doubt that there was some such involvement in both.

This may in part be because of the way that the amount of Dōwa-related money was dwarfed by the amount being paid out in compensation for damage caused to the environment by the mines. A report in the Asahi newspaper in 1986 suggested that there was ¥56,000m being paid out each year by the state for work to repair environmental damage caused by mining in the Chikuhō region, of which 5–10% was skimmed off as a kickback. In one small town neighbouring Q city, 17 people were arrested in 1985–6 on corruption charges, including the mayor and leader of the council. The year before, the head of the Dōwa policy office had been arrested on charges of bribery. The same report goes on to suggest evidence of what it calls 'structural corruption across the whole Chikuhō region'. This is linked not only to the Dōwa policy but more broadly to the programmes that provided compensation for mining damage. The attitude of many involved in the scams is reported to be, 'this is the government's money, we are causing no damage to any of our neighbours, so where's the harm?' (Asahi Shimbun, 3 February 1986).

The Asahi newspaper report discusses the situation in another nearby city where there were 295 designated construction companies. Some owners of these were indignant about the advantages that 'Dōwa related companies' had in winning contracts. One critic said,

> There are a surprising number of Dōwa related firms but they have not been in business long, their technical skills are few and there are hardly any buildings built by them. Most of them further sub-contract the whole work but take a 20% cut. We need the work so we take the contracts but you can't do a good job with that money. And the authorities turn a blind eye.
>
> (Quoted in Asahi Shimbun, 3 February 1986)

Moreover, this involved not just Dōwa project work but general construction projects too. This comment may be in part informed by the sort of prejudices that resulted in widespread envy (*netami*). However, these processes were not (are not?) confined to the Chikuhō region. Kingston noted how a law passed in 1966 resulted in a rapid increase in the number of small construction firms – nationally to 586,000 by 2002. He suggests however that '…these local contractors carry out little of the work they contract; after winning the contract they subcontract entire projects…after deducting a "finder's fee"' (Kingston, 2004, 124–5). This collusion between public works bureaucrats, politicians, and contractors was (is?) an integral part of what McCormack and Kerr refer to as the dark side of the 'construction state' (*doken kokka*) (McCormack, 1995; Kerr, 2001). That it should manifest itself in the Chikuhō region is not surprising but neither is it evidence of special susceptibility of Buraku communities to corrupt practice.

It has to be admitted though that the history of the Dowa project policy has been punctuated by major scandals. In Chapter 6, we referred to the resignation from the Dōtaikyō of the head of the Zen Nihon Dōwakai, Yanai Masao, following revelations 1978–9 about his involvement in the development of a shopping centre in Yamaguchi. In 1981, the Kokura Times newspaper reported on the sale of a plot of land in Yahata involving senior members of the BLL in 1978–9 which generated profits for them of more than ¥270m. This triggered newspaper reports of 20 similar cases over the next months involving local leaders of the BLL and the Zen Nihon Dōwakai, including Yanai's successor as the head, Matsuo Masanobu (Suginohara 754, 2007, 72).

In order to clarify exactly what had happened, Isomura was commissioned by the Kita-Kyushu city council to chair an investigation into Dōwa administration. It examined both the living conditions within Dōwa communities and the process of Dōwa policy administration. The report, published in October 1983, emphasised the importance of ensuring an independent and open policy planning process, that the aims of policy should be to ensure the self-reliance of those within Dōwa communities and the encouragement of links with neighbouring communities but that it was also important to stress human rights protection (Asahi Shimbun, 30 October 1983). Being issued just before the start of the Chiiki Kaizen phase of the Dōwa policy, this report is said to have had great influence on Dōwa policy administration.

However, Suginohara goes as far as suggested that the links that developed more generally between the local BLL leadership and administrators of Dōwa policy amounted to 'structural corruption' pointing to another example in Kyoto city where between 1983 and 1986 seven people were arrested for their involvement in a dubious land deal worth ¥300m (Suginohara, 757, 2007, 75). A search through newspaper archives reveals a number of similar if less spectacular incidents where Dōwa projects were associated with corruption and involvement with organised crime. For example, in January 1994, the head of the Zen Nihon Dōwakai in Tokyo was arrested for conspiring with a local branch of the Yamaguchi-gumi to extort ¥13m from a construction company. The outcome of the case is not recorded (Asahi Shimbun, 29 January 1994). In Yukuhashi, a city less than an hour's drive from Q city, the prefectural branch of the Zenkairen reported their suspicions to the police that in 1995 a leader of the Yukuhashi BLL had demanded a payment of ¥2.47m into his personal account in return for a contract worth ¥212m to construct an irrigation pump. Later the same year, he requested a 'kick back' of over ¥7m from a seedling planting machine manufacturer who received an order worth ¥106m as part of a Dōwa project. The case came to court in December 1998. The judge criticised the accused for his breach of trust and sentenced him to three years imprisonment. However out of court, he had agreed to return the money so the sentence was suspended (Asahi Shimbun, 13 October, 23 December 1998).

What cemented the impression of the link between organised crime and Dōwa policy in the minds of many people was the well-documented and high-profile case which came to light in 2006 and is known as the Asuka-kai incident.[3] It linked the BLL and Dōwa construction projects in Osaka to the *yakuza* on the one hand and the banking system on the other and involved breathtaking amounts of money. In May 2006, Konishi Nobuhiko (b. 1933) was arrested on charges of having embezzled large sums which he spent supporting a luxurious lifestyle for himself and his family. At the time, he was the head of the Asuka branch of the Osaka BLL and a welfare organisation, the Asuka-kai, which was recognised by Osaka city as eligible to receive grants to support Dōwa-related projects. It was alleged that Konishi had used his position within the local BLL to personally benefit from Dōwa grants. Moreover, he pressured the manager of the local branch of the Sanwa bank to extend unsecured loans worth several billion yen, many of which were never repaid.[4] The deputy manager of the bank was also arrested. In June 2006, Konishi was further charged with having conspired with the head of the Asuka Human Rights Center to arrange for a *yakuza* leader to receive seven medical certificates in connection with an old people's care home that they were jointly responsible for.

The Asuka-kai was first established in 1960 to support local welfare projects and to run the public baths (*sentō*). Konishi, known to be an active member of a *yakuza* organisation during the 1970s and 1980s, became the head of the Asuka chapter of the Osaka BLL in 1967 and changed the Asuka-kai into a non-profit foundation which was given permission by Osaka city in 1974 to manage a parking lot near Shin-Osaka station. He became a key intermediary for major construction companies who needed to liaise with local contractors for which services he would charge a fee of typically 5%. The 350 members of the Osaka-fu Dōwa Kensetsu Kyōkai (Osaka Prefecture Dōwa Construction Association) held a virtual monopoly over the projects funded by the SML and Konishi was reputed to play the key role in deciding who would receive the contracts.

Following his arrest on 10 June 2006, Konishi was expelled from the BLL which launched an internal review. Its report published in October insisted that the corrupt behaviour was the actions of an individual that did not represent the BLL. He was later found guilty and sentenced to six years in prison on 24 January 2007. He appealed the verdict but during the summer that year, he was hospitalised suffering from lung cancer and died at home in November. The manager of the Bank of Tokyo Mitsubishi UFJ (BTMU) Awaji branch never appeared in court but in February 2007 the Financial Services Agency announced that it was taking 'administrative action' against BTMU ordering it to cease offering loans to new corporate clients in the Osaka region for several months.

For the successors to the Zenkairen and their supporters in the JCP, this incident reinforced all their criticisms of the BLL and Dōwa policy: that it was a waste of local authority (and tax payers') money, inextricably involved corruption, fostered connections with organised crime, ensured dominance of the Dōwa communities by Buraku 'bosses', and demonstrated how members of the mainstream community such as the bank manager were fearful of what might happen if they refused the demands of a BLL boss.

The relationship between Dowa policy, Buraku communities, and criminal activity was further complicated by the activities of *ese-Dōwa* groups that often purport to be associated with the BLL and demand payments in the name of Dōwa activity. At the peak, there were thought to be more than 200 such groups. Their number increased rapidly in the early 1980s at the time of the coincidence of the extension of Dōwa policy with the revision of laws that restricted the activity of *sōkaiya*, gangsters who demanded payments from company executives for preventing shareholders asking awkward questions at the annual meetings. Typically, the group would adopt a name that included the words 'Dōwa' and 'Zenkoku' or 'Zen Nihon' to give the impression that it was part of a national organisation. Sometimes, it would involve people from Buraku communities, sometimes not. Takagi gives as examples of the kind of activity they became involved in: charging high fees for obtaining 'change of use' certificates in the process of urban development, pressuring financial institutions to provide investment in the name of a Dōwa project then taking large fees when passing it on, charging high fees for the provision of teaching material (books and magazines) or in-house seminars following alleged examples of discrimination by an employee of the company (Takagi, 1986, 92–3). The common factor in all of these activities was their exploitation of the widespread prejudice that Burakumin are '*kowai*' – scary. As we saw in Chapter 6, what to do about *ese-Dōwa* activity exercised Isomura and the Chitaikyō in the 1980s. A liaison council was established within central government in 1987 and continued into the twenty-first century.

Close examination of local newspapers would no doubt reveal more reports about other examples of corrupt practices linked to the allocation of Dōwa project contracts, some of them involving *ese-Dōwa* groups. This is yet another aspect of Dōwa project administration that requires further research although it is not clear how it could be conducted.

No-one doubts that there were and probably still are members of Buraku communities who were recruited into criminal groups or that there were examples of corrupt practice in the administration of Dowa policies. In the Chikuhō region in particular, criminal groups had played a role disciplining the mining workforce and, when the pits closed, employment within them was one of the few alternatives for those who did not want to move to seek employment elsewhere in Japan. But, to repeat, it is not obvious that there was more corruption in the implementation of Dōwa policy-related projects in the Chikuhō region, or anywhere else in Japan for that matter than in any of the other construction projects that took place in Japan across the final decades of the twentieth century.

Notes

1 For examples of the accusations that have been made during the first decade of the twenty-first century, see the four volumes published between 2003 and 2005 with the title *Dowa Riken no Shinsō* (The Truth about Dowa Graft), edited by Terazono Atsushi, Ichinomiya Yoshinaka and Group K-21, Tamashimasha.
2 Reports on the construction industry in the early 1990s suggested that a 2% kickback was standard practice, Far Eastern Economic Review October 7, 1993.
3 Two books have been published which shed light on the background to this incident and its consequences: Kadooka Nobuhiko, *Pisutoru to Keirin*, Kōdansha 2012, Mori Isao, *Dōwa to Ginkō*, Kōdansha, 2009.
4 The Bank of Tokyo Mitsubishi UFJ (BTMU) took over Sanwa bank in 2002–4.

Bibliography

Asahi Shimbun.

Far Eastern Economic Review October 7, 1993.

Kadooka N., (2012) *Pisutoru to Keirin* (Pistols and the Flag of the Crown of Thorns), Tokyo: Kōdansha.

Kerr A., (2001) *Dogs and Demons: Tales from the Dark Side of Japan*, New York: Hill and Wang.

Kingston J., (2004) *Japan's Quiet Transformation: Social Change and Civil Society in the Twenty-first Century*, London: RoutledgeCurzon.

Mainichi Shimbun.

McCormack G., (1995) 'Growth, Construction, and the Environment: Japan's Construction State', *Japanese Studies*, vol. 15, no. 1, 26–35.

Mori I., (2009) *Dōwa to Ginkō* (Dōwa and the Bank), Tokyo: Kōdansha.
Suginohara J., (2007) 'Sengo Dōwa Gyōsei no Tenkai to Shihai Seisaku' (The Evolution of Postwar Dōwa Administration and Ruling Policies), *Jinken to Buraku Mondai*, Kyoto: Buraku Mondai Kenkyūjo, No. 754, January 2007, 69–78; No. 757, March 2007, 75–80.
Takagi M., (1986) *Dōwa Mondai to Dōwa Dantai* (The Dōwa Problem and Dōwa Groups) Tokyo: Doyō Bijutsusha.
Terazono A., Ichinomiya Y., and Group K-21 (eds.), (2002) *Dōwa Riken no Shinsō* (The Truth about Dowa Graft), Tokyo: Tamashimasha.

10 Conclusions

The aim of this book has been to provide an overall account of the policies devised to ameliorate conditions within the Buraku communities. These began with the *kaizen*/*Yūwa* policies of the late nineteenth and early twentieth centuries but our account has focused mainly on the development of Dōwa policies of the 1950s and after. Understandably, much has been made of the agenda-changing impact of the report published in 1965 known as the Dōtaishin although, as we have seen, its impact was significantly reduced in the process of translating its recommendations into legislation and operating procedures between 1965 and 1969. Moreover, too much focus on the programmes implemented in the 1970s tends to undervalue the significance of the projects that had been pioneered since the 1950s by several local governments particularly in the Kinki region. As we saw in the accounts of the formation and implementation of Dōwa policy in Osaka and Nara, local governments had been working with their local Buraku communities for around 20 years before the provision of substantial funding by central government enabled these local projects to be expanded such that they could seriously address the disadvantages experienced by Buraku community residents. That they did is not subject to debate. Even the government's fiercest critics within the BLL concede that the living environment in most Dōwa districts has been improved to the extent of eliminating most of the differences between them and their neighbours even if there remains room for debate about whether this has resulted in the elimination of discrimination and prejudice. In this concluding chapter, I want to begin by referring back to the considerations set out in Chapter 2 in order to bring out some of the characteristic features of Japan's attempt to implement an assimilation policy.

Just to repeat, the five approaches discussed in Chapter 2 to which reference has been made periodically in the preceding narrative were:

- the influence of constitutional and international human rights commitments;
- the changes in that international context and its impact on Japan;

DOI: 10.4324/9781003127994-10

- the relationship of Dōwa policy to other policies which aimed to improve social welfare;
- the nature of the relationship between central and local governments as shown in the implementation of Dōwa policy; and
- the extent to which it is helpful to consider Dōwa policy as a response to a 'socially constructed Dōwa problem'.

Let us take these in turn.

Taking rights seriously I

Human rights provisions make up about one-third of the document adopted in 1946 as the Constitution of Japan. However, during the 1950s the Buraku liberation movement, led by the NCBL from 1946 and then the BLL from 1955, mainly adopted a Marxist perspective which paid little attention to human rights. Meanwhile, although the Japanese government and LDP were not hostile to these concepts, within the Cold War context of the alliance with the USA, they tended to limit their endorsement of human rights to formulaic assertions of commitment to democratic values and support of civil and political rights. During the period immediately prior to and during the period of the *shingikai's* deliberations, human rights advocacy both in Japan and in the wider world had not achieved the currency it would have later in the century. Still, it is notable from what we know of the discussions within the *shingikai* between 1961 and 1965 that both the representatives of the Buraku communities and liberals such as Isomura insisted on the inclusion of explicit reference to Japan's constitutional commitments to human rights often in the face of the opposition of the conservatives and bureaucrats. Having succeeded in embedding those commitments in their report, they were able to use them as leverage to commit the state to supporting measures that would (to borrow Fredman's words) break 'the cycle of disadvantage associated with outgroups'. However, the government was much less enthusiastic about taking positive measures to intervene in the public domain to deter discrimination between citizens in marriage and employment. We will return to this point in our comments on current issues.

Taking rights seriously II

It cannot be said that there was much international influence on the thinking of the *shingikai* members. Within the UN, there was increased attention being paid to the elaboration of human rights ideas and their incorporation into international documents during the 1960s. The CERD was approved by the UNGA in December 1965 and came into effect in 1969 when it had been ratified by 27 countries. But Japan was not one of them and would not ratify it until 1995. The two covenants on civil and political, and social, economic, and cultural rights were both passed by the UNGA in 1966 and came into effect ten years later when they had been ratified by 35 states. Again, Japan was not one of them although it would ratify them in 1979. Japan was also conspicuously slow in its adoption of the conventions on the rights of women, children, and the disabled over the next 40 years.

Apart from the intriguingly full response that the government provided in 1951 on the *Prevention of Discrimination and the Protection of Minorities in Japan*, Japan showed little awareness or interest in the attempts to create the UN-based human rights framework and mostly followed the lead of its Cold War ally. Even after Japan did finally ratify the two basic covenants in 1979 (with some significant reservations), its initial report was minimally brief: only 12 pages in all compared to the 28-page document submitted in 1951.

The *shingikai's* report made passing reference to the 'universal principles of freedom and equality' in its introductory section but thereafter focused exclusively on the domestic policy agenda. During the 1980s, the BLL sent representatives to attend meetings of the United Nations Economic and Social Council ('EcoSoc') sub-commission on the Prevention of Discrimination and Protection of Minorities invited to speak there by groups which already had UN recognition such as the Anti-Slavery League. From the late 1980s, the BLL supported the formation of the IMADR which in 1993 was granted consultative status enabling it to take part in formal functions at the UN in its own right. Parallel to this process, and possibly encouraged by the way the BLL and similar groups representing Ainu and Zainichi Koreans were drawing attention to their plight to the embarrassment of Japanese diplomats, the reports to UN committees about human rights issues produced by the Japanese government under its obligations became more comprehensive.

The debates and demonstrations about civil rights in the 1960s that were defining political discussion in the USA as well as many European and Australasian countries had minimal impact in Japan, not even on the debate about responses to demands for anti-discrimination policy. It is difficult to demonstrate that knowledge of events outside Japan had much influence on the evolution of Dōwa policy until the 1990s. Isomura as an urban sociologist was no doubt aware of contemporary developments in America and Europe but he does not refer to policy there as providing examples that Japan might adopt or adapt. He was publicly critical of Japan's reluctance to ratify the two basic covenants in the late 1970s as part of his demands that the government take a more pro-active approach to the elimination of discrimination. He then made direct reference to them in discussions on the need to extend the SML in December 1981 (see, for example, Asahi Shimbun, 24 October 1978; 11 December 1981). However, it is only in the 1990s and in particular following publication of the Iken Gushin of 1996 that Dōwa policy and the need to address lingering discrimination against Burakumin are discussed in the context of Japan's international human rights commitments.

Meanwhile, the BLL was also starting to think about its activities within an international context. For example, in February 1994, we find the Asahi newspaper quoting Oga Masayuki of the BLL theory committee saying,

> With the end of the Cold War the international situation has changed and it is time for the movement to give priority to values common to all humanity such as human rights and the environment rather than a class struggle perspective.
>
> (Asahi Shimbun, 24 February 1994)

As the BLL developed this idea, it became more committed to the international human rights movement through the IMADR which argued powerfully within conferences held by the UN Committee on the Elimination of Racial Discrimination (CERD) that 'descent' as mentioned in the text of the CERD should be interpreted as including 'discrimination against members of caste and similar groups based on social stratification of hereditary status' (Tsutsui, 2018, 206–7). The Japanese government does not accept this argument and rejects the claim that Buraku discrimination is covered by the CERD.

It is then difficult to argue that the way Dōwa policy was either made or criticised owed much to any transnational influences, at least until the 1990s. It is only in the twenty-first century that there has been any Japanese impact on the international human rights framework.

Dōwa as welfare policy

In Chapter 2, we suggested that it might be appropriate to think of Dōwa policy as an example of time-limited welfare policy targeted at a particular section of the population. As we noted in Chapter 5, Ogata Tadashi, committee member of the Shin Seikatsu Undō Kyōkai (New Life Campaign Association), was a member of the *shingikai* 1960–5 and Kimura Chujirō, a former high-ranking official of the MHW and deputy chair of the Japan National Council of Social Welfare, was its first chair. Kimura continued to serve on the Dōtaikyō until May 1974 and thereafter there was always at least one person with a social welfare (and MHW) background on the council. We cannot trace the influence they had on specific recommendations of the report or the implementation of policy but their presence on these councils suggests that its deliberations were informed by knowledge of social welfare policy elsewhere in government which from 1962 was starting to turn its attention to the problems faced by those living on incomes below the poverty line.

The surveys conducted by the PMO for the Dōwa policy *shingikai* in 1963 demonstrated that, as the BLL had been vociferously arguing, Buraku communities were indeed significantly disadvantaged compared to most mainstream Japanese. Its conclusion was that unless special measures were enacted, this 'disadvantage' would not be overcome, they would continue to lag behind, and this would perpetuate prejudices and discrimination.

The result was a diverse set of policies whose implementation involved eight separate ministries. And yet when we looked in some detail on where most of the money was spent, it became clear that the bulk of it paid for the up-grade of roads, bridges, irrigation systems, and sewage piping none of which had much to do with the specific problems encountered by Burakumin. Moreover, in parallel with these infrastructural improvements within Dōwa districts local governments were engaged in very similar projects across the mainstream community. This was most clearly demonstrated in Q city where the construction of housing for Burakumin residents of the *tanjū* was just part of a city-wide strategy to re-house all of those living in slum housing. Similarly, while Buraku communities benefited from the installation of piping to deliver drinking water and take away liquid waste, elsewhere similar projects were being implemented to improve the domestic hygiene of everyone in the city. One could make similar comments about the public works projects that improved roads and irrigation systems. The outcome was that, although it may have been that some Buraku communities had their living environments up-graded somewhat sooner than their neighbours which may have given rise to feelings of 'envy', by the end of the twentieth century, there were very few observable differences between Buraku and non-Buraku districts in villages, towns, and cities across the country – which of course was the objective.

Moreover, from the late 1980s onwards, the various schemes which had provided personal grants to Buraku individuals and families as documented by Upham, were gradually phased out. Either they disappeared entirely or, as, for example, in the case of grants provided to support attendance at schools and colleges after compulsory education, they were opened up to all children from families with incomes below a certain threshold. This contributed to the reduction in feelings of unfairness but at the same time reduced the role played by the local branch of the Buraku organisation in controlling the distribution of the benefits of Dōwa policies. With the incentives for joining these groups reduced, their membership has gone into steep decline.

But to return to the notion of Dōwa policy as welfare policy: in the first half of the 1960s, government put in place a range of policies designed to provide low-cost access to healthcare, pensions for all and gave notice that it would give particular attention to those families who existed below the 'poverty line'. There were clearly some elements of Dōwa provision that were welfare-linked in a narrow sense: the provision of child-care, special educational provision especially in primary schools, the erection of buildings that served in whole or in part as clinics, and the funding of periodic health checks – *ningen dokku*. But the public works projects also provided employment for many of those in the Dōwa communities who anyway were more likely to rely on the construction industry for employment and can be regarded as functionally equivalent to welfare policies in the sense of creating jobs and an income for those who otherwise would have been unemployed. Thus, Dōwa policy was both directly and indirectly supportive of the welfare of those in Dōwa districts at a time when the state was starting to pay attention to developing a broadly focused set of welfare policies and should be regarded as being connected to them.

Dōwa policy and the Japanese state

Following the abolition of a centrally guided Yūwa policy by the US occupation authorities, local governments in the Kansai region, despite being desperately short of resources, did what they could to address the most egregious examples of disadvantage such as the prevention of such communicable diseases as trachoma. Urged on by campaigns coordinated by the BLL and its predecessor, the quantity of the funding and quality of the Dōwa projects incrementally increased during the 1950s and 1960s. Local governments engaged with representatives of their Buraku communities to devise effective ways to deliver improvement strategies. In Osaka, the creation of the prefectural and city Dōsokkyō whose membership overlapped with but was not identical to the BLL produced an obvious partner for Dōwa policy administrators to work with. In Nara, the Dōwa policy council formed in 1951 worked at the prefectural level to incorporate views of local politicians with those of the Muikakai at the time when groups of residents were being formed within Buraku communities to work with local governments in the formulation and implementation of Dōwa projects. No Dōwa projects seem to have operated in Q city in the 1950s and 1960s and it is not clear when the process of regular consultation with the Shikyō commenced there.

At the national level, immediately following the debates in the Diet and elsewhere on the appropriate response to the *shingikai* report that led to the passage of the SML, cabinet approved instructions to prefectures to implement Dōwa policy projects on 31 July 1969 (Dōwa Gyōseishi Henshū Iinkai, 2002, 324–5). For local governments in Osaka and Nara, adapting administrative structures to implement the new provisions was relatively straightforward. In Q city, it took a couple of years before an office was created to supervise Dōwa policy which itself was part of the broader 'comprehensive plan' to regenerate the city in the aftermath of the mine closures.

Working through a local administrative apparatus that either already existed or was newly created for the purpose allowed the Dōwa policies to be implemented quite rapidly with minimal additional expenditure at the national level. It was cheap. It kept the state small. It also pushed most decisions down to the level of municipalities which empowered Buraku communities to exert influence over them, including even whether or not to launch a suite of Dōwa projects. There was then a very strong 'bottom up' dimension to decision-making albeit mediated through branches of the Dōsokkyō, Shikyō or whatever. On the positive side, this made the Dōwa policy process democratically responsive to the needs of Burakumin. However, this very devolved system of governance made it vulnerable to corrupt practice.

The overall result of this was that a high cost and, in a positive sense, very intrusive set of policies was implemented by the Japanese state over three decades in a way which added very little to the size of the state structure at the national level. Nearly 20 years after the termination of the SML, there is virtually no trace of Dōwa policy administration. Had there been a more solid base for Dōwa policy within central government, for example, the equivalent of the Gender Equality Bureau within the Cabinet Office, one can imagine it allying with such NGOs as the Jiyū Dōwakai or the BLL or maybe both, to argue the case for the need for continued vigilance to resist a future rise of Burakumin intolerance or more positively support a human rights agenda that embraced other issues. It could have provided a nucleus around which a human rights commission could have been constructed.

Dōwa policy as a response to a 'socially constructed' Dōwa problem

How the social problem, the 'Buraku mondai', was defined within postwar Japanese society is particularly important given that, however fragile the categories of race, ethnicity or gender may be, there was no equivalent way of conceptualising Burakumin. Some sociologists suggested that it was fruitful to think of it at a theoretical level *as if* it were a racial issue but this does not help much in policymaking still less policy implementation. For this reason, we looked to the social constructivist literature for guidance. Out of that large literature, we selected two insights. First was the importance of the process of problem definition and second the distinction made between three phases of policy implementation: the political – the process that leads to the passage of a law or creation of a new organisation, the administrative – the formulation of the rules to determine the process of resource allocation, and the operative – the technical task of applying the resources.

The first stage in the process of having Dōwa policy enacted at the national level was to get the Buraku problem recognised as something that was both undesirable and amenable either to resolution or at least attenuation. Putting the issue onto the political agenda was largely achieved by the end of the 1950s following the campaigns led by the BLL with the support of the JSP and also perhaps following evidence from local governments that Dōwa projects could make a difference. Once government and the LDP had been persuaded to recognise the problem, they adopted the standard bureaucratic response of appointing a policy council, a *shingikai*, to provide advice. The formation of such a council had also been part of the BLL/JSP demands but they had sought a membership that would include JSP Diet members. Instead, a body was appointed consisting of eleven serving bureaucrats and nine 'persons of learning of experience' who included academics, retired bureaucrats but also four representatives of Buraku communities.

One suspects that the strategy of senior policymakers was to use this *shingikai* to generate a consensus about Dowa policy among the spending ministries and perhaps even create a coordination mechanism with the lesser aim being to satisfy demands from the opposition parties and pressure groups. Schwartz notes the 'amateur', or perhaps better put, 'generalist' nature of the Japanese bureaucracy which makes it second nature to reach out for specialist advice from academics (Schwartz, 1998, 52). Moreover, the presence of the BLL and Dōwakai representatives would help to legitimate the council's conclusions. However, the *shingikai* was by no means a docile body despite the majority coming from the bureaucracy and the Burakumin representatives were apparently able by force of personality to resist the bureaucratic domination of the proceedings. Soon after it began its work and decided that it needed more accurate information about the state of the Buraku communities, a sub-committee was set up chaired by the urban sociologist Isomura that co-opted Yoneda Tomi from the BLL. This ensured that the survey research design did not generate results simply in order to validate the administrative measures preferred by the bureaucrats and conservative politicians.

The result was a set of recommendations that were closely tied to the human rights clauses of the constitution and defined the issue as being concerned with the violation of the fundamental civil and political rights and freedoms of the residents of Buraku communities. The obligation to resolve those underlying problems was defined as the 'responsibility of the state'. Moreover, the report made clear that a solution would have to involve more than mitigating the deficiencies of their communities but also require changes in the attitudes of majority society, including greater respect for human rights. This went much further than simply setting rules to enable coordination between government departments and set challenging standards by which Dōwa policy could be assessed.

Although it expressed some reservations, the BLL broadly welcomed the report as promising funding for the kind of targeted interventions that it had been demanding since the early 1950s. However, this was not the end of the political phase of the policy process. During extensive debate between 1965 and 1969, the LDP-led government first promised to and then declined to put in place a legal commitment to the proposals and aspirations of the 1965 report in the form of a basic law. In the end, the political process of the translation of the report's recommendations into administrative rules resulted in a skeletal Long-Term Plan that set out the division of bureaucratic responsibilities between the ministries and a Special Measures Law that promised finance for the projects they proposed in collaboration with local governments. No mechanism was created that could hold government accountable to the standards set out in the report.

Nevertheless during the first decade of its implementation, the Dōwa Policy Advisory Council, the Dōtaikyō, continued to contain representatives of the Buraku organisations both on its main panel and on its sub-committees. This may account for its research activity and production of quite extensive reports on such matters as Dōwa education which ran to several hundred pages. However, the Dōtaikyō authorisation expired in May 1978 and when it was reconvened in June 1981 no Buraku representatives were appointed. From this point, the advisory council is engaged less in the critical appraisal of the implementation of Dōwa policies and more in overseeing their administrative and operative processes: setting the rules and overseeing their application.

This was not the whole story though. During the brief interlude 1994–6 when Murayama Tomiichi was PM and members of the JSP served in cabinet posts, political debate on the future of Dōwa policy was revived within a Human Rights and Discrimination 'project team' that was established by Diet members from the LDP, JSP, and Shintō Sakigake. Later, a new *shingikai* was formed to report on human rights education and the creation of a system of redress for human rights infringements. This opened up the prospect that Dōwa policy after 2002 might be embraced within a body with a broad remit to promote and protect human rights, a human rights commission perhaps. Hashimoto Ryūtarō replaced Murayama as PM in January 1996 but for the time being discussions on how to promote human rights education and provide relief for victims of human rights violations continued. The Dōwa policy (or rather Chiiki Kaizen) advisory panel delivered its final report in May and ceased to exist in February 1997. The next five years saw the gradual running down of all the Dōwa projects until in March 2002 the only remaining part of central government with responsibility for Dōwa policy, the 'office' in the Sōmushō, was dismantled. One of its final tasks was to publish a collection of documents tracing the history of the policy. In its afterword, it concludes with the hope that the publication will be of use to all those with an interest in Dōwa policy and that it will stimulate the renewed development of a human rights administration (Dōwa Gyōseishi Henshū Iinkai, 2002, 983). However, as Croydon shows, in 2003 the LDP abandoned plans to establish a Human Rights Commission and no subsequent government has been able to revive them (Croydon, 2017).

However, at the level of local government, where most of the administration of Dōwa projects took place, elements of the 'political' never went away. Representatives of Buraku communities had played a role in Dōwa policy formulation and implementation from the 1950s and they continued to be involved in Dōwa projects up to and sometimes beyond 2002. Moreover, many prefectural and municipal authorities during the 1980s and 1990s have adopted resolutions and administrative regulations that forbid investigations into people's personal backgrounds and since 2016 have passed bylaws on the promotion of the elimination of Buraku discrimination.

In the twenty-first century, the question of who defines the Buraku issue and how has acquired a transnational dimension. Across the 1990s the BLL increasingly directed its energy to contributing to the global human rights movement and from 2001 led the campaign for the international recognition of 'discrimination based on work and descent' as a new norm within the remit of the CERD. In its first report to the CERD committee in 2000, the Japanese government did not mention Burakumin at all and in its reports of 2010 and 2014 it argued explicitly that they did not fall under CERD jurisdiction. Since then, the BLL has supported a triennial conference on caste issues and the IMADR is a supporter of the International Dalit Solidarity Network, while the Japanese government show no signs of accepting Burakumin as a group protected under the CERD (Tsutsui, 2018, 203–7).

The 'Buraku Question' today and tomorrow

Finally, we turn to whether the Dōwa policy has succeeded in solving the Buraku Question. Inevitably, this takes us back to the problem of definition, the dearth of recent reliable and comprehensive information, and to the war of words that continues to exist between two wings of the liberation movement, one formerly known as the Zenkairen linked to the JCP and the other still called the BLL with the centrist Zenkoku Jiyū Dōwakai existing uncomfortably somewhere in between them. Those working within the tradition of the Zenkairen while no longer invoking such concepts of 'feudal remnants' or 'working class solidarity' nevertheless argue that the material conditions that supported prejudices and discrimination against Burakumin no longer exist and interpret evidence about current living conditions and changing attitudes to support their 'national integration thesis' (*kokumin yūgōron*). Following the expiration of the SML in 2002, they declared that Buraku discrimination had been largely resolved and that the movement should move on from Buraku-focused activism and remedies to a commitment to universal human rights principles. Consequently, they dissolved their old organisation creating in its place the *Zenkoku Chiiki Undō Sōrengō* (National Confederation of Human Rights Movements in the Community). Their members have since argued that it was inappropriate for local governments to continue funding Dōwa projects and in 2016 the JCP opposed the proposals to enact a law to make Buraku discrimination illegal. Their case is that it is counter-productive to focus attention on the issue at a time when awareness of it is slipping from the public consciousness.

The regional case studies showed how Dōwa policy faced different challenges from place to place. In areas to the north of Tokyo and indeed in much of Tokyo itself, it may be true that an awareness of Buraku issues barely exists. However, that is not the case in the Kansai region or Shikoku or Kyushu. And, even where members of the majority community are blithely ignorant of this issue, this is not the case for residents of those communities who have to deal with the social stigma of their membership of a Dōwa community. These individuals need to make a decision for themselves and sometimes for their children. Do they choose to keep the stigma of Buraku identity hidden, be assumed to be part of the majority but with the constant anxiety of being 'outed'? Or do they share knowledge about their background considering it to be nothing to hide. It may not be a binary choice. One might be open to one's close friends but not to one's employer or colleagues. Such a decision will have consequences that go beyond the individual: someone who 'comes out' about her background also exposes her siblings and even her as yet unborn wider family to potential discrimination. This then comes back to the question of the need to change the attitudes of the majority population. As has been argued since the time of the formation of the Suiheisha, the task of 'liberating' Burakumin from discrimination is not just about changing material conditions within their communities. Imoto Rinshi, one of the leaders of the pre-war and post-war movements, used to say in criticism of placing too much faith in the Dōwa projects that it would not advance the cause of liberation to 'gold plate' existing Buraku communities if outside attitudes did not change.

This takes us to the complex but crucial discussion about Buraku identity. In the mid-twentieth century, Burakumin were defined as people who have ancestors who had discriminated status in the early modern (Edo) period. As we saw, the SML and its subsequent iterations left the definition about who should qualify for Dōwa benefits deliberately vague. Nevertheless, at the end of the 1960s, it became important to have a working definition of Burakumin and their communities in order to implement the Dōwa schemes. A minimal definition seemed to be someone who was discriminated against as a Burakumin and resided in a designated Dōwa community as verified by a Buraku-based organisation, often but not always the BLL. As the SML was about to expire the influential sociologist, Noguchi Michihiko, suggested this definition be expanded to 'A Burakumin is someone who is regarded as a Burakumin and discriminated against *or someone who is highly likely to be discriminated against*' (Noguchi, 2000, 16; my emphasis). Some 13 years later, the BLL in Osaka suggested a further extension of the definition to include 'all those people who have any connection to Buraku land and all those who might be subject to discrimination'. These changes expand the definition to also include all those who have 'Buraku heritage' whether or not they live in Dōwa-designated communities but also all those who by virtue of having been resident in such a community have come to be regarded as Burakumin despite a lack of 'Buraku heritage' no matter where they currently reside. They suggest that the aim of policy should be to create a society where people can 'self-identify' as Burakumin and talk about their backgrounds if they so wish without fear of discrimination (Yamamoto, 2020, 211). This is just a modern re-statement of the principle announced in the Suiheisha declaration of 1921 that the aim was to create a time when 'we can be proud to be *eta*'. However, although there have been such individuals from the time of Matsumoto Jiichirō in the early twentieth century to Kadooka Nobuhiko who writes about Buraku issues in the twenty-first, it is, as Bondy points, out far more common to encounter attempts by both members of Dōwa communities and the mainstream to shroud the issue in silence in a way that stifles discussion and inhibits research (Bondy 2015).

A definitive answer to the question about the existence of Buraku discrimination is not possible in the absence of a comprehensive survey of conditions in Dōwa districts. In our conclusion to the chapter looking at three regional case studies, we saw that although the evidence was rather fragmentary, it would be premature to conclude that problems no longer existed. Indeed, the passage of the law against discrimination in December 2016 suggested that the government too accepted that this is the case. Clause six of that law stipulated that, 'The state in cooperation with local authorities should conduct a survey of the reality of Buraku discrimination to contribute to the creation of policies to eliminate Buraku discrimination'. This task was given to the Jinken Kyōiku Keihatsu Suishin Sentaa (Center for Human Rights Education and Training) which the following year set up a six-person committee to advise on the aims and methods of that survey. Its report delivered in March 2018 explicitly advised that the survey should **not** consider the Buraku living conditions just discrimination (Jinken Kyōiku Keihatsu Suishin Sentaa, 2018, 31–2). It was to look at reports of cases of discrimination, for example, as reported to CLCs (Jinken Yōgoin) or similar local government counsellors, the incidence of discrimination on the internet, and levels of prejudice and discrimination among the general population. Very briefly, it found very few incidents being reported to the CLC system or similar bodies serving local governments but it concluded that on the internet, while,

> …not everyone searching for information about Buraku discrimination is doing so with an intention to discriminate, it could not be denied that there was a possibility that contact with misinformation or information that promotes discrimination and prejudice could instil discriminatory attitudes.

Similar to the local surveys reported in Chapter 8, it found that 85.8% of those questioned who were aware of the Dōwa issue regarded Buraku discrimination as unjust but of these 15.7% would want to know if an acquaintance or marriage partner was 'from a former Dōwa district'. The report concluded with the suggestion that there is a need to consider what more needs to be done to eliminate Buraku discrimination (Hōmushō Jinkenkyoku, 2020, 187–9).

But when trying to re-think the Buraku 'question' we need to define what the elimination of discrimination might consist of. We noted that when the Japanese government implemented the recommendations of the 1965 report through the SML it committed itself to breaking the cycle of disadvantage associated with out-groups. This Fredman lists as one of the four kinds of measures we might expect to see when a state accepted its obligation to take positive measures to protect and promote equality. Both the Japanese state and the liberation movements agree that this has been largely achieved; the cycle of deprivation and discrimination has been if not broken then substantially weakened. But Fredman then goes on to itemise:

- Facilitating full social participation,
- Accommodating/positively affirming/celebrating their identity with the community,
- Promoting respect for the equal dignity and worth of all.

(Fredman, 2008, 179)

Interestingly, these features are not dissimilar to a checklist proposed by the Zenkairen in the late 1990s to assess whether the Dōwa problem has been resolved:

- The elimination of differences in living standards, employment patterns and educational achievement compared to their neighbours,
- A situation where words and deeds based on unscientific ideas and prejudices towards the Buraku problem are not accepted within the community or workforce,
- The removal of a 'closed' outlook from the attitudes and custom of Buraku residents,
- The realisation of open interaction and socialising across communities.

(Yamamoto 2020, 210 quoting a Zenkoku Chiiki Jinken Undō Sōrengō document of 2013)

Zenkairen's supporters argue that the first has been achieved and the rest are in the process of achievement.

The main difference between the position taken by Fredman and others in Japan, not all of them members of the BLL, and the Zenkairen surrounds the issue of identity. When Buraku residents eliminate their 'closed outlook' what remains of their identity? Two points about this: first, is the Zenkairen position anything more than a slightly more sophisticated version of a pattern of thinking about the issue that defines Burakumin terms of their deficiencies? Second, are we seeing here the re-emergence of the sameness/difference conundrum that Kurokawa has elaborated so eloquently but the Zenkairen has not engaged with? (Kurokawa 1999; see also Tsutsui, 2018, 200). Once material differences no longer exist, are Burakumin left only with 'sameness'? Do they have nothing to celebrate or positively affirm?

Stuart Hall's definition of identification may be useful here.

> Though they seem to invoke an origin in a historical past with which they continue to correspond, actually identities are about questions of using the resources of history, language and culture in the process of

> becoming rather than being: not 'who we are' or 'where we came from', so much as what we might become, how we have been represented and how that bears on how we might represent ourselves.
>
> (Hall, 1996, 4)

Hall was not talking about Japan but the account in this book has suggested that the way Burakumin have been represented has often been 'as if' they were a different race. Their reaction to that has been to argue the case for respect for the equal dignity and worth of all. That struggle is 'where they have come from' and that is something that many may want to identify with. How they choose to represent themselves is surely a choice for each family and individual. For some, it may be an important part of who they are and for others totally irrelevant to their circumstances. But until the situation exists when they can make that choice freely without fear of negative consequences, the Buraku problem will not have been solved, liberation not achieved.

Bibliography

Asahi Shimbun 24 October 1978; 11 December 1981, 24 February 1994.

Bondy C., (2015) *Voice, Silence, and Self: Negotiation of Buraku Identity in Contemporary Japan*, Cambridge MA: Harvard University Press.

Croydon S., (2017) 'Progress or Prevarication?: The Move Toward the Establishment of a Human Rights Commission in Japan', *Human Rights Quarterly*, vol. 39, no. 2, 369–92.

Dōwa Gyōseishi Henshū Iinkai (Dōwa Administration History Editorial Committee), (2002) *Dōwa Gyōseishi* (A History of Dōwa Administration), Tokyo: Sōmuchō Daijin Kanbō Chiiki Kaizen Taisakuhitsu.

Fredman S., (2008) *Human Rights Transformed: Positive Rights and Positive Duties*, Oxford: Oxford Scholarship Online.

Hall S., (1996) 'Who Needs "Identity"?' in S Hall and Paul du Gay (eds) *Questions of Cultural Identity*, London: Sage, pp. 1–17.

Hōmushō Jinken Hogokyoku, (2020) *Buraku Sabetsu no Jittai ni Kakawaru Chōsa Kekka Hōkokusho* (Report on the Results of the Survey on the State of Buraku Discrimination), Tokyo: Hōmushō Jinken Hogokyoku.

Jinken Kyōiku Keihatsu Suishin Sentaa, (2018) *Buraku Sabetsu Kaishō Suishinhō Rokujo no Chōsa ni Kakawaru Chōsa Kenkyū* (Survey Research for The Survey Stipulated in Clause Six of the Law to Promote the Elimination of Buraku Discrimination), Tokyo: Jinken Kyōiku Keihatsu Suishin Sentaa.

Kurokawa M., (1999) *Ika to Dōka no Aida* (Between Difference and Assimilation), Tokyo: Aoki Shoten.

Noguchi M., (2000) *Buraku Mondai no Paradaimu Tenkan* (Changes in the Paradigm of the Buraku Problem), Tokyo: Akashi Shoten.

Schwartz F. J., (1998) *Advice and Consent: The Politics of Consultation in Japan*, Cambridge: Cambridge University Press.

Tsutsui K., (2018) *Rights Make Might: Global Human Rights and Minority Social Movements in Japan*, Oxford: Oxford Scholarship Online.

Yamamoto T., (2020) *Jūmin Undō to Gyōsei Kenryoku no Esunogurafi* (An Ethnography of Residents Movement and Administrative Power), Kyoto: Kōyō Shobō.

Appendix

Principal Dōwa policy projects 1969–81

This was the period of the launching of the Dōwa projects followed by rapid growth in terms of both the number of projects that were funded and the amount of money that was made available for Dōwa policy. Ministries developed Dōwa projects such that in the course of the first phase of the programme, their total number increased from 38 to 100.

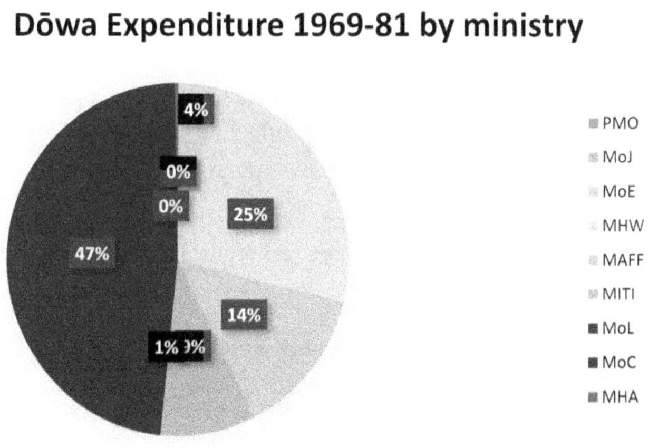

Figure A.1 Total spend over the period 1969–81.
Source: Dōwa Gyōseishi Henshū Iinkai (2002, 109).

Table A.1 Description of Main Projects 1969–81

(A) Projects concerning the improvement of living conditions
Ministry of Construction
Policies relating to town planning and housing
- Parks, infrastructure for sewage etc. construction of public housing, improvement of housing

Ministry of Health and Welfare
Projects to establish facilities for environment improvement
- Roads within communities, sewage and drainage, provision of drinking water, provision of other related facilities

Ministry of Local Government
Provision of Fire Pumps and Hydrants

(B) Projects concerning the improvement of social welfare and public hygiene
Ministry of Health and Welfare
- Provision and management of Rinpokan, subsidies for site acquisition and management
- Equipment of social welfare facilities and their management: kindergarten, children's centres
- Projects linked to public hygiene: trachoma prevention projects, projects to provide mobile health care advice and leadership

(C) Projects to promote industry in Dōwa communities
Ministry of Agriculture, Forestry and Fisheries
Projects related to agriculture, forestry and fishing, addressing the modernisation of agriculture and forestry by the provision of basic facilities
Projects to provide basic facilities to modernise the fishing industry
Projects to improve port facilities
Afforestation projects and forest road provision
Ministry of International Trade and Industry
Projects to develop SMEs: management leadership provided by management specialists, overseas market surveys, product development, provision of capital

(D) Projects related to the promotion of employment
Ministry of Labour
Instruction to employers on the use of 'standard application forms'
Provision of careers advice to school leavers from Buraku communities
Support for employment promotion
Provision of employment training facilities

(E) Projects related to the improvement of educational culture
Ministry of Education
Projects relating to education in schools: the training of Dōwa education leaders, designation of Dōwa education promotion districts, provision of finance to support attendance grants for senior high schools
Projects relating to public education: provision of places to provide adult education to the residents of Dōwa districts, encouragement of Dōwa discussion groups.

(F) Projects relating to human rights protection
Ministry of Justice
Investigation into human rights violations, provision of human rights advice, promotion of human rights ideas, training of people to promote and administer human rights protection (the Civil Liberties Commissioners)

Source: Dōwa Gyōseishi Henshū Iinkai (2002, 117).

Regional improvement policy projects 1982–6

The 1980s was the peak of overall Dōwa spending. Although there was some contraction towards the middle of the decade, some very large projects nevertheless began. Following the review of Dowa policy in 1981, the total number of projects was reduced from 100 to 82.

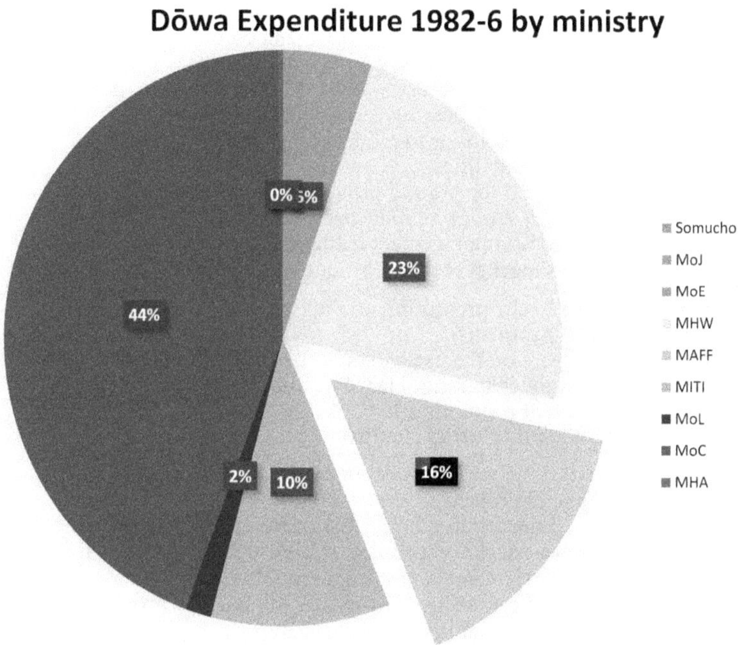

Figure A.2 Total spend over the period 1982–6.
Source: Dōwa Gyōseishi Henshū Iinkai (2002, 109).

Table A.2 Description of Main Projects 1982–6

(A) Projects concerning the improvement of living conditions
Ministry of Construction (16 projects)
Policies relating to town planning and housing
- Parks, infrastructure for sewage etc. construction of public housing, improvement of housing
- Provision of streets and roads

Ministry of Health and Welfare (14 projects)
Projects to establish facilities for environment improvement
- Roads within communities, sewage and drainage, provision of drinking water, provision of other related facilities

(*Continued*)

Ministry of Local Government (1 project)
Provision of Fire Pumps and Hydrants

(B) Projects concerning the improvement of social welfare and public hygiene
Ministry of Health and Welfare (9 projects)
- Provision and management of Rinpokan, subsidies for site acquisition and management
- Equipment of social welfare facilities and their management: kindergarten, children's centres
- Projects linked to public hygiene: trachoma prevention projects, projects to provide mobile health care advice and leadership

(C) Projects to promote industry in Chiiki Kaizen communities
Ministry of Agriculture, Forestry and Fisheries (10 projects)
Projects related to agriculture, forestry and fishing, addressing the modernisation of agriculture and forestry by the provision of basic facilities
Projects to provide basic facilities to modernise the fishing industry
Projects to improve port facilities
Afforestation projects and forest road provision
Ministry of International Trade and Industry (8 projects)
Projects to develop SMEs: management leadership provided by management specialists, overseas market surveys, product development, provision of capital

(D) Projects Related to the promotion of employment
Ministry of Labour (12 projects)
Instruction to employers on the use of 'standard application forms'
Provision of careers advice to school leavers from Buraku communities
Support for employment promotion
Provision of employment training facilities

(E) Projects related to the improvement of educational culture
Ministry of Education (9 projects)
Projects relating to education in schools: the training of Dōwa education leaders, designation of Dōwa education promotion districts, provision of finance to support attendance grants for senior high schools.
Projects relating to public education: provision of places to provide adult education to the residents of the target districts, encouragement of discussion groups.

(F) Projects relating to human rights protection
Ministry of Justice (2 projects)
Sorifu [Sōmuchō] (1 project)
Investigation into human rights violations, provision of human rights advice, promotion of human rights ideas, training of people to promote and administer human rights protection (the Civil Liberties Commissioners)

Source: Dōwa Gyōseishi Henshū Iinkai (2002, 118).

Regional improvement policy designated projects 1987–91

This five-year period began with a review and re-structuring of Dōwa projects in preparation for the termination of the SML. The overall number of projects was significantly reduced in each category from to 55 overall following a review in 1986–7 and the total amount of funding reduced year by year.

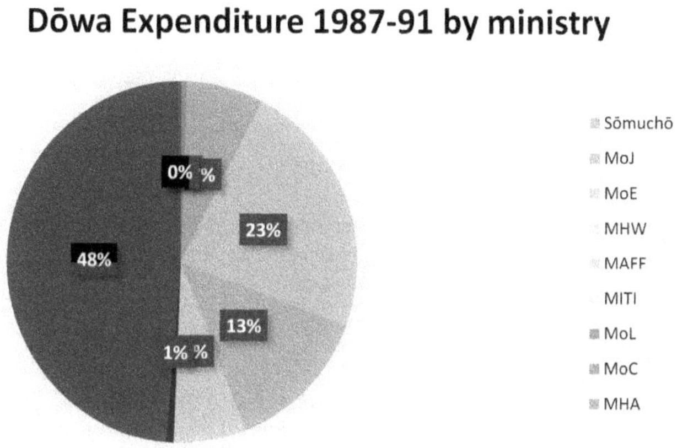

Figure A.3 Total spend over the period 1987–91.
Source: Dōwa Gyōseishi Henshū Iinkai (2002, 111).

Table A.3 Description of Main Projects 1987–91

(A) Projects to improve the living environment
Ministry of Construction (11 projects)
- Housing projects – improvement of facilities in housing, improvement of already complete public housing, provision of capital for new house building
- Town planning projects: streets, parks, sewage, infrastructure
- Construction of roads

Ministry of Health and Welfare (7 projects)
Projects to establish facilities for environment improvement
- Roads within communities, sewage and drainage, provision of other related facilities

Ministry of Local Government (1 project)
Provision of fire pumps and hydrants

(B) Projects concerning the improvement of social welfare and public hygiene
Ministry of Health and Welfare (4 projects)
- Provision and management of Rinpokan,
- Management of social welfare facilities: kindergarten, children's centres

(*Continued*)

- Social research, educational and promotional activity to improve the living standards of district residents

(C) Projects to promote industry in Chiiki Kaizen communities
Ministry of Agriculture, Forestry and Fisheries (9 projects)
Projects to improve the agricultural base, forestry and fishing, addressing the modernisation of agriculture and forestry by the provision of basic facilities
Projects to provide joint-use facilities for the fishing, agriculture and forestry industries
Projects to improve port facilities
Afforestation projects and development of roads in privately owned woods
Projects to provide finance and advice for improvement of management
Ministry of International Trade and Industry (5 projects)
Projects to diffuse improved management techniques, projects to provide advice and training, product development, projects to set up meetings on industry promotion, provision of capital

(D) Projects to promote stable employment
Ministry of Labour (6 projects)
Provision of careers advice to school leavers from Buraku communities
Loans to enable trainees to attend career training courses
Provision of education and leadership for employers

(E) Projects to consolidate education
Ministry of Education (9 projects)
Projects relating to education in schools: designation of education promotion districts, provision of finance to support attendance grants for senior high schools
Projects relating to public education: provision of places to provide adult education to the residents of the target districts, encouragement of discussion groups, training of Dōwa education leaders.

(F) Projects relating to human rights protection
Ministry of Justice (2 projects)
Investigation into human rights violations, provision of human rights advice, promotion of human rights ideas, training of people to promote and administer human rights protection (the Civil Liberties Commissioners)
Sōmuchō (1 project)
Hold lectures and training sessions for employees in central and local government, engage in educational activity produce films, sponsor TV, radio programmes and newspaper adverts about Dōwa issues.

Source: Dōwa Gyōseishi Henshū Iinkai (2002, 119).

Regional improvement policy designated projects 1992–6

In preparation for the termination of the Dōwa programme, the Dōwa policy was reviewed and the number of projects reduced from 55 to 45.

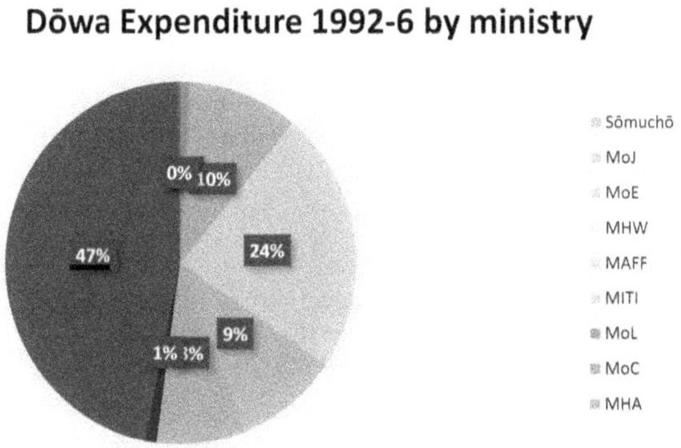

Figure A.4 Total spend over the period 1992–6.
Source: Dōwa Gyōseishi Henshū Iinkai (2002, 111).

Table A.4 Description of Main Projects 1992–6

(A) Projects to improve the living environment
Ministry of Construction (9 projects)
- Housing projects – improvement of facilities in the housing environment, improvement of already complete public housing, provision of capital for new house building
- Town planning projects: streets, parks, sewage infrastructure
- Construction of roads

Ministry of Health and Welfare (5 projects)
Projects to establish facilities for environment improvement
- Roads within communities, sewage and drainage, communal workspace, provision of other related facilities

Ministry of Local Government (1 project) – (partially transferred to general budget)
Provision of fire pumps and hydrants

(B) Projects to improve social welfare and hygiene
Ministry of Health and Welfare (4 projects)
- Provision and management of Rinpokan (promotion of social research, educational and promotional activity to improve the living standards of district residents)
- Management of social welfare facilities: kindergarten, children's centres

(*Continued*)

C Projects to promote industry
Ministry of Agriculture, Forestry and Fisheries (7 projects)
Projects to improve the agricultural base, forestry and fishing, addressing the modernisation of agriculture and forestry by the provision of basic facilities
Projects to provide joint-use facilities for the fishing, agriculture and forestry industries
Projects to improve port facilities
Afforestation projects and development of roads in privately owned woods
Projects to provide finance and advice for improvement of management
Ministry of International Trade and Industry (4 projects)
Projects to diffuse improved management techniques, projects to provide advice training, and product development, projects to set up meetings on industry promotion, provision of capital

(D) Projects to promote employment
Ministry of Labour (5 projects)
Provision of careers advice to school leavers from Buraku communities
Loans to enable trainees to attend career training courses
Provision of education and leadership for employers

(E) Projects to promote educational culture
Ministry of Education (7 projects)
Projects relating to education in schools: designation of education promotion districts, provision of finance to support attendance loans for senior high schools, universities etc.
Projects relating to public education: provision of places to provide adult education to the residents of the target districts, encouragement of discussion groups, training of Dōwa education leaders.

(F) Projects relating to human rights protection
Ministry of Justice (2 projects)
Investigation into human rights violations, provision of human rights advice, promotion of human rights ideas, training of people to promote and administer human rights protection (the Civil Liberties Commissioners)
Sōmuchō (1 project)
Hold lectures and training sessions for employees in central and local government, engage in educational activity, produce films, sponsor TV, radio programmes and newspaper adverts about Dōwa issues

Source: Dōwa Gyōseishi Henshū Iinkai (2002, 120).

Regional improvement policy designated projects 1997–2001

As preparation for what would turn out to be the final phase of the Dōwa policy programme, the number of projects was reduced quite drastically from 45 to 15.

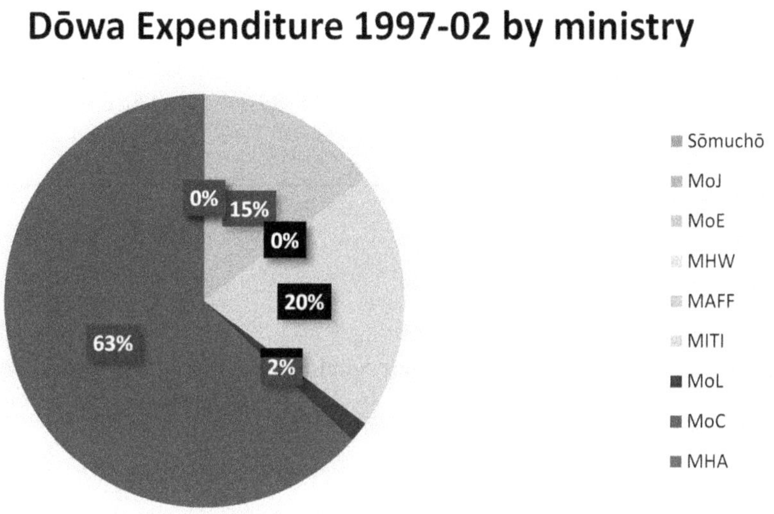

Figure A.5 Total spend over the period 1997–2001.
Source: Dōwa Gyōseishi Henshū Iinkai (2002, 111).

Table A.5 Description of Main Projects 1997–2001

6 material projects
Ministry of Construction
Two housing improvement projects – upgrade parks, roads, and buildings to improve the living environment of densely inhabited residential
areas and smaller communities
Project to provide capital for new housing – in order to improve the facilities in the environment of housing of target areas provide capital for improvement of existing and building of new housing.
Two projects for roads – build and improve roads, both thoroughfares and within communities
Project to improve public sewage provision

9 non-material projects
Ministry of Agriculture, Forestry and Fisheries
Loans for management improvement – low-interest long term loans to improve management in agricultural, forestry and fishing communities

(*Continued*)

Agricultural advice – establish a system of advisers and research groups to assist rural households

Ministry of International Trade and Industry Upgrade regional improvement projects – provide long term, no-interest loans to improve cooperation between SMEs

Disseminate management improvements– provide advice on administration, technology and bookkeeping through chambers of commerce

Ministry of Labour Two projects to provide training to stabilise employment – funding to provide training in various kinds of schools to improve skills and knowledge to stabilise employment

Project to provide employment advisers leading to stable employment

Ministry of Education Funding to support attendance at high schools etc. – loans for support and purchase of goods needed for school attendance.

Ministry of Health and Welfare Livelihood advisor system – to provide support systems that can provide advice to improve their living standards

Source: Dōwa Gyōseishi Henshū Iinkai (2002, 122–3).

Bibliography

Dōwa Gyōseishi Henshū Iinkai (Dōwa Administration History Editorial Committee), (2002) *Dōwa Gyōseishi* (A History of Dōwa Administration), Tokyo: Sōmuchō Daijin Kanbō Chiiki Kaizen Taisakuhitsu.

Glossary

amakudari	'descent from heaven', practice of retiring high-ranking government officials taking lucrative posts in private or semi-private corporations
BLL	Buraku Liberation League, *Buraku Kaihō Dōmei*
CCS	Chief Cabinet Secretary
CERD	Convention on the Elimination of all forms of Racial Discrimination
chimei sōkan	compilation of addresses indicating Buraku locations
Chitaikyō	*Chiiki Kaizen Taisaku Kyōgikai,* Regional Improvement Policy Council
CLC	Civil Liberties Commissioner, *Jinken Yōgoin*
Dōtaikyō	*Dōwa Taisaku Kyōgikai*, Dowa Policy Advisory Council
Dōtaishin	Report of the Dōwa Policy Commission of Enquiry, Dōwa Taisaku Shingikai
ese-Dōwa	fraudulent Dōwa related claims
eta	discriminatory term used in the pre-modern period to refer to marginalised groups often involved in leather production
HC	House of Councillors, *Sangiin*
hinin	discriminatory term used in the pre-modern period to refer to marginal groups usually in urban areas
HR	House of Representatives, *Shūgiin*
Iken Gushin	Comments and Suggestions, for example, by a commission of enquiry
IMADR	International Movement Against all forms of Discrimination and Racism
IRAA	Imperial Rule Assistance Association
JCLU	Japan Civil Liberties Union
JCP	Japan Communist Party
Jinken Kyōiku Keihatsu Suishin Sentaa	Center for Human Rights Education and Training

Jinken Yōgoin	Human Rights Commissioners, Ministry of Justice
JSP	Japan Socialist Party
kawata	discriminatory term used to refer to leather workers in the pre-modern period
keihatsu	public awareness, education
Kinki	region around Osaka, Kyoto, Nara
koseki	family register
kyūdan	literally 'censure', but used to describe the campaigns that the Suiheisha and BLL conducted in protest at instances of discrimination
LDP	Liberal Democratic Party
LTP	Long Term Plan, adopted in August 1969 as a supplement to the Special Measures Law on Dōwa Policies
madoguchi ippon	literally 'single window' used to describe the sole administrative channel through which applications for Dōwa benefits needed to pass.
MHA	Ministry of Home Affairs
MHW	Ministry of Health and Welfare
MITI	Ministry of International Trade and Industry
minsei iin	district welfare officers
MoC	Ministry of Construction
MoE	Ministry of Education
MoF	Ministry of Finance
MoL	Ministry of Labour
NCBL	National Committee for Buraku Liberation – *Zenkoku Buraku Kaihō Iinkai* – name of the Buraku liberation movement 1946–55
OB	Old Boy
PARC	Policy Affairs Research Council (LDP)
PMO	Prime Minister's Office
Rinpokan	'settlement house', multi-purpose community centre constructed in many Buraku communities
Seijōkaren	*Buraku Kaihō Dōmei Seijōka Zenkoku Renraku Kaigi* – Liaison Council for the Normalisation of the Buraku Liberation League, JCP dominated fraction.
shingikai	commission of enquiry
SME	Small- and Medium-sized Enterprises
SML	Special Measures Law
Sōmuchō	General Affairs Agency
Suiheisha	Levellers Association – movement of Burakumin 1922–41
tanjū	cheap housing built for mine workers

TMG	Tokyo Metropolitan Government
Tōhoku	the six prefectures of north Honshu: Akita, Aomori, Fukushima, Iwate, Miyagi, Yamagata
UNGA	United National General Assembly
Yūwa	reconciliation
zaibatsu	industrial conglomerate
Zenkairen	*Zenkoku Kaihō Undō Rengōkai* – National Liberation Movement League, formed in 1976 by the JCP leaning faction of the BLL. In 2003, it became the *Zenkoku Chiiki Undō Sōrengō* National Confederation of Human Rights Movements in the Community.
Zendōtai	*Zen Nihon Dōwa Taisaku Kyōgikai* – All-Japan Dōwa Policy Council, organisation of prefectural representatives involved in Dowa project administration
Zen Nihon Dōwakai	All-Japan Dōwa Association – centrist organisation formed in 1960
Zenkoku Jiyū Dōwakai	National Liberal Dowa Association – centrist organisation formed in 1986

Index

Note: Page numbers followed by 'n' refer to notes.

www.ingramcontent.com/pod-product-compliance
Lightning Source LLC
LaVergne TN
LVHW021121300926
849160LV00010B/808
9780367651367